# PLUTARCH

# ESSAYS

TRANSLATED BY
## ROBIN WATERFIELD

INTRODUCED AND ANNOTATED BY
## IAN KIDD

PENGUIN BOOKS

## PENGUIN BOOKS

Published by the Penguin Group
Penguin Books Ltd, 27 Wrights Lane, London w8 5tz, England
Penguin Putnam Inc., 375 Hudson Street, New York, New York 10014, USA
Penguin Books Australia Ltd, Ringwood, Victoria, Australia
Penguin Books Canada Ltd, 10 Alcorn Avenue, Toronto, Ontario, Canada m4v 3b2
Penguin Books (NZ) Ltd, Private Bag 102902, NSMC, Auckland, New Zealand

Penguin Books Ltd, Registered Offices: Harmondsworth, Middlesex, England

First published 1992
5 7 9 10 8 6 4

Typeset by Datix International Limited, Bungay, Suffolk
Filmset in Monophoto Bembo
Printed in England by Clays Ltd, St Ives plc

# CONTENTS

*Preface and Acknowledgements*                          vii
*Abbreviations*                                          ix
*Introduction*                                           1


ON LISTENING
Introduction                                            19
Essay                                                   27


HOW TO DISTINGUISH A FLATTERER FROM A FRIEND
Introduction                                            51
Essay                                                   61


ON BEING AWARE OF MORAL PROGRESS
Introduction                                           113
Essay                                                  122


WHETHER MILITARY OR INTELLECTUAL EXPLOITS
HAVE BROUGHT ATHENS MORE FAME
Introduction                                           147
Essay                                                  154


ON THE AVOIDANCE OF ANGER
Introduction                                           168
Essay                                                  176


ON CONTENTMENT
Introduction                                           202
Essay                                                  211

# CONTENTS

ON GOD'S SLOWNESS TO PUNISH
Introduction                                              239
Essay                                                     250


ON SOCRATES' PERSONAL DEITY
Introduction                                              294
Essay                                                     308


IN CONSOLATION TO HIS WIFE
Introduction                                              359
Essay                                                     365


ON THE USE OF REASON BY 'IRRATIONAL' ANIMALS
Introduction                                              375
Essay                                                     383


*Bibliography*                                            400
*Textual Appendix*                                        402
*Descriptive Index of Proper Names*                       407

# PREFACE AND ACKNOWLEDGEMENTS

The Greek text used for these translations is that of the Loeb Classical Library, as follows:

*On Listening, How to Distinguish a Flatterer from a Friend* and *On Being Aware of Moral Progress*, from *Plutarch's Moralia* volume 1, by F. C. Babbitt (Loeb Classical Library, London and Cambridge, Mass., 1927).

*Whether Military or Intellectual Exploits Have Brought Athens More Fame*, from *Plutarch's Moralia* volume 4, by F. C. Babbitt (Loeb Classical Library, London and Cambridge, Mass., 1936).

*On the Avoidance of Anger* and *On Contentment*, from *Plutarch's Moralia* volume 6, by W. Helmbold (Loeb Classical Library, London and Cambridge, Mass., 1939).

*On God's Slowness to Punish, On Socrates' Personal Deity* and *In Consolation to His Wife*, from *Plutarch's Moralia* volume 7, by P. H. De Lacy and B. Einarson (Loeb Classical Library, London and Cambridge, Mass., 1959).

*On the Use of Reason by 'Irrational' Animals*, from *Plutarch's Moralia* volume 12, by W. Helmbold (Loeb Classical Library, London and Cambridge, Mass., 1957).

Any occasions where we have translated Greek text which differs from that of these Loeb volumes have been noted in the Textual Appendix (pp. 402–6).

The numbers and letters which appear in the margins of the

translations are the standard means of precise reference to passages of Plutarch's *Moralia*: they refer to the pages and sections of pages of the 1599 Frankfurt edition of *Moralia* (Greek edited by Stephanus, or H. Estienne; Latin translation by Xylander, or W. Holtzman).

The authors take great pleasure in acknowledging the early generosity of Professor Donald Russell, without which this volume would have failed to get started; and considerably less pleasure in acknowledging the collaboration of the National Health Service and London Transport.

# ABBREVIATIONS

| | |
|---|---|
| *CAF* | *Comicorum Atticorum Fragmenta*, ed. T. Kock |
| *CMG* | *Corpus Medicorum Graecorum* |
| *DK* | *Die Fragmente der Vorsokratiker*, ed. H. Diels, W. Kranz |
| *EGF* | *Epicorum Graecorum Fragmenta*, ed. M. Davies |
| *EK* | *Posidonius, The Fragments*, ed. L. Edelstein, I. G. Kidd |
| *FGrH* | *Die Fragmente der griechischen Historiker*, ed. F. Jacoby |
| *IG* | *Inscriptiones Graecae* |
| *ILS* | *Inscriptiones Latinae Selectae*, ed. H. Dessau |
| *PCG* | *Poetae Comici Graeci*, ed. R. Kassel, C. Austin |
| *PLG* | *Poetae Lyrici Graeci*, ed. T. Bergk |
| *PMG* | *Poetae Melici Graeci*, ed. D. Page |
| *SIG* | *Sylloge Inscriptionum Graecarum*, ed. W. Dittenberger |
| *SVF* | *Stoicorum Veterum Fragmenta*, ed. H. von Arnim |
| *TGF* | *Tragicorum Graecorum Fragmenta*, ed. A. Nauck, R. Kannicht, B. Snell, S. Radt |

# INTRODUCTION

Plutarch of Chaeronea has a strong claim to be regarded as the best essayist of the Graeco-Roman world. He may also claim the dubious reputation of being one of the least read today. It was not always so. Indeed Plutarch's literary history has undergone remarkable switchbacks of popularity, from heights where he was unduly admired for quite the wrong reasons to being unduly neglected for no sufficient reason at all.

Things started well for him. He was successful and admired in his own lifetime, invited to lecture and requested for literary and philosophical contributions, known and welcome in the best society for his learned and entertaining company, and died with high honours and a secure reputation. He continued to be read through the late empire as a standard writer by both pagan authors and by the Greek Fathers, who found much of what he wrote sympathetic to their creed, of which he had been unaware. His early popularity is attested by a catalogue of his work which has survived in his transmission, known as the *Lamprias Catalogue*, a compilation which was attributed to a supposed son of Plutarch of that name (Suda, *s.v.* Lamprias). The order of the list of titles, however, betrays a rather crude librarian's system of organization rather than a scholar's grouping, and it is now generally agreed to be a library catalogue, probably of the third or fourth century (see J. Irigoin, *Plutarque, Oeuvres Morales*, I, 1, pp. ccxxviii f., ccciii ff.; F. H. Sandbach, *Plutarch's Moralia*, XV (Loeb)). Its interest lies in the large number of 227 items catalogued, and also because it attracted works of which Plutarch was certainly not the author but nevertheless nestled under the great reputation and protection of his name. It must be admitted, however, that the competence of the compiler is rendered highly suspect by the inclusion in the list of Aristotle's *Topics*, an extreme and witless misplacement of a book which badly needed reshelving. At any rate, at the time of the Byzantine renaissance, manuscripts of Plutarch were still available in some numbers; that so much of his work has been transmitted to us is due mainly to the industrious admiration of the Byzantine monk, Maximus Planudes, who, at the very end of the thirteenth century overlapping to the first years of the fourteenth, hunted down and assembled what was to become the modern corpus. This now comprises forty-eight *Lives* and seventy-eight essays and lectures, masquerading under the conventional title of *Moralia*, a few of which are spurious. This is one of the most extensive survivals of a classical author (it occupies twenty-six volumes of the Loeb edition), and it is due not to chance, but to a continued admiration and affection for Plutarch's works.

In modern literary history his influence was at its greatest from the sixteenth to the eighteenth centuries. He even had some part in the Reformation, for both Melanchthon and Zwingli admired his heroes and actually attempted to bring them by a convenient back door into their Christian heaven, where some at least would scarcely have felt at home. The great humanist Erasmus put him on a par with the Bible, had a hand in the first printing of his work in Greek (1509), and thoughtfully dedicated to Henry VIII of England his Latin translation of *On Flattery*. But one of the most momentous points in Plutarchan history was the translation into French by Jacques Amyot of the *Lives* in 1559 and of the *Moralia* in 1572. This was and is one of the great translations. At that moment Plutarch became a Frenchman, and in the eyes of that nation has remained so ever since. Rabelais, who could read Plutarch in Greek, had already been full of him, but now Amyot introduced Plutarch to the person who was to be his French counterpart, Montaigne. He reached the highest spheres of court and influence, as Racine read Amyot, presumably expurgated in choice of Lives, to Louis XIV; but he also gravitated to the more domestic scene, for even the amiable old philistine in Molière's *Les Femmes savantes*, who had no use whatever for his learned and pedantic sister's books, was yet willing to allow 'a fat Plutarch' as convenient for pressing his neck-bands

(II. 7). Plutarch seemed to be reaching the status of the family Bible in Victorian England.

Meanwhile in England itself, Shakespeare had found him through North's *Lives* (1579) – that is Amyot at one remove, since it was Amyot's version that North translated – and the *Moralia* too was soon turned into English, by Philemon Holland in 1603. Both remain fine translations. Jonson and Bacon show their familiarity with Plutarch, Bacon especially finding him a natural source for aphorisms; and later in the seventeenth century Dryden, in the 'Life of Plutarch' he wrote as a preface to a new set of translations of the *Lives* (not by him, but often known confusingly by his name), recorded his gratitude to Trinity College, Cambridge, for introducing the Chaeronean to him. The Plutarch craze continued in the eighteenth century with writers and thinkers such as Rousseau on the one hand and as a fashionable oracle on the other, providing stagey heroic precedents for the Revolution. And Napoleon was still quoting him on board the *Bellerophon*.

Now Plutarch is a good writer, but not of the highest eminence, and such elevation presaged a fall. It came in the nineteenth century. The causes were no doubt complex, but one lay in the surge of classical historical scholarship in that century, which stopped reading Plutarch for himself, but principally as a source of evidence for the people and times of which he wrote. When it was discovered that he could be both inaccurate and unreliable as a historian, his reputation plummeted and the *Parallel Lives* were discarded from the main classical reading repertoire. This was an unfortunate misjudgement, since Plutarch never claimed to be a historian, and such was emphatically not his purpose or method in writing the *Lives* (see *Life of Alexander* 1.1–3; *Cimon* 2; *Timoleon* 1; *Nicias* 2). But the damage was done, and Plutarch retreated from the rather extreme position of an author whom every person of culture claimed to have read, or at least felt they would read if they ever got round to it, to the opposite pole of the forgotten historical backwoods of literature.

But fashions change. There has been much renewed work on Plutarch, and the *Lives* in particular, Plutarch's greatest sustained work, is being appreciated once more for what it is, with new translations and stimulating commentaries becoming available. The *Moralia* have always tended to ride on the coat-tails of the *Lives*, and so their reputation too, although more slowly, is beginning to revive through scholarly re-examination. But modern translations are lacking, and the purpose of this volume is to offer a selection of the essays in the hope that a new generation may rediscover the attractions of reading them.

But first let us clarify what we are talking about. The conventional title *Moralia* is a Latin translation of a Greek term for 'Moral Pieces' (*ēthika*), which was used as a classificatory title in the Middle Ages for one large group of his essays concerned with popular homilies and disquisitions on themes related to practical ethics. Although the term is not unfair in allusion to the spring of much of Plutarch's writing, it is grossly inadequate and misleading as a description of the collection as a whole, and off-putting as well to modern ears. What we have are Plutarch's surviving essays and lectures on a wide variety of subjects. He was an omnivorous reader, of tireless curiosity and erudition; no subject was alien to him, although naturally some were more attractive and some more suited than others to his intelligence, competence and interests. It is now impossible to date them with any hopes of accuracy, but while a few read like youthful effusions, the great majority appear to date from the time of his mature writing in the later years of the first century AD and the first quarter of the second. His subjects range through philosophy, politics, science, theology, education, rhetoric, literary history and criticism, psychology both human and animal, and antiquarian curiosities. The treatment of these subjects varies from a popular, accessible and practical approach and style to highly specialized and professional hermeneutics and criticism. Some works are lectures, others rhetorical and amusing effusions; some are essays dedicated to influential acquaintances or designed for local youths; some are in the form of the literary epistle, others use the literary dialogue, which had had a continuous and varied history since Plato; another set takes the guise of cultivated and sophisticated table talk; another essay is disguised as a historical novel, while others are the equivalent of the familiar learned article. There is a unifying element for this miscellany and the extraordinary treasure box of riches it contains, but it is not the label *Moralia*. What illuminates them and gives them significance is the personality, character, style and aims of Plutarch himself. Indeed the essays provide one of the clearest displays of a literary personality in the ancient world; and it is the attractiveness of this personality, harmonious in its setting, which is one of the main reasons for reading Plutarch.

One of the first things which strikes the reader is Plutarch's strong sense of rootedness and community. He was born in the mid-forties of the first century AD in the town of Chaeronea in Boeotia, a historic enough place in both Greek and Roman military history, for it occupied a strategic position in central Greece, and incidentally as such enjoyed good lines of communication and access, which Plutarch was able to take advantage of. But it was a provincial backwater nevertheless, gradually recovering from hard times and depopulation in the later Roman republic, by no means a likely centre for a man ambitious for political or social power or aspiring to literary or academic eminence. Plutarch himself wryly admitted this (*Life of Demosthenes* 2.2): if a man intended to be a distinguished historian or researcher, he must live in a capital city with a major library. But Plutarch was at heart a small-town man, and deliberately continued to live in his own little community, 'so that it should not become smaller'.

At the heart of this is the strong impression of a close-knit family that belonged to the place, of whom we have a most affectionate picture scattered through the essays, where they play dramatic roles and form part of the society reflected in *Table Talk*. The family had high social status, claiming descent from or links with ancient local heroes, and was clearly well-off. Domestic memory went back through great-grandfather Nicarchus to the dangerous days before the battle of Actium (31 BC) in the Civil War (*Life of Antony* 68.7), but the first character to blossom, his grandfather Lamprias, is portrayed as a much-loved, many-sided, learned and civilized, affable old gossip (*Table Talk, passim*). Father Autobulus appears to have been much more the country gentleman, but he valued culture and had his sons well educated. Plutarch's elder brother Lamprias probably took after his father – a pugnacious and laughter-loving fellow who enjoyed the good things of life, and took his full part in local affairs. But it was Timon, the younger brother – or perhaps stepbrother, there is doubt about the actual relationship (*On God's Slowness to Punish* 558A) – for whom Plutarch had a special love (*On Brotherly Love* 487D–E). At the core of all was the happiest of marriages. His high valuation of such a union is clear from *Life of Cato the Younger* 7.3, and his love for his wife Timoxena and his appreciation of her companionship shine through his consolatory letter to her on the death of their little daughter (pp. 359–74). They had four sons and probably older girls, all clearly cherished. This is only one side of the picture, the close, loving domestic scene; they also all appear to have been highly cultured and literate and voluble, so that we are constantly introduced into a kind of provincial literary salon or coterie, which Plutarch appears to have extended to a local 'school' of higher education for the most intelligent young men of the whole area, with debating exercises on philosophical and literary issues such as we see in *Are Land or Sea Animals More Intelligent?* And Plutarch himself took his full share of local-community and political office.

Even so, if this had been the extent of Plutarch's influence and interests, he would have remained inward-looking and limited, but it is only the centre of the web. He naturally went elsewhere for his own higher education, to Athens, one of the main intellectual capitals not only of Greece but of the whole Roman Mediterranean world. There he went through the full, and expensive, one may say, higher university training of rhetoric and philosophy, with some introduction to the sciences, of which mathematics interested him, although he had no real talent for it. So Athens remained a main centre for him, to which he returned often; it was, after all, his main library (cf. *On the E at Delphi* 384E). There he became familiar with the best society and a familiar figure in it. He had influential friends such as the public figure Euphanes, to whom he addressed *Old Men in Politics*, and the exiled Prince Philopappus of Commagene to whom *How to Distinguish a Flatterer from a Friend* is dedicated. He was invited to deliver public speeches on great occasions (see p. 147), and was finally awarded honorary Athenian citizenship (*Table Talk* 628A).

But Plutarch was also a deeply religious man, and if Athens was the academic hub of his world, the shrine of Apollo at Delphi, a short distance to the west of Chaeronea in Phocis, was the religious navel of Greece; so Chaeronea was ideally placed between the two centres. Plutarch's family seems already to have had connections with Delphi, but eventually Plutarch had a second house there, was elected to highest office in one of the two permanent priesthoods and again enjoyed honorary citizenship (*Table Talk* 700E; Dittenberger, *SIG*³ 829A; *Old Men in Politics* 792F).

But that was not all. He travelled. He had been to Alexandria and Egypt, possibly to Smyrna in Asia and, most crucially, to Rome, where on the first occasion he lectured, but more importantly began once more to build up a network of friendships and acquaintances in high society. This was a society not simply of literati, but of men of political action, office and influence, such as L. Mestrius Florus, from whom Plutarch obtained Roman citizenship and adopted his Roman *nomen* (*SIG*³ 829A), and who is much to the fore in *Table Talk*; or C. Minucius Fundanus (see p. 174); or the Avidii brothers, Nigrinus and Quietus (see p. 249 and *On Brotherly Love*); or, above all, Q. Sosius Senecio, consul of 99 and 107, to whom he dedicated *Lives* and *Table Talk* (see p. 120). He saw them in Italy; they came to see him in Greece.

So from the centre of *his* world in Chaeronea, his range of concern and participation extended in widening concentric circles to the whole structure of the Roman empire, a situation of considerable interest for us today, in the melding of local patriotism with membership of wider communities. Plutarch's own immediate relationships in his full activities in Chaeronea, and indeed such duties and contacts elsewhere, ensured that his view of wider responsibilities never depended on vague theoretical vapourings, but was rather the portrayal of a society at work through the problems and actions of its individual members. Whether that society in a particular context was domestic, local or international, the treatment and orientation were similar. One should be careful not to mislead and overstate here any case of Plutarchan influence. Plutarch in his far-off, happy, provincial little community, lay distant and disconnected from any real operational power. He could reach his friends' minds anywhere of course by writing, but he was no *éminence grise* in actual politics, rather a touchstone for them of social and political behaviour. Also the picture of society he gives us is no doubt in parts idealized, and certainly focused on a small and extraordinarily highly cultured section, although that section in Plutarch's eyes was or could be the most influential and operative part of it. Even here, what is at stake is not so much Plutarchan influence as the interest of his international attitudes.

The form of the essays is set then by this human framework; Plutarch sometimes uses friends and relatives as vehicles for and embodiments of his thoughts, and frequently also as recipients and targets for his writing. The content, however, is dominated by three themes, with Plutarch's characteristic personal notes.

The first is philosophy. He had been thoroughly trained in rhetoric and may even at one time have considered a professional lecturing or sophistic career. There still survive one or two pieces which seem little more than rhetorical effusions, such as *Which is More Useful, Fire or Water?*, which may come from a youthful period; but more importantly, his mature work retains the techniques and skills inherited from that training. At Athens, however, his philosophy professor, Ammonius, captured his mind for philosophy, and most of his life and work was devoted to its pursuit, but again in characteristic ways. Of the main contemporary schools of philosophy he considered himself a Platonist and member of the Academy (*On the E at Delphi* 387F). He was morally and theologically hostile to Epicureanism and, although attracted to aspects of Stoic ethics, he objected to their more extreme dogmas of absolutism (see *On Being Aware of Moral Progress*). So he could and did write specialized academic essays of philosophical polemic, such as *On Stoic Self-contradictions*, and a companion piece on the Epicureans, or of exegesis, such as *Platonic Questions*. But Plutarch did not have an original or particularly penetrating mind for abstract philosophical analysis and theory; so although these essays are of interest as examples addressed not to professionals but to the highly cultivated society of his time, and although even here, as in his essay on the interpretation of the creation of the soul in Plato's *Timaeus*

(1012a ff.), the individual colouring of his own predispositions show through, one feels that they are not at the heart of his main activity.

He was above all a positive and practical and even pragmatic man, and so his main energy was directed to the application of philosophy as both the canon and the driving force for our whole lives. A fundamental tenet was the one that General Laches saw in Socrates (Plato, *Laches* 188c ff.), and one which in Hellenistic philosophy the Stoics too particularly championed, namely that thoughts and actions must be in tune, and that philosophy be activated in actual behaviour (e.g. *On Stoic Self-contradictions* 1033A–B; and see p. 118); that philosophy is in fact the Art of Life. Accordingly, Plutarch addressed works of popular ethics to individuals, or responded as a consultant for advice, as when Paccius asked for a piece on contentment. An essay may concern itself with domestic relationships, as *Marital Advice*, or with passions (the main topic of Hellenistic ethics) such as rage, sent to the notoriously irascible Fundanus, a passion which affects other people as well as oneself. Another type deals with values and dangers in the relationships between people, like *How to Distinguish a Flatterer from a Friend*, addressed to Prince Philopappus. He is particularly interested in the interaction between two people for the practical moral benefit of both, as in *On Listening*. Fundamentally Plutarch is concerned with the moral well-being of his reader (*On Contentment*), not, however, in the light of an individual in isolation, but rather as springing from the behaviour of that individual in relation to others in his group and society, and how this is interactive. And so the large group of 'moral' essays naturally leads to a group of political essays, such as *Advice on Public Life* (798A ff.), which follow the same principles and have the same aims.

It is in this area of practical ethics that Plutarch's real philosophical gifts emerge. If he lacked theoretical originality, he possessed an acute perceptiveness of individual psychological behaviour. The importance of psychology for ethics had long been a common feature in Greek thought, and one which gained emphasis in Hellenistic philosophy, both in theory (as with Posidonius) and in practical ethics (as with Epictetus). But Plutarch eschews the abstract and indefinite, and displays real insight in analysing the situations and the mental conditions which form the actual springs and causes of the bursts of passion that distort our behaviour, and so in analysing the psychological operations and reactions of individuals in their association with others. This is pursued in quite distinctive ways, as is shown in this volume by the essays *How to Distinguish a Flatterer from a Friend*, *On the Avoidance of Anger* and *On Contentment*, whose Introductions trace the originality of Plutarch's approach to common ethical problems.

Two aspects of this are worth noting. In the first place his advisory and hortatory writing and counselling sprang at least in part from his own practical experience. True to his own principle of putting words into action, he himself engaged in local government and affairs at all levels. He has an amusing tale of how visitors were astonished at the sight of the distinguished writer, magistrate, representative of state, ambassador even, performing on one occasion in Chaeronea a mundane municipal chore as supervisor of roads (*Advice on Public Life* 811B–C). It has been argued (C. P. Jones, *Plutarch and Rome*) that he was also actively committed through his honorary citizenships in offices and responsibilities in the wider communities; but Plutarch himself is reticent on this, and it is perhaps safer to see his main sphere of activities as being in Chaeronea and Delphi. And indeed his 'political' advice not unnaturally seems geared more to local government. His dedications to his powerful Roman friends explored the field of social ethics. But at least he was no armchair guru, regarding his study, as his contemporary, the Stoic Epictetus (3.23.30) did, merely as the equivalent of a medical psychiatric consulting-room. As he says, in a rather different context in *Life of Demosthenes* 2: 'The process may seem strange; and yet it is very true. I did not so much gain the knowledge of things by the words, as words by the experience I had of things.'

The second point is the inverse of this. As his ethical therapeutics and moral guidance for others sprang from personal practical experience as well as from cogitation, so too he regarded such precepts and rules as directed to and indeed necessary for himself. In his time of personal distress at the death of his little daughter, he reminds his wife and himself that it is now that the advice he dishes out to others must apply also to himself (*In Consolation to his Wife* 608F). He is just as explicit with regard to a wider sphere in *Life of Timoleon* 1: 'When I first applied myself to the writing of these *Lives*, it was for the sake of others, but I pursue that study for my own sake, availing myself of history as of a mirror, from which I learn to adjust and regulate my own conduct.'

Such earnest and determined, yet modest, operation of philosophy as a tool for practical instruction explains two other traits. He has sometimes been dubbed a philosophical eclectic because of his willingness on occasion to use Stoic, Cynic or even Epicurean material in a particular presentation or argument. But this is a misleading appellation. He certainly believed himself to be a Platonist and an opponent of the other main schools. But he considered it open to him to bring in relevant support from whatever source to help consolidate or facilitate the understanding of a position he was advocating (cf. pp. 117, 203 ff.). This is revealed starkly by the way he will attack an opponent's view in one essay, yet borrow it positively in another; it depends in either case on the context. But what he will not do is betray for mere rhetorical reasons a fundamental philosophical belief or academic principle. Such borrowing is made possible because there was more shared agreement in the different Hellenistic schools than was immediately apparent from their polemic. Plutarch was prepared to use this in the transmission of his popular philosophy, and in doing so may be said to have helped foster and make use of a kind of philosophical koine in his practical ethics (see pp. 303–4).

Also, since philosophy is pedagogic, and it therefore matters very much to Plutarch that he should *persuade* his audience of what he is saying, he is glad to use what rhetorical skills he can for that end. So, in an educative system and tradition where rhetoric and philosophy contended with and opposed each other for the title and position of the arch science and method of education, Plutarch may be thought to be blurring the edges. But in fact in this period such blurring was not at all unusual. Plutarch's contemporary Dio Chrysostom (The Golden Mouth) of Prusa, was primarily a professional sophist discoursing on themes which included popular philosophy; Plutarch regarded himself primarily as a philosopher, but with rhetorical skills. These skills were formidable and should not be underestimated. Like Plato's literary skills they were at the service of his philosophy. But, as we shall see below, his very method of presentation relied more heavily on literary skills than on argumentation, and so they could distract through their prominence. He was probably aware of this (see p. 26).

The second major ingredient in his essays springs from religion and theology. Since this responds to a similar analysis to that of philosophy, it may be treated more briefly. Again Plutarch's theory and practice arise not only from his own sincere religious sympathies and interests, but also from his personal involvement in high office at Delphi. Indeed he may well be credited with some part in the revival of the fortunes of the great shrine and oracle of Apollo in this period. He wrote a series of 'Pythian' dialogues based on Delphi, such as *The Pythia's Prophecies* and *On the E at Delphi*. Above all he was interested in the impact of the divine on the lives of human beings and, inversely, in the way people's attitude to the divine affected their behaviour. As usual one is impressed by his moderation and abhorrence of extremes. One of his main quarrels with Epicureans was their complete detachment of the gods from human affairs and their consequent denial of any sense of providence (*On God's Slowness to Punish*, init.). On the other hand, like Epicureans, he loathed superstition, on which he wrote an essay (164E ff.). As a believer in the providential operation of the universe, he was naturally drawn to the problem of evil, the existence of which he acknowledged and recognized, not in the abstract, nor in the Platonic and Stoic philosophical theory of self-destruction and corruption, but in the instructive instance of the individual (*Life of Demetrius*, init.) or of the individual in family and society (*On God's Slowness to Punish*). As a priest of Apollo's oracle, he was fascinated by all possible means of communication between gods and men, especially for the guidance of the latter. His penchant for reciprocity led him to set up in a series of myths (see pp. 245–8, 305–6) an imaginative two-world picture, complete with a demonic eschatology, which suggested psychic intercommunication between incarnate and discarnate souls, and so depicted the progression or backsliding of each. Particularly in this area of other-worldly speculation, Plutarch remained almost painfully honest and undogmatic, true to his academic scepticism (cf. *In Consolation to his Wife* 612A–B; p. 241). But there is no doubting the source of strength to him of the faith of his fathers (cf. *Pythia's Prophecies* 402E), which he takes comfort from in the crisis of his daughter's death (*In Consolation to his Wife, fin.*). In the end, I think his aim was to reconcile philosophy and religion, or rather to render them complementary forces for good in our lives. This is depicted, typically in human form, in his portrait of the Theban leader Epaminondas (see p. 303).

The third theme requires development. Let us start from the quite inadequate description of literary magpie or Autolycus (Shakespearean version). Plutarch was clearly a man of insatiable and all-consuming curiosity, and his maw was fed through the conveyor-belt of his voracious reading. He had certainly read all the major Greek authors of classical and Hellenistic literature with thoroughness and appreciation: the epic and lyric poets, the dramatists, the historians, the philosophers, of course, and, although to a lesser extent, the orators. To this may be added more recondite fields, compilations and collections; he is one of the few ancient authors who will on occasion tell us when his information comes second-hand. On top of this was a vast store of anecdote from the oral tradition. A very great deal of this was simply tucked away in his capacious memory; but in addition he kept notebooks of his reading, probably grouped under topics and subjects (*On Contentment* 464F; *On the Avoidance of Anger* 457D–E). It is not easy to understand how easily accessible this ancient form of filing system was for consultation, but he referred to it constantly when writing (*On Contentment* 464F). The result of all this is that in Plutarch we have a kind of living repository of the wisdom of the Greeks and (but to a lesser extent, because of an admitted limited fluency in Latin) the Romans.

Two things worth noting derive from this. The first is that a number of fascinating essays are a direct reflection of his all-embracing curiosity. In them he produces and ruminates on collections of odd stories or strange conundrums in any or every field of human inquiry. Some of these are antiquarian in flavour, like *Greek Questions* and *Roman Questions* and *Brave Deeds of Women*; but his books of *Table Talk* show Plutarch with his family and friends discussing an inexhaustible list of such curious topics and their origins in their after-dinner conversations. There is a rather dilettante air about this, no doubt, although highly civilized, but it does display an astonishing erudition combined with unfading freshness of curiosity and wonder; and this pervades all his work.

The second point is more far-reaching, because the overwhelming mass of reading embedded in his mind affected the very method of his writing and composition. Open any page of Plutarch and you will find it spattered with quotations, anecdote and illustrations heightened by simile and metaphor. But if we read carefully we discover that they are not mere epideictic embroidery or pyrotechnic display; these elements are the very bricks of his persuasion, the actual content of his argument (see pp. 120–21). Plutarch did not have a logical mind; at least he does not develop his case by logical argument. He had, I believe, a pictorial mind (see pp. 152–3). He presents his case by the vividness of illustration, so that the reader is impelled to say, yes, I recognize that, it must be true (cf. p. 209). These persuasive illustrations come from his capacious arsenal; the poets quoted provide their own powerful associations, but the historical and legendary examples and anecdotes are strikingly highlighted by Plutarch's vivid powers of description. He has always and rightly been recognized as a great teller of stories, but the relation of this skill to his method of persuasion has not been adequately appreciated, nor why the virtue he admires most in the historian Thucydides is vividness (see p. 149). The Greeks were well aware of the psychic force of such mental images, and even had a technical name for the process (*anazōgraphēsis*, 'picturing'). In the deployment of this style as argument, Plutarch has no rival in ancient literature.

This is one reason why Plutarch suffers less than some by translation. His actual prose style is careful, elaborate and consciously controlled. He avoids contemporary extremes of archaism and the exotic, and forges a euphonious and dignified style of his own. In translation some of this is missed, and especially a certain sonority of language and sentence (his sentences could be very long), but it is not essential to our appreciation. For his style in the important sense lies in the content and presentation of the images and the vividness of narrative and description, which can to a great extent be captured even in translation. Because of this, too, despite his great display of learning, and manipulation of it, Plutarch is never, at least to my ears, dull. His work is shot through with wit and humour; anyone who doubts whether Plutarch had a sustained sense of humour should address himself without delay to Plutarch's persuasive porker Gryllus in *On the Use of Reason by 'Irrational' Animals*.

So what picture of our essayist emerges from this collection? The most forceful impression is of a humanist. He was primarily interested in human beings, although this for him included their relationship to gods or the divine. He was not concerned with human beings in the indefinite mass, however, but in this or that particular person. I have suggested that this attitude sprang from the immediacy of his relationships in his own small community, which itself was the spring for his suppositions about the wider societies to which he belonged. The influence and impact of Athens and Delphi are clear enough. But what of Rome and his attitude to the Empire? Well, he was clearly not opposed to it (*The Pythia's Prophecies* 408B). He was after all a member and citizen of it. If Chaeronea was his beloved microcosm, Rome and its empire formed his macrocosm. He was a Greek, and proud of the contributions of his nation, as is evident from *Whether Military or Intellectual Exploits Have Brought Athens More Fame*. He was not interested in separatism, however, but rather in fostering a combination of talents in a multiracial, international society. This also appears to be suggested by the *Parallel Lives*: if Romans controlled political power, Greeks could complement this by participation, in so far as it was permitted, and just as importantly, play a full and equal role in the multifarious spheres of living and society.

None of this of course is expressed in theoretical philosophical argument, but by juxtaposing Roman and comparable Greek in

the *Parallel Lives*, yet another example of argumentative illustration, this time in the form of individual historical biographies.
The aim was not historical record, however, but the complementary moral exemplars of good (or bad) Greek and Roman leaders.
So it does seem that his concern for the individual's moral, and
so behavioural, character extends from the personal, domestic
and local context to the social and political context of the international world to which he, his class and his friends, both Greek
and Roman, belonged. And at this level perhaps distinctions
between Greeks and Romans were beginning to blur. In the
small selection of essays included in this volume, one is a personal
letter of consolation to his wife, another is for a local youth;
another is addressed to a princely philanthropist and public figure
in Athens, and four are dedicated to Romans of importance.
There is also a lecture for the Athenian people.

Plutarch's attitude towards his world contrasts revealingly with
the Stoic view, where the individual is enlarged to be a citizen of
the world, that is, of the universe, as Marcus Aurelius put it. But
Plutarch is a citizen of Chaeronea and of Rome. He was concerned, not that his readers should assimilate themselves to the
laws of the universe, but that they should live properly within
their society and if possible conduct themselves effectively in the
political organization and administration of it. So his philosophy
of life and the burden of his writing was dedicated quite simply
to putting his colossal store of information, learning and accumulated wisdom to the practical use of helping his fellow men to
live better in all aspects of their social context.

His humanism is the flower of his own humanity. Plutarch
clearly had the gift of sympathy; again, not in the technical Stoic
sense of being in tune with the divine rational operation of the
universe, but rather a natural empathy with and understanding
of his fellow men, not only his very varied and large list of
friends and acquaintances of all types, stations and degrees, but,
still more remarkably, in imagination, in the case of the countless
earlier figures of literature and history who inhabit his pages.
Also, he shows himself, rather unusually for his times, attractively
humane in his attitude towards what were regarded as lower
members of society, such as women (cf. *Brave Deeds of Women*;

*Dialogue on Love* 769A–F), or of inferior status, such as servants and slaves (see *On the Avoidance of Anger*), and even towards the lower animals (*Life of the Elder Cato* 5; *Are Land or Sea Animals More Intelligent?*). Two qualities which he values highly in his essays, humanity (*philanthrōpia*) and a civilized gentleness (*praotēs*), are characteristic of him himself.

So what glimmers through his work is the portrait of an individual. By that is not meant in any way an eccentric. Plutarch was in fact a rather conservative man. Nor was he an original thinker. But although the content of what he had to say is simply pulled from the whole cornucopia of Greek writers and thinkers before him, it is personalized by his own character, insights and aims. That is what moulded his material, rather than his material moulding him. It is important to realize and acknowledge some of the implications of this. Plutarch is not simply recording the vast riches of detail from the ancient world that come down to us through him; he uses them for his own purposes and so, depending on the context, he will bend and twist this 'evidence' to enhance his structured end and capture the imagination of his readers for their own good (see pp. 204–5). It is not the 'evidence' which is sacred, but the end for which the evidence is produced (*Life of Cimon* 2). The evidence is not produced for itself, but for its effect. It is irrelevant and misconceived to blame Plutarch for this; it is part, and an effective part, of his literary and rhetorical style of persuasion. And after all, even at the purely historical level of everyday factual information, the wealth of reference is still precious gold, but it is gold minted by Plutarch. And since the minting and stamp is Plutarch, what we have in the end is a writer of individuality and imagination, who can outlive his own time, whose essays can still entertain, instruct, stimulate and educate us, and also introduce us to one of the most attractive characters in classical literature.

The sixth-century scholar-poet Agathias was moved to compose a neat epigram for Plutarch which survives in the *Palatine Anthology* (XVI. 331). Dryden translated it in his *Life*, and this is fortunate for us since this is one of the rare cases where the translation is better than the original:

> Cheronean Plutarch, to thy deathless praise
> Doth Martial Rome this grateful Statue raise,
> Because both Greece and She thy fame have shar'd
> (Their Heroes written, and their Lives compared).
> But thou thyself could'st never write thy own;
> Their Lives have Parallels, but thine has none.

Well, true. But readers can resurrect their own Plutarch from his works, and it is in the hope of encouraging the rediscovery of the essays that the following selection is offered.

# ON LISTENING

## INTRODUCTION

From one point of view this delightful, entertaining and instructive essay requires little introduction, for it can stand as firmly on its own merits today as in Plutarch's time; it is as directly applicable and understandable to modern students as it would have been to Plutarch's young friend Nicander and his group. But it can also be set meaningfully within the context of the time it was written. The subject is the neglected art of listening. Most people learn and practise speaking, but ignore its counterpart of listening and assume that one can listen anyhow.

This criticism was especially true of the Graeco-Roman world, where rhetoric and public speaking was one of the most important and valued subjects of higher education, as well as being its main medium and tool. So the young attended lectures, and clearly their behaviour could be disruptively inattentive or their attention could be misdirected. The most vivid extant example of the former comes from the fourth-century professor Libanius, who in his old age described (*Oratio* 3.12–14) the terrible behaviour of some of his students in class: some arriving late; some constantly signalling and passing messages about other more exciting matters; some standing and posing like statues with arms crossed, or picking their noses; others sitting in the general confusion, or forcibly holding down the more enthusiastic; some alleviating their boredom by counting newcomers, staring blankly out of the window or gossiping with a neighbour; some applauding inanely; or finally stamping out, drawing others in their trail. Small wonder that there had grown a recognizable literature on decorum in the young. Philosophers like Zeno, the Stoic (Diogenes Laertius 7.22), discussed such propriety in general terms; but in Plutarch's own century, writers like Pliny (*Letter* 6.17) felt constrained to advise on how to behave in a lecture, how to react with praise and avoid portentous, indolent, envious, arrogant behaviour, or sitting gauche and frozen like deaf-mutes. On the other hand Seneca (*Letter* 52.9 ff.) advocates listening in silence and so submitting oneself to the lecturer mutely as a patient does to the surgeon; while Musonius (F49 Hense = Aulus Gellius 5.1) criticized extravagant shouts and demonstrations of praise for the speaker.

Behind this lies the second common theme of criticism, that a listener may be attending to the lecturer, but attending to the wrong thing, merely to his style and verbal fireworks rather than to his subject-matter (Epictetus 3.23.17 f.). So Aulus Gellius (17.20) used a passage from Plato's *Symposium* to admonish the young student that, marvellous though the style is, he should not be diverted into applauding it instead of penetrating to the depth of what Plato was saying. This seduction by style is seen by some as listening for mere pleasure and entertainment, as if partaking of a gourmet meal (Zeno, Diogenes Laertius 7.22), or going to a concert recital (Musonius F49 Hense); a scathing criticism which goes back to Creon in Thucydides (3.38.7) lambasting the Athenians in their Assembly for 'being captured by the lust of your ears, more like a lounging auditorium before professorial fireworks than a state's councillors'.

This position implies in turn something further: the competition between rhetoric and philosophy in higher education. A lecture, at least if it is given by a philosopher and not by a rhetorician, sophist or guest speaker, is not delivered to entertain, but to instruct and so benefit. Thus Seneca again (*Letter* 108.6) inveighs against people who come to a lecture to hear a speaker, not to learn, as if passing an evening at the theatre. Seneca is speaking here of the large part of the audience who are professional lecture attenders or perpetual students – squatters, he calls them – who regard the philosopher's lecture room as a kind of public lounge. What they are there for is not to improve themselves by ditching their faults or picking up some guidelines for life whereby they can test their characters, but only to enjoy to the full the delectation of their ears. They are fully equipped with their little notebooks, but it is the striking phrase for regurgitation that they enter, the tinkle of empty words, not the meat of the content for their profit.

And that leads to Epictetus 2.24. Epictetus argued that there is a skill in speaking whereby the speaker benefits himself and others, and without which he would do damage, but that even when a speaker has this ability, we still find that some of his audience are benefited and others harmed. This shows that skill in listening is also necessary if the listener is to profit, in much the same way that skill is required when looking at a work of art, which the sculptor has created with his skill. So the effect of what the speaker says also depends on the capacity of the listener to understand and to benefit from it. This is roughly the starting-point for Plutarch's thinking; and since it is evident that there was quite a lively interest in the topic in the literature of the first century AD before Plutarch, much of which we have no doubt lost, including all contemporary Stoic publications in pedagogic theory, it will hardly be surprising if elements from other works recur, as in any common theme (as Plato conceded in *Phaedrus* 235e–236a), especially in an essay written by a man as well read as Plutarch. But these are incidental, grist for his mill, matter for his form, for what he creates is new, individual and typical of himself and his writing.

The first two sections are introductory, and Plutarch immediately strikes dominant and characteristic notes. The message of the essay is given a very personal and intimate touch in its dedication to a teenager called Nicander, whose entry to manhood had recently been formally marked by his change to adult dress. Perhaps he was the Nicander mentioned in *Are Land or Sea Animals More Intelligent?* 965C, and so presumably an attender at the discussion groups in Plutarch's home and may have been destined for lectures at Athens; this was the son of C. Memmius Euthydamus,[1] Plutarch's fellow priest at Delphi (*Table Talk* 700E). In any case the Nicander addressed was well known to Plutarch, and this gives the essay the affectionate familiarity so characteristic of him.

Plutarch points out to the young man that graduation to manhood does not mean a freedom from the imposed disciplines of childhood, but rather the freedom of self-discipline. The

philosophical backgrounds that Plutarch alludes to here are mainly
Platonic and Stoic. The idea that doing whatever we want, in
the sense of abandoning ourselves to the whim of desires, is in
fact subservience to their tyranny, while freedom to do what we
really want depends on self-control and keeping our desires subservient to reason, was the major theme of Socrates' attack on
Callicles in Plato's *Gorgias*. The imagery of the tyranny of desires
when escaped from their fetters may have originated with Socrates (Xenophon, *Oeconomicus* 1.17–23), but it had become popular
again in Plutarch's time (Dio Chrysostom 30.14; Epictetus 1.9.14).
The new ruling principle described by Plutarch as 'following
God' is also Platonic in origin (*Theaetetus* 176b; *Phaedrus* 248a;
*Laws* 716a–b), but his close equation and identification of God
and reason is Stoic, and so is freedom as the power of independent
action, which only the wise and good man has.

So at once Plutarch is clarifying the educative purpose of his
theme and tying it to practical philosophy. Indeed he notes (§2)
that Nicander already has the advantage of being acclimatized to
philosophy, having been brought up in a philosophical home. And
when he then turns to his topic by underlining the general
importance of the sense of hearing, he stresses the susceptibility and
impressionable capacities which make it an instrument of vulner-
ability and possible corruption for the young through their emotions, but also their chief duct for virtuous education through the
reception of rational arguments, by which the tendency to pleasure
in the young is disciplined. It should be remembered that Hellenistic and Roman education, like their literature, was still strongly
oral, and Plutarch mentions that even his written essay began
naturally as a lecture, a progression probably even commoner in
the ancient world (for Plutarch himself: 86C, 1086D, 1107E;
Posidonius T39 EK) than with modern academics. So listening
was the most important medium of reception, and thus also the
main channel for benefit or indeed harm. Therefore learning how
to listen is as much part of the process of education as is learning
how to speak, just as in a ball game thrower and catcher both need
instruction (§3). The subject is now defined and orientated, and its
importance and purpose explained. The rest of the essay follows
and develops from this, and can be dealt with more briefly.

The next few sections (§§4–9) are concerned mainly with proper behaviour in the *reception* of a lecture. Receptive listening requires listening in silence, without offensive or distracting interruptions (§4); it demands clearing one's mind of envy of a speaker's skill (§5) or contempt for his failings; we should be recognizing and responding to excellence to our advantage or, if error is detected, we should be reflecting on how we could do better (§6). On the other hand, uncritical admiration is just as bad; it is likely to be based on the speaker's style and presentation or on other external factors like fashion and reputation, while we should be concentrating on argument and subject-matter for the benefit of our own minds (§§7–9).

The essay now moves to more positive *reaction* to a lecture: asking questions, for example (§§10–12). Questions should not be used to distract, lead off at a tangent or deliberately ask what you know the speaker is incompetent to answer. They are not for showing off cleverness or for scoring points, but to help with a real problem. If necessary the speaker should be approached personally after the lecture.

Applause is also a positive factor (§§13–15). If meagre, it reflects on the listener; if excessive, it can distract the speaker. The particular excellences in a lecture should be signalled by the proper reactions, as a sign that they have struck home. This is not simply a matter of social decorum, but also because the listeners have a function as well as the speaker, just as in a ball game catcher and thrower both have essential roles. They should not sit back while others do the work, like bad party-goers. A lecture depends on cooperation between speaker and listener, so even expressions of praise should respond to the speaker's qualities.

In this double act, the listener must respond properly to pertinent personal criticism, without ignoring it or objecting to it (§16). To outface such criticism brazenly and laugh it off is the mark of an insensitive boor; on the other hand, to bolt into the comforting arms of one's cronies at the first sign of criticism reveals a sensitive flower with no discipline or backbone. It is crazy to undergo the pain of surgery and then get in a panic over the subsequent physiotherapy. It is noticeable that Plutarch sees the reactions of a listener as symptoms of his moral character.

In the last two sections (§§17–18) Plutarch sums up the educational value and purpose of this pedagogic process, which involves the right way to listen to lectures. The first steps in philosophy, as in all learning, can be hard work, confusing and distressful. But perseverance will gradually bring familiarity and enlightenment, and awaken the passion for goodness and excellence without which our life is worthless. The young listener can himself be responsible for failure, either through shyness which prevents him asking questions, but leads to embarrassment and confusion when sheer necessity goads him later to go and ask; or by showing off and pretending to understand when he does not, which only confirms his ignorance. So he must concentrate on trying to understand what is being said, and so gradually progress by continually wrestling with his ignorance, even if he is laughed at. On the other hand he must not swallow everything open-mouthed. The mind is not for filling, but for igniting. Listening is our means of sparking our own original thought. So proper listening is the foundation for proper living: a variation on Plutarch's perennial theme of the connection and harmony between words and action.

It can be seen that topics common to the tradition include general behaviour in lectures, social decorum, reactions of praise, silence or condemnation, criticism of attention to style rather than to matter, the purpose of attending lectures, and the development of the capacity to understand and benefit. In these contexts, Plutarch gives emphasis to the educative benefit to be derived from listening in the right way, rather than to any interest in social decorum; to the advantages to be gained from weighing up the arguments of the philosopher's lecture, rather than to the entertainment value of the brilliant sallies and theatrical presentation of a practised speaker. The end in view is the practical moral education of the student.

Plutarch's major contribution, however, lies in arguing the active collaboration in the lecture room between lecturer and listener. This is different of course from Plato's joint dialectical progression through question and answer in the Socratic dialogues, because Plutarch is using the context of a lecture system, but it is comparable, and the importance of interchange is stressed.

The reaction of students can indeed affect the lecturer, as present-day academics, grateful for what they have gained from their students, can testify. But Plutarch in the main follows his brief in concentrating on the listener's function in self-improvement. He partly clarifies this through psychological states of reaction, but most of all by urging the positive role of the listener himself in cooperation with the lecturer, through using his listening for his own good. The whole approach is very typical of Plutarch's general concern with interrelationship and interreaction between two people for practical moral benefit (cf. Introduction to *How to Distinguish a Flatterer from a Friend*). This positive responsibility of the listener goes far beyond Epictetus' more general capacity for understanding, or Seneca's passive submission to the surgeon; it is more reminiscent of the famous Hippocratic First Aphorism, usually mistranslated and misleadingly truncated: 'Life is short, our science long, opportunity fleeting, experience treacherous, judgement difficult. It is not enough for the physician to do what is necessary, but the patients and the attendants must cooperate as well, and circumstances must be favourable.'

The essay ends with what is surely another Platonic inheritance. Plutarch rightly points out to Nicander that the purpose of attending lectures is not to stuff his mind with second-hand opinions, but to ignite it, kindling his own illumination through active listening to the speaker. Plutarch illustrates this with his own homely simile of a man who had walked over to his neighbour's to borrow a light, and then remained passively warming himself before his neighbour's fire instead of returning to light his own. Not only is the thought Platonic, but the image too is that of the kindling spark of the *Seventh Letter* 341c–d, and of the supposed firing of Dionysius with philosophy at 340b and of the comparable metaphor of *Republic* 498a–b.

It was said of a fine music teacher that he taught his pupils to listen to rather than to hear music. Plutarch's subject is huge, and it may be thought that he has only broached the fundamentals; but it is addressed to a teenager, what he says is indeed fundamental and memorably put, and certainly deserves the attention of a modern audience of students of all ages. *On Listening* is also a highly polished literary production.[2] The liveliness of the writing,

with its constant flow of pithy remarks, allusions, images, quotations, anecdote and graphic illustrations, might ironically, in spite
of Plutarch's explicit warnings, divert the modern reader into
being entertained by the style rather than ignited by the content.
But these characteristic embellishments were intended not as
fancy embroidery, but as a revelatory pattern for his propositions.
After all, a work may be, indeed should be, both instructive and
entertaining.

1. Cf. C. P. Jones, *Bulletin de Correspondance Hellénique* 96 (1972), p. 264.
2. See B. P. Hillyard, *Plutarch: De Audiendo*, pp. xxii–xxxiii.

# ON LISTENING

[1] I have written out and sent to you, Nicander,[1] my lecture on how to listen, to help you to know the correct way to listen to anyone who is trying to persuade you, now that you have been released from guardians and have taken on the mantle of manhood.[2] For lack of rules (which the undisciplined sector of the young call freedom)[3] sets masters over one which are more tyrannical than the teachers and trainers familiar from childhood – these masters are the desires, when they have broken out of prison, so to speak. Just as, according to Herodotus,[4] women discard their inhibitions along with their clothes, so when some young people shed the mantle of childhood, they simultaneously shed inhibition and caution, and no sooner have they divested themselves of restrictive clothing, than they overflow with self-indulgence.

You, on the other hand, have often been told that following God and listening to reason are identical; so bear in mind that for intelligent people the passage from childhood to adulthood is not an abandonment of rules, but a change of ruler: instead of someone whose services are hired and bought, they accept in their lives the divine leadership of reason – and it is only those who follow reason who deserve to be regarded as free. For they alone live as they want, since they have learned to want only what is necessary;

---

1. For Nicander, see the Introduction, p. 21.
2. Literally as well as metaphorically. Nicander would change to the *toga virilis*, or adult dress, with his father's permission, probably at some time between the ages of fourteen and seventeen.
3. The language recalls Plato, *Republic* 560e2–561a4, 562c–e. See the Introduction, p. 22, for the concept.
4. Herodotus 1.8: Gyges' horrified comment when invited by the infatuated King Candaules to spy on his wife naked. However, in a different context (*Marital Advice* 139C), Plutarch disagreed with Gyges.

but undisciplined and irrational whims and actions signify an inferior caste, and there is little freedom of will in often changing one's mind.

[2] Immigrants who are completely new to a country, when they are enrolled into the citizen body, are full of complaints and grumbles about what goes on, whereas resident aliens have been brought up with and acclimatized to the laws, and they readily accept and acquiesce in events. Your case is precisely analogous: you were brought up for a long time in philosophical surroundings, you were thoroughly acclimatized to every lesson and lecture of your formative years being presented with a dash of philosophic reason, and so it is as your friend and relative that you ought to approach philosophy, which is the only thing that invests young people with the manly, perfect and orderly attire that truly stems from reason.

I think you will enjoy a preamble about the sense of hearing. Theophrastus[1] describes it as the most emotional of them all, on the grounds that nothing visible or tasteable or touchable brings the degree of distraction, confusion and turmoil which seizes the mind when the hearing is assaulted by crashing, clattering and booming noises of a certain kind. But in fact it is more rational than emotional. Many bodily regions and parts allow vice to enter through them and affect the mind, but virtue has only one handle – the ears of the young,[2] provided that no flattery has contaminated and corrupted them, and no negative remarks have ever been allowed to fall upon them. That is why Xenocrates[3] suggested that it was children rather than boxers who ought to be equipped with ear protectors: the ears of the latter are marred by blows, but the characters of the former are marred by words. He was not recommending turning a deaf ear or actually being deaf, but he was advising wariness about negative remarks, until other good remarks – picture them as sentinels nurtured by

1. Theophrastus F91 Wimmer. The opinion is unusual, for sight was normally thought to be the most forceful and impressionable of the senses. But Plutarch repeats the view in *Table Talk* 666C.
2. This *mot* may have sprung from a similar quip made by the Stoic Zeno of Citium (Diogenes Laertius 7.24).
3. Xenocrates F96 Heinze. His ear protectors recur in *Table Talk* 706C.

philosophy in one's character[1] – occupy that part of the character which is particularly unstable and credulous.

Bias, too,[2] in times long past, was once told to send to Amasis that part of the sacrificial animal which is simultaneously the best and the worst: the tongue was what he extracted and sent, on the grounds that the maximum harm and benefit are inherent in speaking. And it is very common for people, when they kiss  C small children, to hold their ears and to tell the children to do this to them too[3] – a light-hearted hint that especial love is due to those who confer benefit through the ears!

It goes without saying that a young man who is denied all instruction and never tastes any rational discourse not only remains barren and unproductive of virtue, but also might become marred and perverted towards vice, producing plentiful mental weeds from his unturned and unworked soil, as it were. The reason for this lies in the tendency towards pleasure and the tendency to have reservations about hard work, which are not external tendencies implanted by words, but are (so to speak)  D native sources of countless pathological conditions: if these tendencies are allowed to roam free along the paths they naturally take, if their nature is not disciplined by using good arguments to eradicate or divert them, then there is no wild beast which would not appear tame compared to a human being.[4]

[3] Therefore, since both the benefits and the dangers inherent in listening are equally great for young people, I am of the opinion that listening ought to be a constant topic of discussion in one's own mind and with other people. This is especially so  E because it is noticeable that most people go about the matter in the wrong way: they practise speaking before they have got used to listening, and they think that speaking takes study and care, but benefit will accrue from even a careless approach to listening.

---

1. The conceit originates with Plato (*Republic* 560b).
2. This anecdote of Bias' retort to the king of Egypt was used in a different context at 146F, and is fathered on Pittacus, another of the Seven Wise Men, in *On Talkativeness* 506C.
3. This was known as the 'jug' (or two-handled) kiss (Pollux 10.100), and was a common sign of affection (Theocritus 5.132 f.; Tibullus 2.5.91 f.).
4. The passage is strongly reminiscent of Plato, *Laws* 766a and 808d.

It may be the case that in ball games learning to throw and learning to catch the ball are simultaneous, but in dealing with speech proper receptivity is prior to delivery, just as conception and pregnancy precede the birth of viable offspring.

Where birds are concerned, we are told that the bearing and production of wind-eggs is due to impregnation by certain incomplete and lifeless remnants;[1] and the speech of young people who are incapable of listening and unused to benefiting from listening is truly windy and 'unremarked, unnoticed, is scattered beneath the clouds'.[2] They can tip and turn their cups to guarantee that whatever is being poured in goes in and to ensure that the liquid really falls into their cups rather than out of their cups, but they have no idea how to make themselves ready for a speaker and how to adapt their attention to the lecture to guarantee that none of the useful things said escapes them.

But the most ludicrous thing of all is that if they come across anyone with a story to tell about a dinner party or a procession or a dream or a slanging match he had with someone, they listen in silence and cannot get enough. However, if someone attracts their attention and gives them some beneficial instruction or necessary advice, or tells them off for their misdemeanours, or tries to calm their anger, they become impatient and, if they can, they make a contest out of it, resist his words and try to argue him down; if they cannot do that, they leave to find refuge in further vacuous conversation, filling their ears, as they would mean and faulty cups, with anything as long as it is trivial.

Good trainers turn out horses with mouths amenable to the bit, and children with ears amenable to speech, by teaching them to listen a lot but speak little. The compliment Spintharus paid to Epaminondas is relevant in this context: he said that it was hard to meet anyone who knew more or spoke less.[3] And it is

1. Wind-eggs received their name from a widespread belief that infertile eggs were due to conception by the wind (Varro, *De Re Rustica* 2.1.19). Aristotle (*Historia Animalium* 559b20 ff.) records a theory, which he rejects, that wind-eggs are the residua of eggs previously produced from copulation. But the text of Plutarch is uncertain here.
2. The author is unknown. Guesses have been Empedocles (Wyttenbach) and Callimachus (Frag. anon. 365 Schneider).
3. The anecdote recurs in *On Socrates' Personal Deity* 592F–593A.

said[1] that Nature gave each of us two ears, but one tongue, because we should listen more than we speak.

[4] There are, in short, no exceptions to the rule that for a young man silence is undoubtedly an adornment; and never more so than if he listens to someone else without getting worked up and barking out a riposte but – even if the comments are distinctly unwelcome – puts up with them and waits for the speaker to finish and, once the speaker *has* finished, instead of immediately answering back, leaves an interval, as Aeschines says,[2] to see if the speaker wants to add anything to what he has already said, or to make any changes or take something back. Immediately to lash out in retaliation, however, and neither to listen nor be listened to, but to speak while being spoken to, is scandalous; on the other hand, anyone who has acquired the ability to listen in a self-controlled and respectful fashion is receptive to and retentive of any remarks that are useful, while any that are useless or false are quite transparent to him and easily detectable, because he is – as is obvious – aiming at the truth rather than at winning an argument, and does not pitch in head first for a fight. In this context, there is a valuable saying one occasionally comes across – that those who want to instil something useful should concentrate less on deflating wineskins and more on deflating the pretensions and affectations of young people;[3] without this, young people are full of self-important hot air, and cannot be receptive.

[5] It goes without saying that the presence of the vitriolic and malignant form of envy does no good to anything anyone does, and is an obstacle to all fine actions; but there is nowhere it is a worse colleague and adviser than in listening: there is nothing

1. Zeno of Citium said it (John of Stobi 1, p. 694 Hense; Diogenes Laertius 7.23) and Plutarch repeated it in *On Talkativeness* 502C.
2. This is probably Aeschines the Socratic (F38, p. 183 Dittmar), but the reference is very vague.
3. John of Stobi (3.22.37, p. 593 Hense) attributes the comparison to Socrates. The word *askos* (*uter* in Latin) was the normal term for a wineskin, but such skins were the ancient equivalent simply of bags for putting things in. They were also inflatable and so used, for example, as water-wings or floats (Caesar, *Bellum Civile* 1.48); hence, by transfer, the word could refer to human wind-bags.

less pleasant to an envious person than others speaking well, so envy makes them hear anything beneficial as horrible and disagreeable and unwelcome. Envy, however, is *all* that someone who is irritated at other people's affluence or standing or good looks suffers from, since it is others' good fortune which annoys him; someone who is exasperated by good speaking, however, resents what is to his own advantage. For just as light is a good thing for those who can see, so speech is for those who can hear, if they are prepared to be receptive.

Leaving aside the various undisciplined and faulty mental conditions which make people envious in other respects, envy which is directed at speakers is generated by inopportune and unjustified desire for standing or for recognition, and it discomposes and scatters the mind of anyone who is influenced by these conditions, and so prevents him from attending to what is being said. One part of his mind is surveying its own state to see if the speaker's mind is better; another part is looking at the rest of the audience to see if they are admiring or impressed by the speaker. If their reaction is favourable, his mind becomes upset by their approval and the audience becomes the target of his annoyance. His mind fails to retain and preserve that part of the lecture that has already been delivered, because the memory of it distresses him, and is agitated and worried in case the rest of the lecture turns out to be better than what has gone before. The more excellent the speakers, the more quickly his mind urges them to finish, and when the lecture has ended, his mind does not dwell on any of the points that were made, but takes stock of the audience's comments and attitudes as if they were registering votes. It backs and shies away from those whose comments are favourable as if they were insane,* but pursues and fraternizes with the speeches' detractors, who try to distort what was said; if distortion is out of the question, it uses comparison to claim that others have addressed the same issues better and more capably. The result is that it ruins and violates the lectures, and makes them void of any purpose or benefit they might have had for it.

[6] This is why it is essential for one to call a halt to the

---

* An asterisk indicates a reference in the Textual Appendix on pp. 402–6.

conflict between the desire for instruction and the desire for standing, and to listen to the speaker in a gracious and civilized manner, as if one had been invited to a festival banquet or the opening of a ritual. When the speaker hits the mark, one should acclaim his skill; and one should applaud at least his intention in making public what he knows and in using the arguments he himself has found convincing to try to persuade others. When he does well, we should realize that this is no lucky or random success, but is due to diligence, hard work and study – and such success certainly deserves our admiration and aspiration, and we should reproduce it in ourselves. When he does not do well, however, we must concentrate on the reasons and causes of the error: just as, as Xenophon says, estate-managers gain from both friends and enemies,[1] so people whose attention is alert and focused benefit from both success and its lack in speaking. Sloppy thinking, hollow phrases, cheap figures of speech, excited and tasteless delight in seeking applause, and so on, are more obvious in others when we are listening than in ourselves when we are speaking, so we ought to transfer our scrutiny from the speaker to ourselves, and ask ourselves whether we make the same mistakes without noticing them. There is nothing easier than criticizing one's neighbour, but we might share the same faults, and such criticism is useless and vain if it fails to lead to any improvement or vigilance in these respects. When faced with people making mistakes, one should not balk at constantly repeating to oneself Plato's saying: 'Am I really sure that I'm not like that too?'[2] For just as we see our own eyes reflected in the eyes of our neighbours,[3] so where speaking is concerned it is inevitable that our own mannerisms are mirrored by those of others, and this should stop us rushing headlong into contempt of others, and make us pay closer attention to ourselves when we speak.

C

D

E

---

1. Xenophon, *Oeconomicus* 1.14 f.; repeated naturally by Plutarch at the opening of *How to Profit from One's Enemies* (86C).
2. This does not survive in our Plato. Indeed, it is Stoic (Seneca, *De Ira* 2.28.8; Epictetus 2.21.8 f.). Yet Plutarch uses it in three other places (88E, 129D, 463E) and labels it each time as Plato. He must have had it in his notebooks as such.
3. On the other hand, this conceit does come from Plato (*Alcibiades I* 133a).

In this context, there is benefit to be derived even from the practice of comparison: when we have left the lecture and are on our own, we can take something which we think the speaker coped with poorly or inadequately, and make an attempt at the same thing, and put ourselves in the position of trying to remedy, as it were, deficiency $x$, or to correct fault $y$, or to express $z$ in a different way, or to contribute to the topic in a thoroughly novel fashion (which is what Plato did with regard to Lysias' speech).[1] It is not difficult – in fact, it is really quite easy – to repudiate a speech once it has been delivered; but it is extremely hard work to raise an improved version instead: as the Spartan said, at the news that Philip had levelled Olynthus, 'But raising an equivalent city will be beyond *his* capabilities.'[2] So whenever it becomes apparent that our address on an equivalent topic is not much of an improvement, our contempt wanes considerably and our pigheadedness is curbed, and so is our self-love when tested in comparisons like this one.

[7] Admiration is the opposite to contempt, and it is, of course, a sign of a more reasonable and equable nature; all the same, it too needs quite a lot of caution, and perhaps even more. The reason is that although contempt and wilfulness lessen the benefit to be gained from speakers, yet admiration and innocence increase the possibility of harm; such people bear out the truth of Heraclitus' saying that 'An inane person tends to get excited whatever is being said.'[3]

Openness is essential when extending praise to speakers, but caution is essential when extending trust to what they say. It is crucial to be a kind and artless observer of the debaters' language and diction, but a precise and harsh analyst of the value and truth of what is being said: in this way, the speakers will not take against us, and at the same time their words will not harm us –

---

1. Plato, *Phaedrus* 237a ff. The language suggests that Plutarch thought that the 'speech of Lysias' in *Phaedrus* (230e ff.) was a genuine speech of Lysias and not a parody manufactured by Plato.
2. The sack of Olynthus by Philip of Macedon was in 348 BC. Plutarch uses the story again in *On the Avoidance of Anger* 458C. In Ps.-Plutarch, *Sayings of Spartans* 215B, the Spartan is named as Agesopolis.
3. Heraclitus F87 DK.

amiable trust in speakers often causes us to take in false and
pernicious opinions without noticing it.

When the Spartan government sanctioned a proposal by someone whose life had been bad, they appointed someone else, whose
life and character had earned him a good reputation, to propose
the motion: this was a perfectly sound and politically wise procedure to get the general populace used to being prevailed upon
by how their advisers conducted themselves rather than by what
they said.[1] However, philosophical arguments must be examined
entirely on their own merits, with no reference to the speaker's
reputation, because there is as much illusion in the lecture room
as on the battlefield.[2] The speaker's grey hair, intonation, features
and self-aggrandizement, and especially the audience's cries, yells    C
and stamping, derange the inexperienced and youthful listener,
who is swept away by the current, so to speak.[3]

There is also a deceptive element to style, when the subject is
addressed agreeably and at length, with a certain contrived gravity. When singers are accompanied by flutes, the audience does
not notice most of their mistakes:[4] in the same way, an elaborate
and prepossessing style dazzles the hearer and blinds him to the
actual subject being explained. It was Melanthius, I think, who    D
was asked his opinion of Diogenes' tragedy[5] and replied that his
view had been eclipsed by a crowd of words that prevented his
seeing it; and professional speakers, in their lectures and declama-
tions, not only use words to screen their thoughts, but also make
their voices agreeable by techniques such as assonance, cadence
and balance, and so put their audience into an ecstatic trance —

---

1. Plutarch used the anecdote again with greater detail in *Advice on Public Life*
   801B. He capped it there with a line of Menander (F407.7 Körte), which the
   end of the sentence here is reminiscent of. The earliest form of the story is in
   Aeschines 1.180 f.
2. There is an echo of a well-known proverb, 'Many are the empty alarms of
   war' (Thucydides 3.30.4).
3. The language is very reminiscent of Plato, *Republic* 492c.
4. Exactly the same point is made in Ps.-Aristotle, *Problemata* 922a14 f.
5. According to Diogenes Laertius (6.80), Diogenes of Sinope, the Cynic of the
   fourth century BC, wrote seven tragedies; but if Melanthius was the famous
   Athenian tragedian of the fifth century, contemporary with Aristophanes, he
   could not have seen them. So perhaps the reference is to the tragedian Diogenes
   of Athens, of the late fifth century; but little is known about him.

they give the audience an empty pleasure and receive in exchange an even more empty reputation. Consequently, Dionysius' quip applies to them. Apparently, he went to a performance by an eminent singer and player of the *kithara* and promised to reward the man handsomely, but later gave him nothing, on the grounds that he had already paid his debt: 'For,' he said, 'all the time your songs were giving me pleasure, your hopes were giving you pleasure.'[1] This is the fare with which such lectures satiate the speakers: they are admired as long as they are giving pleasure, and then as soon as the pleasure of listening has evaporated, their reputation forsakes them; one party has wasted their time, the other their life.

[8] It follows that it is important for us to peel off any empty excess of style and go for the actual fruit – that is, we ought to behave like bees rather than garland-weavers. The latter pick★ blossom-laden, sweet-smelling plants, and plait and weave them into something pleasant but transient and barren. Bees, on the other hand, often fly past fields of violets, roses and delphiniums, and swoop down on to that most uncomfortable and acrid of plants, thyme, and alight there 'intent on yellow honey';[2] and once they have taken something useful, they fly away to get on with their work. In the same way, therefore, the dedicated and genuine listener should consider both flowery, showy language and melodramatic, ostentatious topics to be 'the fodder of the drones',[3] the would-be professional speakers, and should ignore such things; instead, he should concentrate on settling his attention on the meaning of the speech and on the speaker's attitude, and should extract from the attitude what is useful and beneficial, and bear in mind that he has not come to a theatre or a concert-hall, but to a school or classroom, with a view to correcting his life under the guidance of reason.

Therefore, he should base an examination and opinion of the

---

1. Plutarch repeats the tale with variations in *Fortune and Virtue in Alexander the Great* 333F f., but the anecdote first appeared in Aristotle, *Nicomachean Ethics* 1164a15 ff., without names.
2. At *On Being Aware of Moral Progress* 79C, Plutarch himself tells us that this comes from Simonides (F88 Page, F47 Bergk).
3. The words are taken from Plato, *Republic* 564e13.

lecture on himself and his own attitude, by considering whether
any of his emotions have been at all pacified, whether any of his
worries have been eased, whether resolution and spirit have been      B
strengthened, whether he has been inspired towards virtue and
goodness. There is no point in his getting up out of a barber's
chair, standing by a mirror and touching his head to check on
the haircut and the difference it has made, but failing, as soon as
he leaves a lecture or a lesson, to observe himself and inspect his
mind, to see whether it has lost any of its troublesome and
unnecessary features, and has become less burdensome and distressing. 'Neither a bath,' says Ariston, 'nor a discussion are any good
unless they are cleansing.'[1]

[9] So a young man's pleasure should be lectures which benefit      C
him – but he must not attend a lecture just for the pleasure of it,
or think that the proper way to leave a philosopher's school is
'humming and grinning',[2] or find ways to splash perfume on
himself when what he needs is a rub-down and a poultice.
Instead, he should be grateful if someone treats his mind, teeming
with dimness and dullness, as if it were a hive, and cleanses it
with the smoke of caustic speech. For even though it is incumbent
upon the speakers not completely to neglect pleasantness and
persuasiveness of style, yet this ought to be the last thing on the
young listener's mind, at any rate at first. Just as it is only after
they have finished drinking that people turn their cups around      D
and inspect the embossing, so it is only later, if you see what I
mean, after a young man has had his fill of opinions and has
drawn breath, that it is all right for him to think about whether
the speaker's style was elaborate and overdone.

On the other hand, anyone who fails to concentrate on the
actual topic, and instead requires the style to be unadorned Attic,
might as well refuse to drink medicine unless the cup has been
made out of Attic clay[3] or refuse to wear an overcloak in winter
unless the wool came from Attic sheep: such a person sits in a

1. The Stoic, Ariston of Chios, *SVF* 1.385.
2. A quotation from Plato, *Republic* 411a8.
3. The Greek word for clay here, *kōlias*, was in fact the name of a promontory in
   Attica, so famed for its pottery clay that it became synonymous with it. Such
   regional appellation of pottery or porcelain is common.

light, thin cloak of Lysian language,[1] so to speak, and is lethargic and
E   sluggish, because he is suffering from the diseases which have caused
a dearth of intelligence, for the most part, and of good sense, and
have filled the schools with pedantry and verbosity, which is what
happens when the younger generation do not concentrate on a
philosopher's life or behaviour or public conduct, but give credit to
style and phraseology and a good delivery, and lack the ability and
the desire to examine whether the content of the delivery is useful or
useless, essential or trivial and unnecessary.

[10] The next subject we meet is the proposing of topics for
F   debate. Anyone who has come to dinner should make do with
whatever is placed in front of him and not ask for something
different or complain, and I would have anyone who comes to a
feast of words listen in silence to the speaker, if it is a set lecture:
people who try to divert the speaker on to other topics and
interrupt with questions and queries are disagreeable nuisances in
the audience of a lecture, derive no benefit from it, confuse the
speaker and make his lecture confusing too. On the other hand,
if the speaker invites the audience to ask questions and propose
topics,[2] then what is important is that it is clear that the topics
one is proposing on any occasion are valuable and essential. It
may be that Odysseus was mocked (in the course of the episode
43A  with the suitors) for 'begging for crumbs rather than swords and
cauldrons',[3] since people who command respect are commonly
held to be recognizable as much by their sizeable demands as by
their sizeable gifts; but more deserving of mockery is a member
of the audience who moves the speaker on to considering trivial
and paltry problems – the kinds of problems some young men
are in the habit of posing out of pedantry, or in order to display
a philosophical or mathematical turn of mind, such as the one

---

1. The orator Lysias had become the ideal model for the plain classical Attic
   style; but the fashionable vogue for aping and admiring it was itself a pretentious concentration on style rather than content.
2. A common move of display sophists and public speakers. It was noted by
   Pliny (*Letter* 2.3 *init.*) as a characteristic of the contemporary Assyrian sophist
   Isaeus, of the end of the first century AD, who specialized in extempore
   speeches.
3. Homer, *Odyssey* 17.222. Odysseus, disguised as a beggar, was taunted as worth
   only a few crumbs. Noble guests would receive fine gifts.

about the logical division of simple indefinite propositions,[1] and 'What is movement that is along the side or along the diagonal?'[2] Applicable to these people is what Philotimus[3] said to someone who had an internal abscess and was consumptive. The man asked him for medicine for a whitlow; Philotimus assessed his condition from his complexion and breathing, and said, 'My friend, the issue in your case is not a whitlow.' And the same goes for you, young man: this is not the time for you to be considering such questions, but how you can stop being opinionated and big-headed, lustful and fatuous, and can secure for yourself a life which is unassuming and salutary.

[11] By far the more proper course is to slant one's questions towards the speaker's expertise or natural ability – those matters in which he excels himself[4] – and not to force off track the philosopher who is inclined towards ethics by introducing topics from physics and mathematics, or the one who prides himself on his physics by drawing him into determining the validity of hypothetical propositions[5] or resolving paradoxes like the Liar.[6] We wouldn't think that anyone trying to split logs with a key or open his door with an axe was meaning the key or the axe harm, but that he was denying *himself* their utility and efficacy; likewise, people who make demands of a speaker which neither nature nor training have equipped him to answer, and who reject and refuse what the speaker has to offer, are, in the first place, doing themselves no good by this behaviour, and moreover are earning a reputation for bad manners and troublemaking.

---

1. This is a logical problem which engaged the Stoics, and Chrysippus even wrote a book on it (Diogenes Laertius 7.197).
2. A question of the interpretation of the movements of 'the Same' and 'the Other' in Plato, *Timaeus* 36c.
3. The doctor's name was actually Philotimus, of the third century BC, and his works were still well known to Athenaeus (e.g. 79A). Plutarch repeats the story in *How to Distinguish a Flatterer from a Friend* 73B, and Galen knew it too (*Commentary on Hippocrates' 'On the Nature of Man'*, CMG V.9.1, p. 85).
4. A reminiscence of a line from Euripides' *Antiope* (F183 Nauck and Snell), and a tag which Plutarch used again: 514A, 622A, 630B.
5. The Greek word is a technical term for hypothetical propositions of the form, 'If it is day, it is light', the validity of which greatly exercised Stoic logicians.
6. The Liar was the recognized label for the logical paradox of the form 'When I am lying and say that I am lying, am I lying or telling the truth?'

[12] One must also be careful not to keep on proposing a host of topics oneself, which is in a way a sign of ostentatiousness. But those who listen without hostility when someone else is doing the proposing are those who enjoy rational discourse and are sociable.[1] One should speak out only if something personal is seething within one and demanding attention – it may be a feeling that needs controlling or something unhealthy that needs curing. For perhaps it is not 'better to hide ignorance', as Heraclitus says,[2] but to expose it and treat it. If anger or an attack of superstition or acrimony towards one's family or manic, lustful

E   desire, 'moving the unmoved strings of the heart',[3] discompose the mind, then we should not avoid scrutinizing them by taking refuge in unrelated discussions, but should listen to set pieces on these very matters, and afterwards go up to the speakers on our own and ask further questions. This is what we must do, and not follow the usual, opposite course of enjoying and admiring philosophers as long as they talk about other issues, but getting irritated with them as busybodies if they disregard the rest of the audience, take one aside and talk openly about things that really

F   matter and remind one of them. Generally speaking, people think that philosophers ought to be listened to in schools, as dramatists are in theatres; but on non-specialist topics they think that the philosophers and they themselves are on a par. This is not an unreasonable feeling where the public speakers are concerned, who, when they get up from the seat of honour without their books and primers and deal with the realities of life, are invariably revealed as unimportant and inferior. But this is not an appropriate feeling to have about true philosophers: it would betray ignorance that in their case a serious tone and a light one, a nod and smile as well as a frown, and especially the words

44A  discharged to an individual in private, are laden with profit for those who have trained themselves to stay put and pay attention.

[13] Expressing approval, to be appropriate, also calls for care: the mean must be found, because too much or too little approval

---

1. The term used seems to have been especially employed by the Stoics.
2. F95 DK.
3. *TGF Adesp.* 361 Nauck, Kannicht and Snell. Plutarch liked the line: 456C, 501A, 502D, 657D.

are both crass.[1] A person who greets everything that is said with obdurate impassivity is a contemptible nuisance in the audience: he oozes hollow conceit and the deep-rooted self-aggrandizement of assuming he could improve upon what is being said, and he neither alters his appearance nor lets slip a sound which might indicate that he is listening with enjoyment and appreciation. Instead, he uses silence, feigned seriousness and posturing to pursue a reputation as a man of calmness and depth, and – as if compliments were cash – he thinks that any compliment he pays someone else is one less for himself.

It is in fact common to misunderstand Pythagoras' dictum and to distort its meaning: *he* said that philosophy had given him the advantage of being amazed at nothing,[2] but *they* concentrate on approving of nothing and valuing nothing – they think that to be high-minded is to look down on things,* and they look for gravity in arrogance. While philosophic reason eradicates the awe and astonishment which inexperience* and ignorance generate, because it investigates and gets to know the cause of everything, it still does not destroy one's good nature, sense of proportion and charity. For those who are truly and unequivocally good, there is no better reward than to reward someone who deserves it, and no more glorious honour than to honour someone who deserves it – this is because they have all the reputation they need, and more than enough. On the other hand, those who are mean in complimenting others immediately give the impression of being bankrupt and starved of their own compliments.

Then there is also the opposite type, who has no discrimination, but gets up on his feet* and cheers word after word, syllable

---

1. The mean as a virtue or excellence between the two extremes of excess and deficiency was a Peripatetic tenet originating in Aristotle's *Nicomachean Ethics*.

2. We are most familiar with the tag 'to be amazed at nothing' from Horace, *Epistle* 1.6.1 f. Nowhere else is it associated with Pythagoras. Strabo (1.31.21) connected it originally with Democritus, but afterwards with all philosophers. Not surprisingly, it was one of the attributes of the Stoic wise and good man (Diogenes Laertius 7.123). An equally strong view was that 'wonder' was the origin of philosophy (Plato, *Theaetetus* 155d; subscribed to by Plutarch himself in *On the E at Delphi* 385C). Plutarch's explanation here suggests (like Aristotle, *Metaphysics* 982b12 f.) that philosophy removes the initial impulse of wonder by understanding and explanation (cf. *Table Talk* 680C f.).

D   after syllable; flighty and twittering, he often displeases the debaters themselves, and always annoys the audience by startling them and making them, against their will, share his excitement – it is as if fear of disapproval forces them to join in with his cheering. His applause distracts his own attention from the lecture, he gets overexcited about it and consequently he derives no benefit from it; there are three possibilities as to what reputation he will leave the lecture with – hypocrite, flatterer or philistine as far as speeches are concerned.

E   A juror at a trial must listen without inclining towards either hostility or favour, but must be rational and impartial;[1] at a professional lecture, however, there is no law or oath stopping us from giving the speaker a kind reception. In fact, Hermes traditionally has a place alongside the Graces,[2] because the main thing discourse demands is a favourable and friendly attitude. It is impossible for a speaker to be so thoroughly ineffective and mistaken that he fails to come out with a commendable idea or quotation or overall topic and plan,[3] or at least a commendable use of language or structuring of his speech – 'just as in the midst

F   of broom and rough restharrow the delicate snowdrop blooms'.[4] There are some who have eulogized vomiting and fever and – hard though it may be to believe – even pots and pans:[5] if they can do so and still be persuasive, then surely a speech given by a man who has any kind of reputation and name as a philosopher must undoubtedly provide kind and charitable listeners with some relief and an opportunity for applause.

---

1. Plutarch has in mind the formal oath sworn by jurymen at Athens.
2. He is thinking of statuary grouping Hermes and the Graces. This is Hermes Logios, in his aspect of god of eloquence.
3. A reminiscence of Plato, *Phaedrus* 235e.
4. The poet is unknown, probably Hellenistic. Plutarch uses the lines again at 485A and 621E.
5. Such show oratory or epideictic was well known from the fifth century BC onwards, but increased in popularity and ingenuity in the first and second centuries AD. Epictetus (F21) reports Agrippinus on fever, and Gellius (17.12) reports Thersites on the same subject, in a general section on ignoble subjects of which the rhetor Favorinus was apparently fond. For pots we have a reference in Alexander, *De Figuris* (p. 3 Spengel); but since there are other echoes of Xenophon's *Oeconomicus* in this essay, Plutarch may have *Oeconomicus* 8.19 in the back of his mind. As for vomiting, it looks as if Plutarch was trying to hit the jackpot himself.

At any rate, as Plato says,[1] youthfulness never fails somehow to affect anyone who is attuned to love – and he finds something in all young men to admire and appreciate. He glosses over their defects and describes pallid young men as 'children of the gods', swarthy ones as 'virile', a hook nose as 'aristocratic', a snub nose as 'pert', sallow skin as 'honey-coloured': any pretext suffices for love, which is as skilled as ivy at self-entanglement. And anyone who loves listening and loves rational discourse will be far more capable of finding some reason for praising each of the speeches and having it clear that his praise is not misplaced. In fact, although Plato could not condone the viewpoint of Lysias' speech, and finds fault with its lack of structure,[2] he still praises its style, saying that 'every word has been lathed until it is clear and rounded'.[3] Archilochus could be criticized for his brief,[4] Parmenides for his awkward verse,[5] Phocylides for his banality,[6] Euripides for his verbosity,[7] Sophocles for his inconsistency;[8] and, of course, the same goes for the speech-writers too, one of whom is incapable of characterization, while another cannot generate emotion and a third lacks artistry. Nevertheless, each of them has his own special and innate way of stirring and moving the audience, and is to be praised for this talent; and therefore there is no shortage of reasons for the audience to treat the speakers with kindness. There is no shortage of means either, since it is not always necessary to articulate this out loud: sometimes all one needs to provide is an indulgent glance or a calm face or an aura of goodwill and satisfaction.

We now come to things which are recurrent, in the sense that they are common to every lecture, even if one is faced with

---

1. An adaptation of Plato, *Republic* 474d f. Plutarch turned to it again in *How to Distinguish a Flatterer from a Friend* 56C f., and refers to it in *On Being Aware of Moral Progress* 84E.
2. Plato, *Phaedrus* 236a, 264a–d.
3. Plato, *Phaedrus* 234e5 ff.
4. By Quintilian 10.1.60, for example; and see Plutarch himself in *How to Study Poetry* 33A f.
5. So Cicero, *Academica* 2.74.
6. Not one of Plutarch's poets. He quotes him only once, at 47E below.
7. This criticism started early, in Aristophanes' *Frogs*, for example.
8. Compare Ps.-Longinus, *De Sublimitate* 33.5.

complete failures: not to sit languidly, but in an upright posture
without slouching; to look directly at the speaker; to remain
actively attentive; to keep one's features impassive, so that one
not only displays no conceit or annoyance, but also does not give
the impression that one's mind is elsewhere and otherwise engaged. Whatever the product, there is no exception to the rule
that beauty is the result of a plurality (to use a mathematical
image) forming a single proportion under the influence of a
certain commensurability and harmony, while ugliness is generated at the precise moment that one of the elements is removed
or any extra and inappropriate element is added.[1] Likewise,
D  where lectures are concerned, not only do scowling, grimacing, a
roving eye, twisting round and crossing one's legs[2] constitute
inappropriate behaviour, but nodding, whispering to someone
else, smiling, yawning, looking gloomily at the floor and all
similar actions are also reprehensible and require plenty of
restraint.

[14] Some people think that the speaker has a function, while
the listener does nothing. They expect the speaker to come with
everything carefully thought out and prepared, while they can
charge in and sit down without a care and with no thought for
proper behaviour, for all the world as if it were a party they
E  were attending, where they could indulge themselves while
others do the work. In fact, however, even a guest at a party has
a function to perform, if he has good manners; and someone
attending a lecture has even more of a function, because he is a
shareholder in the speech and a colleague of the speaker, and he
ought not to cross-examine harshly every error of speech or

---

1. This theory of beauty may at least partly derive from the *Canon* of Polyclitus,
   the Argive sculptor of the fifth century BC, who wrote on rhythm and
   proportion in statuary (*Die Vorsokratiker* 40 DK); but it may also contain Stoic
   ideas (Diogenes Laertius 7.100).
2. In Greek male society, the provocative impropriety of crossing one's legs
   was associated with boys and young men, not with women as in our society.
   This was because youthful male dress admitted indecent exposure by such an
   action, whereas female dress did not. Cf. Aristophanes, *Clouds* 973 f.; Aristides
   2.380; and Clement of Alexandria, *Pedagogus* 2.7 (54.3). The 'moral appropriate-
   ness' of such an action at a lecture was even a topic for debate among Stoics
   (*SVF* 3.711).

action the speaker commits and attempt to criticize them, while his own disgraceful behaviour goes uncriticized and he continues to conduct himself boorishly in many respects at the lecture. Instead, just as in a ball game the catcher must move and change position in a rhythm which responds to that of the thrower,[1] so in the case of speeches there is a certain harmonious rhythm on both the speaker's and the listener's part, if each of them makes sure that his own conduct is appropriate.                                     F

[15] Expressions of praise must not be used thoughtlessly either – even Epicurus offends when he describes his friends' letters as 'provoking uproarious applause'.[2] Some people nowadays import alien expressions into the lecture room, and exclaim 'Awesome!' and 'Inspired!' and 'Out of this world!', as if 'Well said!' and 'Cleverly put!' and 'True!' (the expressions used by Plato, Socrates, Hyperides and their peers to indicate approval) were redundant. This is outrageous, and these people bring the speakers into discredit too, by implying that they need such presumptuous and excessive praise.

Another exceedingly offensive group are those who accompany their favourable verdict on the speakers with an oath, as if they were in a lawcourt. And no less offensive are those with incorrect estimates of speakers' qualities, when they call out 'Smart!' to a philosopher, and 'Neat!' or 'Brilliant!' to an aged speaker: they transfer to philosophers expressions suitable for those who trivialize and flaunt intellectual pursuits, and they praise restrained speeches as they would a prostitute, which is like crowning an athlete with lilies or roses rather than laurel or     B olive.[3]                                                        46A

Once when the poet Euripides was prompting his chorus in a lyrical ode he had composed, and a member of the chorus

1. This comparison with a ball game was especially popular with the Stoics: for example, Chrysippus, quoted by Seneca, *De Beneficiis* 2.17.3, and Epictetus 2.5.15 ff. There is an even closer parallel in Clement of Alexandria, *Stromateis* 2.6 (p. 126 Stählin).
2. F143 Usener. The point is the unsuitable extravagance of the expression in the context; cf. Plutarch, *Against Colotes* 1117A; Diogenes Laertius 10.5.
3. The laurel or bay, as Apollo's tree, crowned victorious athletes at the Pythian Games; the olive, as the tree of Zeus, provided the crowns for the Olympic Games.

laughed, Euripides said, 'It is only your insensitivity and ignorance that make you laugh while I am singing in the mixolydian mode.'[1] And in my opinion a philosopher or a statesman might extirpate the indiscipline of someone in the audience who had got out of hand with the words: 'From my viewpoint you are stupid and uneducated; otherwise, you would not be twittering during my discourse (or homily or discussion) about the gods (or government or authority), and you would not be making my words your dancing partner.' You can see that something must be seriously wrong when passers-by wonder whether applause is for a flute-player or *kithara*-player or dancer, when it is actually a philosopher who is speaking – when they cannot tell, because of the cries and shouts of those inside the hall.

[16] The next point is that one should not turn a deaf ear to criticism and disapproval, or run away from it. People who treat a rebuke by a philosopher with nonchalance or indifference, and laugh at reproof and praise their reprovers (which is how parasites react to their benefactors' insults), are behaving in a thoroughly forward and reckless fashion, and no one mistakes their effrontery for proper, genuine courage. It is true that it is not a sign of bad breeding and lack of education, but of an autonomous and disciplined[2] character, not to get upset and to remain genial when faced with non-malicious banter which is delivered lightly and humorously; but to hear castigation and criticism whose goal is improvement of character and whose damning logic stings like medicine, and not to cower, body sweating and head spinning and mind burning with embarrassment, but instead to remain untrembling and to grin and brush it aside with a laugh, is the mark of a young man whom habitual and continuous deviance has made terrifyingly crass and deaf to conscience, and whose mind is as unreceptive of the lash as hard and callused flesh.

---

1. There is no trace of this story elsewhere. The mixolydian mode (one of the key tunings of the lyre) was characterized by Plato (*Republic* 398e) as a 'wailing mode'.
2. The Greek actually says 'Spartan' (or, to be exact, 'Laconian'). It was common belief that Spartans were not only educated to be disciplined, but in particular to put up with any criticism and with being laughed at (Plutarch, *Table Talk* 631F).

That is what these people are like, and then there are young   E
men with the opposite attitude, who only need to be told off
once and they bolt without a backward glance and run away
from their master, philosophy: their innate conscience provides
them with an excellent foundation for salvation, but is extinguished by their lack of discipline and manliness because they do
not stand up to censure or show their quality by accepting
remedial measures, but turn aside and listen to the comfortable
and untroubling talk of flatterers or professional speakers, who
charm them with words that may be pleasing, but are futile and
worthless.

Imagine someone who runs away from a doctor after surgery
and refuses to submit to bandaging: he has had the pain, but
rejected the beneficial part of the treatment. In exactly the same   F
way, someone whose inanity has been punctured and injured by
reason, and who then refuses to make his inanity available for
reason to heal the sore and cure him, departs from philosophy
with a stinging pain, but with none of the benefit. It is not just
the wound of Telephus which, in Euripides' words, 'is soothed
by the spear's filed flakes':[1] the same rationality which has caused   47A
the injury is also the healer of the pain which philosophy instils
in young men of good character. It follows that a person who is
at the receiving end of criticism ought to feel some discomfort
and pain, but should not be depressed or downhearted: he should
treat it as if philosophy had ritually initiated him, and endure the
preliminary purifications and disturbances, anticipating that his
present discomfort and distress will lead to a delightful and lucid
state. Even if the censure seems unwarranted, it is best to put up
with it and patiently hear the speaker out, and when he has
finished, defend yourself to him face to face and ask him to keep
the force of the candour he has just used on you for some   B
genuine deviance.

[17] Besides, the first steps in learning how to read and write,
or play music, or exercise,[2] bring plenty of distress, hard work

1. From Euripides' lost play *Telephus* (F724 Nauck and Snell).
2. In other words, the traditional basic education of a Greek boy (cf. e.g. Plato,
   *Protagoras* 312b; Aristotle, *Politics* 1337b24; Musonius F2 (Hense); Dio Chrysostom 13.17).

and confusion, and then, as one gradually progresses, increased intimacy and acquaintance (as they do in one's dealings with other people too) make everything familiar, manageable and easy to describe and do. It is no different where philosophy is concerned: despite a degree of inevitable awkwardness and strangeness in the first terms and topics one meets, these early stages should not make one take fright and decamp like a faint-hearted coward, but one should have a go at everything in turn, persevere and work for improvement, and wait patiently for matters to become so familiar that what is good and what is pleasant are identical.[1] This *will* happen before too long, and will cast plenty of light on the subject and induce an intense passion for goodness; and it is only someone consumed with stubborn-ness, or alternatively a coward, who could put up with a life devoid of this passion when he had not been man enough to stick to philosophy.

So although it is probable that for callow youths even the issues are rather opaque at first, nevertheless they have only themselves to blame for nearly all the confusion and incomprehen-sion they get caught up in, as is proven by the fact that people of opposite characters fall into the same traps. Some, motivated by a kind of embarrassment and an unwillingness to involve the speaker, stop themselves asking questions and fixing the speech in their minds, and just nod as if they understood; others, influenced by excessive desire for recognition and vain competitiveness, try to show how sharp they are and how quickly they learn by claiming to understand the speech before they have got the point – and so miss the point. What happens next is that after those retiring, quiet ones have left the room, they upset themselves and feel confused, and end up by being forced by necessity to ap-proach the speakers on another occasion (which causes them even greater embarrassment) and to make a nuisance of themselves by chasing after the speakers to ask their questions; meanwhile, the hotheads who were hungry for recognition are continually having to mask and conceal their deep-rooted ignorance.

1. In *On Exile* 602C, Plutarch quotes the adage 'Choose the life that is best, and familiarity will make it pleasant' as Pythagorean.

[18] We must, therefore, rid ourselves of such stupidity and E
affectation. We must progress towards understanding and concern ourselves with grasping the point of any beneficial talk. We
must endure the scorn of those who give the appearance of
talent, just as Cleanthes and Xenocrates did when they appeared
to be slower than their fellow pupils at school.[1] This did not
make them run away from education, nor did it make them
despair: instead, they were the first to make fun of themselves,
comparing themselves to narrow-necked containers and bronze
engraving-plates, because although it was hard for the words to
get in, yet they were preserved securely and reliably. For it is not
only the case, as Phocylides says, that 'one striving for goodness is
often let down',[2] but it is also inevitable that he will often be F
mocked and belittled, and must grapple with his ignorance and
wrestle it down to the ground with total commitment even
while being the butt of jokes and derision.

Nevertheless, we should not overlook the opposite mistake,
which laziness causes some irritating and annoying people to
make: they are not prepared to stir themselves by their own 48A
devices, and they bother the speaker instead by asking the same
questions over and over again – they remind one of young birds
before they can fly,[3] with their mouths constantly opened towards someone else's mouth, for whom acceptable fare is only
what is ready-made and pre-processed by others. Then there are
others whose inappropriate desire for a reputation for attentive-
ness and sharpness leads them to exhaust speakers with their
chattering and inquisitiveness; they are constantly asking redundant and unnecessary questions and looking for proofs of erudition on trivial matters. 'This is how to make a short journey
long,' as Sophocles says[4] – and not only for themselves, but for B
everyone else too. In taking the lecturer up on each and every
point with superficial and superfluous questions (as if they were

1. A well-known characteristic of both philosophers: for Cleanthes, see Diogenes
   Laertius 7.170; for Xenocrates, see Diogenes Laertius 4.6.
2. Phocylides F13 Diehl, F6 West. Different versions of the line exist.
3. The words recall Homer, *Iliad* 9.323 f., lines which Plutarch used again in *On
   Being Aware of Moral Progress* 80A.
4. *Antigone* 232.

travel companions), they thwart the continuity of the lecture by interrupting and delaying it. These people are like cowardly and tenacious puppies – the image comes from Hieronymus[1] – who tear at hides and shred scraps at home, but go nowhere near the actual animals.

We must encourage those lazy ones, however – once they have grasped the basic points – to interconnect everything else on their own, to use memory to guide original thinking, and to accept what someone else says as a starting-point, a seed to be nourished and grown. For the correct analogy for the mind is not a vessel that needs filling, but wood that needs igniting – no more – and then it motivates one towards originality and instils the desire for truth. Suppose someone were to go and ask his neighbours for fire and find a substantial blaze there, and just stay there continually warming himself: that is no different from someone who goes to someone else to get some of his rationality, and fails to realize that he ought to ignite his innate flame, his own intellect, but is happy to sit entranced by the lecture, and the words trigger only associative thinking and bring, as it were, only a flush to his cheeks and a glow to his limbs; but he has not dispelled or dispersed, in the warm light of philosophy, the internal dank gloom of his mind.

If any further advice about listening is needed, it is for us to remember what has just been said and to combine learning with working towards originality, which will enable us to acquire an attitude which is not merely sophistic and curious, but profound and philosophical – and the basis of this is the view that proper listening is the foundation of proper living.

1. F20 Wehrli.

# HOW TO DISTINGUISH A FLATTERER
# FROM A FRIEND

## INTRODUCTION

Plutarch's topic of flatterer and friend was by no means new, but had well-established literary and philosophical precedents. There were different strands to this, some tracing flattery or friendship alone, others interweaving the two.

The Greek word for flatterer (*kolax*) covers a wide range from sponger, panderer or parasite to toady, sycophant, yes-man and time-server. The social and political phenomenon was well recognized then as now as endemic in all societies, not only in dictatorships, but also in democracies such as at Athens, where demagogues pandered to the public whim, as described by Aristotle (*Politics* 1292a4 ff., 1313b40) and derided by Aristophanes (e.g. *Knights* 40 ff.). So the flatterer achieved literary eminence, particularly in the comic dramatists from the fifth century BC on, in the form of satire or as the comedy of manners, and we know that two of the most famous playwrights, Eupolis and Menander, produced plays with *The Flatterer(s)* as the title. But the philosophers too were interested in the subject in the context of social morality. Plato had used flattery in *Gorgias* (462c ff.) as an example of the tricks designed to gratify merely, and which counterfeit the genuine skills that contribute to the good of body and mind. Aristotle in his *Nicomachean Ethics* (*NE*) (1108a26 ff.) and *Eudemian Ethics* (*EE*) (1221a7; 1233b30) included flattery in his analysis of the moral context of the field of pleasant relationships. His successor Theophrastus, in his gallery of *Characters*, had a portrait of the flatterer which had strong affinities to the social exposures of the comic dramatists. But he also wrote a monograph on the topic (Diogenes Laertius 5.47), and the subject seemed to remain of particular interest in the Peripatetic tradition, as the *Gergithius* of Clearchus of Soli (third century BC; F19 Wehrli) suggests. But it was a common theme, on which the learned diners of Athenaeus' *Deipnosophistae* at the end of the second century AD could regale themselves at length with literary allusion and quotation (VI.234D ff.); and John of Stobi, in his fifth-century-AD collection of *Extracts* (*Eclogae*) from classical authors, has a whole section on flattery (3.4, pp. 468–76 Hense) amassed from seventeen different authors representing dramatists, philosophers, rhetors and scholars ranging from the fifth century BC to the second century AD.

The sweep of friendship in history and literature was still more prominent, but the philosophers took early notice. Socrates discussed it (Xenophon, *Memorabilia* 1.4); Plato devoted a dialogue, the *Lysis*, to the subject, and Aristotle in Books 8 and 9 of his *Nicomachean Ethics* distinguished three kinds of friendship: for ulterior advantage, for pleasure or for mutual good. Only the last is true friendship, and the good and happy man needs friends. This link between friendship and morality continued in Hellenistic philosophy. The Epicureans claimed friendship to be not only necessary for happiness, but also a general factor of social cohesion, utility and pleasure,[1] and Stoics maintained that true friendship was only possible for the wise and good man (Diogenes Laertius 7.124). We know that monographs were written on this popular topic by Theophrastus (running to three books, Aulus Gellius, *Noctes Atticae* 1.3.10), Cleanthes (Diogenes Laertius 7.175) and Chrysippus (Plutarch, *On Stoic Self-contradictions*, 1039B); but only Cicero's *De Amicitia* survives.

However, for Plutarch's essay the most important feature of earlier treatment was the discussion of the intertwining relationship of and distinction between flatterer and friend. The greatest impulse came from Aristotle. For in his ethical map of virtues and vices as a mean between two extremes of excess and deficiency, he placed friendship and flattery on the same scale or continuum. Friendship was the mean, representing the right degree of giving pleasure and being pleasant; flattery was the extreme of excess in this (*NE* 1108a26 ff.; *EE* 1221a7); the other extreme, of deficiency, was the quarrelsome, bad-tempered, annoying fellow. Flattery and friendship were effectively linked for the future as different aspects of the same phenomenon, so that

Cicero, for example, in his essay *De Amicitia* (*De Am.*) turns naturally, towards the end (89 ff.), from friendship to the contrasting but related vice of flattery. The question thus arises as to how to distinguish between the two, and it was Aristotle again who made what was to become accepted as the basic differentiation: the friend aims at our good, the flatterer only at pleasure.[2] Other characteristics emerge as common coin: for example, the imitative pliancy of the flatterer contrasted with the constancy of the friend (Aristotle, *EE*, 1233b30; Cicero, *De Am.* 93); the plain speaking of the friend as opposed to the dissembling flattery of the sycophant (e.g. Cicero, *De Am.* 88 f.). On the other hand the similarities between flatterer and friend, that is between counterfeit and true friend, gave the question of how to distinguish between them such importance and urgency in practical ethics from the first century BC onwards (Cicero, *De Am.* 95; Seneca *Letter* 45.7; Plutarch) that Cicero tells us (*De Oratore* 3.117) that the comparison of friend and flatterer was included as a commonplace in the rhetorical repertoire; and a set example of this is preserved in *Oratio* 14 (Hobein) of the sophist Maximus of Tyre of the second century AD.

It was against this sort of background that Plutarch's essay was written and in the light of which it would be read. A brief analysis may show something of his dependence and his originality. It is addressed to a Syrian prince in exile, C. Julius Antiochus Epiphanes Philopappus, a grandson of the last king of Commagene, Antiochus IV, who had been deposed by Rome in 72 AD, when Commagene was merged with Syria. Prince Philopappus had settled in Athens, where he became a patron of the arts. He is an honoured guest and takes part in the discussion at one of the dinner parties of Plutarch's *Table Talk* (628A ff.), that given by Serapion to celebrate his choral victory with the tribe Leontis (of which Plutarch himself was an adopted member) in a contest which Philopappus had presided over and financed with great munificence. Later he was elected to the archonship in Athens in 96/7 AD,[3] and became a Roman consul in 109. His splendid funerary monument, erected between 114 and 116 AD, still stands on the Mouseion hill in Athens. So Philopappus was not only another of the cultivated members of Plutarch's circle, but a grandee of considerable influence and power, and thus a prime target for flattery. Plutarch as usual gives point to his practical philosophy by personalizing it.

The first lines also introduce a most important key for our approach to the rest of the essay. Typically Plutarch uses a quotation from Plato as a spring for the thought that self-love, self-centredness, leads to the flaw of self-deception, and so makes us receptive to flattery, which operates on self-deceit rather than on truth. In a way we may be said to bring flattery on ourselves. But this, although penetrating, is hardly complimentary to Philopappus, and Plutarch hastens to balance it (§2) with the point that the great and the good are especially vulnerable to flattery, as flatterers fasten on them for their own advancement, and their generous and trustful natures render them susceptible. This sounds a little like flattery itself; but Plutarch hurries on to the main point, that it is men like Philopappus most of all who must be on their guard, to protect themselves beforehand rather than rue it after being hurt. It is typical of Plutarch to be interested in practical ethics as a prophylactic. But to do that one must distinguish between flatterer and friend, and that is by no means easy, as they occupy common ground. Both are pleasing company, both are ready with praise, although the flatterer will not criticize when necessary (a seed forecasting the theme of the last sections of the essay, §§25 ff.). So it is a real and serious problem to be faced, for it is not the obvious sponger and hanger-on who will deceive us, but the expert professional who pretends to be our friend and is the real danger precisely because we think he *is* our friend (§§3, 4).

So the next sections (§§5–10) deal with the theme of flattery and imitation, both the flatterer's imitation of friendship and also his chameleon-like adaptation to his victim; for as friendship is a union of like to like in attitudes and habits, the flatterer ingratiates himself by following and praising the same interests and pursuits as his victim until he breaks him in and renders him docile, as a horse-tamer does (§6). But the difference is that a friend remains consistent and constant; the flatterer changes shape with the object of his flattery like water poured into different vessels. He can and will if necessary play the studious academic or the riotous playboy and man-about-town (§7; a splendidly written and vivid section). But Plutarch has practical advice: you can rumble such a 'friend' by pretending to change back and forth yourself, and seeing whether he will follow you indiscriminately (§8). Also, the true friend imitates and approves only of what is good in his friend and so benefits him; the flatterer concentrates on weakness, encouraging it by imitation, and so harms his victim. As usual memorable stories underline the point: when Dionysius grew dim-sighted, his courtiers started bumping into the crockery and breaking it; one 'friend' even pretended to throw his own wife out, when his friend kicked out his – but was caught maintaining relations secretly by his friend's wife (§9). A variation, illustrated by a string of witty examples, is for the flatterer to claim, when a failing is recognized, that he is still worse, while in good qualities the friend is always lauded as better (§10).

Plutarch now turns to flattery and pleasure, for the giving of pleasure is another factor common to flattery and friendship, and so treacherous. But there is a distinction of purpose: the friend aims at the good of his friend, and will even hurt him for that end; but the yes-man in his own interest always aims at gratification (§11), and the chief weapon for such buttering-up is eulogy. But a man's very character can be damaged by inappropriate praise and he and his future actions fundamentally corrupted, so it is imperative for his own well-being to discriminate how he is being praised. Is such praise consistent? Is it given in his absence? Does it go against his conscience (§12)?

What follows is a practical unmasking of a number of sophisticated methods of toadying, but the real emphasis is on the moral well-being of the victim, who must guard himself against them. There is, for example, praise indirect, such as (a) the flatterer pretending to have heard the praise from someone else (§13); or (b) praise implied by denigrating and ridiculing the opposite qualities (§14); or even (c) silent flattery such as giving up one's seat or giving way to a wealthy or powerful superior (but do they do so to the good, or the poor or the old?) (§15). There is no accomplishment that flattery will not attribute in praise, and yet people who double up with mirth at the thought of the Stoic wise and good man allegedly garlanded with all the accomplishments will swallow the lot themselves with disastrous results. There is a nice story here about wealthy aristocrats being good only at riding and nothing else, because horses unseat riders who are incompetent whatever their rank (§16).

But the matter is not so straightforward, for the opposite of praise is frank and candid criticism, and as candour is the real attribute of the true friend, the flatterer imitates this and so operates a counterfeit candour, as ineffectual in its clout as a stage-prop weapon, but as deceptive. So the flatterer will try to give the impression that he is a hard, uncompromising man in relation to other people; but he will take care to criticize trivial, irrelevant faults, turning a blind eye to major ones (§17). For his aim in pretended candour is not the benefit but the gratification of his duped friend (§18). Another trick (and these are all strikingly illustrated by historical anecdote) is to impute to his friend a fictitious fault which is the opposite of one of his real faults, a particularly poisonous move, since it is likely to inflame the real sore (§19). At this point Plutarch sums up the counterfeit candour section by appealing to philosophy for the solution (§20), confident that Philopappus and his cultivated circle of readers will appreciate this approach. The best method of combating such corruptive 'candour' is to realize that our mind has a rational element and an emotional element. Such psychological analysis derives from Platonic and Peripatetic theories, but the language is especially reminiscent of the Stoic Posidonius, a typical blending of philosophical backgrounds by Plutarch. While the friend supports the rational, the flatterer devotes himself entirely to intensifying the emotional aspect. When we are in an emotional state ourselves and our passions are high, it is difficult to see this, and so we are susceptible. Therefore we must convince ourselves in our rational states, to protect ourselves and forestall the effects of such flattering 'candour'.

Plutarch rounds off this part of the essay with some miscellaneous instances in which flatterer and friend may be distinguished: in actions, for example (§21), where the simple sincerity of the friend is in contrast to the ostentation of the flatterer; or in promises and assistance given (§22). He finally and decisively underlines the real, recognizable difference between the two types as moral purpose and the lack of it (§23). There is antipathy too; for while a true friend will wish to enlarge his circle, the flatterer, conscious of his inferiority, will isolate his companion by driving away his real friends (§24; an idea floated earlier in Plato, *Phaedrus* 232c–d, as a characteristic of the selfish lover).

The essay now seems to change tack, from a description of the wiles of gratification and the counterfeit candour of flattery to the genuine frankness of friendship. For this Plutarch returns to his original point, that since it is self-love which leaves us open to flattery, we must try to recognize this weakness in ourselves. For that purpose we especially need friends to criticize us (§25). But the effective employment of plain speaking is difficult, and the remainder of the essay is devoted to practical advice on how best to be frank with your friend.

The character of some of the points made may be briefly noted: candour must not only be properly motivated, but must be seen to be so (§26). It should be free of sarcasm and ridicule (§27). Timing is important, and so are circumstances, for in some situations sympathy and kindness are more effective than criticism (§28). The right time for plain speaking may depend on both sides, or an opportunity may be created by one (§30). There are subtle, indirect methods of criticism (§31). Your friend should not be exposed before an embarrassing audience (§32). There are tips for making plain speaking more palatable (§33), and the recognition that in friendship openness to frank criticism must be mutual (§34). Criticism should not be diluted with constant nagging, but the impact reserved for important matters (§35). It should be balanced with praise. Candour when remedial should be tactful, but when prophylactic more direct and forceful (§36). In short, to speak frankly is a skill which must be studied just as a doctor studies his science for the benefit of his patient, for candour is the most potent medicine between friends (§§36, 37).

This last part of the essay (§§25–37) raises questions of structure. We seem to have moved from a discussion on how to distinguish a flatterer from a friend to a kind of pocket vademecum on how to speak frankly to a friend without offence and with the most effect and benefit, which does not appear to be immediately related to the title of the essay. So it has been suggested that we may have two separate essays tacked together. Arguments for this have been neatly put by J. Sirinelli,[4] but they seem to me to lack conviction. The charge that the two sections have different philosophical backgrounds and affiliations would be hard to establish; they are both examples of a typical Plutarchan *mélange*. Sirinelli points out that the dominant analogical images in the first part are animal, in the second medical. But similes are moulded by the main subject in either case, the flatterer in one, and candour between friends in the other; and the general variety of illustration in both cases is uninhibited. Most unusually Plutarch quotes the same line of Euripides in both sections (49F and 69A; *Ion* 732); but such carelessness is hardly decisive. The combined parts make an unusually long essay; but not the longest (cf. *On the Obsolescence of Oracles* and *On Isis and Osiris*).

There is no doubt that whatever the history of original drafts, Plutarch intended the two sections to form a whole essay, and took some trouble to point up the linkage with his deliberate references back in §§24 and 25 to his original key position in §1. So the most pertinent question should centre on the relationship of the last section on candour to what has gone before. It is, I believe, the positive development of the account of flattery, and helps us to understand better the whole essay. The flatterer must be detected, distinguished from the friend, avoided and countered because he harms us morally, enlarging our weaknesses by blinding us to them. To recognize this is helpful and self-protective, but still negative. The positive counterpart is a true friend's candour and frank criticism, which by warning us of our failings and encouraging our better qualities helps us to understand ourselves and become better men and women. But as the complex art of flattery is hard but necessary to unmask, so plain speaking, *if it is to be beneficial to the recipient*, is no less an art, and requires as much understanding in the relationship between friends. Flattery may be regarded as a harmful excess of praise, but an excess of critical frankness will be just as destructive. The intimate relationship between two people demands the beneficial mean or virtue of the right combination and degree of praise and candour, which depends on the proper and appropriate employment of candour no less than praise in friendship. This is made plain in both parts of the essay: §2, 50B and §36, 73A. And since this is practical ethics, candour too must be described and understood. Indeed candour is the more important of the two, as it is remedial and prophylactic. So we have a kind of balanced diptych between the two parts of flatterer and friend, in terms of flattery and praise, candour and carping criticism, but really based on the moral dangers of the flatterer and the moral value of a friend. Plutarch makes candour the structural hinge of this diptych, moving from the counterfeit candour (which is really flattery) to the true candour (as distinct from excessive or inappropriate candour or criticism) of the friend.

Of course candour in friendship was already embedded in the tradition of Plutarch's subject (cf. Cicero, De Am. 88 f.), and our analysis has revealed other major ingredients familiar from the pot: for example, the title itself and the emphasis on the importance of distinguishing between flatterer and friend (Cicero, De Am. 95; Seneca, Letter 45.7; Maximus of Tyre, Oratio 14 (Hobein)); flattery in the form of imitation (Aristotle, EE 1233b30 ff.; Cicero, De Am. 93) or counterfeit (Plato, Gorgias 462c ff.); flattery aimed solely at pleasure and gratification, while the friend aims at good (Aristotle, NE 1173b31 ff.; Rhetoric 1361b36 f.; Cicero, De Am. 91 f.); flattery as an excess in relation to friendship (Aristotle, NE 1108a26 ff.; EE 1221a7); even the idea of self-love leading to susceptibility to flattery (Aristotle, Rhetoric 1371b21 ff.; Cicero, De Am. 97). And some of the anecdotes are reused from earlier treatments, as the tale of the 'ladderettes' (50D), which had occurred in Clearchus' Gergithius (F19 Wehrli, Athenaeus 256C–D), and the story of Dionysius' sycophants aping his poor eyesight, which had been used by Theophrastus (Athenaeus 435E); but it was a well-known story (Athenaeus 249F), and it looks as if Plutarch embroidered it. No doubt such details could be amplified had more of the tradition survived.

But Plutarch's essay is far from being cold porridge hotted up. It is highly individual. In the first place it is an excellent example of his style. The liveliness of his treatment, the vividness of his similes and anecdotes, and the piquant seasoning of quotations, revealing the everyday bones of contemporary social life no less than the well-read, civilized and literary man's treasure house of reference and allusion: all this gives as usual a memorable individuality to his practical homily. Surely Philopappus was amused, as we are, certainly intellectually entertained, perhaps instructed, and maybe a little flattered.

But there is more. The matter of the essay shows a new and serious approach to what was almost a hackneyed theme. Plutarch is not concerned with the theoretical abstract examination of concepts. He is not so much interested in flattery and friendship as in the flatterer and the friend. Nor is he concerned with the mere exposure for satire of a recognizable social animal. His aim is practical and so the moral intent is personalized, both in dedication and presentation, and even in the high frequency of historical anecdote. His main concern is the effect one person has on another for good or bad; in other words he explores the psychological operation and effect of flatterer and friend. The flatterer is dangerous and the friend beneficial precisely because of the effect they have on the mind of the partner, in its weaknesses or strengths. So Plutarch's contribution, by focusing on flattery and friendship as psychological phenomena, lies in shifting the emphasis from the flatterer to the victim, in recognizing that reciprocity and reaction are involved in such intimate human relationships. All this is signalled clearly at the beginning of both parts of the essay by the underlining of self-love and knowledge of self. But in practical terms this leads back to the understanding of the arts of flattery or friendship; for the best way to protect oneself against susceptibility to flattery is to examine and understand the psychological conditions which permit flattery to flourish, and, on the other side, the conditions under which plain speaking can strike home and be recognized for what it is intended to be.

1. See Long and Sedley, *The Hellenistic Philosophers* 1.137.
2. *NE* 1173b31 ff.; so, e.g., Cicero *De Amicitia* 91 f., Maximus of Tyre *Oratio* 14, p. 170 f. Hobein.
3. J. A. Notopoulos, 'Studies in the Chronology of Athens', *Hesperia* 18 (1949), p. 12, from *IG* II², 1759.
4. *Plutarque, Oeuvres Morales* I.2.68 ff., Budé.

# HOW TO DISTINGUISH A FLATTERER
# FROM A FRIEND

[1] It is true, Antiochus Philopappus,[1] that Plato says[2] a high degree
of self-love is universally forgiven; but he also says that it engenders a
very serious flaw (not to mention the multitude of lesser flaws) –
namely, there is no way that a person in love with himself can make
a fair and impartial assessment of himself. Unless education has
accustomed one to prefer goodness, and to make this one's goal,
rather than what is inbred and innate, then 'Love is blind where the
beloved is concerned'.[3] This lays the domain of love or friendship
wide open to the flatterer; self-love provides him with a perfect base
camp against us, since self-love makes each person his own primary
and chief self-flatterer, and makes it easy for us to allow someone else
under our guard – someone else to testify to and corroborate and
support us in our beliefs and aspirations. To call anyone, as an insult,
'fond of flattery' is to say that he is excessively in love with himself,[4]
since his fondness for himself leads him not just to aspire to
everything, but to believe that he already has everything: the
aspiration is not odd, but the belief is treacherous and needs a great
deal of caution.

If truth is indeed divine and is the source, in Plato's words, 'of
all good things for gods and all for men',[5] then the flatterer is
likely to be inimical to the gods and especially to the Pythian
god, since a flatterer is perpetually ranged in opposition to the
saying 'Know yourself':[6] he instils in everyone self-deceit and

1. See Introduction, p. 53, for Philopappus.
2. *Laws* 731d-e.
3. Plato, *Laws*, 731e5, slightly changed from our text of Plato.
4. This echoes Aristotle, *Rhetoric* 1371b21 ff.
5. *Laws* 730c1.
6. 'Know yourself' was a motto inscribed on Apollo's temple at Delphi, but
   claimed as a philosophical principle by Socrates (Plato, *Protagoras* 229e, *Phaedrus*

ignorance both of oneself and of those things which are good and bad for oneself – he makes the former impossible to achieve and accomplish, and the latter impossible to rectify.

[2] Now, if a flatterer were like most other bad things and exclusively or largely seized on the dregs and dross of mankind, he would not be so terrible or hard to resist; but just as it is soft, sweet woods that woodworms prefer to penetrate, so it is C generous, good and fair characters which admit and nourish the parasitic flatterer. Besides, as Simonides says, 'It is not with Zacynthus that horse-farming goes, but with fertile fields':[1] it is noticeably no different in the case of flattery, which steers clear of poverty, obscurity and ineffectuality, and traps and infects mighty houses and weighty affairs, and not uncommonly deposes kings and rulers. It follows that trying to ensure that flattery is ferreted out before it harms or corrupts friendship is not an unimportant task and requires considerable forethought.

Lice leave a dying person and abandon his body when the D blood which nourishes them dries up, and the chances of seeing flatterers involved in business which has no sap or warmth are minimal, but they cling to reputation and authority and they flourish there – until things change, when they waste no time in slithering away. It is important, however, that one does not just wait for that experience, which is at the best pointless, and is more likely to be hurtful and even dangerous, in the sense that the realization, at precisely the time when one needs friends, that they are no friends is hard to endure, since there is no chance then of exchanging the unreliable, counterfeit friend for one who is good and reliable. No, the friend that you have, just like the coin in your pocket, should have been assayed before the need

---

229e; Xenophon, *Memorabilia* 4.2.24; Plutarch, *Against Colotes* 1118C; Aristotle F709 Gigon), and so adopted by the Academy, Plutarch's own philosophical school, which was originally founded by Plato. But like the other most famous Delphic maxim 'Nothing too much', it was common coin (Plutarch, *Banquet of the Seven Sages* 164B).

1.  Simonides F86 Page. Zacynthus (which depends on plausible emendation of the text) is a hilly island in the Ionian Sea off the north-west coast of the Peloponnese. Both Homer and Virgil give it the epithet 'woody', which would be unsuitable for horses.

arises, rather than being tested by the need when it arises. The   E
realization ought not to occur because we have been hurt; we
ought to have already acquainted ourselves with and observed
the flatterer, and so avoid being hurt. Otherwise, our experience
will be no different from that of people who realize the facts
about lethal drugs by sampling them first: death by suicide is the
price they pay for their conclusion.

This attitude is not the only type we cannot commend: there
are also people whose premiss is that friendship is fine and
useful, and whose conclusion is that those who are pleasing
company are thereby self-evidently guilty of being flatterers. But
a friend does not have to be unpleasant or unpalatable, nor does   F
friendship gain its significance by being harsh and uninviting: it
is rather the case that it is pleasant and attractive precisely because
it is fine and significant. 'Its neighbours are the Graces and
Desire',[1] and it is not only for someone who is down on his luck
that, in Euripides' words, 'it is pleasing to look into the eyes of a
kindly man':[2] where friendship is present, it brings pleasure and
joy in good times to the same degree that it removes the pain
and confusion of bad times. On the analogy of Evenus' maxim   50A
that the best relish is the cooking-fire,[3] God's fusion of friendship
with life makes everything heart-warming, pleasing and attractive, since friendship is there as a partner in the pleasure.

There is no possible explanation why the flatterer disguises
himself in pleasing masks, except that he has noticed that friendship never excludes pleasure. But just as fool's gold and counter-
feits imitate only gold's gleam and sheen, so the flatterer can be
seen as imitating the pleasant and attractive aspects of friendship,   B
always putting on a cheerful, vivacious face and never being
negative or recalcitrant. But it is false to conclude from this
that people who praise others are immediately to be suspected
simply of flattering them: when either is called for, approval and

1. Hesiod, *Theogony* 64.
2. Euripides, *Ion* 732.
3. The *mot* of Evenus, an innovative sophist and elegiac poet of the fifth century
   BC, pleased Plutarch who used it again three times: 697D (again in the context
   of friendship), 1010C and 126D, where he forgot the provenance and ascribed
   it to another fifth-century sophist, Prodicus.

disapproval are equally appropriate within friendship – or rather, although captiousness and disparagement are inevitably inimical to friendship and compatibility, we are still perfectly content to put up with criticism and someone speaking their mind, provided there have been earlier manifestations of kindliness unstintingly and enthusiastically expressing approval of deeds well done; and the reason we are content to do this is because we trust – with no hint of anxiety – that anyone who is happy to express approval expresses disapproval only when compelled to do so.

C [3] At this point someone might comment that it is difficult to distinguish the flatterer and the friend, since they both equally provide pleasure and express approval; in fact, it is noticeable that flattery often outdoes friendship in favours and acts of service. We will reply as follows: of course it is difficult, because we are after the genuine flatterer, the one who approaches the matter cunningly and artfully; we are not falling into the usual trap of regarding as flatterers those who carry their own oil-flasks (as the epithet goes),[1] those spongers and scroungers whose voices (as someone has put it) are heard only once hands have been washed for dinner,[2] and whose vulgarity, with its concomi-
D tant sarcasm and rudeness, becomes obvious before the first course and first drink are over. For there never could be the slightest point in investigating Melanthius, the parasite of Alexander of Pherae, who replied, whenever he was asked how Alexander had been killed, 'Through the ribs and into my stomach'; or those who besiege a well-endowed table, whom 'neither fire nor iron nor bronze prevents from turning up regularly for a meal';[3] or those female flatterers from Cyprus who, having travelled across to Syria, earned the name of 'ladderettes' for bending over and allowing

1. Greeks rubbed their bodies with oil before taking exercise (see also p. 83, n. 1), and so when they went to the gymnasium or sports ground, a slave carried an oil-flask for this purpose. If you had to carry your own flask, that was a sign of poverty and dependence.
2. Plutarch's *Life of Phocion* 8.3 clarifies the allusion: kings listen to their flatterers only once dinner has begun, that is after serious business discussions are over and hands have been washed for dinner.
3. According to Plutarch elsewhere (*Philosophers and Princes* 778E), this is from Eupolis' *The Flatterers* (*PCG* F175 Kassel and Austin, F162 Kock).

the royal women to use them for climbing into their carriages.[1]   E

[4] Of whom, then, ought one to be careful? Of the person who does not appear to be a flatterer, and does not let on that he is; who cannot be found near the kitchen or be caught counting the minutes before dinner; who does not fall about drunk all over the place, but is invariably sober; who sticks his nose into everything and thinks that he ought to be involved in things and wants to be privy to secrets – in short, of the man who acts the part of friend in a serious manner rather than comically or farcically. As Plato says, 'The ultimate dishonesty is the false appearance of honesty':[2] it is not overt, light-hearted flattery that   F must be regarded as problematic, but the covert, straight-faced version, which can corrupt even true friendship if we do not watch out, because its behaviour coincides to a large extent with that of friendship.

When Gobryas[3] tumbled into a dark room along with the Magus he was chasing and found himself entwined with his opponent, he told Darius, who was near by and did not know what to do, to use his sword, even if it wounded both of them. We, however, can never under any circumstances at all condone the attitude of 'Never mind what happens to a friend, just so long as an enemy suffers';[4] so if we want to rid ourselves of the flatterer, then, given that he is intertwined with the friend by many threads of similarity, we ought to be exceedingly careful   51A that we do not somehow either throw out the good with the bad or open our doors to danger by indulging what we feel comfortable with. I imagine that when uncultivated seeds which are nearly the same shape and size get mixed up with wheat, it makes cleaning the wheat difficult, because a fine sieve does not eliminate the seeds, and a wide sieve eliminates both the seeds and the wheat; it is just the same with flattery, which is hard to

1. Details in Athenaeus 256C–D. There is a play on the Greek words *kolakides* (female flatterers) and *klimakides* (female ladders).
2. *Republic* 361a.
3. Plutarch remembered this anecdote from the vivid account by Herodotus (3.61–79) of the usurpation by impersonation of the Persian throne by two Magian brothers, and the revenge of Darius, Gobryas and five other Persians.
4. *TGF Adesp*. 362 Nauck.

separate from friendship because it has infiltrated every one of our moods, activities, needs and habits.

B [5] However, it is because friendship is the most gratifying thing in the world and nothing affords one more pleasure, that the flatterer's domain is pleasure and pleasure is what he uses as bait. And it is because goodwill and service are inseparable from friendship (hence the saying that a friend is more essential than fire and water), that the flatterer undertakes tasks and tries hard always to appear well-meaning, determined and enthusiastic. And since the chief factor in forging friendship at the beginning is similarity of interests and attitudes, and enjoying and avoiding the same things is usually the initial bond which brings people together, through affinity, then because the flatterer is well aware C of all this, he patterns and forms himself as if he were some kind of material, in an attempt to match and mirror whoever he plans to beset by means of imitation; and he is so malleable and plausible in his mimicry that he provokes the comment: 'You are no son of Achilles, but the man himself!'[1] However, the most iniquitous aspect of all his iniquity is that, because he has noticed that speaking one's mind is both claimed and believed to be a mode of speech specific to friendship – just as animals make specific sounds – and that someone who avoids speaking his mind is held to be unfriendly and unforthcoming, then he proceeds to imitate this too; just as skilful cooks use sharp and bitter flavours as seasonings to get rid of the cloying nature of sweet foods,[2] so D flatterers employ a candour which is false and does no good, but is, so to speak, no more than a wink and a tickle.

These are the reasons, then, that the man is hard to spot: he is like one of those animals which can naturally change their colour so as to be assimilated with the shrubs* and environment around them. But because his imposture and invisibility are based on similarities, it is our job to use discrepancies to reveal him and expose him for, in Plato's words, 'embellishing himself with others' colours and forms through lack of any personal to himself'.[3]

1. *TGF Adesp.* 363 Nauck. Plutarch used it of Alcibiades in *Life of Alcibiades* 23.
2. The point of the analogy, that cloying flattery is masked with stinging forthright speech, is made even more explicit in *Life of Antony* 24.
3. Plato, *Phaedrus* 239d.

[6] We should, therefore, begin the inquiry right from the beginning. As already mentioned, the beginning of friendship is invariably when temperament and nature are so much in unison E that they cleave to habits and attitudes which are, within reason, identical, and enjoy the same interests, activities and pastimes. It has even been said, concerning this unison: 'An old man most enjoys the voice of another old man, a child that of a child; woman is in concord with woman, invalid with invalid, and one overtaken by disaster enchants another in tribulation.'[1] So, because the flatterer knows that if people enjoy the same things they are bound to form a relationship and take pleasure in each other's company, his first tactic for getting close to a given F individual and pitching tent near him is as follows: he treats it like an exercise in breaking in animals, and patiently makes his approach (by means of the same interests, pastimes, pursuits and occupations) and finally strokes his quarry, and keeps at it until the other submits and becomes docile and accustomed to his touch. The flatterer criticizes the activities, ways of life and people he sees the subject disliking, and is extravagant in his praise for whatever the other likes, to ensure that he is seen to express more than his share of astonishment and incredulity; and 52A he insists that his likes and dislikes are carefully thought out rather than being emotional reactions.

[7] So, given that we are dealing with no actual similarity or even potential similarity, and that this is all just camouflage, how can we put the flatterer to the test? What actual discrepancies are there, in which he can be ensnared? Above all, one should see whether his intention is consistent and constant, whether he always enjoys the same things, approves of the same things and guides and organizes his life with regard to a single model, which is proper behaviour for someone who is autonomous and who desires friendship and familiarity with a like-minded person. If he does all this, he is a friend. On the other hand, since the flatterer has no single foundation for his attitudes as a source of stability and his way of life is not of his own choosing but is derived from someone else, and since he moulds and adjusts himself B

1. *CAF Adesp*. commentary on 1206 (III.606) Kock; or *TGF Adesp*. 364 Nauck.

by reference to someone else, then he is not straightforward or single, but complex and multifaceted; he is always streaming from one place to another (like water in the process of being poured) and the only form he has is given by the vessels that receive him.

A horned owl,[1] apparently, is caught as it tries to copy a human being and move and dance along with him; a flatterer, on the other hand, is the one who inveigles others and leads them into the trap, by playing a variety of parts: he dances and sings with one person, but wrestles and rolls in the dust with another. If he has caught someone who is keen on stalking and hunting, he joins in and comes close to bellowing out Phaedra's lines, 'Oh, how I adore hallooing the hounds when I'm hot on the heels of the dappled deer',[2] and is not in the slightest concerned with the beast, but enmeshes and traps the hunter himself. If he is after a studious young academic, he changes tack, surrounds himself with books and lets his beard grow down to his feet; arrayed in the requisite threadbare cloak and indifference to the world,[3] he spouts mathematics and Platonic right-angled triangles. If an idler bursts into his life, a rich carouser, he changes again, 'and cunning Odysseus divests himself of his rags':[4] the cloak is discarded, the beard is pruned like an unproductive fruit-tree, and their place is taken by wine-coolers, drinking-bowls, conversations laced with laughter, jokes at the expense of philosophers.

It was just the same, as the story goes, in Syracuse during Plato's visit, when Dionysius was seized by an intense passion for philosophy: the palace was filled with clouds of dust raised by the hordes of geometers.[5] After Plato's 'impertinence', however, when Dionysius had rejected philosophy and rushed back to

---

1. It seems that Plutarch dictated 'monkey' here, but Aristotle, *Historia Animalium* 597b22 ff. (and cf. Pliny, *Naturalis Historia* 10.68; Athenaeus 391A; Aelian, *Varia Historia* 15.28) shows that the reference should be to the horned owl. Plutarch himself got the owl right explicitly in *Are Land or Sea Animals More Intelligent?* 961E and in *Table Talk* 705A. But he does sometimes misremember a reference recorded correctly elsewhere.
2. Euripides, *Hippolytus* 218 f.
3. The threadbare cloak was the recognized uniform of the philosopher, and 'indifference to the world' translates a technical Stoic term.
4. Homer, *Odyssey* 22.1.
5. They were drawing diagrams in the dust.

wine, women, trivial conversation and sensuality, it was as if    E
Circe had transformed them all: everyone without exception was
overtaken by uncultured oblivion and foolishness. The point is
further illustrated by the actions of the greatest flatterers and
demagogues, of whom the most outstanding was Alcibiades: in
Athens, he had fun, bred horses and lived a witty and elegant
life; in Sparta, he had a crew cut, wore a thin cloak and washed
in cold water; in Thrace, he drank and was aggressive; and when
he arrived at Tissaphernes' court, he adopted the soft life of
luxurious indulgence and pretension. By this process of assimilation and adaptation, he kept on ingratiating himself with everyone and currying their favour. People like Epaminondas and    F
Agesilaus provide the contrast; they interacted with a great many
people, cultures and lifestyles, but they never failed to preserve
their own character in the ways they dressed, behaved, spoke and
lived. Likewise, Plato in Syracuse was no different from Plato in
the Academy, and Dionysius saw the same man that Dion did.

[8] It is very easy to expose the octopus-like transformations of
the flatterer:[1] all you have to do is appear to be mutable yourself,
by criticizing a lifestyle you previously commended and by suddenly embracing activities, behaviour and language you had de-    53A
plored. You will see that the flatterer has no constancy, that he is
not his own man and that his likes and dislikes, pleasure and
distress, are not aroused by innate feeling, but that he resembles a
mirror: the only reflections he admits are those of external feelings, lifestyles and actions. Here is an example of his behaviour: if
you criticize one of your friends to him, he says, 'It took you a
long time to see through him; I've never liked him.' And if you
later change your mind and you compliment your friend, he will
– though it defies belief – say that he's glad too and vicariously
grateful for your compliment and that he trusts your friend. And
if you say that you need to change your way of life, for instance    B
from political service to quiet inactivity, he says, 'Yes, we're
long overdue for a break from ructions and rivalries.' And if you
later give the impression of being strongly inclined towards activity and oratory, his response is: 'There's a project worthy of you!

1. Plutarch liked this octopus simile: 96F, 916B, 978E–F.

It's nice to do nothing, but it doesn't bring fame or recognition.' We must lose no time in saying to someone like that: '"Stranger, you now seem to me different from before."[1] I have no need of a friend who changes place when I do and nods in agreement when I do; my shadow is better at that. I need a friend who helps me by telling the truth and having discrimination.'

So that is one type of test that can be applied, [9] but we must also watch out for a second discrepancy when he is imitating someone else. A genuine friend does not imitate everything or praise everything enthusiastically: he approves only of the best things. As Sophocles says, 'He was born for mutual love, not mutual hatred'[2] – and, without a doubt, for mutual integrity and conscientiousness, not for mutual deviance and connivance. The only exception is if, just as eye infections can spread, he is unconsciously contaminated with a defect or imperfection by some contagious discharge, simply because of his proximity to and association with the source. This, of course, explains why (as the stories go) Plato's associates used to copy his slumped shoulders, Aristotle's his lisp, King Alexander's his cocked head and harsh conversational tone: some people unconsciously get most of their characteristics from others' attitudes and styles.

A flatterer, however, behaves exactly like a chameleon. A chameleon can assimilate itself to every colour except white; a flatterer leaves nothing contemptible unimitated, because he is altogether incapable of making himself resemble anything worth ascribing importance to. Just as inferior artists, who lack the skill to achieve beautiful results, summon up representations of their subjects by resorting to wrinkles and moles and scars, so a flatterer imitates lack of self-control, superstition, rage, severity towards servants, mistrust of kith and kin. This is because he is innately inclined towards the worse sides of a person; and the fact that he imitates despicable behaviour means that he avoids a reputation for being critical of it, since it is people who strive for improvement* who are suspected of being disappointed and aggrieved at their friends' mistakes. This is why Dion, Samius and

1. Homer, *Odyssey* 16.181.
2. Sophocles, *Antigone* 523.

Cleomenes, in their relationships respectively with Dionysius, Philip and Ptolemy, fell from grace and were killed.[1] But anyone who wants to be, and also wants to be seen to be, good-tempered and trustworthy at the same time puts on an overdone display of enjoying the worse sides of a person, the implicit message being that his overwhelming fondness for the other person makes him tolerate even his less desirable aspects and share his feelings and    F
inherent attitudes towards everything. That is why such people assume that they should be involved even in unchosen, chance events: they flatter people who are ill by pretending to have the same illness; if they are in the company of people who are partially blind or deaf, they pretend to be unable to see or hear well, just as when Dionysius' sight was weak, his flatterers used to bump into one another and drop their plates during meals. Some prefer emotional contact as a means of infiltrating themselves further, and they go so far as to use secrets to make their feelings indistin-    54A
guishable from the other person's. If they see cases of ill-starred marriage or of mistrust of sons or family, they moan unstintingly about their own children or wife or relatives or family and let drop some secret reasons for the problem, because affinity makes people emotionally close, and if someone has been trusted with a secret, he is more inclined to disclose a secret of his own; and once he has made such a disclosure, a relationship has been formed and there is fear of loss of trust. I personally know someone who even threw his wife out because a friend of his had dismissed *his* wife (but the friend's wife got at the facts, and he was discovered to be    B
surreptitiously visiting his wife and writing to her!). It is obvious that anyone who thinks that the following riddle refers only to a crab and not to a flatterer knows nothing about flattery: 'With a body which is nothing but stomach and with eyes that peer in all directions, a creature that scuttles on claws.'[2] This is a perfect description of a parasite – 'of those whose friendship extends from frying-pan to meal end', as Eupolis puts it.[3]

1. Dion was the friend of Dionysius of Syracuse. Samius (or occasionally Samus) was a foster-brother and 'friend' of Philip V (late third century BC). The reference is to Ptolemy IV Philopator, also of the late third century BC.
2. *PLG* III, p.669, *Carmina Popularia* 35B.
3. *PCG* V, p. 505, Eupolis F374 Kassel and Austin.

[10] However, this is not the proper part of the discussion for these remarks. What we must do now is not overlook a particular device the flatterer uses when imitating others: if he does imitate any of the good points of the person he is flattering, he makes sure that the balance is in favour of the other person. True friends are not rivals and do not envy one another: whether or not one is as successful as the other, he reacts with even temper and equanimity. The flatterer, however, is constantly aware that he is the understudy, and so, even while imitating the other person, he makes himself less than equal, insisting all the time that he is inferior and defective in every respect except for badness. Where bad features are concerned, he does not let anyone take first place away from him: if the other person is grumpy, he calls himself depressive; if the other person is superstitious, he calls himself spellbound; if the other person is in love, he calls himself besotted. 'Your laughter was excessive,' he says, 'but I nearly died laughing.' Where good features are concerned, however, it is the other way round: he says that although he is a fast runner, the other person zooms along;[1] that he is a reasonably good horseman, 'but no match for this Centaur here'. Or 'I'm a natural poet, and the verse I write is pretty good, "but causing thunder is Zeus' job, not mine".'[2] What is happening is that he is intending to demonstrate simultaneously the irreproachability of the other person's predilections, by imitating them, and the invincibility of the other person's abilities, by being outclassed.

Anyway, when he is imitating someone else, a flatterer's discrepancies (which distinguish him from a friend) take that kind of form. [11] But, as I have already mentioned, there is also the issue of pleasure, which is equally relevant to both the flatterer and the friend, because a good man enjoys his friends to the same degree that a bad man enjoys his flatterers. So we must proceed to make the distinction in this context too, and we find the distinction in referring the pleasure to its purpose. Look at it this way: perfume smells nice, of course, but so does medicine. The

---

1. Lucian (*Soloecista* 7 and *Lexiphanes* 25) regards this verb as a barbarism: hence the slangy translation.
2. Callimachus, *Aetia* F1.20 Pfeiffer.

difference between them is that the one has no *raison d'être* except pleasure, while in the other case the fact that what counteracts impurities or chills or emaciation smells nice is neither here nor there. Or again, artists blend their paints into vivid hues and tinctures, and some medicinal potions are vivid to look at and appealing in colour. So what is the difference? It is surely obvious that we can distinguish them by their functional purpose.

In exactly the same way, although the charm of friendship is,    F
so to speak, vivid as well as delightful when the issues are fine and beneficial, still there are times when friends interact by means of trivia, food, drink – even jokes and idle talk – which act as a kind of seasoning for the fine, important issues. This is the context of the line 'They rejoiced in telling tales to one another',[1] and also the line 'There is nothing else which could have separated us two in our mutual love and enjoyment.'[2] The function and purpose of the flatterer, however, is *always* to concoct and prepare    55A
some trivial event or expression, as if they were spicy sauces, with pleasure as the goal and objective.[3]

In short, while the one thinks it is his duty to bend over backwards to be liked, the other always does his duty, and although he is often liked, he is often disliked too – not that he sets out to be disliked, but he does not refrain from it if it is the better course of action. If it helps patients improve, a doctor gives doses of saffron or spikenard and often even soothes them with baths and generously recommends nourishing foods; there are circumstances, on the other hand, in which he eschews these prescriptions and forces castor[4] down the patient's throat, 'or hulwort, whose strong smell is disgusting',[5] or he pounds some hellebore and makes him drain the cup. In neither case, how-    B
ever, does he regard the distress or the pleasure as an end; both are means by which he single-mindedly guides his patients

1. Homer, *Iliad* 11.643.
2. Homer, *Odyssey* 4.178.
3. The language, analogy and direction of the argument of this sentence are reminiscent, no doubt deliberately, of Plato, *Gorgias* 465b ff.
4. From beavers, it was used as a stimulant and anti-spasmodic.
5. Nicander, *Theriaca* 64. Pliny, *Naturalis Historia* 21.44 and 145, reports on the efficacy of this herb.

towards the goal of improvement. In exactly the same way, a friend sometimes spends all his time lionizing and delighting the other person, using praise and compliments to guide him towards goodness: examples are when someone said, 'Teucer my dear friend, Telamon's son, leader of your people – strike like this',[1] and 'How, then, could I overlook godlike Odysseus?'[2] On the other hand, when severity is called for, a friend latches on to the other person with words that bite and candour that smacks of the guardian: 'Menelaus, you may be protected by Zeus, but you're out of your mind: there's no need for such stupidity.'[3] There are also circumstances in which a friend acts as well as speaks his mind: Menedemus taught the son of his friend Asclepiades a lesson by locking out the degenerate, insubordinate young man without actually ticking him off, and Arcesilaus banned Baton from his school for composing verse mocking Cleanthes, and relented only when Baton had reassured Cleanthes and had had a change of heart.

The point is that one should upset a friend only when it does him good, and should not let the upset destroy the friendship, but should use sharpness like a medicine, to preserve and protect the patient. This is why a friend is like a musician: in retuning his instrument for the mode of goodness and benefit, he loosens here and tightens there, and consequently, although he may often be likeable, he *always* does good. By contrast, because a flatterer is used to constantly playing his pleasing and likeable accompaniment in one mode only, he does not know how to use resistance or hard words: someone else's preferences are his only guides and all the notes he sings or plays are in unison with that other person. We should, therefore, behave like Agesilaus, in Xenophon's account,[4] who was happy to be complimented by people who were also prepared to criticize him: we too should regard a pleasing and delightful nature as indicative of friendship only if it is accompanied by the ability to upset us and resist us, and we should be suspicious of a relationship which is constantly

1. Homer, *Iliad* 8.281.
2. Homer, *Iliad* 10.243 and *Odyssey* 1.65.
3. Homer, *Iliad* 7.109.
4. Xenophon, *Agesilaus* 11.5.

gratifying and which tends purely towards pleasure, with no   E
admixture of hurt; and we most certainly ought to keep in mind
the Spartan's comment on praise of King Charillus: 'Of course
he's not a good man: he doesn't get cross even with bad
people.'[1]

[12] It is said that gadflies insert themselves into bulls' ears and
fleas into dogs' ears; flatterers fill the ears of ambitious people
with their expressions of approval and, having once become
attached, are hard to scratch off. It follows that it is particularly
important to have one's discriminatory apparatus alert and checking whether the approval is for the man or for his behaviour. It   F
is for the behaviour if they prefer to praise us in our absence
rather than in our presence; if they share the same desires and
ambitions themselves, and therefore do not restrict their approval
to us, but praise everyone for the same behaviour; if they do not
turn out to be inconsistent in what they say and do; and most
importantly if we ourselves are conscious of no remorse for the
behaviour for which we are being praised and of no embarrassment or hankering to have said or done the opposite (for if our
innate conscience impugns and spurns the praise, then it is un-
affected, untouchable and unassailable by the flatterer). Incred-   56A
ibly, however, not only do most people reject advice when they
are out of luck and prefer to be surrounded by sorrow or grief,
but also, when they transgress and do wrong, they regard as an
enemy and a detractor anyone who uses reproof and criticism to
instil qualms and contrition, while they embrace and regard as a
well-meaning friend anyone who commends and praises them
for their actions. People who readily praise and join in the applause for an action or sentiment or anything, whether seriously   B
or humorously intended, are only fleetingly and immediately
harmful; but those whose compliments reach a man's character
and whose flattery even touches his temperament are doing exactly what slaves do if they steal from the seed-corn rather than
from the stock: since disposition and character are the seed of

---

1. There are variants of this legendary tag elsewhere in the Plutarchan corpus.
   The Spartan's name is given as Archelaus in *Life of Lycurgus* 5.9, and as
   Archidamidas in 218B.

conduct,[1] they are corrupting the foundation and source of a person's life by clothing vice in words proper to virtue.

In times of civil and external wars, as Thucydides remarks,[2] 'They changed the way words had usually applied to behaviour, and justified the change: irrational foolhardiness was considered

C  to be courage born of love for one's comrades; circumspection was regarded as specious cowardice; self-restraint as a mask for gutlessness; the desire to understand everything as the desire to do nothing.' And in cases of flattery we must watch and be wary of wastefulness being described as 'generosity', cowardice as 'caution', capriciousness as 'quickness', small-mindedness as 'a sense of proportion', a lustful person as 'sociable and affectionate', a short-tempered bully as 'courageous', a good-for-nothing lackey

D  as 'altruistic'. Likewise Plato says somewhere[3] that a lover (who is a flatterer of his beloved) calls a snub nose 'pert', a hooked nose 'aristocratic', swarthy people 'virile' and pallid people 'children of the gods'; and 'honey-coloured' is nothing but the invention of a lover trying to gloss over and make light of a sallow complexion. Still, if an ugly person is persuaded that he is goodlooking, or a short person that he is well built, he does not have

E  to live with the lie for a long time, and the wound is not deep or irremediable. But praise that conditions a person to treat vice as virtue – and to do so gladly, not reluctantly – and that does away with one's sense of shame at wrong-doing, is the praise that brought the Sicilians low, by describing Dionysius' and Phalaris' cruelty as 'righteous indignation'; and it is the praise that corrupted Egypt, by naming Ptolemy's effeminacy, entrancement, chanting and striking of hand-drums 'devotion' and 'worshipping the gods';[4] and it is the praise that came within a hair's breadth of overturning and effacing what it was then to be Roman, by glossing over Antony's promiscuous, self-indulgent

---

1. The metaphor of the house slave stealing the seed-corn is vivid, but the moral, that character is the seed and source of action, is commonplace (e.g. 100C, 477A–B) and Stoic (SVF 1.203).
2. Thucydides 3.82.
3. Republic 474d.
4. This is Ptolemy IV Philopator, whose dissolute court became proverbial (Polybius 5.34; Plutarch, Life of Cleomenes 33).

and self-glorifying ways as the sparkling and genial fun* of one
blessed with unlimited power and good fortune. What else    F
equipped Ptolemy with mouthpiece and pipes?[1] What else supplied Nero with a tragic stage and dressed him in mask and
actor's boots? Was it not the praise of flatterers? In the majority
of cases, isn't a king called an Apollo if he can warble, a Dionysus
when he is drunk, a Heracles for his wrestling? And isn't it
enjoyment of this flattery that diverts him into utterly scandalous
behaviour?

[13] It follows that approbation is the main aspect of the
flatterer against which we must protect ourselves. But he is
aware of this too, and is clever at protecting *himself* against    57A
suspicion. If he latches on to some overdressed swank or rustic
innocent in a thick leather jacket, he indulges in all-out sarcasm,
just like Strouthias when he tramples on Bias and gloats over his
insensitivity with compliments like 'You could drink King Alexander under the table' and 'I see you're one up against the
Cypriot – that's rich!';[2] despite this, when he is dealing with
more sophisticated people, he notices that this is the respect in
which they particularly scrutinize him and that this is the region
and area in which they are particularly on their guard, and so
he does not deploy his praise in a frontal assault, but pulls it back
a long way, performs an encircling movement and 'makes as    B
stealthy an approach as any animal',[3] brushing by in an experi-
mental manner. On one occasion, he reports the compliments
that *others* have been paying the person – like an orator availing
himself of someone else's personality – and explains how he had
been delighted to have met in the agora some strangers or men
of venerable age who had, in admiring tones, had many a complimentary tale to tell about him. On another occasion, he pursues
the opposite course and the lies he invents consist of superficial
complaints against the man – made up by the flatterer as if he
had heard them from others: he rushes up to find out whether
the imputed words or deeds really happened. The person denies
it, of course, and then the flatterer jumps in and introduces his

1. This is Ptolemy XII Auletes (Strabo 17.1.11).
2. Menander, *Kolax* F3 Sandbach, F2.2–3 and F3 Körte, F297 Kock.
3. Menander, *Kolax* F6 Sandbach, F6 Körte, F298 Kock.

C   accolade: 'I could hardly believe that *you* had abused one of your friends, when you're constitutionally incapable of abusing even your enemies, or that *you* had been after someone else's goods, when you're so generous with your own.'

[14] Others behave like artists who enhance the light, bright parts of their paintings by juxtaposing them with shade and darkness; in much the same way, some flatterers implicitly approve and perpetuate their victims' current flaws by depreciating and reviling, or ridiculing and mocking, the opposite qualities. If they are with spendthrifts, they denigrate restraint as provincial; if they are with greedy criminals, whose source of wealth is

D   contemptible and evil practices, they denigrate self-sufficiency and morality as cowardice and ineffectiveness in the world; however, when they are in the company of idle layabouts who shun the limelight of politics,[1] it causes them no embarrassment to describe political activity as 'annoying interference' and ambition as 'pointless vainglory'. Furthermore, flattery of an orator might call for mocking a philosopher, and the way to gain prestige among loose women is to call monogamous and faithful wives 'frigid and drab'.

Flatterers surpass themselves in amorality, however, in that they do not even go easy on themselves. Just as wrestlers prostrate

E   themselves in order to trip others up, so flatterers worm their way into their neighbours' admiration by self-criticism: 'At sea, I'm a cowardly creature; I give up easily when faced with hard work; I can't control my temper if someone slights me. But nothing,' he goes on, 'makes this man here afraid, and no task is too hard: he is extraordinary – he puts up with everything without anxiety or distress.'

Now imagine someone who thinks he is very clever, who sets out to be forthright and blunt – under the guise, of course, of integrity – and whose constant watchword is 'Son of Tydeus, you must find the middle course between eulogizing me and

F   maligning me.'[2] The skilful flatterer does not approach such a

---

1. Plutarch's phrase here is an echo of Plato, *Gorgias* 485d5. He used it again in 777B.
2. Homer, *Iliad* 10.249.

person in the way we have been describing, but there is another stratagem available to him: he treats him as prodigiously intelligent and goes to ask his advice about his personal business; he claims that although he has closer friends, still he has no choice but to impose upon him – 'When we need words of wisdom, where are we to go? Whom can we rely on?' Then, once he has heard what he has to say, he leaves with the declaration that he has been given no mere advice, but an inspired utterance. Or again, if he sees that the man fancies himself as a literary expert,   58A he gives him a piece he has written, and asks him to read it and correct it. When King Mithridates was keen on medicine, some of his associates allowed him even to perform surgery on them and cauterize them: this was flattery – albeit of a physical rather than verbal kind – because the fact that they entrusted themselves to him was assumed to be evidence of his expertise. 'The gods have many guises',[1] and this sort of non-apparent praise needs rather cunning safety measures: it must be exposed by deliberately drafting outlandish plans and projects and by making irrational suggestions as to how things might be improved. If he contradicts   B nothing, but assents to and accepts everything, and greets each proposal with a cry of 'Well said!' or 'Fine!', then he is obviously 'pursuing a hidden agenda, while asking about the code'[2] – that is, he is actually wanting to praise the other person and play a part in inflating his ego.

[15] Moreover – and I am reminded of the definition of painting as silent poetry[3] – there is a kind of praise which stems from silent flattery. Just as hunters are more likely to deceive their quarry if they disguise themselves as travellers or shepherds or farmers, so flatterers get a particularly secure grip with their praise when they do not appear to be praising, but to be doing something else. Imagine, for instance, someone who gives up his chair or his seat to a later arrival, or who, while addressing the Assembly or the Council,[4] sees that someone affluent wants to   C

1. A commonplace in Euripides: *Alcestis* 1159, *Andromache* 1284, *Helen* 1688, *Bacchae* 1388.
2. *TGF Adesp*. 365 Nauck and Snell.
3. A sentiment attributed to Simonides at 346F. Plutarch liked it: 17F, 748A.
4. The two main political bodies in democratic Athens.

speak and so breaks off in mid-speech and hands over the rostrum and the topic to him: despite his silence, he is showing more clearly than if he shouted it out loud that he regards the other person as better than him and intellectually superior. So the reason these people can be seen occupying the front seats at lectures and plays is not that they think they deserve them, but so that they can flatter affluent people by getting up out of them; and they can be seen at gatherings and meetings starting out on a line of argument, but then giving way as if faced by people with a better case, and changing over, with no difficulty at all, to the opposite line – if the person taking the opposite line is powerful or wealthy or famous. And this shows us by far the best method of exposing this servility and submissiveness, as we must – because they do not defer to experience or excellence or age, but only to wealth and reputation. Once, when Megabyzus sat down next to Apelles the painter and tried to start a conversation about line and shading, Apelles said, 'You see these lads here who are grinding pigment? They could hardly take their eyes off you while you were quiet, and were impressed by your purple-dyed clothes and golden jewellery; but now they are laughing at you for having embarked on a conversation about matters you don't understand.'[1] And when Croesus asked what happiness is, Solon replied that Tellus (an Athenian with no public prominence) and Cleobis and Biton were more fortunate than him.[2] Flatterers, however, make public their view that kings and rich men and political leaders are not only successful and fortunate, but are also outstandingly intelligent, skilful and so on for every virtue.

[16] Some people cannot abide even *hearing* the Stoics claim that the wise man is *ipso facto* a rich, good-looking, well-born king; but flatterers explicitly *say* that an affluent man is *ipso facto* an orator and a poet, or (if the fancy takes him) a painter and a musician, or a sportsman and an athlete, by letting themselves be

1. The anecdote, which recurs in *On Contentment* 472A, has the details confused. The Persian commander Megabyzus lived in the first half of the fifth century BC, but the painter Apelles in the second half of the fourth century BC. Aelian (*Varia Historia* 2.2) gave Zeuxis as the painter, which fits better.
2. Herodotus 1.30 ff.; Plutarch, *Life of Solon* 27.6 ff.

thrown at wrestling or fall behind at running – as Crison of Himera[1] let himself be overtaken in a race against Alexander (but Alexander realized what he was up to and was infuriated). Carneades used to say that the sons of wealthy men and of kings learn nothing but horsemanship, and that the reason they learn nothing else properly and well is that while their teacher flatters them with compliments during their lessons and their wrestling opponent submits to them, their horse neither knows nor cares who is an ordinary citizen or who is a political leader, who is rich or who is poor, and simply bucks off all incompetent riders. It follows that Bion's words are foolish and fatuous:[2] 'If eulogiz-    59A
ing a field guaranteed its productivity and fertility, then it would not seem wrong for someone to do this★ rather than to dig and make trouble for himself. So it would not be odd for someone to praise a man either,★ if that man is useful and thoroughly productive for those who praise him.'★ This is fatuous because although a field does not deteriorate by being praised, a person is made egotistical and is corrupted by false and unjustified praise.

[17] Anyway, so much for these topics – the next step is to consider the issue of candour. Patroclus dressed himself up in    B
Achilles' armour and drove Achilles' horses to battle, but forswore the Pelian spear,[3] which was the only weapon he refused to handle; likewise, when a flatterer is equipped and disguised with his friend's marks and tokens, he ought to leave behind only candour, and not handle it or imitate it, but treat it as an instrument special to friendship, 'weighty, massive and sturdy'.[4] But since they steer clear of the area where unalloyed laughter,★

1. The most famous sprinter Crison of Himera won at the Olympics in the middle of the fifth century BC (Pausanias 5.23.4) and could not have raced with Alexander over a hundred years later. The anecdote on Crison and reference to the complete virtues of the Stoic wise man recur in *On Contentment* 471E–472A, along with the Megabyzus/Apelles tale we have just met, thus betraying a cluster in one of Plutarch's notebooks. Since goodness for a Stoic was a settled state of character, the completely good man had all the virtues. Paradoxically, Stoics appear to have added that he also had all the accomplishments and was omnicompetent. One wonders whether this may have arisen from an opponent's sally.
2. Bion of Borysthenes F50 Kindstrand.
3. Made from an ash tree on Mount Pelion in Thessaly.
4. The description of Achilles' spear in Homer, *Iliad* 16.141.

jokes and levity are the means of reproof, and they elevate the
C  business straight to a serious level and are frowning flatterers
who adulterate levity with criticism and rebuke, then we must include this issue in our investigation. In my opinion, just as in
Menander's comedy[1] Noheracles comes on with a club that has
no solidity or strength, but is an empty, hollow imitation, so when
we test the flatterer's candour, we will find it feeble, flimsy,
flabby and identical in effect to those pillows women use, which
look as though they can stay firm and resist heads, but in fact
D  give way and cave in. In the same way, the hollow, illusory and
unreal bulk of this counterfeit candour makes it overblown and
distended, so that when it is deflated the force of its collapse can
capture and suck in anyone who is swept into it. Errors are the
domain of the true candour of friendship, and if it is cruel, that is
only because it is helpful and kind: like honey, it makes injuries
sting and cleanses them, but that is its only painful aspect, and
otherwise its action is benign and pleasant.[2] We will spend some
time on this type of candour later.[3]

As for a flatterer, however, in the first place he lets it be
known that in his dealings with other people he is a hard man,
impatient and uncompromising. He is stern with his servants,
fiercely cracks down on his friends' and relatives' mistakes, and
E  allows no one else to impress him or win his admiration, preferring to sneer at them; he is unforgiving and rude enough to
provoke anger in other people. What he wants is to be known
for his hatred of anything bad, and to be recognized as someone
who would not readily relinquish his candour, or do or say
anything ingratiating.

In the second place, he pretends to be completely unaware of
and unacquainted with genuine, important flaws, although he
ferociously springs on trivial, irrelevant oversights: he energeti-

1. Menander F458 Körte, F523 Kock.
2. Honey was familiar in the ancient world for medical properties (Dioscorides
   2.82; Pliny, *Naturalis Historia*, 21.79, 84; 22.42; 24.23. See also R. J. Forbes,
   *Studies in Ancient Technology*, V.81, 86, 89 f., 94). In fact, it is somewhat acid
   and has mild antiseptic properties, and so is still used in the treatment of burns
   and lacerations and as a surgical dressing.
3. Sections 25 ff.

cally and forcefully lambasts the culprit if he sees a tool out of
place, a case of poor housekeeping, or someone not bothering to   F
have a haircut or dressing carelessly or paying inadequate attention to a dog or a horse. He is totally unconcerned, however, if
someone neglects his parents, ignores his children, humiliates his
wife, sneers at his relatives and ruins his assets: these situations
find him tongue-tied and helpless. He is like a coach who lets an
athlete get drunk and live an undisciplined life, and then makes
an issue of the oil-flask and strigil;[1] or he is like a schoolteacher
who scolds his pupil for his writing tablet and writing instrument,
while ignoring his flawed and faulty language. A flatterer, typically, has nothing to say about the actual speech of a ludicrously
awful orator, but criticizes the sound of his voice and takes him to   60A
task for ruining his throat by drinking cold water; or if he is told
to go through an atrocious script, he criticizes the roughness of
the papyrus and the careless untidiness of the writer. So when
Ptolemy[2] was playing a studious role, they used to keep an
argument with him going until midnight about some linguistic
or prosodic or historical point, but none of them, however many
there were, stood up to him in his times of sadism and arrogance,
or when he was beating his hand-drums and playing the mystic.
Flatterers, in short, bring candour to bear where there is no
capacity for distress or pain – which is no different from using a   B
scalpel to trim the hair and fingernails of someone with malignant
growths and abscesses.

[18] In the third place, we find worse insincerity in the case of
those who use their candour and criticism for the other's gratification. When Alexander rewarded some comedian very generously,
Agis the Argive was prompted by his envy and hurt to cry out,
'How incredibly odd!' The king turned to him in anger and said,
'What exactly do you mean?' Agis replied, 'I admit that I get
upset and cross when I see how all you descendants of Zeus
enjoy flatterers and buffoons; Heracles got pleasure from some   C
Cercopes, Dionysus from Sileni, and it is clear that you too think
highly of people of that ilk.' And once, when Tiberius Caesar

1. The Greeks oiled their bodies before exercise from a flask, and then scraped
   the oil and dirt off afterwards with a strigil, or scraper.
2. Ptolemy IV Philopator.

went to the Senate, one of his flatterers stood up and said, 'It is
the duty of free men to speak candidly and not to hold back or
keep quiet about any worthwhile matter.' This made everyone
alert, and as soon as there was an expectant silence and he had
Tiberius' attention, he went on, 'Listen, Caesar, to what we
unanimously accuse you of, but no one dares say out loud: you
neglect yourself, you expend your physical energy and exhaust
D    yourself by worrying and working for us, day and night without
stopping.' It is said that, while he was going on and on in this
vein, the orator Cassius Severus commented, 'This candour will
be the death of that man.'[1]

[19] In fact, these are all fairly trivial aspects of flattery, but
there are also aspects which are formidable and dangerous to
anyone thoughtless, when flatterers accuse their victims of having
afflictions and defects which are the opposite of what they are
actually suffering from. The flatterer Himerius, for instance, used
to stigmatize the person who was the most miserly and avaricious
of the Athenian plutocrats for being extravagant and reckless and
E    destined to reduce himself and his children to starvation. Or on
the other hand flatterers might reproach extravagant spendthrifts
for being mean and cheap, which is what Titus Petronius did
with Nero. Or they might tell rulers who treat their subjects
with savagery and brutality to refrain from acting so fairly, with
such ill-timed and inexpedient leniency. A similar case is when
someone treats an innocent, stupid halfwit as a terrible schemer,
and pretends to be wary and afraid of him. Then there is the
man who comes up to some malcontent (who delights in constantly slandering and criticizing people, but who has on this
occasion been inspired to praise someone of high repute), and
F    tells him off for his defect of praising even utterly undeserving
people: 'I mean, who is that man, after all? Has he really said or
done anything outstanding?'

Flatterers are particularly insistent and inflammatory where
their victims' hearts are concerned. If they see people arguing
with their brothers, despising their parents or having a low

1. Actually, Cassius Severus must have been in exile at the time. 'That man' in
Severus' remark refers to Tiberius, so the meaning is that flattery will be
Tiberius' undoing.

opinion of their wives, they do not tell them off or blame them, but they aggravate the emotion by saying, 'You don't think of yourself' and 'It's your fault: you're always seeing what you can do for other people and putting yourself down.' And if anger and jealousy cause some friction between a man and his lover or   61A
mistress, then flattery – armed with its bright candour – is right by his side, making sure the fire stays blazing, justifying the friction and accusing the lover of commonly behaving in unaffectionate, hard-hearted ways which demand retribution: '"You ungrateful wretch, after all the countless kisses!"'[1] So it was that Antony's friends tried to convince him that the Egyptian woman (with whom he was passionately in love) loved him too. They would insolently call him insensitive and distant,[2] and say, 'The woman has given up her grand kingdom and her blissful way of life: she is pining away as she accompanies you on your cam   B
paigns, playing the part of a concubine. "But you have in your heart wits proof against charm"[3] and you ignore her pain.' These complaints of unfair behaviour pleased him and, because he enjoyed being accused rather than praised, he was unwittingly corrupted by a semblance of reproof.[4]

Candour of this sort resembles the bites of loose women, since it stimulates and arouses pleasure by pretending to cause pain. Undiluted wine, taken separately, counteracts hemlock, but if it is added to hemlock and stirred in, then it makes the effect of the   C
drug utterly irreversible, since the heat conveys the effect to the heart;[5] this is an analogy for how unprincipled people know that candour goes a long way towards counteracting flattery and therefore use candour itself as a form of flattery. That is why even Bias did not give a satisfactory answer when he was asked which is the most formidable creature: he replied that the tyrant is the most formidable wild creature and the flatterer the most

1. *TGF* Aeschylus F135 Radt; from *The Myrmidons*, probably spoken by Achilles over the dead body of Patroclus. Compare Plutarch, *Dialogue on Love* 751C.
2. See Plutarch, *Life of Antony* 53.8. The 'Egyptian woman' is, of course, Cleopatra.
3. Homer, *Odyssey* 10.329.
4. Compare *Life of Antony* 24.11 f.
5. For this medical lore, compare *Table Talk* 653A, *On Talkativeness* 509D–E; Pliny, *Naturalis Historia* 25.152; Dioscorides 4.78.1.

formidable domesticated creature.[1] But it would be more true to
say that there are two categories of flatterer: the domesticated

D  ones are those who gather around someone's bath and table; but
the flatterer who stretches his interference, slander and malevolence, like so many tentacles, into someone's inner chambers and
into the women's quarters is wild and savage and hard to tame.

[20] One protective measure, I believe, is to appreciate and
constantly remember that the mind consists of one part that is
trustworthy, principled and rational, but another part that is
irrational, unprincipled and emotional.[2] A friend acts as an adviser
to and champion of the better part (just as a doctor develops and
maintains health), but a flatterer sides with the emotional, irra-

E  tional part: this is what he stimulates and titillates and tempts,
and he drives a wedge between it and rationality by devising for
it shoddy, sensual indulgences. Consequently, just as there are
foods which cannot be assimilated by either blood or breath and
fortify neither muscles nor marrow, but stimulate the genitals,
excite the belly and produce flesh that is infirm and internally
unsound, so a flatterer's words – as will be obvious to any
observant person – fail to fortify intelligence and the rational
mind, but cultivate some erotic pleasure, or intensify thoughtless
passion, or provoke spiteful envy, or expand and increase vain
self-regard, or offer support to distress, or use slander and menace

F  to sharpen malevolence, keep dependency cowed and pander to
the fears of an untrusting nature. For he is forever lying in wait
for some emotion which he can fatten up, and like a tumour he
arrives when the mind is rotten and inflamed: 'If you're angry,
lash out; if you want something, buy it; if you're afraid, let's run
away; if you're suspicious, you might well be right.'

The intensity and power of these emotions discompose one's
rational faculty and this makes the flatterer hard to detect; but his
behaviour is similar when he concerns himself with lesser emotions too, so here he gives us a better opportunity. Suppose

62A  someone suspects himself of drinking or eating to excess, and is

---

1. Compare Plutarch, *Banquet of the Seven Sages* 147B.
2. The language is reminiscent of the Stoic Posidonius (Frs. 31, 33, 158, 166, 168
EK), but Posidonius' unorthodox psychology followed Platonic and Aristotelian structures. Compare Plutarch again at 943A and 441D.

in two minds about bathing or dining: a friend will restrain him with the suggestion that he should take care and be circumspect, but a flatterer drags him off to the baths, or tells him to lay on some dish he is unused to and not to harm his body by fasting. And when he sees someone's resolve weakening with regard to a journey or a voyage or some enterprise, he will say that there is no hurry, and that delay or sending someone else instead will make no difference to the outcome. And if someone has promised to lend or give some money to a relative and is regretting the promise but ashamed to break it, a flatterer tries to tip the scales towards the worse alternative, supports the person's tightfisted-ness, and eliminates his remorse by telling him to be thrifty because he has many expenses and there are many people he has to satisfy. Hence, if we notice when we are coveting something, ashamed of something or afraid of something, then we will notice the flatterer at work too, because these are the feelings he is constantly championing and whose outcomes he is constantly describing with candour. Anyway, it is time to move on to another topic.

[21] Let us turn now to his undertaking jobs and attending to tasks, because this is an area where a flatterer makes the difference between himself and a friend very opaque and unclear, since he seems to be ready, willing and available for anything. But a friend's manner is 'straightforward' (as Euripides described 'words of truth')[1] and uncomplicated and sincere, while a flatterer's manner is actually 'diseased within itself and requires clever medi-cine' – and indeed, no ordinary medicine and in no ordinary doses. So, one can imagine an occasion of a friend meeting someone else and, without any exchange of words but solely by looks and smiles, he conveys through his eyes his inner goodwill and cordiality (which are reciprocated) and then walks on by. A flatterer, on the other hand, starts running and chasing and waving when he is still a long way off, and if he is not the first to do the spotting and the greeting, he apologizes profusely, calling frequently on men and gods to witness his innocence. Likewise where day-to-day business is concerned, friends do not

1. *The Phoenician Women* 469; 472 follows.

bother with the trivial details: they do not complicate matters by insisting on precision, nor do they insist that they themselves must attend to everything. A flatterer, however, works in this area without stopping, pausing or resting, and allows no one else the space or room to attend to anything; he longs to be told what to do, and the lack of such instructions puts him on edge – or rather makes him utterly depressed and morose.

E    [22] This, then, is all evidence, for intelligent people, of a kind of friendship that is false and immoral – excessively ready to play the prostitute and embrace another person. However, we must, first, be aware of how the two types differ when they promise to do something. An old author has expressed it nicely: a friend's promise is 'If I can do it, and if it is something that can be done', whereas a flatterer's is 'You only have to tell me what you want.'[1] Comic playwrights also portray people like that on stage: 'Nicomachus, set me up against the soldier and see if my whip and I don't tenderize him all over, if I don't make his face softer than a sponge!'[2]

F    Second, no friend lends a hand without first lending advice and having assessed the enterprise and helped in ensuring that it is appropriate and useful. A flatterer, however – even if he is given the opportunity to join in assessing the matter and to have a say about it – wants to make himself less important than the other person and to gratify him, and furthermore does not want to give the other person the impression that he is not keen and is trying to wriggle out of working, so he puts up no resistance, but fans the other's enthusiasm with his own. For no rich man or 63A    ruler is readily able to say, ' "I wish I could find a beggar, or preferably someone meaner than a beggar, who through goodwill towards me will fearlessly speak what is in his heart." '[3] Instead, like tragic playwrights, they need a chorus – a chorus of friends singing in unison – or an audience applauding as one. That is why Merope in the play suggests: 'Make sure you have friends who aren't obsequious in their speech, and keep beyond

---

1. The first quote is Homer, *Iliad* 14.196 (or 18.427, or *Odyssey* 5.90); the second is part of the line preceding each of these three lines.
2. *CAF Adesp.* 125 Kock.
3. Euripides, *Ino* F412 Nauck.

the locked door of the house those wicked people who pander to your pleasure.'[1] But they do the opposite: they anathematize   B people 'who aren't obsequious in their speech' but who resist for their own good, and they admit 'wicked people who pander' – servile charmers – not only within 'the locked door and the house' but even within their hearts and their personal affairs.

Some of these flatterers – the more guileless ones – set out only to be attendants and assistants, because they do not think it right and proper to advise on such important matters; others, however – the less principled ones – stand there and mirror the other person's puzzled frowns and head-shaking, but actually say nothing. But if the other person expresses his opinion, they say, 'Good heavens! That's exactly what I was going to say. You took the words out of my mouth.' Just as mathematicians say that surfaces and lines do not in themselves bend or extend or   C move (since they are immaterial concepts), but can bend and extend and move along with the material bodies whose limits they form,[2] so you will find that the parts a flatterer plays, the opinions he expresses, even his pleasures and passions, always conform to the other person; consequently, in these areas at any rate, the difference between him and a friend is easy to detect.

They are even easier to distinguish by the way they attend to things. A favour from a friend is like a living creature: its most important potential lies beneath the surface, and there is nothing   D showy or ostentatious on the outside. However, just as a doctor often cures someone without the patient knowing it, so a friend's interventions and solutions often benefit someone who remains unaware of the friend's attention. Arcesilaus was this kind of friend, especially when he discovered that Apelles of Chios, who was ill, was running out of money; he paid him another visit, this time with twenty drachmas, sat down beside him and said, 'Everything in the world consists only of those Empedoclean elements – "fire, water, earth and ether, gentle and sublime"[3] – but in your

1. Euripides, *Erechtheus* F362.18–20 Nauck. But it is difficult to see how Merope appeared in this play. The lines were probably spoken by Erechtheus' wife Praxithea, and Plutarch's memory was playing tricks again.
2. Plutarch used the same illustration in *Marital Advice* 140A.
3. Plutarch's recollection of Empedocles F17.18 DK.

case they are awkwardly arranged.' Meanwhile, he was rearranging the pillow, and he slipped the money underneath it without Apelles noticing. When Apelles' old servant found the money, she wondered how it got there and told him about it, and Apelles laughed and said, 'Arcesilaus is the perpetrator of this sleight of hand!'[1]

Furthermore, 'children take after'[2] those who are their parents in philosophy. At any rate, Lacydes (who was a member of Arcesilaus' circle) was among Cephisocrates' friends, all of whom stood by him in court when he was informed against and consequently prosecuted. When the prosecutor asked to see Cephisocrates' ring, he quietly dropped it on the ground; Lacydes noticed this, and stepped on the ring to hide it, since the prosecution's case depended on the ring. After the verdict, when Cephisocrates was greeting the judges, one of them, who had apparently seen what had gone on, told Cephisocrates that he should be grateful to Lacydes and explained what had happened, although Lacydes had told no one. Likewise, I think, most of the blessings the gods confer are unnoticed by the recipients, since for the gods benevolence and charity are innately pleasant.

On the other hand, a flatterer's activity is never honest, genuine, straightforward or generous; instead, it generates sweat, noise and frenetic scampering about, and a face that is tense with the superficial appearance of laborious and earnest service. (He reminds one of an elaborate painting which evokes an impression of clarity by means of lurid colours and angled folds, wrinkles and corners.) And then he recounts all the trips the business has caused him to make, how worried he has been, and how he has put others' backs up, and lists the innumerable efforts he has made and the ordeals he has endured, and ends up declaring that it was not worth it. In all this he is obnoxious, because any favour which is turned to criticism is obnoxious, repellent and intolerable, and a flatterer's favours contain an element of criticism and of wanting the other person to feel ashamed even while

---

1. Diogenes Laertius (4.37) has another version of this anecdote with different details.
2. Hesiod, *Works and Days* 235.

they are being performed, not with hindsight. However, if a    B
friend is required to talk about the matter, he gives a restrained
report, and says nothing about himself. This was the way in
which the Spartans sent grain to the inhabitants of Smyrna when
they needed it: when the Smyrnaeans expressed astonishment at
their charity, the Spartans replied, 'It was nothing momentous: we
voted to deprive ourselves and our draught-animals of the midday
meal for one day, and it added up to what we sent you.'[1] This
kind of charity is not only generous, but also more gratifying to
the recipients, because they think that their benefactors are not
being hurt to any great extent.

[23] Anyway, the flatterer's nature is most recognizable not in
the obnoxiousness with which he attends to matters, nor in the
ease with which he makes promises, but rather in whether he    C
undertakes jobs for good or despicable purposes and contributes
towards someone's benefit or his gratification. For a friend will
not think (as Gorgias used to put it) that his friend ought to
work for him in moral ways and then himself go on to serve
his friend in all sorts of immoral ways:[2] 'He was born for mutual
virtue, not mutual imperfection.'[3] In other words, he is more
likely to try to dissuade his friend from unsuitable action, and if
he fails, there is Phocion's fine comment to Antipater: 'You
cannot treat me as both a friend and a flatterer'[4] – that is, as a
friend and not as a friend. For a friend is there as a colleague not
a co-rogue, to consult with not to conspire with, for support in
spreading facts not fictions – and yes, even to share his adversity
not his perversity. If it is not even desirable to know about    D
friends' despicable actions, how could it be desirable to take part
in them and share the disgrace? In other words, a friend behaves
like the Spartans: when they had been defeated by Antipater and
were negotiating terms with him, they had no objection to his
imposing any penalty he liked upon them, provided that it did
not disgrace them; and a friend has no objection to being the first

1. The anecdote reappears in Ps.-Aristotle, *Oeconomica* II.1347b16 ff. but of
   Spartan generosity towards the Samians.
2. Gorgias F21 DK.
3. A rather free recollection of Euripides, *Iphigenia in Aulis* 407.
4. Plutarch liked this *mot*: 142B, 188F, 532F; *Life of Phocion* 30.3; *Life of Agis* 2.4.

to be called upon and thinks he ought to be involved and makes no excuses and is enthusiastic when a job crops up which entails expense or danger or hard work, but when the job entails disgrace, all he asks is to have nothing to do with it and not to be

E   involved. But flattery, on the contrary, backs away from tasks which entail hard work or danger, and if you tap flattery to test its quality, it sounds flawed[1] – a result of making excuses – and cheap. But if you abuse a flatterer and trample on him, having set him to despicable, demeaning, disreputable menial tasks, he does not think it at all awful or insulting.

Consider a monkey. Because it cannot guard property like a dog, or endure weight like a horse, or plough land like cattle, abuse and sarcasm and jokes are heaped upon it, as a self-created catalyst of laughter.[2] In much the same way, a flatterer is incapable of backing anyone up verbally, or contributing money, or siding with anyone, and stops short whenever hard work and

F   effort are called for; but he is wholehearted – in underhand actions; he can be relied on – to facilitate a love affair; he is precise – when it comes to paying a whore; he takes care – when elucidating his calculation of the cost of a drink; he is no sluggard – when meals need preparing; he is attentive – to people's mistresses; he is strong-willed and unshakeable – when told to taunt the in-laws or help in expelling a wife. Consequently, here too

65A  the man's behaviour gives him away, since he is ready to give freely of himself when told to attend to any disreputable, despicable matter you may care to mention, so as to gratify the person who is giving him the order.

[24] One of the chief areas in which a considerable difference between a flatterer and a friend becomes obvious is in their attitude towards other friends. It is a source of great pleasure for a friend to be far from alone in liking and being liked, and what he constantly spends his time trying to achieve for a friend is a wide circle of friends and considerable public recognition, because he thinks that friends share things and therefore ought above all

---

1. A metaphor perhaps remembered from Plato, *Theaetetus* 179d.
2. This seems to have been a not unusual reaction. Monkeys amused Posidonius too (F245 EK).

to share friends. A flatterer, however, is false, phony and debased,    B
because he is well aware that he is mistreating friendship by
using it as a counterfeit coin. He is naturally envious, but it is
people similar to himself that he relates to in an envious fashion,
by striving to beat them in a contest of jokes and gossip; on the
other hand, he stands in fear and trembling of anyone better than
himself, but certainly not because 'he is a foot-soldier marching
beside a Lydian chariot',[1] but because (in Simonides' words) 'he
does not even have unalloyed lead to compare with purified
gold'.[2] So since he is a shallow, superficial impostor, then when
he is compared and investigated in close proximity to genuine,
substantial, solid-wrought friendship, he patently does not make    C
the grade, and so he behaves just like the man who painted an
abominable picture of some cocks and told his slave to shoo all
the real cocks as far away as possible from the painting: the
flatterer shoos real friends away and refuses to let them get close.
If he cannot do that, then in public he cringes, and is at their
beck and call, and stands in awe of them, because they are better
people than him; but in private he spreads and scatters lies about
them.

And once the chafing of covert talk has produced a festering
wound (even if it takes time to produce such an extreme result),
he bears in mind and cherishes Medius' role. Medius was, so to
speak, the ringleader and chief mentor of the chorus of flatterers
who surrounded Alexander and who ganged up against those of    D
good character.[3] He told his troupe to go all out for afflicting
and hurting their victim with their lies, on the grounds that even
if he healed the wound, the lies would still have caused a lingering
scab. And it was indeed these scabs – or rather gangrene and
cancers – that consumed Alexander and caused him to execute
Callisthenes, Parmenion and Philotas;[4] he then entrusted himself
wholeheartedly to people like Hagno,[5] Bagoas, Agis★ and
Demetrius, who contrived his downfall by prostrating themselves

1. This is from Pindar, as we learn at *Life of Nicias* 1.1; F206 Snell and Maehler.
2. Simonides F87 Page.
3. Compare *Life of Alexander* 75.4, 76.2 and 23.7, 53.1.
4. *Life of Alexander* 55 and 49.
5. *Life of Alexander* 40 and 55.

E  before him, dressing him up and presenting him as if he were some Eastern idol.[1] Pandering to pleasure has that much power, and nowhere does it have more, apparently, than on people with the greatest public images, because the belief that one has the best qualities, coupled with aspirations towards them, gives a flatterer confidence and encourages him as well. Although high ground is hard for those with designs upon it to approach and reach, nevertheless elevated opinions in a mind which, thanks to external or innate factors, lacks common sense are particularly accessible to pettiness and meanness.

[25] This is why I now repeat the advice I gave at the beginning of this discourse — that we should eliminate self-love and
F  self-importance from ourselves, because it prepares the ground for external flatterers by flattering us first and softening us up for them. However, if we trust the god and appreciate how extremely precious for each of us is the precept 'Know yourself',[2] and if we also survey our character, upbringing and conditioning to see how in countless respects they fall short of goodness and include bad, unchosen behaviour, speech and moods, then we will make it hard for flatterers to trample on us. Alexander said that his sleeping and having sex were the prime reasons for his disbelieving those who called him a god, since in these respects he was more dependent and passive than he should be;[3] and if
66A  we observe how often and in how many respects our own attributes are disgraceful, distressing, imperfect and wrong, we will constantly discover that we do not need a friend to commend and compliment us, but to take us to task and speak candidly — yes, and even critically too — about our misdeeds.

This need arises because there are few who have the courage to speak candidly rather than gratifyingly to friends, and again, even among the few, it is far from easy to find people who really know how to do this, rather than those who think they are using candour when they are merely being rude and critical. In fact,
B  however, candour is no different from any other medicine: if it

1. Cf. *Life of Alexander* 45.
2. See p. 61, n. 6.
3. Again in *Life of Alexander* 22 and *Table Talk* 717F.

is not administered at the right time, the result is distress and disturbance with no benefit, and its effects are in a sense only a painful version of the pleasant effects of flattery. Inopportune criticism is just as harmful as inopportune praise, and is a prime factor in making people susceptible, easy targets for flattery, when they flow like water off the forbidding slopes and towards the undemanding valleys. This is why candour must be tempered by tact and must be rational, so that it is not overdone and so that its impact is diluted, as if it were bright light: otherwise, because people are upset and hurt by those who criticize everything and disparage everyone, they turn for shelter to the shadow of the flatterer and incline towards freedom from distress.

You see, Philopappus, the means of sheltering from every    C kind of vice is virtue, and not the opposite vice:[1] some people imagine they can use coarseness to escape timidity or slickness to escape rusticity, and can position their attitudes as far away as possible from cowardice and effeminacy if they appear to be as close as possible to impudence and audacity. Others make atheism their defence against superstition and unscrupulousness their defence against silliness, and so their inexperience of anything straight and upright distorts their character, as if it were a piece    D of wood, so that instead of being warped one way it is warped the opposite way. And the most despicable way that flatterers dissemble is by causing distress with no accompanying benefit; and to use unpleasantness and severity to avoid losing face and demeaning oneself in friendship is a sure sign of clumsiness and incompetence as regards affectionate relationships, and resembles an emancipated slave in a comedy, who thinks he should make use of his right to address others on equal terms by addressing them in defamatory terms.

So since both involving oneself in flattery (by trying to gratify someone) and avoiding flattery (but in the process destroying friendship and affection by excessive candour) are despicable; and since we must allow neither of these to happen, and candour is

1. The following passage is founded on the Aristotelian moral theory of virtue being a mean between excess and deficiency, as expounded in *Nicomachean Ethics* 2.6–7.

no exception to the general principle that the mean is where

E   virtue is found; then this topic – in so far as it requires developing – turns out to provide our essay with a natural conclusion.

[26] Candour, therefore, is plainly beset by rather a lot of fatal defects, and the first one to remove from it is self-love: we must make absolutely sure that no one could think that we were merely being rude because of some personal reason such as unfair or hurtful treatment. For any words spoken for personal reasons are assumed to be provoked not by goodwill but by anger, and to constitute disparagement rather than rebuke – the difference being that candour is altruistic and high-minded, while disparagement is self-centred and petty, which is why candour earns respect and admiration, while disparagement earns recrimination and

F   contempt. For instance, Agamemnon refused to put up with Achilles' apparently moderate candour,[1] but when Odysseus lays into him savagely with the words 'You loser! How I wish you were in command of another pitiful army!',[2] he gives in and lets him get away with it, because he is humbled by the goodwill and sense of what he says. For Odysseus had no grounds for a

67A   personal grudge and spoke his mind for the good of Greece, whereas Achilles gave the impression of having personal reasons for getting so angry. Still, Achilles himself, despite his 'lack of sweet or indulgent disposition',[3] and although he was 'a dreadful man, liable to accuse even the innocent',[4] often quietly let Patroclus inveigh against him with remarks such as: 'You pitiless man! The horseman Peleus was not your father, nor was Thetis your mother: the grey sea and the sheer cliffs gave you birth, as is proved by your merciless mind.'[5]

B   The orator Hyperides used to recommend that the Athenians consider not just whether he was being harsh, but whether or not he had reason to be harsh;[6] and likewise, because a friend's rebukes are free of any personal feelings, they command respect

1. It was hardly moderate: see Homer, *Iliad* 1.225 ff.
2. *Iliad* 14.84.
3. *Iliad* 20.467.
4. A Homeric line made up from memory of *Iliad* 11.654 and 13.775.
5. *Iliad* 16.33 ff.
6. Hyperides F212 Jensen; quoted in *Life of Phocion* 10.6.

and are valued and cogent. If it is clear that your candour in speaking to a friend owes absolutely nothing to the fact that he has wronged you, and that this plays no part at all, but you are taking him to task for other misdeeds of his and not stopping yourself from making him feel remorse for what he has done to others, then the energy of this candour is overwhelming, and because you, as rebuker, are being so agreeable, you intensify the harshness and severity of the rebuke. So, although it is right that it is particularly important to do or plan something useful and appropriate for *friends* when we are angry or arguing with them, yet it is just as relevant to friendship, on occasions when we ourselves are being overlooked and ignored, to speak candidly on behalf of *others* who are also being ignored, and to remind our friends of them.

So there was a time when Plato and Dionysius were looking askance at each other and getting into arguments. Plato asked Dionysius for an appointment, which Dionysius granted, but he was thinking that Plato wanted to go through a catalogue of self-centred complaints. Plato, however, started a conversation with him, as follows: 'Dionysius, if you heard that someone had sailed to Sicily with a grudge, and was wanting to do you harm, but hadn't found the opportunity, would you let him sail away? Would you give him the chance to get away scot-free?' 'Not at all, Plato,' replied Dionysius. 'It is important to disapprove of and punish not only one's enemies' actions, but also their intentions.' 'So,' Plato went on, 'if someone has come here with warmth in his heart for you and wanted to do you good in some way, by his own agency, but you hadn't given him the opportunity, does he deserve to be let go without thanks or due regard?' When Dionysius asked whom he meant, Plato said, 'Aeschines – in character as equable a man as any of Socrates' circle, and as capable of improving his acquaintances by his conversation; but although he sailed a considerable distance to get here, so as to make your acquaintance on the basis of philosophy, he has been ignored.' Dionysius was so stirred by this, and so impressed by Plato's benevolence and magnanimity, that he immediately embraced Plato and hugged him, and also gave Aeschines the proper consideration suited to his stature.

[27] The second defect to remove from candour – in order to

purify it, as it were – is any trace of insolence and mockery and ridicule and sarcasm, which spice up candour in a contempt-
F  ible way. For just as when a doctor performs an operation, it is important that a certain delicacy and precision inform his actions, and that his hand is free of the superfluous suppleness suitable for a dancer or for wild and random gestures, so candour admits cleverness and wit (as long as this charm preserves the dignity of the candour), but perishes and is utterly destroyed[1] at the ap-proach of belligerence, sarcasm and insolence. So the lyre-player found a convincing and elegant way to shut Philip up when he was trying to argue with him about how to pluck the strings; he
68A  said, 'I hope, my lord, that you never suffer such misfortune that you become more expert than me on these matters.'[2] Epicharmus, on the other hand, was wrong in his remark to Hieron: Hieron once had some of his associates killed, and a few days later invited Epicharmus to dinner; Epicharmus said, 'You didn't invite your friends when you were performing a sacrifice the other day.' And Antiphon was wrong too, in replying to the question what the best kind of bronze is – when this inquiry occurred in Dionysius' presence – 'The bronze from which the statues of Harmodius and Aristogiton were made at Athens.'[3] These re-marks cause distress and pain with no benefit, and their sarcasm and levity cause no pleasure either; all behaviour of this kind
B  originates in lack of self-control when it is fostered by hostility and blended with bad manners and insolence, and those who make use of such behaviour also ruin themselves, dancing as they are on the brink of a chasm. In fact, Antiphon was executed by Dionysius and Timagenes fell from Caesar's favour – Timagenes, who never uttered a non-derivative phrase, but at any party or during any discussion kept on using friendship as specious justifica-tion for abuse, for no serious purpose at all, 'but because it drew more laughter from the Argives'.[4]

1. The language of the metaphor is reminiscent of Plato, *Phaedo* 103c ff.
2. Plutarch rightly enjoyed this story and used it elsewhere: 334C–D, 634D (and cf. 179B). Aelian (*Varia Historia* 9.36) told it of Antigonus.
3. Harmodius and Aristogiton were popularly known as the tyrannicides and liberators of Athens.
4. Homer, *Iliad* 2.215.

Now, the comic poets often composed harsh, socially pertinent messages to address to the audience; but because they mixed sarcasm and humour together, like an obnoxious mixed sauce for   C
food, they wasted their candour and destroyed its potential benefit, and consequently the poets were left only with a reputation for spite and rudeness, and the audience was left with no profit at all from the poets' words. Jocularity and humour are all right to use among friends on the odd occasion, but candour must preserve its seriousness and its own character; and if it is focusing on rather important matters, then your words must be made convincing and stirring by your use of emotion, gesture and tone.

Bad timing is always extremely harmful, and never more so than when it destroys the point of candour. It is patently obvious that we must take care in this regard if we are ever drinking and getting tipsy. A person makes blue skies overcast if he   D
interrupts light-hearted fun by starting up a discussion that furrows brows and tautens faces as if it were hostile to the god of freedom,[1] who, in Pindar's words, 'frees the fetters of anxious cares'.[2] Bad timing is also extremely dangerous, because wine makes minds teeter on the brink of anger, and inebriation often annexes candour and converts it into hostility. And in general it is not a sign of calibre or courage, but of cowardice, to speak one's mind only at the table and never when sober: this is how craven dogs behave. Anyway, there is no need to carry on with this topic.

[28] Many people do not think it right – or do not have the   E
courage – to try to control friends whose affairs are going well: they regard success as completely beyond the reach of rebuke. However, when a friend stumbles and trips, they oppress and ride roughshod over him, now that he has been humbled and brought low: they release their candour upon him all in a rush, like a stream which had been unnaturally dammed, and because of his former superciliousness and their former weakness, they relish the opportunity to take advantage of his change of fortune. It follows that it is rather important to discuss this matter too,

1. Plutarch uses an epithet of Dionysus meaning 'Loosener' or 'Liberator'.
2. Pindar F248 Snell and Maehler.

and to find a reply to Euripides when he says, 'When God grants success, what need is there of friends?'[1]

F   The answer is that successful people have a particular need of friends who speak their minds and deflate any excessive pride, since success and sound judgement rarely go together: in the majority of cases, while luck is inflating and destabilizing people, sense needs to be imported and rationality to be forced on them from outside. On the other hand, when God lays them low and divests them of their pretensions, events themselves contain an inherent rebuke and a stimulus to remorse; so there is at that time nothing for friendly candour or serious, caustic words to do, but on occasions of change of fortune of that order, it is 69A really 'pleasing to look into the eyes of a kindly man',[2] if he is being supportive and encouraging. Clearchus was a case in point: according to Xenophon, the sight of his kind and considerate face during battles or when danger was imminent used to put heart into his threatened men.[3]

However, the employment of candid and caustic speech on someone out of luck is like applying a stimulant to an afflicted and inflamed eye: it does not cure anything or alleviate the pain, B but adds to the pain the extra element of anger and makes the sufferer worse off. At any rate, there is no way that a healthy person gets cross or fierce with a friend for criticizing the company he keeps and his drinking, or his laziness, unfitness, constant bathing and excessive eating at the wrong times of day; but it is not just intolerable for someone who is ill, but even increases his illness, to be told that his present condition is due to his indulgence, effeminate lifestyle, rich food and womanizing. 'You certainly know how to pick a bad moment,' he responds. 'Here am I, writing my will and having castor or scammony, perhaps, prepared for me by my doctors;[4] and you start telling me off and getting all philosophical!' So this is an example of how the actual

1. Euripides, *Orestes* 667.
2. Euripides, *Ion* 732, already quoted at 49F above.
3. Plutarch cooked this titbit plucked from Xenophon, *Anabasis* 2.6.11, differently in *Table Talk* 620D.
4. Castor (from beavers) was used as a stimulant and antispasmodic; scammony was a purgative.

circumstances of people who are out of luck make candour and
stating the obvious unacceptable: what is required is a considerate     C
and helping hand. When children fall over, their nannies do not
run up to give them the rough edge of their tongues, but they
pick them up, wash them clean and calm them down, and only
then do they tick them off and scold them.

There is a story that when Demetrius of Phalerum[1] had been
exiled from his homeland and was spending time near Thebes,
with no public prominence and occupying himself with lowly
affairs, he once saw Crates approaching and was not pleased,
because he expected to be on the receiving end of some typically
Cynic candour and rough words. Crates, however, greeted him
civilly and struck up a conversation about how exile was not
inherently bad or worth getting upset about, since one is released     D
from risky, insecure circumstances: he was encouraging him not
to be depressed about himself and his situation. Demetrius' spirits
rose and he cheered up; he told his friends that he regretted those
affairs and occupations of his which had prevented his getting to
know a man like Crates.

'From friends comes kindly conversation when one is distressed, and rebuke when one is excessively foolish.'[2] That is
how exemplary friends behave, but inferior, worthless flatterers
of successful people are, as Demosthenes puts it, 'like fractures     E
and sprains: they are aroused whenever the body later suffers any
ill'.[3] So flatterers latch on to changes in fortune as though they
enjoyed them and found them a source of fulfilment. If the past
needs to be brought up at all when a bad plan has laid someone
low and it was his own fault, then these words are enough: 'This
was not in accordance with our will – in fact, for my part, I
often spoke strongly against it.'[4]

[29] Under what circumstances, then, ought a friend to be
forceful? When should he use the power that candour carries?
Whenever he is presented with the opportunity to stem the tide
of hedonism or anger or arrogance, or to curtail venality or     F

1. F59 Wehrli.
2. At 102B we are told that these lines are from Euripides (*TGF* F962 Nauck).
3. Demosthenes 18.198.
4. Nestor in Homer, *Iliad* 9.108 f.; the quotation is continued at 73F below.

restrain stupid thoughtlessness. An example is Solon's candour when he told Croesus, who had been corrupted and spoiled by transient success, to look to the end.[1] This is also how Socrates used to restrain Alcibiades, and he elicited tears of genuine remorse by showing him the error of his ways and made him turn over a new leaf.[2] Cyrus' treatment of Cyaxares was similiar,[3] and so was Plato's of Dion: when Dion's glory was at its most resplendent, and the sublimity and grandeur of his actions were 70A  attracting the attention of the whole world towards himself, Plato recommended that he should be wary and fearful of 'wilfulness, because isolation lodges with it'.[4] Speusippus too wrote in a letter to Dion[5] that he should not be proud at being a frequent topic of conversation among children and women, but should make sure that he embellished Sicily with religiousness, morality and the best laws, and so 'won renown'[6] for the Academy. On the other hand, as long as Perseus was successful, his courtiers Euctus and Eulaeus constantly conducted themselves with a view to his gratification: they were yes-men and followed his lead like everyone else. But after his catastrophic encounter with the Romans at Pydna[7] and his subsequent flight, they used to afflict him with their harsh criticisms and remind him of his mistakes and oversights, casting each and every one of them in his teeth, B  until, tormented by pain and fury, the man struck them both with his short-sword and did away with them.[8]

[30] So we have by now discussed the parameters of opportunities for candour which occur thanks to both parties at once; but opportunities are commonly created by one party in particular, and a caring friend should not let them pass, but should exploit

1. Life is so uncertain, according to Solon, that it is only after someone's death that you can truly assess whether or not he had a good life. For the full story, see Herodotus 1.30 ff. (and cf. *Life of Solon* 27).
2. Plato, *Symposium* 215e. Plutarch recalled the passage again in *On Being Aware of Moral Progress* 84C.
3. Xenophon, *Cyropaedia* 5.5.5 ff.
4. Plato, *Fourth Letter* 321C1.
5. A collection of such letters survived under Speusippus' name according to Diogenes Laertius 4.5.
6. A tag lifted from Euripides, *The Phoenician Women* 1742.
7. In 168 BC.
8. Recounted in *Life of Aemilius Paulus* 23.

them. For there are occasions when a question, a description, and a criticism or commendation of similar traits in others prepare the ground, so to speak, for candour. For instance, there is a story that Demaratus went to Macedonia at a time when Philip was quarrelling with his wife and son; when Philip greeted him and asked about the state of inter-Greek *entente cordiale*, Demaratus (who was concerned for Philip and knew him well) replied, 'It is really very good of you to ask about the rapport between Athens and Sparta, and to disregard the fact that your own household is overrun with so much conflict and disharmony.'[1] Diogenes did well too: he once arrived at Philip's camp – Philip was marching to fight the Greeks – and was taken to him; Philip did not know who he was and asked if he was a spy. 'I most certainly am a spy, Philip,' he said. 'I spy on your absence of wisdom and common sense, which is the only thing forcing you to go and gamble your kingdom and your life in a single moment.'[2]

It may be that this was over-forceful. [31] Opportunities for rebuke also arise, however, when people have been berated for their mistakes and are feeling humble and deflated. A subtle person comes up with an elegant use of this situation: he deflects the people who were berating his friend, sends them packing, and once he has got his friend to himself, he reminds him that he ought to be careful, even if the only reason for doing so is to put an end to his enemies' presumption: 'I mean, what occasion can there be for them to utter a word, what can they say against you, if you banish and rid yourself of the things which give rise to the slanders against you?' In this way, anything hurtful is credited to a berater, and anything beneficial to a rebuker.

An even more clever tactic is used by some people: by criticizing others, they make their acquaintances repent, because the faults they find in the others are those which they know their friends commit. My teacher Ammonius once found out during an afternoon lecture that some of his pupils had eaten a variety of dishes at midday: he told his freedman to whip his (Ammonius') slave,

---

1. Philip paid heed, according to 179C.
2. The anecdote recurs in *On Exile* 606C.

and adduced as a reason his inability to eat without also drinking. And he simultaneously looked at us, so that the reprimand went home to those who deserved it.

[32] The next point to note is that care must be taken about using candour towards a friend when there are a lot of people F around – one should bear in mind what happened to Plato. Once Socrates laid into one of his associates rather forcefully while talking near the banking stalls. Plato said, 'Wouldn't it have been better to have said that in private?' Socrates replied, 'Wouldn't it have been better for *you* to have spoken to me like that in private?' And there is a story that Pythagoras once attacked a pupil rather harshly when there were a lot of people around and the young man hanged himself; from then on, Pythagoras never again told anyone off in the presence of anyone else.

The point is that deviance should be regarded as a disfiguring disease, and should be chastised and exposed only in secret, not as 71A if it were a public festival or display, or in such a way as to attract witnesses and an audience. It is not a friend, but a sophist, who enhances his own reputation by others' failures and preens himself in front of the audience: this is the behaviour of those doctors who perform operations in theatres so as to make money. Leaving aside the arrogance (which is never justified in any form of treatment), one must also consider the contentiousness and wilfulness that accompany character flaws. It is not just that (as Euripides puts it) 'the more love is disapproved of, the more it stimulates',[1] but that public and plentiful disapproval makes anyone, whatever his defect or condition, disregard decency. B Therefore, just as Plato thinks it a prerequisite for elderly people who are trying to inculcate decency in the younger generation to behave decently themselves towards the young people,[2] so the sensitive candour of friends is the best instigator of sensitivity, and a careful, calm approach and assault on a deviator undermines and eradicates his flaw, which becomes infected by respect for the respect shown it. That is why it is best to 'put your head

1. *TGF* F665 Nauck.
2. Plato, *Laws* 729b–c; a precept again given in *Marital Advice* 144F and *Roman Questions* 272C.

close, so that the others might not hear'.[1] And the most disgraceful behaviour of all is to expose a husband within his wife's     C
hearing, a father when his children can see, someone in love
when the object of his affection is present or a teacher in the
presence of his pupils, because pain and fury make them completely forget themselves when they are censured in front of
those whose good opinion they expect.

In my opinion, in Clitus' case too, it was not so much the wine that
made him irritating as that he appeared to be telling Alexander off
when there were a lot of people present.[2] And because Ptolemy's
teacher Aristomenes[3] once woke him up with a slap when he was
nodding off in front of a delegation, he let in Ptolemy's flatterers,
who pretended to take Ptolemy's side and to be cross, and said, 'If
you fell asleep after all your hard work and sleepless nights, we ought     D
to reprimand you in private, not lay hands on you in front of so
many people.' Ptolemy sent a cup of poison to the man and told him
to drink it. Moreover, Aristophanes says that Cleon found fault with
him, and tried to incite the Athenians against him, for 'slandering the
state in the presence of foreigners'.[4]

It follows that this is another thing to watch out for, along
with the others we have discussed, if one wants to avoid exhibi-
tionism and currying favour with people, and concentrate on
using candour as a means of beneficial treatment. In fact, it ought
to be possible for people who use candour to say what Thucy-     E
dides had the Corinthians say about themselves: 'We are in a
position to criticize others.'[5] That is quite right: as Lysander
apparently said to the Megarian who, at a meeting of the allies,
was speaking candidly on behalf of Greece, 'Your words need a
city to back them',[6] so any person's candour presumably needs

---

1. A recurring line in Homer's *Odyssey*: e.g. 1.157, 4.70, 17.592.
2. Clitus, a Macedonian noble who had earlier saved Alexander's life, in a large
   drunken party one evening went too far in plain-spoken criticism of Alexander
   and provoked the king to lose his temper and kill him. It remained a notorious
   incident and is given full coverage in Plutarch's *Life of Alexander* 50 f.
3. This is Ptolemy V Epiphanes; see Polybius 15.31, 18.53; Diodorus Siculus
   28.14.
4. Aristophanes, *Acharnians* 503.
5. Thucydides 1.70.
6. Also told in *Life of Lysander* 22.1.

moral authority – a saying that is nowhere more true than in the case of those who rebuke others and try to instil self-responsibility in them. At any rate, Plato used to say that his way of life was his means of reprimanding Speusippus;[1] and likewise, of course, Xenocrates needed only to be seen by Polemon during a lecture,
F     and to glance at him, to convert him and change his life.[2] On the other hand, if anyone whose character lacks authority and goodness employs candour in his speech, the inevitable response is 'a healer of others with sores erupting all over his own body'.[3]

[33] Nevertheless, there are many situations which induce people, even though they themselves are less than perfect, to rebuke others similar to themselves with whom they are associating: here the most reasonable tactic would be one in which the person speaking his mind is somehow simultaneously implicated and embraced in the accusation. This is the context of the line 'Son of Tydeus, what has happened to us? Why have we forgot-
72A    ten our fierce heroism?',[4] and also of the line 'At the moment, all of us together are no match for Hector by himself.'[5] An example of a similar principle is how when Socrates used to refute his young associates, he never supposed that he was immune from ignorance himself, but thought that he ought to accompany them in concentrating on virtue and searching for truth. The point is that warmth and trust are inspired by people who seem to have the same flaws and seem to be correcting themselves along with their friends, whereas anyone who, while castigating someone else, adopts an elevated position, as if he were some pure and dispassionate entity, comes across – unless he is considerably advanced in years or has acknowledged standing because of
B     his virtue and reputation – as offensive and oppressive and consequently is no help at all. That is why Phoenix disingenuously

1. This is elaborated in On Brotherly Love 491F–492A: Plato's example reclaimed Speusippus from self-indulgence.
2. From libertinism to philosophy. Diogenes Laertius (4.16) offers more details.
3. A line from Euripides (TGF F1086 Nauck) which erupts elsewhere in Plutarch: 88D, 481E, 1110E.
4. Odysseus to Diomedes, attempting to stem the drive of Hector in Homer, Iliad 11.313.
5. Agamemnon trying to rouse the Greeks, Iliad 8.234.

included the disasters that had happened in his own case, when anger impelled him to try to kill his father and he quickly relented 'in case the Greeks dubbed me parricide',[1] because he did not want to give the impression, while reprimanding Achilles, of being himself beyond the reach of anger and altogether fault-less. For that is the way to get through to and affect someone's character, and people are less likely to resist someone who seems to have the same feelings and does not give the impression of despising them.

A bright light should not be brought close to an inflamed eye, and neither can a mind which has been taken over by the emo-tions submit to candour and undiluted reproof. Therefore, one of the most useful ways to be of assistance is to blend in a pinch of praise, as in the following lines: 'You are the best men in the army, so you can no longer do well by refraining from fierce heroism. For my part, I have no argument with anyone who refrains from fighting – provided he is a weakling; but in my heart I am furious with *you*.'[2] There are also the lines: 'Pandarus, where is your bow? Where are your winged arrows? Where is your fame, which no man here can contest?'[3] There are also lines like the following, which issue a clarion call of encouragement to people under pressure: 'What has happened to Oedipus and his famous riddles?'[4] and 'Are these the words of Heracles, who has often proven dauntless?'[5]

Speaking like that not only softens the harshness and bossiness of the criticism, but also sets up an internal rivalry: he is made to feel shame for his disgraceful aspects by being reminded of his fine aspects and by making himself an example of better conduct. However, comparisons with others (of the same age, for example, or country or family) aggravate and exacerbate the contentious-ness which accompanies any flaw, and which invariably retorts angrily: 'So why don't you shove off to my betters, and leave me in peace?' When employing candour, therefore, one must be

1. Homer, Iliad 9.461.
2. Poseidon rallying the Greeks in Iliad 13.116 ff.
3. Aeneas to the Trojan archer Pandarus in Iliad 5.171 f.
4. Antigone to Oedipus in Euripides, The Phoenician Women 1688.
5. Theseus to Heracles in Euripides, Heracles 1250.

careful about praising others – unless, of course, those others are the person's parents. That is why Agamemnon says, 'Tydeus

E  certainly fathered a son who scarcely resembles him',[1] and in *The Scyrians* Odysseus says, 'Here you are, bringing the bright light of your family into disgrace by knitting, when your father is the greatest man in Greece.'[2]

[34] The most unsuitable behaviour of all is to repay a rebuke with a rebuke and candour with candour, because it makes tempers rapidly flare and provokes argumentativeness, and in general this kind of bickering can give the impression of stemming not from an attempt to retort with candour but from an inability to

F  abide candour. It is preferable, therefore, to let a friend get away with it, when he seems to be telling you off, because if at a later date he goes wrong himself and needs telling off, then the situation itself in a sense allows candour to be candid: if, without bearing a grudge, you remind him that he himself has tended not to stand idly by when his friends go wrong, but rather to censure them and take them in hand, he is more likely to submit and be open to correction, and will see it as repayment stemming not from angry recrimination, but from charitable goodwill.

73A  [35] There is also the point that Thucydides makes when he says, 'Anyone who, in pursuing the highest goals, tolerates envy has the right priorities.'[3] It is correct for a friend to put up with the hostility his reprimands generate, when crucially important issues are involved. However, if he gets irate at everything, whatever the situation, and relates to his acquaintances as if they were his pupils rather than his friends, then when very important issues arise and he tries to deliver a reprimand, he will be feeble and ineffective – he has used up his candour, like a doctor who dispenses in many minor and unessential cases medicine which,

B  though harsh and bitter, is essential and valuable. So he will, first, be very careful about being constantly critical himself;

---

1. Homer, *Iliad* 5.800. But it was Athena, not Agamemnon, speaking. The son in question is Diomedes.
2. Odysseus to Achilles sitting among the girls in Scyrus, from *The Scyrians*, possibly by Euripides (*TGF Adesp.* F9 Nauck; Euripides F683a Snell). Plutarch filled out the quotation differently in *How to Study Poetry* 34D.
3. Pericles in Thucydides 2.64.5.

second, where other people are concerned, if someone else fusses and nags about everything, he will use this as a stepping-stone, so to speak, to approach the other person's more important flaws. When the doctor Philotimus was shown a sore finger by a man with an abscess on his liver, he said, 'My friend, the issue in your case is not a whitlow';[1] so too, given the opportunity, a friend can say to someone who carps at trivial, worthless things, 'Why are we making an issue of merry-making, carousing and incidentals? My friend, if he would only get rid of his lover, or stop gambling, we would find him exceptional in all other respects.' The point is that leniency over minor matters makes a friend's candour about more important matters not unwelcome, whereas constant harassment, continual severity and ill-humour, and making it one's business to know everything and to interfere in everything, are not only more than flesh and blood can stand, but are intolerable even to slaves.

[36] As Euripides says,[2] not every aspect of old age is bad; and the same goes for one's friends' fallibility. Therefore we must observe our friends when they do right as well as when they do wrong; and our starting-point should certainly be to be ready to praise them. Cooling contracts iron and hardens it into steel, provided it has first been made tractable and fluid by heat; similarly, friends who have been relaxed and warmed by praise must later be calmly treated to a cooling bath, so to speak, of candour. Given the opportunity, we must say, 'Do you think there is any comparison between these two types of behaviour? Can you see what kind of harvest goodness yields? We who are your friends demand that behaviour from you: it is proper to you, it is your birthright. But you must banish the other kind "into the mountains or into the waves of the roaring sea".'[3]

A considerate doctor would rather use sleep and diet than castor and scammony to relieve a patient of illness, and by the same token a good friend, a conscientious father and a teacher enjoy using praise rather than criticism as a means of moral

1. See p. 39, n. 3.
2. *The Phoenician Women* 528, but the context is quite different.
3. Homer, *Iliad* 6.347.

improvement. The one thing above all which makes candour hurt as little as possible, and be as remedial as possible, is to deal in a tactful and kindly fashion, without any trace of rancour, with people who are making mistakes. That is why it is important not to criticize them harshly if they deny their faults, or to stop them defending themselves: one should even help them in some way to come up with plausible excuses and should make room for a more moderate reason by distancing oneself from the worse one. This is what Hector did when he said to his brother,[1] 'What are you up to? It is wrong of you to have stored up this anger in

F  your heart' – as if his withdrawal from the battle was not a cowardly bolt, but was prompted by anger. In the same vein, Nestor said to Agamemnon, 'You succumbed to your proud-hearted temper.'[2]

The point is that it is more likely to have an effect on someone's character to say 'It didn't occur to you' and★ 'You didn't know' rather than 'That was a criminal act' and★ 'You acted disgracefully'; 'You shouldn't emulate your brother' rather than 'You

74A shouldn't be jealous of your brother'; and 'You should avoid the corrupting influence of that woman' rather than 'You should stop corrupting that woman.' But although this is the path candour looks for when it is trying to remedy a defect, nevertheless when its goal is preventive,★ it takes the contrary route. When what is necessary is to divert people who are poised to go wrong, or when we want to energize and motivate people who are being won over★ when faced with some powerful impulse which is tending in a direction opposite to what is required, or who are being weak and disconsolate with regard to correct conduct, then we must attribute the situation to motives which are out of character and discreditable. Thus, when Odysseus is inciting Achilles in Sophocles' play,[3] he says that it is not the case that the meal has made him angry, but 'As soon as you caught sight of

B  the buildings of Troy, you were afraid'; and again, when Achilles is livid at this and announces his intention to sail away, Odysseus

1. Homer, *Iliad* 6.326; the brother is Paris, the abductor of Helen.
2. Homer, *Iliad* 9.109.
3. From Sophocles' *The Dining Companions*, F566 Radt.

says, 'I know what you're running away from, and it's not slander: Hector is close – you're right not to stay.' In other words, threatening to let it be known that a courageous hero is a coward, or that a restrained and disciplined man is a libertine, or that a generous and munificent person is petty and avaricious, inspires them towards correct conduct and deters them from contemptible conduct, provided that one is demonstrably moderate in irremediable circumstances and distressed and sympathetic, rather than critical, when speaking candidly, but forceful, implacable and unwavering when trying to prevent errors and when resisting emotions, since this is the right time for unquenchable goodwill and true candour.

It is noticeable that enemies too use criticism of past behaviour against one another – and so Diogenes used to say[1] that for safety's sake no one ought to have either good friends (to take one in hand) or fervent enemies (to tell one off). However, heeding advice and consequently taking care not to make mistakes are preferable to being berated and consequently regretting one's mistakes. That is why one should apply oneself to candour with the dedication due to a craft, to the extent that it is the most important and effective medicine available to friendship; but it constantly requires accuracy of timing, above all, and also dilution to prevent it being too strong.

[37] So since, as we have said before, candour inevitably often hurts the person undergoing the treatment, medical practice provides an important model: when doctors perform an operation, they do not abandon the part that has been operated on and leave it aching and sore, but they apply soothing lotions and poultices; and tactful critics do not run away either, after they have employed their harsh and painful treatment, but they use conversation of a different kind, consisting of tempered words, to allay and disperse the hurt, as sculptors smooth and polish the parts of their statues where tools have been used and bits of stone broken off. If someone has been marked by having the tool of candour used on him, and is left with rough edges, bumps and

1. He says it again in *On Being Aware of Moral Progress* 82A; but in *How to Profit from One's Enemies* 89B he has turned into Antisthenes.

uneven surfaces, he will be angry and therefore unresponsive and recalcitrant at a later date. It follows that this is another thing – one of the most important – for critics to watch out for: they should not leave too soon, or make anything hurtful and provocative the conclusion of their association and relationship with their acquaintances.

# ON BEING AWARE OF MORAL PROGRESS

## INTRODUCTION

This essay begins deceptively. It plunges straight into an attack on three notorious Stoic ethical paradoxes of a highly technical nature, of which Plutarch gives special prominence to their dictum that 'the wise (i.e. perfectly good) man may be unaware that he has attained virtue'. These were precisely the kind of topics which Plutarch had raised in his professional philosophical essays against the Stoics and Epicureans, as at *On Stoic Self-contradictions* 19, 1042E ff., and *On Common Conceptions* 9–10, 1062B ff. So are we to expect another similar philosophical polemic against the Stoics? But no, this turns out not to be the case. After the first two sections Plutarch slides into a style typical of his popular moral essays, abandoning the Stoics and offering instead a collection of signs or indications of moral progress that may be gleaned from our behaviour. The explanation for this transition and for the consistency of the essay should become apparent from a closer look at its structure. But it is first necessary to disentangle the complexity of the Stoic theories in question, and assess the character of Plutarch's response to them.

In section 1 two Stoic theories are attacked: (i) the wise man may be unaware that he has attained virtue; (ii) anyone who has not attained virtue is bad. Plutarch assumes that they imply: (*a*) we are then unaware of any progress to virtue; (*b*) we would be unaware of having passed even in an instant from extreme turpitude to perfect virtue.

But Plutarch's assumptions are false. (*a*) The Stoics did not deny progression to virtue; indeed it was they who sealed the technical name for it (*prokopē*), and progression was a whole section of their philosophy. Nor did they anywhere say that you could not be aware of your progression, which is of course different from saying that you might not be aware of the actual crossing of the boundary to perfect virtue, the transition from fallibility to infallibility. (b) It is important to recognize that the Stoic use of the word 'badness' was not equivalent to vice or viciousness. Since virtue for them was absolute and the only good, everything else (both immoral and amoral) was not-good, that is, bad in respect to virtue. So in that sense anyone not absolutely good is bad. But this latter huge area is not homogeneous in itself, and some of the acts it covers are naturally preferable to others, in a relative sense, that is, but not absolutely so. So we progress by choosing morally appropriate acts, but because we do not have perfect moral knowledge, we do not really know the reasons for our choice and we often go wrong. So since virtue is a state of mind fortified by infallible knowledge of absolute value, it is only once we have obtained that, if we ever do, that we can be sure of infallibly behaving morally, and so always choosing the right thing to do. Nevertheless, as we are always progressing with our appropriate acts, and since although not all appropriate acts are right acts, but all right acts are morally appropriate, the Stoics believed that it was possible to achieve the transition to an infallible state of mind without at first being aware of it. The change was indeed crucial, but since progression (of which one was aware) had been going on for a long time both in practical ethical action and in the development of rational understanding of moral theory, it was certainly not a change from complete scoundrel in the morning to saint in the evening (75D). Now Plutarch does not here engage these Stoic theories at their deeper level, nor indeed does he attempt to argue against them as he does in his Stoic essays. He simply attacks by cutting repartee, on the level of a powerful presentation of the reaction of ordinary common sense to what must have seemed an outrageous Stoic paradox to many intelligent men of the period.

Section 2 develops what Plutarch regards as the Stoic elimination of moral progression, by attacking another allied Chrysippean *mot* (from *Ethical Questions* 4), that all moral mistakes or faults are equal. Plutarch infers from this that in that case, apart from the perfectly good man, everyone else is placed in a single undifferentiated category of vice by the Stoics, and that therefore there is no room for moral progression. This was a famous and well-chewed bone of contention. The Stoic position was more complex and subtle, but invited controversy. Chrysippus, one suspects, had, rather like Socrates, a penchant for outrageous paradoxical statement. By 'all mistakes are equal' he seems to have meant that all mistakes are equally mistakes or faults in missing the mark. A miss is as good as a mile – or rather, an inch in a miss is as good as an ell. On a golf-course green, a putt that lips the hole is as much a miss as one that runs off the green. But the Stoic does not imply that all moral mistakes are equally bad, to be valued equally, any more than all missed putts are equally bad putts (although not all Stoic illustrative arguments helped with this distinction: Cicero, *De Finibus* 4.75 f.). So when Diogenes Laertius 7.127 stated that for the Stoics there is nothing between virtue and vice (i.e. badness), whereas the Peripatetics maintain that between virtue and vice there is progression (*prokopē*), we should not infer that Stoics eliminated progression, which they obviously did not, but rather that it took place within the area of 'badness'. But there is a crucial distinction: Peripatetics and Academics thought of virtue or goodness as the end of a progression through accumulative degrees; Stoics believed that perfect goodness and virtue was an intellectual state different in kind from all that preceded its attainment, and was in no sense a matter of degree. In that sense, as the Stoics said, a stick is either straight or crooked, an action is either right or wrong; in *that* sense the putt is missed, you drown an inch below the surface as much as ten fathoms deep (see Plutarch's different polemics in *On Common Conceptions* 1062E ff.). But the category of not-good was by no means undifferentiated within itself. Vice itself is different from the material on which moral judgements worked, the so-called 'indifferents' or 'intermediates', and in this latter group there were natural criteria of comparative value. This was the area of progression. But all this was of relative value, different in kind from the absolute value of goodness and virtue, and so in the category of not-good (or bad), although preparatory to virtue. Again Plutarch does not engage in argument at the deeper, more sophisticated level, but appeals to apparent fact. It was generally believed, indeed it was obvious, that Stoics behaved and acted upon the assumption that moral progress was possible, and so Plutarch accuses them of acting in a manner opposed to, or rather in contradiction to their theory. This insistence on the harmony of words and action, or of philosophical theory and practical behaviour, is a most characteristic Plutarchan stance, and sets the theme and character for the rest of the essay.

So section 3 marks a transition to his own position by affirming that all vice admits of degrees, and that therefore moral progress is possible. But what he means by progression is clarified in purely practical terms as a gradual advance in stages, pushing back the darkness of imperfection like the gradual illumination controlled by a dimmer switch. One should mark the stages of one's progress as in a voyage. His quotation of Hesiod, *Works and Days* 361–2, shows that he really does think of virtue as the end of a staged progression by degrees, an accumulation of goods and actions. So the most important factor is habituation, which must be continuous and unremitting. This established, the rest of the essay follows as a kind of urbane sermon or popular diatribe on conscious moral improvement.

The basic structure becomes stereotyped: we are given a succession of 'signs', pointers or indications of progress. These signs arise from our behaviour as evidence for the state of our moral character. The first group of signs (§§4–6) concerns general attitudes in our training, such as whether or not we give up in the face of breaks and setbacks, and whether we welcome or feel pain at our separation from training (§4); or again (§5), how do we face up to initial difficulties, with or without depression or weakness? Then (§6), what is our resilience to external factors, such as friends' advice and enemies' attacks? To what extent do we envy the public success of others? Are we improving by ceasing to conform to popular values because they are admired by the majority? What is so typical of Plutarch in all this is that he eschews all general philosophical theories on external goods, such as success, social standing and reputation and simply plants before the reader particular practical instances to be recognized immediately.

The next three sections (§§7–9) offer signs of progress in

training in the use of words and arguments. Are we beginning to stop playing with them for their own sake, merely as ammunition for debate, and starting to see that they have an inward reference for our own improvement (§7)? Are we becoming less occupied by style and more with subject matter (§8), so that our reading of poetry, for example, is not merely for pleasure, but for instruction, in sharpening our recognition and judgement of our good? The position is again very Plutarchan in its dependence on proceeding from practice to theory (not the other way round), so that one's behaviour and practice serves as a kind of proof of one's views and, moreover, one's opinions and views are formed by experience. Thirdly (§9), how do we react to an audience, to its size or lack of it, its response, noise and so on? Do we play to an audience merely for our own glorification?

Actions, like arguments, also give signs (§10). Are we acting more from showmanship or self-advertisement, or for truth? Is there any sign that we realize that a good deed does not need an audience or boasting? Do we resist bribes or pressure? Are we acting with more restraint, rejecting a drink or a kiss from a pretty girl? Plutarch makes the point, presumably leading from 'awareness' of moral progress, that what is important is self-recognition. So his next 'sign' (§11) is whether we accept and welcome criticism, which itself leads to a recognition of faults and ignorance, and so to an opportunity to face up to them. Having nothing to do with criticism is a bad sign, like someone who is mentally ill thinking he has no need of a doctor. Dreams too (§12) are a sign, as they reveal our unconscious desires.

In a rather more complicated section (§13) Plutarch turns to passion as a sign. He says that if freedom from excessive emotions (*apatheia*) is the divine state, at least progress can be seen in alleviating and taming them. This can be observed in two ways: (i) if we notice that a present emotion is less intense than a former occurrence; (ii) if we compare different emotions, and find that we are becoming more subject to more respectable emotions than to more disgraceful or objectionable ones. We still err if we feel them to excess, but we are at least progressing.

So far, so clear. But a puzzle has been seen here[1] in Plutarch's apparent praise of Stoic *apatheia* as a great and divine state, whereas in other passages in his writing he condemns the theory of the eradication of passions and insists that we need passions so that we can attain virtue by taming and modifying them; in other words he normally maintains a Peripatetic and Platonic stance against the Stoa. But although variations or even contradictions arising from different contexts in Plutarch are hardly rare, I think it doubtful here. Where Plutarch does support the eradication of passions, he is careful to define such passions as 'diseased' (e.g. *On Curiosity* 515C; *On Superstition* 165C). This partly, but only in part, follows the lead of the Stoics, who defined *all pathē*, or excessive passions, as diseases. As usual in Hellenistic philosophy there was more common ground than is sometimes acknowledged. But here Plutarch's praise of complete lack of passion (*apatheia*) as divine is probably ironic. It is 'divine' as being notoriously the ideal state of the Stoic ideal man. Plutarch concentrates wholly on the practical and natural ethical task of controlling and balancing passions for the attainment of virtue. But it is worth noting that what the Stoics tried to eliminate was not all emotion, but all excessive passions, which they regarded as a sign of sickness and distortion of reason. There were good emotions (*eupatheiai*) felt by the ideal man; so his *apatheia* was freedom from passion (or imperturbability), but not from emotion. A later Stoic, Posidonius, whose works were known to Plutarch, argued that an irrational emotive factor was a natural element of human beings, so it could not be eradicated, but had natural ends which were of relative value subject to the control of reason, but never absolutely good in themselves.

The essay's final 'signs' come under the heading of motivation. Progress is shown by our readiness to translate words into action, to be so excited by our admiration of good men that we try to emulate them. This again is very Plutarchan. Words and arguments (i.e. philosophizing) are insufficient in themselves; it is important to put them into action, to translate mere theory into behaviour. This is an extension of the harmony of words and action (which goes back at least to Plato, *Laches* 188c ff.) to words motivating action. The idea is also strong in Plutarch's rough contemporary Epictetus (frequently stated, but see his essay *On Progress* 1.4). Plutarch may have been following up a common topic, and one increasingly popular in his own period, but he made it particularly his own. Still more characteristic of Plutarch is his insistence that we should admire, and be motivated by, good men rather than abstract goodness (as in Plato). So he continues (§15) that progress is further signalled when our admiration for good men is not deflected by minor blemishes in them or even by major mishaps to them. So good men become practical exemplars for our own behaviour, acting as reflector, standard and check. All this is immediately recognizable as the very touchstone of Plutarch's own *Lives*. And the reverse of this would be (§16) our wish to show our own whole life and actions to those whom we most revere and admire.

Various things emerge from this analysis. The first is a clarification of the problem of the first two sections. For it is now apparent that the essay is not a polemic against the Stoics; what Plutarch is attacking is not a Stoic philosophical paradox or sophism, but what he regarded as a major and fundamental impediment to all moral education and improvement. If awareness of progress and improvement is removed, the very possibility of progress is removed. The Stoic *mots* of 'the virtuous man unaware' and 'all moral mistakes are equal' are simply used to emphasize the importance of his own position. So Plutarch is not here engaged in dialectical discussion with the Stoics, or in trading arguments with them, or even in attempting to show up their self-contradictory arguments, as he does in his polemical essays. He uses them as a springboard (with scathing denial of fact) for his own purposes, namely the illustration of the actual occurrence of moral progress as signalled by the awareness of our behaviour. It is remarkable after all that Plutarch nowhere even names the Stoics in this essay. It is also surely true that Plutarch was not unaware of the deeper and more subtle aspect of the Stoic paradoxes; but he pays no attention to that, because he is not investigating their truth or falsity but using them at crude face value to fortify his own advocacy of moral training and progression. So this essay is by no means to be grouped with Plutarch's specialized philosophical essays against the Stoa, such as *On Stoic Self-contradictions* and *On Common Conceptions*, but with his more popularized disputations on moral behaviour and improvement, with all the characteristic traits noted above as common to these works. There is, to be sure, an implicit but conscious contrast between the brilliant moral theorist Chrysippus and Plutarch the pragmatic behaviourist; we are meant to see, through the first two sections, the supposed mess and ineffective confusion engendered by Stoic theory contrasted with the practical approach of moral advance through the recognition of behavioural facts, training and habituation, and the example of good men (§2, 75F).

There is indeed little argument in this essay, and the idea of moral progress itself is not clearly distinguished from the outward signs of virtuous or moral behaviour, or rather from a perceptive account of how we tend to judge a man's character. But, after all, it is 'awareness' of moral progress that is the subject of this essay, and it is this awareness of character that became for Plutarch a major educative force when combined with the motivation given by the example of good men we admire. The final stress on this in the essay links it so markedly with the moral purpose of Plutarch's *Lives* that one cannot help thinking that *On Being Aware of Moral Progress* has a latish date. This conviction is strengthened by the dedication to Q. Sosius Senecio, one of Plutarch's most notable Roman friends, who was most prominent under Trajan and consul in 99 and 107 AD, for the *Lives* of Theseus and Romulus, Demosthenes and Cicero, Dion and Brutus were addressed to him. He was a highly educated man; Plutarch also dedicated his nine books of *Table Talk* to him, and he appears frequently as a participant in the discussions in them. The dedication to Sosius also explains why Plutarch at the beginning of the essay plunges directly in with sophisticated allusion to an unnamed Stoic paradox. Sosius' name indicates that the essay was no school effusion destined for the young and immature, but was aimed at an educated and intelligent adult audience.

The absence of argument makes the bare analysis of content above somewhat banal, but this is because it has been gutted of Plutarch's presentation. As elsewhere Plutarch makes his points not so much by argument as by vivid illustration; or rather, he 'argues' by quotation, simile and anecdote, in the hope that the reader will 'see' or recognize from the illustration that what is said is so. Quotation in this essay is relatively modest for Plutarch: two from the *Iliad* and one from the *Odyssey*; Hesiod, *Works and Days*, twice; Simonides, Sappho and Semonides of Amorgus; one from Aeschylus; three from Sophocles; Euripides twice; Thucydides; Democritus; Plato, *Symposium*, and twice from *Republic* and *Laws*. But there is a vivid and rich variety of similes and images, some of them sustained, from medicine, doctors and chemists, diseases; music; sea journeys and voyaging; sea motion; farming, crop growing, harvesting, plant growth, farm animals; scientists and the path of planets; boxing; literacy; sex change; bricklaying; scales and balance; bees and honey; clothing; perfume; being in love; siege of soul by vice; light and darkness; waking and dreaming; initiation into the mysteries. The most notable presentational feature of this essay, however, is the abundance and brilliance of anecdote. It is significant that none occur in the first two 'Stoic' sections, nor indeed in the next two transitional sections; but in the remaining eleven sections there are twenty-seven anecdotes, some prolonged, and in two sections (§§6 and 11), there is actually an accumulation of five in each. Apart from the number, a comparison with other authors' use of a familiar anecdote shows Plutarch's mastery of the genre (see e.g. notes on 77E).

Plutarch, as we know (*On Contentment* 464F; *On the Avoidance of Anger* 457D–E), compiled notebooks with quotations and references from his wide reading for his own literary use. And so some quotations and anecdotes from this essay reappear in others. The most striking example of this may be found in the short section 14, 84B–D, where the anecdote on Themistocles resurfaces four times elsewhere (*Life of Themistocles* 3.4; 92C, 185A, 800B), and the quotation from Semonides reappears at 136A, 446E, 790F, 997D, F210 Sandbach. Nevertheless, none of these are parallel in context. They are not repetitive decoration. Plutarch uses them each time in a particular context, and with different slants for that context. Plutarch stacks his own ammunition, selects and fires it for his own purposes.

1. E.g. by D. Babut, *Plutarque et le Stoïcisme*, pp. 321 ff.

# ON BEING AWARE OF MORAL PROGRESS

75A [1] Is there any argument, Sosius Senecio,[1] which will salvage
B one's sense that one is improving and approaching virtue, if in
fact progress causes no relief from folly, but vice circumscribes
every stage and exactly counterbalances the progress and 'drags it
down as lead does a fishing-net'?[2] Take, for example, music or
literacy: there can be no recognition of improvement here either,
if the lessons do nothing to whittle away one's ignorance of these
subjects, and one's incompetence remains perpetually at a constant
level. And if medical treatment fails to relieve a patient's discomfort or in some way alleviate the illness and cause its remission
and decrease, then it cannot afford the patient any sense that his
C condition is changing for the better, until his body has completely
recovered its strength and the treatment has engendered the opposite condition with no trace of illness at all.

In fact, however, people do not make progress in these domains
unless they perceive the change, since the instrument of their
progress is relief from what was weighing them down (as if they
were on a balance, and were being carried upwards as opposed
to their former downward movement). And likewise, in philosophy, no progress or awareness of progress can be assumed if
the mind is not freeing and purifying itself of fallibility, but is involved in absolute vice right up to the moment when it secures
absolute, perfect virtue. Of course, it takes only a moment, a

1. See Introduction, p. 120, for Sosius Senecio. The Greek word for 'salvage' is a
   pun on the name Sosius.
2. See Introduction, pp. 113–14, for the Stoic theories attacked here. The Greek
   word used here for 'progress' is a technical term in Stoic ethics. Vice 'counterbalances' moral progression, just as lead counterbalances the buoyancy of the
   net's corks; the quotation comes from Sophocles (*TGF* F840 Radt).

split second, for the wise man to change from the worst possible    D
iniquity to a state of consummate virtue! And in an instant he has
totally and utterly escaped from the vice which he did not even
partially eliminate over a lengthy period!

Still, I am sure you already know that the authors[1] of *these*
assertions turn out to find 'the wise man who is unaware'[2]
extremely awkward and problematic, thanks to their own assertions. Consider a person who has not yet grasped the fact that he
has become wise, but is unaware and uncertain in this regard,
because it has escaped his notice that, by a gradual and lengthy
process of subtracting this and adding that, progress has taken
place and has steadily led him, as if it were a road, to an appointment with virtue. But if the speed and size of the change were so    E
great that someone who is the worst of sinners in the morning
can become a perfect saint in the evening, or if change occurred
in such a way that someone could go to bed worthless and wake
up wise and, with his mind freed of yesterday's fallibility and
liability to error, could say, 'Goodbye, false dreams; I now see
that you were nothing'[3] – if all this were so, how could anyone
not realize that a change of this magnitude had happened within
himself and that wisdom had enlightened him all at once? I
would sooner believe that someone like Caeneus, whose prayer
to change sex from female to male is granted, could fail to notice
the transformation, than that someone who had become controlled, wise and courageous instead of cowardly, stupid and    F
weak-willed, and who has in an instant exchanged a life at a
bestial level for one at the level of the gods, could be unaware
of himself.

[2] No, it is a correct saying that one should 'Fit the stone to
the line, not the line to the stone.'[4] But the people who refuse to
fit their views to the facts, and instead force facts into unnatural

1. The Stoics.
2. A Stoic technical phrase: 'the wise man who is unaware ⟨that he has attained
virtue⟩'. Plutarch's common sense was outraged by the idea: 1042F, 1058B,
1062B.
3. Euripides, *Iphigenia in Tauris* 569.
4. A proverb, apparently (Leutsch-Schneidewin, *Paroemiographi Graeci* II, 625,
n. 88a), but it also occurs in the Sicilian comic writer Epicharmus, of the fifth
century BC (F276 Kaibel). Modern bricklayers follow the same procedure.

conformity with their hypotheses, have infected philosophy with
plenty of puzzles: the one which fits everyone, with the sole
76A    exception of the perfect man, into a single undifferentiated category of vice is only the greatest of these puzzles.[1] This puzzle
makes the term 'progress' opaque: what they call 'progress' is a
state little short of sheer inanity, and a state which makes all
those who have not rid themselves★ of every emotion and defect[2]
still just as miserably off as those who have not escaped even any
of the very worst vices. Anyway, these thinkers refute themselves,
because in their lectures they place Aristides on a par with Phalaris
in respect of immorality, and Brasidas with Dolon in respect of
B    cowardice, and even go so far as to claim that Plato and Meletus
are utterly identical in respect of ignorance;[3] but in their lives
and actions[4] they refrain and abstain from the behaviour of the
latter set of people, which they acknowledge to be heartless, and
attach themselves to and trust the former set, whose example, as
they agree, is in the most important respects of great value.

[3] We, on the other hand, can see that 'more and less' can be
attributed to every kind of vice, and especially to mental vice,
which is a genus comprising an indeterminate, limitless number
of species;[5] and we can see that this is also what makes different

1. This is a false assumption derived from the Stoic dictum that all moral
mistakes are equal. By that they meant that they were all equally mistakes
with regard to goodness, not that they were all equally bad in their own
sphere, where relative values operated. See Introduction, pp. 114–15.
2. The Greek word for emotion (*pathos*) could also mean 'disease' or 'defect', so
this is a philosophical hendiadys (as Cicero recognized at *De Finibus* 3.35; see
also *Tusculanae Disputationes* 3.23). The emotions or passions from which the
Stoics wished to be freed were the excessive, diseased passions by which our
moral judgement is distorted. It is a modern myth that a Stoic wished to banish all emotions from the life of the good man; of course the good man feels
emotions, but they are those which are consonant with his moral judgement.
3. The names are chosen as polar opposites in popular legend for the states
mentioned: the probity of the Athenian statesman Aristides compared with the
cruel injustice of the Sicilian tyrant; the bravery of the Spartan general compared with the legendary coward of the *Iliad*; the wise judgement of the
philosopher compared with the ignorant folly of the accuser of Socrates.
4. This is a very Plutarchan criticism: he constantly stressed the importance of
harmony between philosophical beliefs and daily action and behaviour (e.g.
*On Stoic Self-contradictions* 1033A).
5. There are verbal echoes of Plato, *Philebus* 24 ff., where 'more and less' character-
izes that which is not marked by limit. But the phrase became stock Greek for

stages of progress different, as reason gradually illuminates and purifies the mind by pushing back imperfection as if it were darkness. Consequently, we do not find illogical the notion that people who are being carried upwards out of an abyss, so to speak, are aware of the change, and we think that this awareness has definite, describable principles.

C

Here, without further ado, is the first such principle to consider. Just as those who are running under sail in the open sea use the time along with the strength of the wind to calculate how much of their voyage they are likely to have accomplished, given that $x$ amount of time has passed and they are being driven by $y$ amount of power, so in philosophy one can, to satisfy oneself, take as evidence of progress the continuity and constancy of the journey, and the fact that it is rarely interrupted by pauses followed by fresh effort and impetus, but is perpetually pressing forward smoothly and evenly, and using reason to secure its passage without stumbling.[1] The advice 'If you add even a small amount to a small amount and do this often'[2] is valuable for more than just the accumulation of money: it is universally effective, and nowhere more so than in the development of virtue, when to reason is added plenty of habituation, which is what produces results.[3]

D

Any unevenness and dullness, however, on the part of philosophers makes them not only wait and linger on the journey of progress, so to speak, but even turn back, because vice seizes every opportunity to ambush anyone who gives in and takes

anything relative which admitted of degree; as such it was contrasted with what was absolute and only differed in kind (Aristotle, *Politics* 1259b37 f.). The Stoics regarded perfect virtue as absolute, differing in kind from moral progression; Plutarch believed in straight progression by degrees from vice to virtue.

1. 'Smoothly' and 'without stumbling' are perhaps remembered from Plato, *Theaetetus* 144b3, of the young Theaetetus' progress.

2. Hesiod, *Works and Days* 361 f.

3. Habituation in ethical training was stressed by Aristotle (*Nicomachean Ethics* 2.1 ff.) and the Peripatetics. Its importance was also underlined by the Stoic Posidonius (Frs. 31, 164, 165, 168, 169 EK). But Plutarch himself advocated it elsewhere, since it appealed to his preference for practical ethics rather than abstract moral theory.

time off, and to carry him away in the opposite direction.[1] Mathematicians[2] tell us that when the planets stop moving forwards, they become stationary, but in philosophy, when progress ceases, there is no gap, no stationary mode. Since human nature is constantly in motion, it tends to tilt as if it were on a pair of scales: it is either fully extended by its better movements or, thanks to the opposite movements, it plummets towards its worse aspect. So if — as in the oracle uttered by the god which stated, 'Fight against the Cirrhaeans every day and every night'[3] — if you are aware of having resisted vice day in and day out without stopping, or at least of having rarely let down your guard or of having only occasionally admitted into your presence certain pleasures or amusements or diversions with a view to making a deal with them, as if they were envoys from the army of vice,[4] then you have every reason to proceed towards the future undaunted and in good heart.

[4] Nevertheless, even if breaks occur in one's philosophical activity, if later there is more stability to it and longer stretches of time are spent on it than before, then this is a good indication that hard work and repeated effort are squeezing laziness out. The other alternative, however, is bad — when after a short while setbacks frequently and continually occur, with enthusiasm shrivelling, so to speak. A reed starts growing with a huge spurt[5] whose result is a smooth, unbroken length, and at first it is rarely thwarted or retarded and only at long intervals; but then (as if it had difficulty breathing up there)[6] it grows weak and consequently starts to fail and its growth is hampered by the formation of many protuberances, with little room between them, as its

---

1. Exactly the same point was made by Seneca, *Letter* 71.35, 72.3.
2. For example, Geminus 1.20, 12.23; Theo Smyrnaeus, p. 148 Hiller; and cf. Ptolemy, *Tetrabiblos* Aη'2, Bα'6.
3. The story is in Aeschines' speech *Against Ctesiphon* 107 ff. Cirrha in Phocis (near modern Magoula), at the head of the Crisean Gulf, served as a harbour for Delphi. At the time of Solon of Athens (*c.* 595 BC) the people of this area committed some outrage against Delphi. At the invitation of the Delphic oracle, unremitting war was waged against the town until it had been destroyed.
4. Compare the metaphor of siege in Plato, *Republic* 560b.
5. Compare Plato, *Laws* 765e.
6. Compare Plato, *Republic* 568d1–2.

life-force encounters bumps and shocks. This is an analogy for what can happen in philosophy: anyone who starts with a series of energetic charges, and then continually encounters drawbacks and interruptions in large numbers, while seeing no improve-   B
ment, gets fed up and gives in. 'On the other hand, he gains wings'[1] applies to anyone who is motivated by the benefit of philosophy and who, with strength and enthusiasm generated by achievement, cuts through the excuses as if they were a crowd of nuisances.

When you are with someone you find attractive, it is not happiness that is a sign of falling in love (since this is not unique to love), but pain and distress when you are cut off from that person;[2] and likewise, plenty of people are drawn to philosophy and apparently set about learning with a great deal of zeal, if nothing else, but if other matters or diversions drive them away, that emotion drains out of them and their mood becomes one of indifference. On the other hand, 'anyone smitten by love for his beloved'[3] might strike you as placid and tame while you are   C
together, sharing in philosophical discussion, but you should see him when he has been cut off and separated from philosophy: he is feverish, restless, dissatisfied with every matter and every diver-sion; his longing for philosophy impels him, as though he were a mindless beast, to forget his friends.★ The point is that what is required is not that people treat discussions as they do perfumes and enjoy them when they are there, but do not go out of their way for them, or even have a positive distaste for them, when they are not there; what is important is rather that, when one is cut off from philosophical discussions (whether it is getting mar-ried or a sea journey★ or forming a friendship or military service that causes the separation), one should feel something similar to hunger and thirst, and so stay in contact with the genuine cause   D
of progress. For the greater the gain from philosophy has been, the greater the displeasure at separation.

[5] What we have been saying is basically identical or very

1. Homer, *Iliad* 19.386.
2. The comparison between philosophy and being in love goes back to Plato's *Symposium*.
3. *TGF* Sophocles F841 Radt.

similar to the ancient description of progress in Hesiod[1] – that the path ceases being steep or excessively sheer: it becomes easy, level and manageable. It is as if repeated effort levels the path, and as though the journey creates a light and a brightness in philosophy, to replace the perplexity, uncertainty and vacillation which students of philosophy come across at first, like sailors

E   who have left the land they know, but cannot yet see the land which is their destination. For they are in the position of having left behind what is normal and familiar, but of having not yet become acquainted with and in possession of what is better: they are going round in circles in the intermediate area, and in the process often turn back towards where they have come from.

Sextius the Roman was a case in point:[2] the story goes that on account of philosophy he had abandoned his offices and positions of authority in the political arena, but on the other hand was, while in the philosophical arena, in a bad way and was finding the subject difficult; he came very close to throwing himself off the top of a building. And there is a similar story about Diogenes of Sinope[3] when he was embarking on his study of philosophy: it was an Athenian holiday, and they were having fun and staying awake all night, with meals laid on by the state, plays at

F   the theatres, and parties with one another; Diogenes was curled up in a corner of the agora,★ trying to sleep, and he found himself thinking decidedly upsetting and self-destructive thoughts, trying to work out how, under no external compulsion, he had of his own free will taken on a gruelling and unnatural lifestyle, and was sitting there excluded from all those good things. Just then, however (as the story goes), a mouse crept up and occupied itself with the crumbs from his bread; Diogenes started to use his mind and reconsider, and said to himself, in a

78A   critical and disparaging tone, 'What are you getting at, Diogenes? Your leftovers are a feast for this mouse, yet you, a man of stature

1. Hesiod, *Works and Days* 289–92; of Hesiod's language, Plutarch reproduces only the words 'sheer' and 'easy'.
2. Seneca too (*Letter* 98.13) has the story of Sextius' rejection of public life for philosophy; but Plutarch embroiders it with more vivid detail.
3. A comparison with the versions of this anecdote in Aelian (*Varia Historia* 13.26) and in Diogenes Laertius (6.22) shows Plutarch's mastery of this literary device.

– are you complaining and moaning just because you're not lying over there on soft, gaudy blankets, getting drunk?' So when that sort of bad mood occurs only rarely, and the mind quickly steps in to cancel it out and repel it (changing defeat into victory, as it were), and has no difficulty in getting rid of the agitation and restlessness, then one ought to regard one's progress as being on a firm basis.

[6] Their own weakness, however, is not the only factor which can make students of philosophy waver and double back. The earnest advice of friends and the mocking, bantering attacks of critics can also, on their occurrence, warp and sap resolve, and have been known to put some people off philosophy altogether. Therefore, a good indication of an individual's progress would be equanimity when faced with these factors, and not being upset or irritated by people who name his peers and tell him how they are prospering at some royal household, or are marrying into money or are going down to the agora as the people's choice for some political or forensic post. For anyone who is not dismayed or swayed in these circumstances has clearly been suitably and securely gripped by philosophy, since it is impossible to stop trying to conform to behaviour the majority of people admire unless one has become accustomed to admire virtue instead; even anger and insanity give some people the ability to stand up to others, but disdain for affairs commonly admired is impossible without a high purpose, truly and securely held.

This is also the context of the proud comparisons people make between the two concerns, as when Solon said, 'We will not exchange our virtue for their wealth, since the one is permanent and stable, but different people have money at different times.'[1] And Diogenes used to compare his moves from Corinth to Athens and back again to the great king's residency at Susa in the spring, at Babylon in the winter and in Media in the summer. Then there is Agesilaus' remark about the great king: 'He is a greater man than me only if he is more moral.' And in a letter to

1. Solon F15 Bergk, F15 West, F4.10–12 Diehl. We will meet the lines again in *On Contentment* 472D–E; and they also crop up in *Life of Solon* 3.1.

Antipater about Alexander, Aristotle wrote that the fact that
Alexander rules over a lot of people does not make him the only
one who can legitimately feel proud: anyone whose thinking
about the gods is correct has just as much right.[1] And when
E    Zeno saw that Theophrastus was admired for the number of his
students,[2] he said, 'Although his chorus is larger, mine is more
harmonious.' [7] Anyway, when the contrast between virtue and
externals has enabled you to eliminate from yourself envy and
jealousy of others, and all the things which commonly irritate
and undermine beginners in philosophy, you can take this too as
a clear indication of your progress.

Another not unimportant sign is a certain change where arguments are concerned. Almost without exception, beginners in
philosophy tend to look for ways of speaking which will enhance
their reputation. Some behave like birds: because they are lightweight and ambitious, they swoop down on to the brilliant
heights of science. Others behave 'like puppies', as Plato says:
F    'they enjoy dragging things around and tearing them apart',[3] so
they head for controversies and puzzles and sophisms. A great
many beginners immerse themselves in philosophical arguments
and use them as ammunition in casuistry. Occasionally, beginners
go around collecting quotable phrases and stories, but just as
Anacharsis used to say that, in his experience, the only reason the
Greeks have money is to count it, so these people – in respect of
the arguments they employ – are short-changed and short-change
others, and accumulate nothing else which might do them good.

79A    The result of all this is illustrated by Antiphanes'[4] saying, in its
application to Plato's circle. Antiphanes used to tell an amusing
story about a city where, as soon as anyone spoke, the sound of
his voice was frozen solid, and then later, when it thawed out in
the summer, they heard what had been said in the winter; likewise, he added, what Plato said to people when they were still

1. See p. 228, n. 2.
2. According to Diogenes Laertius 5.37, two thousand used to attend his lectures.
3. Plato, *Republic* 539b; cf. *Philebus* 15d–e.
4. Probably the fourth-century writer of comedies, who became an Athenian citi-
    zen, rather than Antiphanes of Berge, the teller of tall tales scorned by Strabo,
    who probably lived later. The conceit resurfaced in later European literature:
    Rabelais, *Pantagruel* 4.55; Addison, *Tatler* no. 254 (23 November 1710).

young only just got through to most of them much later, when
they were old. People also have this experience when faced with
philosophy in any form, and it stops only when their discrimination becomes sound and steady, and begins to encounter the
factors which instil moral character and stature, and starts to seek
out arguments whose tracks (to borrow Aesop's image) tend
inwards rather than outwards.[1] Sophocles used to say that he      B
first lightened Aeschylus' heaviness, then the austerity and affectedness of his own* style, and only then did he, as a third step, try
to change the actual nature of the language, which has the most
bearing on morality and virtue;[2] this is an analogy for the fact
that it is only when students of philosophy stop using arguments
for display and affectedness and turn to the kinds of argument
which have an impact on the character and the emotions that
they begin to make genuine, unassuming progress.

[8] In the first place, then, you must make sure that when you
are reading philosophical works and listening to philosophical      C
lectures, you do not concentrate on the phraseology and exclude
the subject-matter, and that you do not pounce on awkward,
odd phrases rather than those which are useful, meaty and beneficial. Secondly, you must be careful, when you spend time on
poetry and history, in case you overlook any well-expressed
point which might improve your character or ease the weight of
your emotions. For just as a bee spends time with flowers, as
Simonides says, 'intent on yellow honey',[3] whereas everyone else
appreciates and takes in no more of the flower than its colour
and scent, so, although everyone else's involvement with poetry
has the limited aim of pleasure and fun, nevertheless if someone
by his own resources discovers and gathers from it something
worth taking seriously, then it is by this token plausible to

1. Aesop, *The Lion and the Fox* 147 (Hausrath), 142 (Perry), 196 (Chambry), 246
   (Halm).
2. This is a difficult and uncertain sentence, about which different views have
   been held: Wilamowitz, *Lesefrüchte* 115 (*Kleine Schriften* 4, 204 f.); C. M.
   Bowra, 'Sophocles on His Own Development', *American Journal of Philology*
   66 (1940), 385–401; T. B. L. Webster, *Introduction to Sophocles* (2nd ed.), 143 ff.;
   M. Pinnoy, 'Plutarch's Comment on Sophocles' Style', *Quaderni Urbinati di
   Cultura Classica* 45 (1984), 159–64.
3. F47 Bergk, F88 Page.

D    suggest that his training and love for what is good and congruent
with his nature have brought him to the point of recognizing
what is good and congruent.

There are people, for example, whose concern with Plato and
Xenophon is limited to their language, and who glean no more
than their pure Attic diction (which is, as it were, the dew and
down on the flower). The only comment one can make about
such people is that they appreciate the nice, flowery smell of
medicines, but fail to ingest, or even recognize, their analgesic
and purgative properties. By contrast, those whose progress is
ongoing are capable of benefiting, and of gathering what is
congruent and useful, not just from the written or spoken word,
E    but from any sight and any situation at all.

Anecdotes about Aeschylus and others of similar stature illustrate the point. For instance, Aeschylus was watching a boxing-
match at the Isthmian games, and whenever either of the boxers
was struck, the audience yelled out loud; Aeschylus nudged Ion
of Chios and said, 'Do you see what practice can do? The man
who has been struck remains quiet – it is the spectators who cry
out!' Brasidas once picked up some dried figs which had a mouse
among them; the mouse nipped him and he dropped it: 'Incredible!' he remarked. 'No matter how small or weak a creature is,
it will live if it has the courage to defend itself.' When Diogenes
saw someone using his hands to drink, he took his cup out of his
bag and threw it away.[1]

F    These stories illustrate how attention and repeated intense effort
enable people to notice and absorb the implicit virtue in everything. This is more likely to happen if they supplement theory
with practice – not just 'by studying in the school of danger', as
Thucydides puts it,[2] but also by giving themselves a practical
demonstration of their views – or preferably, forming their views
by experience – whenever they are faced with pleasure and
argumentativeness, or involved in decision-making, advocacy in

1. This is Diogenes of Sinope, the famous founder of the Cynic school of
philosophy. The story recurs in Seneca (*Letter* 90.14) and Diogenes Laertius
(6.37), where its point is plainer: Diogenes realized that his cup was one more
material possession he could do without.
2. Thucydides 1.18.3.

court and political authority. As for those who, even while they are    80A
still students, occupy themselves with considering what they can
take from philosophy and recycle without delay in the political
arena, or to entertain their young friends, or at a reception given by
the king, they are no more entitled to be regarded as philosophers
than sellers of medicines are entitled to be regarded as doctors; or
perhaps a better description is to say that a sophist of this kind is
basically altogether identical to Homer's bird, because he regurgi-
tates for his pupils, as if they were his 'flightless chicks', anything he
takes in, 'and fares badly himself',[1] if he fails to consider his own
advantage and to absorb or digest anything he takes in.

[9] It is therefore essential for us to make sure, first, that we    B
approach words in a way that is beneficial to ourselves, and
second, where other people are concerned, that we do so not
because we want empty glory or public recognition, but rather
because we want to be taught and to teach. Above all, we must
make sure that, when investigating issues, there is no trace of
rivalry and contentiousness, and that we have stopped supplying
ourselves with arguments as if they were boxing thongs or
padded gloves[2] to be used against one another, and no longer
prefer bludgeoning others to the ground to learning and teaching.
Reasonableness and civility during discussions, neither embarking
on conversations competitively nor ending them in anger, neither    C
crowing if an argument is won nor sulking if it is lost – all this is
the behaviour of someone who is progressing nicely. Aristippus
gives us an example: once he was outmanoeuvred in an argument
by a man who did not lack self-confidence, only intelligence and
sense; Aristippus saw that the man was delighted and had got
big-headed, so he said, 'I am going home now: I may have been
argued down by you, but I will sleep more peacefully tonight
than you, for all your success.'

When we speak, we can also assess ourselves by seeing whether

1. Homer, *Iliad* 9.323 f.
2. Greek boxers wore leather thongs around their knuckles and arms, mainly for
   protection; when sparring in training, they wore padded gloves: Plato, *Laws*
   830b; H. A. Harris, *Greek Athletes and Athletics*, 98 f. Plato too used the confrontational sports as an analogy for eristic argument as opposed to philosophical
   discussion (e.g. *Euthydemus* 277d).

or not we get afraid and hold back if a large crowd unexpectedly gathers round us, whether or not we get depressed if there are only a few to hear us debate, and whether or not, if called upon to address the Assembly or a person in authority, we throw the opportunity away by being inadequately prepared with respect to what language to use. This latter point is illustrated by stories about Demosthenes[1] and Alcibiades. Alcibiades was extremely adept at knowing what topics to address, but less confident about what language to use and, as a result, used to trip himself up while he was addressing topics; often, even in the middle of speaking, he used to search for and hunt after an elusive word or phrase, and so get booed. By contrast, Homer was not bothered about publishing an unmetrical first line:[2] his talent gave him plenty of self-assurance about the rest of the poem. It is therefore fairly reasonable to suppose that those who are striving for virtue and goodness will make good use of the opportunity and the topic, by being completely indifferent to any tumultuous, noisy response to their language.

[10] The same applies to actions as well as to words: everyone should try to ensure that they contain more usefulness than showmanship, and are more concerned with truth than with display. If genuine love for a young man or for a woman does not seek witnesses, but reaps its harvest of pleasure even if it fulfils its desire in secret, then it is even more likely that someone who loves goodness and wisdom, who is intimate and involved with virtue because of his actions, will be quietly self-assured within himself, and will have no need of an admiring audience. There was a man who summoned his serving-woman at home and shouted out, 'Look at me, Dionysia: I have stopped being big-headed!' Analogous to this is the behaviour of someone who politely does a favour and then runs around telling everyone about it: it is obvious that he is still dependent on external appreciation and drawn towards public recognition, that he does

1. In fact, no anecdote on Demosthenes is given, but his stress on preparedness was notorious (Plutarch, *Life of Demosthenes* 8).
2. Plutarch appears to refer to the scansion of the word *Pēlēïadeō* in the first line of the *Iliad*. It is, however, usually accepted that it may scan – – ˇ ˇ – by synizesis of *-eō*.

not yet have virtue in his sights and that he is not awake, but is acting randomly among the illusory shadows of a dream[1] and then presents his action for viewing, as if it were a painting.

It follows that giving something to a friend and doing a 81A favour for an acquaintance, but not telling others about it, is a sign of progress. And voting honestly when surrounded by corruption, rejecting a dishonourable petition from an affluent or powerful person, spurning bribes and even not drinking when thirsty at night or resisting a kiss from a good-looking woman or man, as Agesilaus did[2] – quietly keeping any of these to oneself is also a sign of progress. A man like this gains recognition from himself, and he feels not contempt, but pleasure and contentment at being self-sufficient as a witness, and spectator too, of his good deeds; this shows that reason is now being nourished within B and is taking root inside him, and that he 'is getting used to being his own source of pleasure', as Democritus puts it.[3]

Farmers prefer to see ears of corn bent over, nodding towards the ground; they regard as worthless impostors the light ones which stand up straight. Young would-be philosophers are just the same: it is those who are particularly insubstantial and lightweight who cut a dash, pose and strut, faces full of contempt and disdain which spare nothing and nobody; but when they start to fill out and gain in yield from the lectures, they shed their ostentatious pomposity. And just as the air inside empty vessels C into which liquid is introduced is squeezed out and goes elsewhere, so when people are filled with genuinely good material, their pretensions are pushed aside and their self-esteem starts to crumble; they stop feeling proud of their beard and threadbare gown,[4] and instead make their minds the object of their efforts;

1. The conceit contrasting waking and dreaming runs through Greek literature from Homer (*Odyssey* 19.547; 20.90) on, but is especially frequent in Plato.
2. Xenophon, *Agesilaus* 5.4. But denying yourself a drink, or a kiss from a pretty girl or boy, was commonplace Cynic and Stoic training (e.g. Epictetus 3.12.11, 3.12.17), as also was not telling anyone.
3. F146 DK.
4. The threadbare gown and unshaven beard had been adopted especially by Cynics as a mark of their disdain for externals. But by now the combination had come to stand for the badge and uniform designating any philosopher (e.g. Epictetus 3.1.24); see also p. 68, n. 3.

and they use the caustic, harsh side of their nature on themselves above all, and treat anyone else they come across with greater leniency. They put an end to their former habit of usurping and

D   confiscating for themselves the name of philosophy and the reputation of studying philosophy; instead, if an innately good young man is even called 'philosopher' by someone else, he will be so dismayed that he will say with a smile, overcome by embarrassment,★ ' "Look, I am no god. Why do you compare me to the gods?" '[1] As Aeschylus says, 'When a young woman has experienced a man, the heat in her eyes gives her away';[2] and when a young man has experienced genuine philosophical progress, these lines of Sappho's are relevant: 'I am tongue-tied, and delicate fire plays over my skin'[3] – despite which, his gaze is unworried and his eye calm and you would want to hear him speak.

At the start of the initiation ceremony, as the candidates assemble, they are noisy, call out and jostle one another; but when

E   the rituals are being performed and revealed, then they pay attention in awestruck silence. Likewise, you can see plenty of disturbance and chatter and self-assurance at the beginning of philosophy, on the threshold, with some people rudely and roughly jostling for acclamation; but anyone who finds himself inside and in the presence of a great light, with the sanctuary open, so to speak, changes his attitude and becomes quiet and transfixed, and 'with humility and restraint complies'[4] with reason, as he would with a god. Menedemus' joke seems to apply rather neatly to such people. He said that the numerous people

F   who sail to Athens to study go through the following progression: they start wise, then become philosophers,[5]★ and as time goes on, they become normal people, by gradually laying aside their self-esteem and pretensions in proportion to the hold they have on reason.

1. Homer, *Odyssey* 16.187.
2. From Aeschylus' lost play *Toxotides* (*TGF* F243 Radt).
3. F2.9 Bergk, F31.9 Lobel-Page, Campbell.
4. Plato, *Laws* 716a.
5. There is a play on words here: we start wise, and then become lovers of wisdom (philosophers), which, as Plato's *Symposium* tells us, implies that we realize that we do not possess wisdom.

[11] When people need healing,[1] if it is a tooth or a finger that is hurting, they go straight to the doctor; if they have a fever, they summon the doctor to their house and ask him to help; but if they are suffering from an extreme case – melancholy or brain fever or delirium – they sometimes cannot even stand the doctor coming to visit them, but chase him away or avoid him, because the severity of their illness prevents them even being aware that they are ill. The same goes for people with faults: it is the incurable ones who get angry and behave aggressively and fiercely towards anyone who tries to rebuke and reprimand them, whereas those who put up with rebuke and do not resist are in a more composed state. And when someone with faults puts himself in the hands of critics, talks about his defects, does not hide his iniquity and does not relish getting away with it or enjoy being unrecognized for what he is, but admits it and begs for someone to take him and reprimand him, this must be a significant sign of progress. This is surely why Diogenes used to say that anyone concerned about safety ought to try to find either a proper friend or a fervent enemy, so that one way or another – either by being rebuked or by being treated – he might steer clear of badness.

Imagine someone with an obvious stain or mark on his clothes or a torn shoe affecting self-deprecation as a pretence to the outside world, or someone thinking that by making fun of his own short stature or slumped posture he is showing a carefree spirit: as long as he does all this, but disguises the internal blemishes of his mind, the defects* of his life, the pettiness, hedonism, malice and spite, and hides them away as if they were boils, without letting anyone touch them or see them because he is afraid of being rebuked, then his involvement in progress is minimal, or rather non-existent. On the other hand, anyone who comes to grips with these defects, and primarily anyone who has the ability and the desire to supply his own distress at and censure for his faults, but secondly anyone who has the ability and the desire to put himself in someone else's hands for castigation, and

1. The following analogy occurs in quite similar terms at the end of St Basil's essay to his nephews, *On Gaining Benefit from Reading Greek Literature.*

sticks with it, and is purified by the criticism, is precisely the person who seems to have a genuine loathing for iniquity, and to be really trying to eradicate it.

It is, of course, important to feel embarrassed at, and to avoid, even a reputation for badness; but someone who dislikes actual iniquity more than he dislikes an adverse reputation does not avoid being reproached, and reproaching others himself, if the object is moral improvement. For instance, there is Diogenes' nice remark to a young man he saw in a pub, who ran away
D    – but into the pub: 'The further inside you run,' he said, 'the more you are going to be in the pub!'[1] And the more a person denies any defect, the more he immerses and imprisons himself in the vice. It is obvious that anyone who is poor, but who pretends to be rich, increases his poverty by his masquerade; but Hippocrates, who wrote down and published the fact that he did not understand the skull's sutures, is a model for anyone who is genuinely progressing,[2] because he thinks it quite wrong for
E    Hippocrates to help others avoid the situation he found himself in by publicizing his own failing, while he – a person who is committed to immunity from error – does not dare to be castigated or to admit his fallibility and ignorance.

In fact, it is arguable that Bion's and Pyrrho's assertions refer not to progress, but to a better, more perfect state. Bion told his friends that they deserved to think they were progressing when they could listen to abuse and be affected as if what was being said was '"My friend, you don't seem bad or foolish, so I wish you health and great joy, and may the gods grant you prosper-
F    ity."'[3] And there is a story about Pyrrho that once when he was

1. The anecdote is repeated in Diogenes Laertius 6.34, but typically of anecdotes the detail changes: the boy becomes Demosthenes (so also in Ps.-Plutarch, *Lives of the Ten Orators* 847E). Apparently, eating and drinking in pubs was not regarded as respectable (e.g. Isocrates, *Areopagiticus* 49).

2. In our Hippocratic corpus the apposite reference is *Epidemics* 5.27. But this story about Hippocrates had passed into the anecdotal tradition (Celsus 8.4.3; Julian, *Letter* 59, 444d). This trait of Hippocrates is also noted by Quintilian (3.6.64), but without the details.

3. This is a cento combined from Homer, *Odyssey* 6.187 and 24.402. Cynic authors like Bion were fond of quoting Homer, and regarded the enduring Odysseus as a kind of Cynic hero; so Bion F15 Kindstrand. It was also very much part of Cynic training to school oneself to indifference in the face of abuse.

endangered by a storm at sea, he pointed to a piglet which was happily tucking into some barley that had been spilled, and told his companions that anyone who did not want to be disturbed by events should use the rational mind and philosophy to develop a similar detachment.[1]

[12] You should also notice what Zeno said – that a person's dreams ought to make him aware that he is progressing, if when asleep he sees himself neither enjoying anything discreditable, nor conniving at or doing anything awful or outrageous, but if instead he feels as though he were in translucent depths of tranquil stillness and it dawns upon him that the imaginative and emotional part of his mind has been dispersed by reason.[2] Plato also apparently realized this point, before Zeno, and he described in outline the imaginative, irrational aspect of an innately tyrannical mind and the sorts of things it does when asleep: 'He tries to have sex with his mother', feels compulsions for all kinds of foods, transgresses convention and acts as though his desires, which by day are shamed and cowed into restraint by convention, had been set free.[3]

Draught-animals which have been well trained do not attempt to stray and deviate, even if their master lets the reins go slack: they press forward in an orderly fashion, obedient to their conditioning, and unfailingly keep to their course. In the same way, people whose irrational aspect has been tamed and civilized and checked by reason find that it loses its readiness to use its desires to act outrageously and unconventionally even when dreaming or when under the influence of illness; instead, it watches protectively over its conditioning and remains aware of it, since it is conditioning which gives our attention strength and energy. If, as a result of training, detachment can gain control over even the

83A

B

1. This story about the Sceptic Pyrrho was told by the Stoic philosopher Posidonius (F287 EK), from whom it passed into the anecdotal tradition (Diogenes Laertius 9.68).
2. The language here (the 'emotional part of his mind') betrays a later expansion or interpretation, perhaps by Posidonius or by Plutarch himself, of an anecdotal tradition about Zeno. On dreams and moral progress, see also Epictetus 3.2.5.
3. The Platonic passage in mind is *Republic* 571c–572a. It was clearly well known in the first centuries BC and AD. Cicero, *De Divinatione* 1.61 f., translates it at length.

body – over the whole body and any of its parts – so that eyes faced with a harrowing sight resist weeping and a heart sur-
C    rounded by horrors resists lurching, and genitals modestly keep still and cause no trouble at all in the company of attractive men or women, then naturally this increases the plausibility of suggest-ing that training can take hold of the emotional part of the mind and, so to speak, smooth it and regularize it by suppressing its illusions and impressions at all levels, including dreaming.[1]

There is a story about the philosopher Stilpo which illustrates the point. Once he dreamed he saw Poseidon and that Poseidon was angry with him for having omitted to sacrifice an ox (which was a standard offering to Poseidon), but Stilpo was not per-turbed in the slightest and said, 'What do you mean, Poseidon? Don't you think it's childish of you to come and complain that I didn't bankrupt myself and fill the city with the smell of burnt
D    offerings, but instead sacrificed to you on a moderate scale at home, drawing on what I actually had?' And then he dreamed that Poseidon smiled, extended his right hand[2] and said that, because of Stilpo, he would create for Megara a bumper crop of sardines.

So anyway, when people have dreams which are pleasant, clear and untroubled, and sleep which brings back no trace of anything frightening or horrible, or malicious or warped, they say that these features are beams of the light of progress; but they say that the features of distressing and bizarre dreams – frenzy, agitation, running from danger like a coward, experiencing child-ish delights and miseries – are like breakers and billows, and originate in a mind which does not yet have its own regulator, but is still being formed by opinions and rules, so that when it is
E    asleep and as far from these formative influences as it can be, it is again dissolved and unravelled by the emotions. Now, you must join me in considering, by yourself, whether this phenomenon I

1. For habituation in ethics, see p. 125, n. 3. The stress on training (askēsis) as a kind of conditioning by habituation was especially advocated by the Cynics. But it was also elaborated in Posidonian Stoicism and by Epictetus. So Plutarch is using a common topic, but one that particularly appealed to his natural leaning towards practical ethics.
2. A Greek gesture accompanying making a promise.

have been talking about stems from progress or from a state which already has the steady, solid strength which comes of being based on reason.

[13] Since absolute detachment is an exalted, divine state, and progress towards it is, as I say,* like a kind of alleviation and taming of the emotions,[1] then it is important for us to examine our emotions and to assess their differences, comparing them with themselves and with one another. We must compare them with themselves to see if the desires and fears and rages we now experience are less intense than they were before, given that we are using reason rapidly to extinguish their violence* and heat; and we must compare them with one another to see if our sense of disgrace is now more acute than our fear, and whether we prefer to emulate people rather than envy them, and value a good reputation more than we value money. In short, we must compare them with one another to see if, to use a musical analogy, we err on the side of the Dorian rather than the Lydian mode,[2] whether our lifestyle inclines towards asceticism rather than indulgence, whether our actions tend to be slow rather than hasty, and whether we are astounded by rather than contemptuous of arguments and people. Where ailments are concerned, it is a good sign when the disease is diverted into parts of the body where it will not prove fatal;* and likewise where vice is concerned, it is plausible to suggest that when people who are making progress find that their vices now engage more respectable emotions, those vices are gradually being eliminated. When Phrynis strung two extra strings on the lyre, in addition to the usual seven, the ephors[3] asked him whether he was prepared to

F

84A

---

1. 'Detachment', or complete lack of excessive emotion or passion, was a notorious characteristic of the Stoic ideal man, and so an ideal or divine state. There is a strong flavour of irony here. Plutarch, as elsewhere (e.g. *On Moral Virtue* 451C ff.), concentrates on the Aristotelian and Platonic theme of the taming of the passions individually and on a gradation between them; see further the Introduction, pp. 117–18.

2. The reference is to different tunings of the lyre producing different 'modes' or keys. The Greeks believed that different modes produced different emotive effects on listeners, and thus affected their behaviour, and so could be an educational instrument. The Lydian was thought to be a relaxed, effeminate mode, the Dorian a manly, disciplined, warlike one (e.g Plato, *Republic* 398e9 ff.).

3. Spartan officials.

let them cut off the top two *or* the bottom two; but the first point to make about ourselves is that what is required is, as it were, that the top ones *and* the bottom ones are cut out, if we are going to settle on an intermediate, moderate position;[1] and the second point is that progress begins with the lessening of our emotions' extremity and intensity, 'lusting after which,' as B Sophocles says, 'makes one overwrought'.[2]

[14] Now, we have said that translating decisions into actions and not allowing words to be just words without turning them into deeds is particularly typical of progress. What is significant in this context is modelling our behaviour on what we commend and being keen to do what we express admiration for, while being unwilling even to connive at what we find fault with. For example, although it was not surprising that Miltiades' courage and bravery were universally applauded in Athens, nevertheless, C when Themistocles said that Miltiades' trophy stopped him sleeping and allowed him no rest,[3] it was immediately obvious that he was doing more than just expressing approbation and admiration: he was also moved to emulate and imitate Miltiades. So we must regard our progress as minimal as long as our admiration of success lies fallow and remains inadequate in itself to spur us towards imitation.

The point is that physical love is not a force for change unless it is accompanied by the desire to emulate; and commendation of virtue is also tepid and ineffective unless it nudges us and goads us to stop being envious and instead to want − with a desire that D demands satisfaction − to emulate good behaviour. Alcibiades stressed the importance of the heart being moved by a philosopher's words and of tears being shed,[4] but that is not all that is

1. The aim for the intermediate was especially characteristic of Aristotelian moral theory: *Nicomachean Ethics* 1106a26 ff.; in general, *Politics* 1295b4.
2. *TGF* F842 Radt.
3. The restless ambition of the Athenian general Themistocles was fired to rival his compatriot Miltiades' victory over the Persians at Marathon (490 BC). The story, in much the same terms, had become stock, and is already in Cicero (*Tusculanae Disputationes* 4.44) and Valerius Maximus (8.14.ext.1), and repeated in four other places by Plutarch himself.
4. The reference is to Plato's *Symposium* 215e, where Alcibiades so describes the effect on himself of Socrates' words.

important: anyone who is making genuine progress compares his own conduct with the deeds and actions of a man who is an exemplar of goodness, and is simultaneously aggravated by the awareness of his defects, happy because of his hopes and aspirations, and full of a restless compulsion. Consequently, he is liable to 'run like an unweaned foal close to a horse' (to use a line from Semonides),[1]* because he longs to be virtually grafted on to the good man. In fact, this experience is typical of genuine progress – dearly to love the character of those whose conduct we desire to imitate, and always to accompany our wanting to be like them with goodwill which awards them respect and honour. On the other hand, anyone feeling competitively envious of his betters must realize that it is jealousy of a certain reputation or ability that is provoking him, and that he is not respecting or admiring virtue.

[15] So when our love for good men starts to be such that we not only, as Plato says,[2] count as blessed both the responsible man himself and anyone who listens 'to the words emitted by a responsible mouth', but we also admire and cherish his posture, walk, look and smile, and long to attach and glue ourselves to him, so to speak, then we can legitimately consider ourselves to be making genuine progress. This is even more legitimate if we do not admire only the successful aspects of men of virtue, but behave like lovers who are not put off if those they find attractive have a speech defect or a pallid complexion:[3] despite the tears and misery brought on by her grief and misfortune, Pantheia still thrilled Araspes,[4] and in the same way we should not be repelled by Aristides' exile,[5] Anaxagoras' imprisonment,[6] Socrates'

1. Semonides F5 West and Bergk.
2. Plato's Athenian in *Laws* 711e is praising Nestor, the wise old man in the Greek army of Homer's *Iliad*.
3. A reminiscence of Plato, *Republic* 474d–e, which was much echoed (e.g. Lucretius 4.1153 ff.; Horace, *Satires* 1.3.38 ff.; and cf. Éliante in Molière, *Le Misanthrope*, II.4). In this volume, see also *On Listening* 45A and *How to Distinguish a Flatterer from a Friend* 56C.
4. The story is told in Xenophon, *Cyropaedia* 5.1.4 ff. Pantheia was a captive Assyrian lady put under the guard of the Mede Araspes by Cyrus, the Persian king.
5. Aristides 'the Just' was ostracized and exiled from Athens in 483/2.
6. The philosopher Anaxagoras, teacher and friend of Pericles, was indicted for impiety (Diogenes Laertius 2.12; Diodorus Siculus 12.39.2; Plutarch, *Life of Pericles* 32); but Pericles helped him avoid imprisonment by escaping to Lampsacus.

poverty[1] or Phocion's condemnation,[2] but because we regard virtue as desirable even under these circumstances, we should draw near to it, quoting Euripides' line whenever the occasion demands 85A — 'It's incredible how high-minded people find nothing bad!'[3] You see, someone who is inspired enough to admire and want to imitate even apparently awful things, rather than be put off by them, can certainly never be deterred from good things ever again. It has already become such a person's practice, when he is embarking on some course of action, or taking up office, or taking a risk, to picture truly good men of the past★ and to wonder, 'What would Plato have done in this situation? What would Epaminondas have said? How would Lycurgus or Agesi-

B laus have come across?' He uses each of them as a kind of mirror, before which he puts himself in order, or adjusts his stance, or refrains from some relatively petty saying of his, or resists an emotion. Some people learn the names of the Dactyls of Mount Ida and steadily recite each one, as a spell to ward off fear;[4] but if thoughts and memories of good men readily occur to people who are making progress and make them think again, then they keep them true and safe, whatever emotions and difficulties beset them. It follows that this is another mark by which you can tell someone who is morally improving.

[16] Moreover, to have stopped getting all flustered, blushing
C and hiding or rearranging some idiosyncrasy when a person who is famous for his self-control unexpectedly appears, but instead to go up to such people confidently, can corroborate one's aware-ness. Alexander apparently once saw a messenger running to-wards him with his right hand extended and looking very

---

1. Socrates could not in fact have been poor, since he served as a hoplite in the Athenian army; but he no doubt neglected his property in his pursuit of philosophy (cf. Plato, *Phaedo* 82c–d), and then his poverty became a literary commonplace, beginning shortly after his death, from Plato and Xenophon onwards.

2. Phocion 'the Good' was condemned to death by the restored democracy in 318 BC.

3. *TGF* Euripides F961 Nauck.

4. The Dactyls were magician smiths of folklore connected with Mount Ida in Crete or with the homonymous mountain in Phrygia. It appears that their number was quite uncertain, ranging from five or six to thirty-two or even a hundred. No doubt this practice too helped to concentrate the mind.

pleased. 'What news, my friend?' said Alexander. 'Has Homer
come back to life?' For he thought that the one thing his exploits
lacked was a voice that would give him undying fame.[1] But the
love which fills the character of a young man who is improving
is, above all else, love of showing off before truly good people    D
and of displaying his home, board, wife, children, occupation
and spoken and written compositions; and consequently it is a
source of pain for him to remember that his father or his tutor is
dead and cannot see him in his present condition, and the one
thing in particular he would pray to the gods for would be that
they might come back to life and so witness his lifestyle and
conduct. On the other hand, people who have taken no responsibility for themselves and who have been spoiled are quite the
opposite: they cannot even dream about their relatives calmly
and without anxiety.

[17] There is another mark, no minor one, for you to add,    E
please, to the ones we have already discussed. It is to have stopped
regarding any of one's faults as trivial, and instead to take thorough care about and to pay attention to all of them. People who
do not expect to become affluent have no qualms about spending
small amounts, because they think that adding to the small
amount they already have will not produce a large amount,
whereas anticipation joins with savings to increase love of affluence the closer it gets to its goal. It is the same with conduct
which pertains to virtue: if someone scarcely gives in to 'What's
the point?' and 'That's it for now – better next time', but applies
himself on every occasion, and gets fed up and irritated if vice
ever worms its way, with its excuses, into even the slightest of    F
his faults, then he is obviously in the process of acquiring for
himself a certain purity and wants to avoid being defiled in any
way whatsoever. On the other hand, thinking that nothing is, or
can be, especially discreditable makes people nonchalant and careless about the little things. In fact, when a wall of some kind or
other is being built, it does not make any difference if the odd
piece of wood or ordinary stone is used as infrastructure, or if a
stele that has fallen off a tomb is put in the footings, which is

1. As Homer had celebrated Achilles (so Cicero, *Pro Archia* 24).

analogous to the conduct of degenerates who jumble together into a single heap any old business and behaviour. But people who are progressing, and who have already 'fashioned a fine foundation'[1] for their life (as if it were a home for gods and kings), do not admit things chosen at random, but use reason as a straight-edge by which to apply and fit every single part together. And this, in my opinion, is what Polyclitus was referring to when he said that those whose clay is at the stage when fingertips are required have the hardest task.[2]

86A

---

1. Pindar F194 Maehler, F184 Bowra.
2. It seems that the final stage in clay modelling rested on the sensitivity of the fingertips. But the phrase (literally 'to the nail') was also applied to masonry, where fingertips tested the perfect join or fit. The phrase passed on to Latin, and Horace (*Satires* 1.5.32; *Ars Poetica* 294) used it for 'to a nicety', 'to perfection'.

# WHETHER MILITARY OR
# INTELLECTUAL EXPLOITS HAVE
# BROUGHT ATHENS MORE FAME

## INTRODUCTION

This is an example of something quite different in Plutarch's work; it is not an essay, but a public oration. The opening of section 2, and the exclusively Athenian events, writers and artists cited, show that the speech was delivered at Athens on some public occasion; we do not know which, but a reasonable guess would be one of the annual festivals of thanksgiving, alluded to in section 7, on which the Athenians celebrated their great historical victories. Plutarch's theme is that Athens gained more fame from her military achievements than from her literary glories. This has so scandalized some and puzzled others, coming from the pen of a man of letters, that the speech has been passed off as a mere declamation or epideictic *tour de force*, but in fact it is highly characteristic of Plutarch.

The opening and end of the speech are missing (the outer page(s) having been lost at some stage of transmission), for it starts in mid-anecdote and ends in mid-sentence. But probably not much has gone, and the structure is clear. Plutarch's position is asserted at the start: men of action have priority over writers, because without the former the latter would not exist. Plutarch is not arguing the modern thesis that without men of action writers would have neither the security to give them leisure to write nor the wealth to support them (literary genius has in any case survived without these); he is putting forward the more radical position that without historical events historians would have nothing to record. It is at once apparent why Plutarch starts his literary review with historians because in that genre the connection between actual events and literature, and the dependence of the one on the other, is obvious and immediate. Historians, like actors, present the deeds of others.

But Plutarch's basic explanatory analogy is with painting (§2), which is singled out because it was thought to be the prime example of representational art. It was a copy of reality (346F). So his list of artists at Athens in the fifth and fourth centuries BC gives prominence to men like Apollodorus, who by introducing new techniques such as shading was regarded as striving to produce a *trompe-l'oeil* likeness of what he was painting. The general theory of painting as a mimetic art is taken from Plato, *Republic* 10, but it was common critical belief among Plutarch's own approximate contemporaries in the first century AD that the main object of the school of painters to whom Plutarch refers was to create the perfect illusion of reality. So Pliny (*Naturalis Historia* 35.65) tells the famous story of Zeuxis (not in Plutarch's list because he was regarded as an Ionian rather than an Athenian painter) painting grapes so deceptively that birds flew down to peck at them, and Zeuxis himself being deceived by Parrhasius' painting of a curtain, which he wanted to draw. So Plutarch's illustrative analogy would not seem extravagant or contrived to his audience, nor indeed would it be foreign to his own thinking. He chooses two paintings for special notice and comment: Euphranor's 'Theseus' and his 'Cavalry Engagement at Mantinea'. Both were extremely well known to Plutarch and his audience, for they were in the Stoa of Zeus Eleutherius at Athens (Pausanias, *Guide to Greece* 1.3.3). They are vividly recalled, but in typically different ways, the 'Theseus' by citing Euphranor's own memorable comparison (346A) of his 'Theseus' ('beef fed') with that of Parrhasius ('fed on roses'), and the 'Engagement' with a long (346B–E), seemingly disproportionate, description building up to the climax of the relief of Mantinea by the Athenian cavalry. Plutarch in fact is transposing and transforming into words and oratory the powerful visual impact of the painting in giving the illusion of reality. But then the actuality has the priority.

Plutarch has just demonstrated by his own skill that painting is an exemplar for literature. As Simonides said, painting is silent poetry and poetry voiced painting; that is, the purpose is the same, it is only the media which are different. So he can now return to historians in section 3 with the judgement that the best historian is the one who best imitates reality. Historical narrative is word painting using characters and emotions. The prime virtue which Plutarch singles out for the great Athenian historian Thucydides is vivid presentation (*enargeia*). The modern reader will be astonished that such things as historical judgement and the handling of evidence are ignored for a concentration on narrative technique, but the values stressed by Plutarch were not uncommon for his time. The importance of vivid presentation in particular was much stressed by the literary critics, not only with reference to Thucydides (Dionysius of Halicarnassus, *Letter to Pompeius* III. 776R) but in general: Ps.-Longinus, *De Sublimitate* 15; Demetrius, *On Style* 209 ff.; Quintilian 8.3.62; 6.2.29. But Polybius (2.56.7 ff.) gave a historian's estimate of this stylistic feature. Plutarch, however, repeats his characterization of Thucydides at the opening of his *Life of Nicias*.

After the historians, the poets (§4); but they are still further from reality. According to Plutarch, poetry, like history, sets out to simulate actual events, but by fiction, and its power lies in its storytelling, not in its poetic language and tropes. Poetry is feigned history, and poets are thus as inferior to historians as historians are to men of action. They are another stage even more remote from reality. Now Plato, in *Republic* 10, also represented poetry and artists as mimetic art twice removed from reality; but Plato's scheme started from the ultimate reality of the paradigmatic universal, 'imitated' by particular objects, which were themselves in turn imitated by painters and writers. This section of Plutarch should also be compared with Aristotle's *Poetics* 9, where Aristotle states (1451b27 ff.) that the poet must be a poet by virtue of his stories (i.e. plots) rather than of his verses, in so far as he is a poet by imitation. In the same chapter Aristotle too compares and distinguishes the poet and the historian: the historian writes about particular (i.e. actual) events; the poet is concerned with universals, that is, with what such and such a character will probably or necessarily say or do. This is why Aristotle says that poetry is more philosophical than history. Thus, as so often, Plutarch is working within a kind of tradition, but has given it an individual stamp with an interpretation of his own.

But this is Athens, so Plutarch dismisses from consideration all poetry except tragic drama (§5); epic and lyric poetry are excluded because Athens produced none of note, and comedy as being vulgar and trivial. The latter omission is a surprise, since Old Comedy and Aristophanes in particular (often quoted by Plutarch) could be politically satirical and so related to actuality, and Menander and New Comedy clearly attracted him. But Plutarch concentrates on the clash of the most powerful opponents. It was generally accepted, and, to judge by the multitude of quotations throughout his works, endorsed by Plutarch, that it was the tragic dramatists who won the widest literary acclaim for Athens. Plutarch subtly, within the limits of his theme, gives them their due: they are honest illusionists who can make their deluded audience wiser. But dramatic art is still a deceitful illusion; it is the statesmen and generals who deal with reality.

The dramatic context is now superbly used for the centrepiece of the speech (§§6–7), in a marvellously vivid extended image of the two opposing sides progressing on stage to confront each other as if they were two Choruses. From the one side comes the Entry of the Dramatists, with their pampered and expensive paraphernalia of the theatre, like the retinue of retainers, beauticians and camouflage artists for some rich woman. More is lavished on a single production than on a military campaign, and for what? A savaging by the critics if a failure, a tripod if successful. From the other wing comes the Procession of the Commanders, and for them everyone makes way. They bring victories, cities, islands, countries, great prizes. The examples now enumerated to give weight to the triumphs of Athens are nearly all from the victories and expansion of Athens in the fifth century BC, from the Persian and Peloponnesian Wars; that is, some five hundred years before the Athens of Plutarch's time. It is as if the English were to regard Agincourt or the defeat of the Spanish Armada, or the Scots the battle of Bannockburn, as the apex of national glory (as indeed some do). Of course Plutarch must have known that it was precisely those long-distant but still reverberating echoes which would stir in his Athenian audience the most emotional patriotic response. After all, Plutarch adds, it is these exploits which are annually commemorated in the

Athenian festivals of thanksgiving throughout the year, and compared with them the contributions of the poets are no more than amusing toys.

But an important literary class remains (§8), the orators, some of whom might claim, like Demosthenes, to have activated events as statesmen through their political oratory. At first Plutarch rebuts this on familiar grounds, by concentrating on orators simply as rhetors, so that Hyperides' rhetorical Plataean speech is put in the same category as the work of tragedians and poets, and opposed to Aristides' victory over the Persians at Plataea. Plutarch can make derisive capital out of this by concentrating on Isocrates, no man of action, who spent his long life immured in his study battling with his literary style. But then he returns to the much more interesting ground of Demosthenes as orator and statesman, and infuriatingly it is at this point that the speech breaks off, so that we do not know whether or not he allowed some kind of compromise in such cases, and if so how. After all, Demosthenes and Cicero keep company with the men of action of Plutarch's *Lives*.

A speech of this kind is shaped by three factors: the occasion, the audience and the author. It is likely that the theme and its direction were dictated or at least suggested by the occasion, such as a festival celebrating past military glory. If the speech was addressed not to a small highly cultivated circle but to a large popular audience, we immediately have the explanation for the absence of the erudite display of quotation and allusion which is usually such a prominent feature of Plutarch's essays. The exploits described were known to all Athenians, enshrined in annual celebration and depicted in their public buildings. Literary reference is mostly to well-known writers and to particularly famous works with which the audience would have been familiar, whether or not they had actually read them. Their patriotism is roused by emotive word-painting, not by argument. Such national gatherings celebrate their days of thanksgiving, independence or freedom won gloriously long ago, not their poets; the Scots are unusual in their national celebration of the birth of Burns. In the late first century AD Athens, although still highly respected, was shorn of all political and international influence, so

that memories of her past glories grew more tenacious and roman-
ticized, and were indeed fostered and pandered to by literary
movements like the Second Sophistic, attracting works in the
second century like Aelius Aristides' *Panathenaicus* and *On the
Four*.[1] After all, Athens could still claim, and the claim was
recognized, that she was the donor of freedom to Greece and the
Western world.

But if the style and theme are shaped to the audience, they are
by no means alien to Plutarch himself. The basic presumptions,
although perhaps exaggerated, are characteristic: his treatment of
mimetic art, for instance, and the analogy between painting and
literature. One example from this speech will suffice, the reason
for the extraordinary length of his account of the cavalry engagement at Mantinea in section 2. This passage is not produced for
historical information. In fact Plutarch telescopes events, implying
that Epaminondas' foray into the Peloponnese happened just after
his victory over the Spartans at Leuctra in 371 BC. And indeed
Epaminondas did invade the Peloponnese in 370/69 (and with a
force of 70,000, 346B), and again in 369 and 366, but it was not
until 362 that he mounted the expedition which culminated in
the battle of Mantinea. Plutarch was not unaware of all this (at
least when he wrote his *Life of Agesilaus*, §§31 ff.). He also fails to
add that although the Athenians repulsed the Thebans in the
famous initial cavalry engagement by which Epaminondas had
hoped to take Mantinea by surprise, it was Epaminondas and the
Thebans who won the final decisive battle of Mantinea, in which
also Epaminondas lost his life. But his account is not history, it is
word-painting to match the impact on his audience of
Euphranor's painting, a picture that is built up to the climax of a
brave feat of arms, between the confident, conquering Thebans
holding the initiative in the Peloponnese and the weary, unpre-
pared, but valorous Athenians; he thus attempts to fix the vivid
picture (like Euphranor) of the shock of engagement in a famous
national exploit. The power of such vivid mental images was
recognized in Hellenistic philosophy: Posidonius, the Stoic
philosopher of the first century BC, called them *anazōgraphēsis*,
or mental pictures, and stressed their importance in influencing
our actions; earlier Chrysippus had written a book about them

(Diogenes Laertius 7.201 = *SVF* 2.17); see also Strabo 8.3.30 and Epictetus 2.18.16. This is precisely what Plutarch means by vivid presentation (*enargeia*), and it is typical of his style in general. It is a style of illustration rather than of argument, modelled to create mental images fixed by human examples, by anecdote and simile. The comparison with painting is explicitly repeated in introductions to his *Lives*, as in *Alexander and Caesar* 1 and *Cimon and Lucullus* 2. And indeed the outstanding characteristics which he selects for Thucydides, namely vivid presentation, emotions and characters, are apparent also in his own *Lives*.

Finally, should we doubt that Plutarch himself gave priority to men of action over men of letters, despite his admiration of Athenian literature? First, the theme is Platonic (*Republic* 599a ff.); more importantly, Plutarch consistently maintained that words without deeds were empty, and his last great work, the *Lives*, is a gallery not of writers but of men of action.

1. In general see E. L. Bowie, 'Greeks and Their Past in the Second Sophistic', *Past and Present* 46 (1970), pp. 3–41.

# WHETHER MILITARY OR
# INTELLECTUAL EXPLOITS HAVE
# BROUGHT ATHENS MORE FAME

345C  [1] ⟨We hear that Themistocles once told the following story:
'In the course of an argument between Day-after and Holiday,
Day-after pointed out that whereas Holiday was all hustle and
bustle, *she* provided the opportunity for leisurely, peaceful enjoyment of everything that had gone into Holiday. "That's true,"
Holiday replied, "but *you* wouldn't exist without me."'⟩ He was
right to say this to the military commanders who succeeded him,
because by expelling the Persians and freeing Greece he had
opened a passage to their later actions; and it would be equally
right to say the same to people who pride themselves on their
literary output, since if you do away with men of action, you
will have no writers. Get rid of Pericles' statesmanship, Phormio's
D   naval successes at Rhium, Nicias' courage at Cythera, Megara
and Corinth, Demosthenes' Pylos, Cleon's four hundred
prisoners-of-war, Tolmides' circumnavigation of the Peloponnese, Myronides' victory over the Boeotians at Oenophyta – and
you have expunged Thucydides. Get rid of Alcibiades' bold ven-
tures at the Hellespont and Thrasyllus' near Lesbos, Theramenes'
elimination of the oligarchy, Thrasybulus' and Archinus' and the
Phyle Seventy's insurrection against Spartan rule,[1] Conon's
E   putting Athens to sea again – and you have deleted Cratippus.

It is true that Xenophon became his own historical subject, by
writing about his own command and successes – and about how

---

1. In December 404 BC, seventy exiled Athenian democrats seized the frontier
fort of Phyle, which was the first move towards the restoration of independent
Athenian democratic government in 403 by Thrasybulus, in place of the
oligarchic dictatorship of the Thirty and a Spartan garrison which had ruled
Athens since her capitulation at the end of the Peloponnesian War in April
404 BC.

Themistogenes the Syracusan had composed the book (the device of representing himself in the third person and giving someone else the credit for the writing had the purpose of increasing credibility).[1] But all the other historians – Clidemus,* Diyllus, Philochorus, Phylarchus and so on – have played the part of actors in the dramas of others' exploits, by reciting the deeds of commanders and kings and by dressing themselves up in what others left behind, so as to share in a certain brightness and light, as it were, in the sense that external fame rebounds and reflects, as an image, back from men of action on to writers, when their words act like a mirror, as a medium in which the exploits appear.

F

[2] Now, this city, in its benevolence, has been mother and nurse of many arts and techniques, some of which it was the first to invent and discover, while to others it contributed vitality, prestige and growth; and one of the more important arts to have been developed and organized by it is painting.[2] The painter Apollodorus was the original inventor of tinting and shading, and he was Athenian – he is the one whose works carry the epigram, 'Better a critic than a mimic.'[3]

346A

Then there were Euphranor, Nicias, Asclepiodorus and Pleistaenetus (who was Phidias' brother), whose subjects were victorious commanders, or battles, or heroes. Euphranor, for instance, compared his Theseus to Parrhasius' with the comment that Parrhasius' was fed on roses, but his was fed on beef.[4] In fact, Parrhasius' Theseus has been painted rather daintily and does look rather hungry!* But the sight of Euphranor's Theseus prompted from someone the apposite quote, 'People of great-

B

---

1. The reference is to Xenophon, *Hellenica* 3.1.2. There is no direct evidence of this supposed Syracusan historian, and most people agree with Plutarch that Xenophon used Themistogenes as a pseudonym for his own *Anabasis*; cf. M. MacLaren in *Transactions of the American Philological Association* 65 (1934), pp. 240–47.

2. For the list of painters which follows, compare Pliny, *Naturalis Historia* 35.53 ff. and the excellent notes in the edition of J.-M. Croisille.

3. Pliny, *Naturalis Historia* 35.63, assigns this saying to the painter Zeuxis.

4. A famous *mot*: cf. Pliny, *Naturalis Historia* 35.129. Euphranor's painting of Theseus was in the Stoa of Zeus Eleutherios in Athens (Pausanias, *Guide to Greece* 1.3.3).

hearted Erechtheus, whom Zeus' daughter Athena once looked after . . .'[1]

Euphranor has also painted, with considerable inspiration, the cavalry battle of Mantinea against Epaminondas. This is what happened.[2] Epaminondas of Thebes became puffed up with pride after the battle of Leuctra and wanted to trample on Sparta, now brought low, and tread the city's conceit and self-esteem under-foot. His first move was to invade with seventy thousand men from his army: he devastated the land and caused a revolt of their subjects. Then he tried to get the opposing troops, who were stationed near Mantinea, to meet him in battle, but they refused: they had no stomach for the fight, and were expecting reinforcements from Athens. So Epaminondas struck camp under cover of darkness and took all his men down into the Spartan plain, and his assault brought him very close to taking and occupying the undefended city. But the allies found out what was happening and quickly went to help the city, so he pulled his men back as if he was going to return to ravaging and destroying the land. The trick worked: once he had neutralized the enemy in this way, he withdrew from Sparta, raced across the intervening territory and appeared at Mantinea – much to the inhabitants' surprise, because they were trying to decide on the best moment for sending help to Sparta! Epaminondas lost no time in ordering his Thebans to prepare for battle. So the Theban troops, with all their proud prowess in battle, bore down on the city walls and surrounded them. There was pande-monium, screaming and stampeding among the Mantineans: there was no way they could repel this massed force which was descending upon them like a torrent, and help was inconceivable.

At precisely this opportune moment, the Athenians were coming down from the hills into the Mantinean plain; they had no idea of the critical knife-edge on which the contest was balanced, and were marching along at a leisurely pace. Then one of the Mantineans sprinted out of the city and alerted them to

---

1. Homer, *Iliad* 2.547, from the description of the Athenian contingent of the Greek army at Troy. It implies the grandeur, toughness and beefiness of the Athenian warrior in contrast to Parrhasius' delicate flower.

2. For Plutarch's treatment of this event, see the Introduction, pp. 152–3.

the danger. Although the Athenians were few in comparison with the huge numbers of the enemy, and although they were tired from their journey, and although none of their allies were near by, they immediately formed themselves into ranks, all except for the cavalry, who got ready and charged on ahead, and engaged in a fierce fight under the very gates and wall of the city. They were victorious and wrested Mantinea from Epaminondas' grasp.

This was the event that Euphranor portrayed, and his picture allows one to see the battle's mêlée and the clash of forces, with all their might and will and spirit. But I doubt that you would give priority to the painter rather than to the commander, or would put up with people preferring the picture to the trophy and the copy to the reality. F

[3] Now, Simonides calls painting silent poetry, and poetry voiced painting,[1] because whereas painting presents us with events as if they were actually happening, words describe and relate the same events in the past. It is true that the presentation★ in the one case depends on colours and shapes, and in the other on words and phrases, so that they differ in the material and means they employ to imitate reality; nevertheless, they both basically have the same purpose: the best historian is the one who uses emotions and characters to make his narrative a reflection of events, as a painting is. 347A

Thucydides, at any rate,★ is constantly striving for this vividness in his writing, because he is eager to turn listeners into spectators, as it were, and to produce in his readers the emotional disturbance and turmoil which the witnesses to the events went through. For instance,[2] here is Demosthenes marshalling the Athenians right on the beach at Pylos; Brasidas urgently ordering his B

---

1. A very well-known saying (Plutarch, *How to Study Poetry* 17F), alluded to again in *How to Distinguish a Flatterer from a Friend* 58B, and, with the application transferred to dancing, in *Table Talk* 748A. It recurs in the *Rhetorica ad Herennium* 4.39 (first century BC), and in Ps.-Plutarch, *On the Life and Poetry of Homer* 216. For the common comparison of painting and poetry by the ancients, see C. O. Brink, *Horace on Poetry* II, 369 (on *Ars Poetica* 361), and cf. Lessing, *Laokoon, Vorrede*. For what follows, compare also Aristotle, *Poetics* 1447a16 ff.
2. Thucydides 4.10–12.

helmsman to run the ship aground, stepping out on to the gang-plank, being wounded and slipping unconscious into the outrigger; the land-fighting Spartans at sea and the sea-fighting Athenians on land. Or again, in the account of the Sicilian expedition:[1] 'While the sea battle hangs in the balance, both sides' infantry, watching from the land, are in a state of considerable★ mental conflict and tension, and because of the prolonged uncertainty★ C  of the struggle, even their bodies reflect their terror and sway in exact time with their thoughts.' There is something of the vividness of a painting in his delineation and description of events. Consequently, if it is inappropriate to compare painters with commanders, then we should not compare historians with them either.

Heraclides of Pontus records that it was Thersippus of Eroeadae★ who brought the news of the battle of Marathon. The majority of the sources, however, tell us it was Eucles who ran in full armour, although he was already hot from fighting, burst through the doors of the leaders' meeting-room, and had time only to say, 'Greetings! Victory is ours!', before expiring.[2] Now, this man came to deliver the news himself of a battle in which he D  had been a contestant. But what if some goatherd or peasant had witnessed the battle from a distance, standing on some peak or vantage point, and had realized the importance – the indescribable importance – of what was happening, and had arrived, unwounded and unbloodied, in the city with the news? And what if he had then expected to receive the recognition which Cynegeirus, Callimachus or Polyzelus received, just because he had delivered the news of their courage, their wounds and their deaths?[3]

1. Thucydides 7.71.
2. This is our Marathon runner (the distance between Marathon and Athens is about forty kilometres), but he occurs nowhere else in the surviving literature apart from Lucian, Pro Lapsu 3, who, however, gives the messenger the name Philippides (or Phidippides), thus confusing him with Herodotus' 'Marathon runner' who ran from Athens to Sparta and back before the battle to ask for help (6.105). Plutarch was well aware of Herodotus' Philippides (On the Spite of Herodotus 862A), and so here he is recalling another tradition, perhaps embroidered in the patriotic revivals of the fourth century BC, but certainly established lore in Plutarch's Athens.
3. The three heroes of Marathon not only feature in Herodotus' account (6.109–17), but were portrayed for all to see in the famous painting of the battle by

Wouldn't one's opinion be that he was inordinately impertinent? (In fact, we hear that the Spartans sent the person who told them about the victory at Mantinea – the one recorded in Thucydides' history[1] – a piece of meat from the public refectory as a reward for being the bearer of good news.) And yet writers simply bring news of events in an eloquent manner, and achieve their successes merely on paper, thanks to the excellence and power of their writing; and the first time people encounter them and read    E their histories, they owe them the reward for being bearers of good news. There is no doubt that it is people who achieve success at something who are responsible even for the praise writers earn when they are being recited and read, because words do not create deeds, but it is the deeds which cause the words to be regarded as worth listening to.

[4] Poetry too is appreciated and respected in so far as its words simulate actual events (one is reminded of Homer's 'While speaking, he made up plenty of lies to resemble the truth').[2] Also relevant is a story about Menander: one of his friends said to him, 'Menander, it's not long till the Dionysia, and you haven't composed your comedy, have you?' He replied, 'Yes, of course I have. The plot is under control; I just need to find the lines to    F accompany it.' That is, even poets regard events as more essential and important than words.

Once, when Pindar was still young and snobbish about his literary abilities, Corinna told him off for being uneducated and for failing to tell stories, which is conventionally what poetry should do, and for relying instead on prettifying events with dialect words, catachresis, metonymy, music and metres. Pindar    348A was extremely impressed by what she was saying, so he composed the famous poem which starts: 'Of Ismenus, or Melia with her golden distaff, or Cadmus, or the sacred race of Sown Men, or

---

Panaenus or by Micon in the Painted Portico in Athens (Pliny, *Naturalis Historia* 35.57; Pausanias, *Guide to Greece* 1.15.3; Aelian, *De Natura Animalium* 7.38).
1. Thucydides 5.64–74; but Thucydides does not have the anecdote, which Plutarch used again in his *Life of Agesilaus* 33. The date is 418 BC.
2. Homer, *Odyssey* 19.203.

the great might of Heracles, or the joyous cult of Dionysus . . .'[1]
When he showed it to Corinna, she said with a smile that seeds
ought to be sown by the handful, not the sackful – the point
being that Pindar had in fact concocted and amassed a kind of
farrago of stories and poured them into the poem.

The claim that poetry's domain is storytelling was also made
by Plato.[2] A story sets out to be a fictional account which
resembles a true account; therefore, it is at a considerable distance
B   from the facts, given that an account is an account of a fact, and
a story is a simulation and a reflection of an account. Writers of
fictional deeds are as inferior to writers of history as writers of
historical accounts are to the actual performers of deeds.

[5] Anyway, Athens has had no famous craftsman of epic or
lyric poetry: Cinesias seems to have been a terrible dithyrambic
poet. Although his family was unremarkable and he himself was
insignificant, he has gained a rather unfortunate reputation as a
result of being mocked and reviled by the comic poets.[3] As for
dramatists, comedy was regarded as so undignified and demeaning that it was illegal for any Areopagite[4] to compose comedies.
C   But tragedy flourished and won acclaim; it developed into a
marvel for the ears and eyes of the people of that time. By means
of the stories and emotions it portrayed, it produced an illusion
in which, as Gorgias says,[5] the illusionists are more honest than
sincere people, and the deluded are wiser than the undeluded.
The illusionists are more honest because they have done what
they promised to do; and the deluded are wiser because it requires
sensitivity to be susceptible to literary pleasures.

How, then, did these excellent tragedies benefit Athens, when
compared with Themistocles' shrewdness in building a wall
around the city, Pericles' solicitude in adorning the Acropolis,
D   Miltiades gaining freedom for the city, Cimon raising it to a

1. Pindar F29 Snell and Maehler. There is a fuller version of the opening of this
   hymn in Ps.-Lucian, *Demosthenis Encomium* 19, and an apparent reference to it
   as the first of Pindar's *Hymns* in Lucian, *Icaromenippus* 27.
2. *Phaedo* 61b.
3. For example, Aristophanes (*Birds* 1373 ff.).
4. The Areopagus was an ancient council and court composed of former holders
   of high office and men from the upper classes of Athenian society.
5. F23 DK.

position of leadership? If Euripides' craftsmanship, Sophocles' eloquence and Aeschylus' command of words performed a similar service and freed the city of any of its problems or added any extra lustre, then it is appropriate to draw a parallel between their plays and trophies, to juxtapose the theatre and the military headquarters, to compare edification with decoration for valour.

[6] Would you like us to introduce the men themselves, carrying the tokens and insignia of their activities, and to allow each type its own proper entrance? From the one side, then, let the poets approach, declaiming and singing to the accompaniment of pipes and lyres – 'Anyone who is unacquainted with such sacred speech, whose intention is impure, who has neither sung nor danced the rites of the noble Muses, or who is uninitiated in the linguistic revelries of bull-eating Cratinus, must now keep silence and make way for our choruses'[1] – and carrying their equipment, masks, altars, stage contraptions, revolving backdrops and triumphal tripods. With them, let their tragic actors come – men like Nicostratus, Callippides, Mynniscus, Theodorus and Polus – as beauticians and attendants of tragedy, as if she were a wealthy woman; but perhaps we should see them as following behind, in the role of painters and gilders and dyers of statues. And let them be furnished with an unruly crowd and expensive patronage, for their equipment, masks, purple-dyed robes, stage contraptions, chorus-leaders and walk-on parts.

A Spartan once noticed all this and made the nice comment that Athens was making a mistake in wasting serious amounts on trivial pursuits – that is, in spending on extravagant patronage of the theatre the amount required for major campaigns and for supplying expeditions abroad. If the cost of each production is calculated, it will turn out that Athens has spent more on Bacchant women, Phoenician women, various Oedipuses and Antigone,★ and on Medea's and Electra's troubles, than it spent on fighting foreigners for supremacy and freedom. For instance, army commanders often led their men into battle with instructions to bring provisions of uncooked grain; and naval commanders certainly equipped their rowers with pearl barley and a

1. Aristophanes, *Frogs* 353–6.

savoury of onions and cheese, and then boarded them on their ships. Patrons of plays, however, used to serve up for their players baby eels, lettuce hearts, ribs of beef and marrow, and used to feed them well for a long time, while they trained their voices and became spoiled. If a patron's play failed to win, he was savaged and jeered at; if it did win, he got a tripod which was (as Demetrius says) not a prize for victory, but a monument* to his squandered life and a cenotaph for his forsaken household. These are the rewards of poetry; there is nothing more splendid to be gained from it.

[7] But now let us imagine the commanders approaching from the other side. And as they approach, people who are unacquainted with action and political and military life, anyone who lacks the courage required for these activities, whose 'intention is impure', and who 'is uninitiated in the revelries' of Mede-slaying Miltiades and Persian-killing Themistocles, must really 'keep silence and make way'. This is Ares' troupe, weighed down with infantry regiments and naval contingents, with mingled spoils and trophies.

'"Hear me, Battle-cry, daughter of War, harbinger of spear fight, on whose altar men are offered in the ritual sacrifice of death."'[1] So spoke Epaminondas of Thebes, when they were preparing themselves for the finest and most glorious contest of all – to fight for their country, their ancestors' tombs and their temples. I seem to see their victories approaching, and the prizes these victories bring in their train are not cows or goats, nor is ivy their garland or Dionysian dregs their scent. They bring whole cities, islands, countries, priceless temples and colonies populated by countless people; and their garlands are trophies and plunder of every description. Their badges and tokens are, for instance, the vast Parthenon, the South Wall, the docks, the Propylaea, the Chersonese, Amphipolis.[2] Marathon comes first in

1. Pindar F78 Snell and Maehler.
2. The Parthenon and Propylaea were part of Pericles' grand building project (447–432 BC) of restoring the temples of Athens destroyed in the Persian invasion. The South Wall ran from Athens to Phalerum on the coast, and together with the North Wall to Piraeus secured the safety of Athens' corridor to her port. They were built between 461 and 456. Curiously, the subsequent building of the Middle Wall parallel to the North Wall (see p. 167, n. 1)

the train of Miltiades' victory, and Salamis in Themistocles', whose basis is the wrecks of a thousand ships. Cimon's victory brings a hundred Phoenician warships from the Eurymedon, Demosthenes' and Cleon's brings from Sphacteria Brasidas' captured shield and prisoners-of-war, Conon's strengthens the city's defences, Thrasybulus' leads the people from Phyle to freedom, E Alcibiades' victories resuscitate the city from its Sicilian lapse. It was as a result of Neileus' and Androclus' battles in Lydia and Caria that Greece appreciated Ionia's potential. And if you were to ask each of the victories I have not mentioned what benefit it had brought the city, you would get a string of answers like: Lesbos, Samos, Cyprus, the Black Sea, five hundred warships, ten thousand talents – with additional gifts of reputation and trophies.[1]

These are the events for which public holidays and sacrifices are instituted, rather than for Aeschylus' or Sophocles' victories. It is not the day of Carcinus' success with *Aerope*, nor Astydamas' with *Hector*, but on the sixth day after the beginning of Boedromion the city still, after all this time, has a holiday to celebrate the victory at Marathon;[2] and on the sixteenth day of this month a libation of wine is performed in remembrance of Chabrias' victory in the sea battle at Naxos;[3] and on the twelfth F they used to perform a sacrifice, an offering in thanks for their freedom, since that is the anniversary of the return from Phyle. On the third day after the beginning of the month, they

---

reduced the military importance of the South Wall, which fell into disrepair. The naval dockyards were at Piraeus. The Chersonese was cleared of Persians and brought under Athenian control by Cimon in the mid-460s. Amphipolis was colonized by Athens in 437.

1. It is remarkable that this list of Athenian victories and proud glories is confined to the Persian and Peloponnesian Wars of the fifth century BC, some five hundred years before the time of the Athenians Plutarch was addressing. The strange exceptions are Neileus and Androclus, who were in Athenian legend sons of King Codrus and founder colonists of Miletus and Ephesus very much earlier.

2. Boedromion was the third lunar month in the Athenian calendar year, which began approximately after the summer solstice. So the Marathon Thanksgiving Day fell about the end of August; the battle itself had been fought earlier in August.

3. Over the Spartans in 376 BC.

won the battle of Plataea.[1] They made the sixteenth day of Munichion sacred to Artemis, since that was the day when the goddess shone as a full moon on the Greeks in their victory at Salamis.[2] The battle of Mantinea has made the twelfth day of Scirrophorion even more sacred to Athens, given that during the battle, although the rest of the allies were overwhelmed and routed, the Athenians alone were victorious in their field of operations and erected a trophy seized from the dominant enemy.[3] These are the events which brought Athens to its heights of fame and pre-eminence. These are the reasons Pindar described Athens as 'the backbone of Greece';[4] it was not because of any prosperity Athens afforded Greece with the tragedies of Phrynichus and Thespis, but because, as Pindar himself says, Artemisium was the first occasion when 'Sons of Athens laid the gleaming foundation of freedom'; and once they had solidly established Greece's freedom at Salamis and Mycale and Plataea, they bequeathed it to the rest of mankind.

[8] But someone may assert that although what poets do is not to be taken seriously, nevertheless the work of orators does have some importance, when compared to that of military commanders – and this is the context of Aeschines' reasonable mockery of Demosthenes for asserting that he would call for a suit to decide the claim of the speakers' podium to control the military headquarters.[5] So is it appropriate to give precedence to Hyperides' Plataean speech over Aristides' victory at Plataea?[6] Or to

1. The final decisive infantry victory over the Persians in 479 BC.
2. Munichion was the tenth month of the Athenian calendar, and so the Salamis festival was in April; Themistocles' great naval victory, however, actually took place in September 480 BC (20th Boedromion), as Plutarch himself stated in his later *Life of Camillus* 19. Was he unaware of that when he delivered this earlier effusion?
3. Scirrophorion was the twelfth Attic month and covered the latter part of June and early July. For the engagement, see section 2 and the Introduction.
4. This line (F76 Snell, Maehler) and the following two (F77 Snell, Maehler) became extremely famous, as one may imagine, in Athens. The grateful Athenians even went to the length of erecting a statue of Pindar (Pausanias, *Guide to Greece* 1.8.4), and of rewarding him handsomely (Isocrates, *Antidosis* 166) for his compliments.
5. Aeschines, *Against Ctesiphon* 146.
6. No other reference to a Plataean speech by Hyperides has survived. Isocrates wrote one, but it voices an imaginary appeal from Plataeans to Athens after

Lysias' speech against the Thirty[1] over Thrasybulus' and Archinus' extermination of those tyrants? Or to Aeschines' speech against Timarchus for prostitution over Phocion's intercession in C Byzantium, which enabled him to prevent the sons of our allies becoming victims of Macedonian drunken lust?[2] Or are we to compare Conon's★ chaplets, which he received for liberating Greece, with Demosthenes' speech *On the Chaplet* – in which, in fact, the orator has composed extremely clear and eloquent remarks on this issue, when he swore 'by those of our ancestors who in the past faced danger at Marathon',[3] rather than by those who in the past taught our young men at school? That is why it is not people like Isocrates, Antiphon and Isaeus whom the city buried with public memorials, but the others – the ones whose bodily remains the city felt responsible for, and whom the orator treated as gods by swearing by them in his oath, because he D could not aspire to be like them.

Isocrates once said that those who in the past faced danger at Marathon had fought as if their lives did not belong to them,[4] and he celebrated their courage and their disdain for life; nevertheless, it is said that when he had grown old, someone asked him how he was, and he answered, 'The state I'm in is that of a man who is over ninety years old and regards death as the greatest of evils.' For he had not grown old honing a sword, sharpening a spearhead, burnishing a helmet, or playing a part in the army or the navy, but stringing together and composing antitheses, clauses balanced in length and words whose endings rhyme, and almost polishing and shaping his clauses with chisels and files. How E could anyone not be afraid of the crashing of arms and the clash

---

Thebes had destroyed their city in 373 BC. Aristides' victory was in 479. But elsewhere in this paragraph, Plutarch compares events which are not contemporaneous; and we have no reason to doubt that Hyperides wrote on what was probably a common rhetorical subject.
1. Lysias, *Against Eratosthenes*.
2. Phocion intervened with Athenian forces in 339 BC to save Byzantium from Philip of Macedon. Plutarch gives details in his *Life of Phocion* 14.
3. Demosthenes, *On the Chaplet* 208, a passage of great fame in Athenian literature; see Ps.-Longinus, *De Sublimitate* 16.
4. Isocrates, *Panegyricus* 86.

of regiments in battle, when he is afraid of letting vowel encounter vowel and of producing clauses whose equivalence is a syllable short?[1]

Miltiades set out for Marathon, and on the next day he joined battle and arrived victorious back at the city with his army; Pericles took nine months to subjugate Samos[2] and thought more highly of himself than he did of Agamemnon, who had captured Troy in the tenth year; but Isocrates spent almost twelve years writing his *Panegyricus*,[3] and during this period he did not take part in any military campaigns, or act as an ambassador, or found a city, or lead a naval expedition, even though the period saw countless wars. Instead, while Timotheus was liberating Euboea, Chabrias was fighting sea battles around Naxos, Iphicrates was massacring the Spartan contingent and the Athenian people – now that they had liberated all Greece – gave everyone the same voting rights as themselves,[4] Isocrates was sitting at home using words to reshape a book, and taking the same time about it that Pericles took to construct the Propylaea and his vast edifices. Still, Cratinus ridiculed even Pericles for

1. Isocrates' preoccupation with the avoidance of hiatus, and with balance and rhythm, was notorious: cf. Dionysius of Halicarnassus, *Demosthenes* 4; Cicero, *Brutus* 32 ff.; Quintilian 10.1.79. However, Plutarch's own care to avoid hiatus is equally noticeable.

2. 440–439 BC. This anecdote of Pericles' pride is told again in Plutarch's *Life of Pericles* 28.7, on the authority of Pericles' contemporary, the tragedian, poet and historian Ion of Chios.

3. This prolonged literary gestation was notorious. The usual figure given is ten years (c. 390–380 BC): Ps.-Longinus, *De Sublimitate* 4.2; Dionysius of Halicarnassus, *De Compositione Verborum* 25, 208; Quintilian 10.4.4; Ps.-Plutarch, *Lives of the Ten Orators* 837F. But the last three add that ten years was the lowest estimate.

4. The list in this sentence seems carelessly inaccurate. The main reference appears to be to the establishment of the Second Athenian Confederacy ('voting rights') in 377 BC. With this is linked the battle of Naxos in 376. But Iphicrates' destruction of the Spartan hoplite garrison detachment outside Corinth took place in 390. And the best-known intervention of Timotheus to liberate Euboea against Thebes was in 358/7. But in Demosthenes, 13.22, the same triad of Timotheus, Iphicrates and Chabrias with their engagements recurs, except that Timotheus takes not Euboea but Corcyra, and that expedition occurred in 376. Even so, since Isocrates' *Plataean Oration* was delivered in 380, only Iphicrates' clash of arms could properly be said to have taken place within the gestation period. It is doubtful whether Plutarch's audience either knew or cared.

taking a long time to complete his works, saying something like the following about the Middle Wall: 'It's coming along fine in Pericles' speeches, but there's no progress at all in fact.'[1] Consider how narrow-minded the orator was, then, to spend a ninth of his life on a single speech.

So again, is it particularly appropriate to compare the speeches of Demosthenes the orator with the achievements of Demosthenes the general? The former's speech accusing Conon of assault with the latter's trophies at Pylos?[2] The former's speech against Arethusius on the subject of slavery[3] with the latter's enslavement of the Spartans? The age at which he wrote his speeches about his guardians was Alcibiades' age when he got Mantinea and Elis to cooperate in opposition to Sparta.[4] Nevertheless, his public speeches are remarkable in this respect, that in the *Philippics* he enjoins action and elsewhere he commends Leptines' activity . . .[5]

1. Cratinus F300 Kock. The quip reappears in *Life of Pericles* 13, where Plutarch gives more details. The Middle Wall was built about 455 BC and ran from Athens to the port of Piraeus (a distance of about four miles) and thus secured Athens' communication with her port.
2. On the bay of Navarino where in 425 BC, during the Peloponnesian War, Demosthenes established and maintained a strategic garrison on Spartan territory. In doing so, a valued contingent of prime Spartan troops was captured.
3. Demosthenes, *Against Nicostratus*.
4. Plutarch's age correspondence is somewhat elastic. Demosthenes' father died when he was seven, and the estate was left in the hands of trustees who mismanaged it. Demosthenes prosecuted when he came of age – the first case, *Against Aphobus*, was in 364 BC when he was twenty. Certainly the matter dragged on for years; on the other hand, Alcibiades must have been about thirty in 420 BC when he contrived the Mantinean alliance.
5. The *Philippics* called for Athenian action against Philip of Macedon. But the last phrase of the broken sentence must be corrupt. Demosthenes spoke against Leptines for introducing legislation which repealed freedom from taxes granted to the families of benefactors of the state.

# ON THE AVOIDANCE OF ANGER

## INTRODUCTION

The topic of anger provided one of the most popular subjects for dissertations, monographs and essays in Hellenistic philosophy and literature. And this is not surprising; it is after all a mental state with which everyone is only too familiar, and bitterly aware of the human problems caused by it. The Greeks had been fascinated by it from the very first words, the wrath of Achilles, of their earliest literary masterpiece, the *Iliad*. The philosophers, Plato and Aristotle, gave it their attention. But it was in subsequent Hellenistic philosophy that anger became a prime topic. This was because the Stoics elevated the discussion of the passions, as the crucial distorting factors in human moral behaviour, to central prominence in ethical philosophy (cf. Posidonius F30 EK). And of course anger is the most obvious and widespread of the passions. Members of all the leading Schools produced monographs: among others, Hieronymus and Sotion of the Peripatetics; Antipater, Posidonius and Seneca of the Stoics; Philodemus, the Epicurean; and popular moralists like Bion of Borysthenes.[1] Plutarch himself wrote a second essay *On Anger* (*Lamprias Catalogue*, 93). In 60/59 BC Cicero in a letter to his brother Quintus (1.1.37) excuses himself from a lengthy sermon on anger by pointing to the numerous authors on the subject. Most of this has now disappeared, apart from Seneca's three books *De Ira*, and part of Philodemus' monograph on papyrus. But enough has survived to show that inevitably the genre had gradually accumulated a stock of common and shared elements through convenience, habit and custom.

This can be illustrated briefly through comparison of Plutarch's essay and Seneca's *De Ira*. Common ingredients include shared topics (physical reactions, 455F/Sen.2.35.3 ff.; anger and the unexpected, 463D/Sen.2.31.1); common fields of dispute (ethical ambiguity of anger, 456F/Sen.1.20.1); anecdote (Antigonus, 457E/Sen.3.22.2 and 458F/Sen.3.22.4 f.; with variations even of attribution: Diogenes/Cato, 460E/Sen.2.32.2); instance (Socrates' behaviour, 455A/Sen.3.13.3; murder of Clitus, 458B/Sen.3.17.1); illustration (epileptic fits, 455C/Sen.3.10.3; mule kicks, 457A/Sen.3.27.1; runaway slaves, 459A/Sen.3.5.4; cold bread, 461C/Sen.2.25.1; illegible writing, 464B/Sen.2.26.2); comparisons (ants and mice, 458C/Sen.2.34.1); imagery (mirror, 456B/Sen.2.36.1–3; retractable knives, 458E/Sen.2.35.1); even phraseology (lip-biting, 458D/Sen.1.19.3).

Such common elements have led scholars to search for common sources.[2] But this to my mind is to misconstrue the situation. There was no single common source, but a shared literature and field of debate from which in general was culled a common armoury of argument and illustration. Plutarch's reading was enormously wide; he took notes as he read and, as we all do, he often reproduced such notes in various ways as he needed them. We should not forget, either, the power and force of memory in the ancient world, and writers' dependence on it; and memory relies on familiarity. And indeed we are all ourselves aware of the advantages in debate of employing well-known instances and illustrations. So it is more interesting to note and accept the common elements, and try to assess the individuality of their use in the composition and presentation of the whole.

An immediate hint of the character of the essay is given by the initial setting. The Roman Fundanus is to give an account of how he managed to tame his notoriously violent temper. So this is not to be an abstract philosophical dissertation or analysis of anger. The Greek title of our essay is literally *On Negation of Anger* (*Peri Aorgēsias*); the Latin version is *On the Restraint of Anger* (*De Cohibenda Ira*). It is to be a practical homily, similar to Plutarch's other essays in popular philosophy.

The structure, however, is lax and repetitive. It is possible to see a kind of division between sections 2–11, which are mainly concerned with a prophylactic approach to avoiding or forestalling rages, and sections 12–15, which are more related to cure by understanding what anger is, how it arises and what its effects are.

But common elements recur in both sections, and separate major themes obtrude.

The first point to be made is that self-cure is essential, which must spring from our own volition and practice (§2). Also, since once in the full grip of rage we are powerless, we must practise trying to forestall it. Anger grows, so immediate opposition is necessary to deny it fuel by attempting to keep quiet and calm (§§3–5). Shame and loathing can be produced by watching the horrible physical effects which mark people mad with rage (§6). Above all, we must bridle the tongue before it is too late (§7). At this point (§8) there is an intrusion of a stock topic, the ethical ambiguity of anger: some accord it a good side. Plutarch will have none of this, and maintains that it always springs from weakness and mental disease. The next section (§9) is devoted to the moral assistance to be derived from contemplating historical examples of controlling temper. But then (§10) yet another intrusive topic is introduced: anger as retaliation, retribution and punishment, for which it was often approved as an essential ingredient. Plutarch denies this, and dissociates 'righteous indignation' from courage and manliness. Anger as a retributive force is self-destructive. He now at last (§11) returns to his main theme: practice and constant schooling of temper. It is most convenient and effective to practise on your servants. Do this by forcing yourself to delay between losing your temper at a misdemeanour and passing judgement.

But if delay is helpful in protecting oneself from making mistakes, it is not a cure. A cure would demand recognition and understanding of what causes anger: a belief that we are being slighted, ignored, despised or unjustly treated (§12). Such belief is promoted through being self-centred and discontented, that is, by weakness of character, fostered by a spoilt and pampered way of life (§13). One must also understand the effects of anger: the distortion of all contacts and relationships. And it cannot be countered by calling it pretty names like 'righteous indignation' (§14). Finally, we should understand what it is, a mental disease (§14). In fact it unites in it elements from the other passions, and so is the most disagreeable of them all, particularly in its involvement with cruelty and pain. It is a desire to hurt and destroy others, even at risk to oneself (§15).

The last section (§16) seems to sum up and bring together earlier elements. Again righteous indignation is dismissed. *All* excess must be eradicated. But it can arise from what might seem a creditable although mistaken impulse, expecting too much from other people and then feeling betrayed. But this is a form of overconfidence. We are all fallible and weak human beings. To realize this in oneself as well as in others is a helpful safeguard. We should also try to be less interfering in what does not concern us. But above all, the only remedy lies in training and habituation. Yet we also need to understand that passion leads to mental confusion and unnatural actions, and that an even temper is a greater blessing even for the possessor than for the lucky recipients of its effects.

Now as far as structure goes, this is a curious mixture of sound common sense, humanity, practical tips and advice, and an entanglement in the historical development of philosophical debate on the subject. But within the structure are revealing topics and presentation.

One such topic concerns the ethical ambiguity of anger. This started with Plato, for whom anger was derived from 'the passionate or spirited part' of the mind, which under the control of reason also engendered courage. In Plato's famous metaphor of the soul in *Phaedrus* 246b, where the charioteer of reason drives the horses of passion and desire, the passionate horse is the good horse, the other the bad. And in *Laws* 731b–d Plato talks of a righteous indignation where you can let your anger off the leash. Aristotle in *Nicomachean Ethics* (*NE*), 4.5, 1125b26 ff., praises 'good' anger, where you are angry at the right things, with the right people, in the right way, at the right time. Further, in Aristotle's ethical theory of a mean between two extremes, anger or rage (*orgē*) is the extreme of excess; lack or negation of anger (*aorgēsia*) is the equally censured extreme of deficiency (*NE* 1126a3). In post-Aristotelian philosophy the battle lines were clear between Peripatetics and Platonists, who defended morally praiseworthy anger, and Stoics and Epicureans, who condemned all anger as an excess springing from mental weakness and moral distortion and degeneration. The debate continued well into the Christian era of course (e.g. Lactantius, *De Ira Dei* 17.12 ff.).

Seneca (*De Ira* 3.3.1) called Aristotle 'Anger's Champion'; for Peripatetics and Platonists saw anger in the form of righteous indignation as a necessary ingredient of moral character and action. It produced the spirit to stand up for yourself (Aristotle, *NE* 1126a7), an ingredient of manliness and courage (Plato, *Republic* 411b; Aristotle, *NE* 1126b1 f.), as Achilles' anger was heroic until it became excessive, compared with the 'soft' fighter Menelaus (*Republic* 411b). And so anger was the 'mind's sinews' (Plato, *Republic* 411b), the 'whetstone of courage' (Cicero, *Tusculanae Disputationes* 4.43, on the Peripatetics). In this essay Plutarch is on the side of the Stoics. He will have nothing to do with righteous indignation (§8, 456F; §14, 462E f.; §16, 463B, E), which can serve as a cloak for and incitement to passion. As Stoics defined passion as 'excessive impulse' (*SVF* 3.462, 479; Posidonius F34 EK), so Plutarch stresses the excessive element of anger (§16, 463B); like the Stoics, Plutarch claims that anger always springs from weakness (§8, 456F–457B) and is itself a mental disease (§14, 462F; so Posidonius F163 EK) and causes confusion leading to unnatural behaviour (§16, 464C). He expressly denies that anger is the mind's sinews (457C, referring to Plato, *Republic* 411b, but without naming Plato), and goes out of his way to separate it from courage (§10, 458E; §8, 456F). The term used by Aristotle, and perhaps invented by him (*NE* 1126a3) for his censured extreme of deficiency, *aorgēsia*, negation of anger, becomes the Greek title handed down to us for Plutarch's essay, as the goal for which we should aim; the term in any case is used in the essay (464C), and may be compared with the Stoic use in Epictetus 3.18.6; 3.20.9 and 10.

Now we should perhaps remember that the speaker is Fundanus, the honoured dedicatee, and Fundanus may have been a Stoic, since he quotes Musonius in familiar fashion (453D). Also linguistic terminology in this area is deficient, as Aristotle noted (*NE* 1125b26 ff.). The Greeks tended to use 'anger' for a whole ethical spectrum of emotion. But in Hellenistic philosophy *orgē* was especially referred to rage, excessive violent anger. If Plutarch is elsewhere willing to give anger a moral role,[3] the context of this essay is against that. So even although Plutarch employs in his didactic historical examples the Peripatetic term 'moderation of passion' (*metriopatheia*, 458C), and even Aristotle's word for the 'mean' of anger (458C, 458E), he dissociates all this from and contrasts it with anger/rage. But further, Aristotle's word for the mean, 'gentleness' or 'mildness' (*praotēs*, *NE* 1125b26), had become in Stoic philosophy equated with 'negation of anger' (*aorgēsia*), as in Epictetus 3.20.9. And so indeed with Plutarch in this essay. Of course, neither Plutarch nor the Stoics were negating emotion altogether and advocating insensibility. So the point again is the context: Plutarch's theme is not theoretical analysis, but practical advice or therapeutics on the cure of irascibility. For a man with a violent temper, *all* anger becomes excessive (463B) and needs taming (459B).

Context also shapes another common topic, where special prominence is given to anger as revenge in section 10. This too was an Aristotelian theme (*NE* 1126a6–8, 1126a21 ff.), but the Stoics brought it very much to the fore by actually defining anger as desire for revenge on someone you believe to have done you undeserved wrong (Diogenes Laertes 7.113; Posidonius F155 EK). Plutarch again uses this for his own purpose in his own context to highlight the danger for a quick-tempered man of the Peripatetic advocacy of anger as a spur and propulsion for retaliation and punishment. Rather it propels to self-destruction; whereas courage needs no tincture of gall (458E). He also isolates and stresses with the Stoics that the belief that one has been unjustly wronged is the cause of anger (§12, 460D).

Plutarch's main practical therapy lies in constant training and habituation (§11; §16, 464B–C). This too was something of a commonplace in Hellenistic philosophy. It had long been a feature of Peripatetic ethics, and was central to Cynic practice as *askēsis*, or the prophylactic confrontational training of body and mind to keep them in fighting trim against inessential desires. Later Stoicism too supported such training, for Posidonius argued that the irrationality of passion was responsive only to the irrational schooling of custom (Frs. 31.16–19; 169.106–17; 168; 165.172–89; 162 EK); and Epictetus gave similar advice. Plutarch's Fundanus follows such practical exercises, gradually extending his rageless periods (464C). But Plutarch's main presentation of his theme is entirely characteristic, the presentation of vivid pictorial examples to the mind. The description of the disgusting and frightening appearance of raving men (455E) is intended to deter, just as pictures of lung cancer are used today to discourage smoking. More typically, positive historical anecdotes illustrate the successful resistance of rage; section 9 pours out eight of these. Now two of these anecdotes are clearly common property as they also turn up in Seneca, *De Ira*; five of them are used by Plutarch elsewhere, a couple resurfacing together in *On Moral Virtue*, suggesting a grouping in Plutarch's notebooks. None of this matters; the whole section is entirely and characteristically welded to his context. The essay is peppered with such anecdotes and they drive the reader effortlessly through the loose structure. They are not merely decorative. The imagery is didactic, and some, like that of C. Gracchus and his vocal tuner (456A) are unforgettable.

Another strong Plutarchan feature is the stress on human relationships. The note of friendship is struck right at the start (453A f.), and the effect of anger in distorting all relationships is emphasized (§14, 462B ff.). Particularly noticeable is Plutarch's humanity, in the long sections concerning domestic relationships with slaves and family (§11, 459B ff.; §13, 461A ff.); and by chance, the same theme of slaves and wives appears again in F148 Sandbach from Plutarch's lost essay, *On Anger*. The hint of divine vows and resolutions at the end led Erasmus, who translated this essay in 1525, to suggest that 464B–D was a Christian appendix. But it is no more than a characteristic extension of Plutarchan humanity to divine contact and reference.

One factor remains, the dialogue form, or rather the lack of it. As was customary, from Plato's invention of the genre on, the participants were real people. Sextius Sulla was a Carthaginian (727B; *Life of Romulus* 15), based in Rome and a friend of such standing as to hold a dinner party for Plutarch on his arrival in Rome after a long absence. Clearly a cultivated man in both philosophy and science, he crops up again not only in *Table Talk,* but also as a leading participant in *On the Face on the Moon.* C. Minucius Fundanus was a Roman of some importance, suffect consul in 107 AD, and proconsul of Asia in 122/3. But the dialogue form is unusually bare. The organic character of the

Platonic dialogue, which gave form to the dynamic interchange of argument, declined in Hellenistic philosophical literature to a static medium presenting opposed positions, or to conversation pieces. *On the Avoidance of Anger* is not even that. After a brief exchange setting the scene, the essay becomes a monologue by Fundanus on how he tamed his temper. The advantage of this lies not in argument but in the verisimilitude of a personal declaration, a giving of testimony, within an initial setting of pretended actuality. This is in tune with Plutarch's personalization of moral problems. It might be thought odd to honour an influential Roman by making him the central spokesman on bad temper. But the compliment was obliquely strong. Fundanus' temper was clearly notorious anyway (453B f.), and a hot temper was an imperious fault (Aristotle, *NE* 1126b1–2); but to have a violent temper and then cure it was very praiseworthy, and a shining example to all.

Fundanus was also a friend of the younger Pliny, and this helps to date our essay.[4] For Pliny in a letter to him (*Letter* 5.16) mentions the death of Fundanus' much-loved younger daughter in terms which indicate that Fundanus was already a widower. But Fundanus in Plutarch's essay refers to the sudden realization of the effect his temper has on his wife and little daughters (455F). From Pliny's letter and the girl's funerary urn (*ILS* 1030), we know that she died when she was barely thirteen. Since Pliny's letter appears to have been written about 105/6 AD, Plutarch's essay must have been written after 92/3; and since it is hardly possible that Plutarch would be so insensitive as to make his friend refer to a much-loved little daughter as if she were there when she had recently died, it was probably written in the late nineties. So it is, as we would expect anyway from the part of Fundanus, a work of Plutarch's maturity, and indeed of a prolific period of his writing.

1. For a fuller list, see Kidd, *Posidonius* II, p. 179.
2. See, for example, and with further illustration: A. Schlemm, 'Ueber die Quellen der Plutarchischen Schrift περὶ ἀοργησίας', *Hermes* 38 (1903), pp. 587–607; J. Fillion-Lahille, *Le De Ira de Sénèque*, Paris, 1984; Philodemus, *De Ira*, ed. C. Wilke, Teubner, 1914; Filodemo, *L'ira*, ed. G. Indelli, Naples, 1988).
3. E.g. *On Moral Virtue* 451E; cf. D. Babut, *Plutarque et le Stoïcisme*, p. 96.
4. See C. P. Jones, *Journal of Roman Studies* 56 (1955), pp. 61 f.

# ON THE AVOIDANCE OF ANGER

452F [1] SULLA: Fundanus,[1] I think the painters' practice of periodically examining their paintings before adding the finishing touches is commendable. Continuous familiarity hides the ways in which something might vary slightly from what is required; so by interrupting their viewing, they use repeated discrimination to
453A keep the viewing fresh and more likely to catch minor variations. But it is impossible for a person to apply himself to himself only periodically, by separating himself and interrupting the continuity of his self-awareness – and this is the main reason why everyone is a poorer judge of himself than of others. Therefore, a second-best course is for him periodically to inspect his friends and to make himself available to them for the same purpose, which is not to see if he has suddenly grown old or if his body is in a better or worse condition, but for them to examine his habits and character, to see if over a period of time any good features have been added or bad ones subtracted.

Anyway, I've come back to Rome after over a year away, and I've been with you for over four months now. I don't find it particularly surprising that the good points you were already innately endowed with have developed and increased so much;
B but when I see how much more amenable and submissive to reason that strong, fiery temper of yours has become, I am inclined to comment on your impetuosity by quoting the line, 'It is amazing how much more gentle he is.'[2]

Nevertheless, this gentleness has not made you ineffective or

---

1. See Introduction, p. 174, for the participants.
2. The quotation from Homer, *Iliad* 22.373, is witty. The line was spoken by Greek warriors over the dead body of Hector, the Trojan champion who had terrorized them while alive. Fundanus must have had quite a temper.

languid, but it has replaced your notorious sudden changes of mood with a smooth surface and an effective, productive depth – like a cultivated field. It is also clear, therefore, that your temper is not waning because advancing age has made it start to decline, or because of any other automatic factor, but because it is being treated by good rational advice. But I must confess that when our mutual friend Eros told me this about you, I suspected that his warmth towards you was making him attribute to you qualities which truly good people ought to have, even though you didn't have them – and I thought this despite the fact that, as you know, he is the last person to renounce an opinion just in order to please anyone. But I now see that he is not guilty of perjury. Since we have nothing else to do while we're travelling, I wonder if you would explain how you made your temper so tame, moderate, and amenable and obedient to reason – what regimen you followed, so to speak.

FUNDANUS: You're too kind, Sulla. Are you sure that *your* warm friendship towards me is not blinding you to some aspects of my character? I mean, even Eros himself often fails to restrain his temper and 'keep it steadily compliant' (as Homer puts it);[1] it is righteous indignation that makes it boil over. So it is possible that I seem amenable compared to him on these occasions, just as high notes can take the place of low notes, relative to other high notes, when one scale changes into another.

SULLA: Neither of these are realistic possibilities, Fundanus. Please, as a favour to me, do what I asked.

[2] FUNDANUS: All right. Musonius came up with some excellent suggestions, Sulla, and one of them, as I recall, was that a life of constant therapy guarantees immunity.[2] The point is that when reason is the therapeutic agent, it should not – in my opinion – be flushed out of the system along with the illness, as hellebore is, but should remain in the mind and contain and watch over our decisions. In its effects, the analogy for reason is not medicine, but nourishing food, since anyone who becomes accustomed to

---

1. Homer (*Odyssey* 20.23) uses the phrase of Odysseus, still in disguise, controlling his anger with difficulty in the face of the suitors' insulting behaviour in his house.
2. F36 Hense.

it gains energy[1] and well-being from it, whereas when emotions are at a peak of fermentation, advice and reproof struggle long and hard for slight gains, and exactly resemble smelling-salts, which arouse people who have a fit and fall unconscious, but don't get rid of the actual ailment.

Still, even at the time of their peak, all the other emotions do in a sense fall back and make way when reason with its reinforcements enters the mind from outside; but anger does not act in quite the way Melanthius says – 'It displaces intelligence and then commits criminal acts';[2] in fact, it does so after having replaced intelligence altogether, and shut it out of the house. And then the

F   situation is similar to when people burn to death in their houses, in the sense that anger makes the inside full of chaos, smoke and noise, with the result that the mind is incapable of seeing or hearing anything beneficial. This is why it is easier for an aban-

454A   doned ship to take on a helmsman from outside in the middle of a storm and in the open sea, than it is for someone who is being tossed in the sea of fury and anger to accept reason from an external source, unless he has made his own rationality ready. People who anticipate a siege and expect no help from outside accumulate and amass all the useful things they can; similarly, it is particularly important for people to gather from far and wide everything philosophy has to offer that will help combat anger, and to store it up in the mind – because the time when the need is crucial is also when they will not readily find it possible to introduce such assistance. I mean, the din stops the mind even hearing anything external, unless the mind has reason of its own, like an internal

B   ship's boatswain who smartly picks up and understands every instruction; otherwise, even if the mind does hear anything, it despises quiet, gentle words and bridles at any which are more defiant. The point is that since a temper is arrogant, wilful and

1. The Greek word *eutonia* (literally 'good tension') had particular significance for a Stoic. Since the active principle of reason was material, its beneficial effects on the mind and character could be physically expressed as producing a good or proper tension (e.g. *SVF* 3.471, 473).
2. Wilamowitz (*Hermes* 29.150 ff.) argued that the line comes from the second-century Academic and tragedian Melanthius of Rhodes, rather than from the fifth-century Athenian tragedian (*TGF* p. 760 Nauck). Plutarch quotes the line again in *On God's Slowness to Punish* 551A.

hard for an external agent to dislodge, it is like a secure tyranny which can be brought down only by an internal, inbred agent.

[3] If anger becomes constant and resentment frequent, the mind acquires the negative condition known as irascibility, which results in prickliness, bitterness and a sour temper – that is, when the emotions become raw, easily distressed and hypercritical:     C
think of a piece of iron which is already weak and thin being further filed. On the other hand, if rational discrimination immediately defies and bears down on any outburst of anger, it not only remedies the current situation, but also gives the mind energy and detachment for the future.

In my own case, at any rate, what happened is that once I had defied anger two or three times, I experienced what the Thebans did: once they had repulsed the apparently invincible Spartans for the first time,[1] they were never subsequently defeated by them in battle. I mean, I gained the firm conviction that rationality can win. I saw that Aristotle's claim that anger ends when cold water is sprinkled on it is not the whole story:[2] it is also     D
quenched when faced with fear. Moreover, of course, the onset of happiness frequently causes the instantaneous 'melting', to use Homer's term,[3] and dispersal of anger. The net result was that I became convinced that, provided the will is there, this emotion is not entirely irredeemable. You see, anger might well be aroused by something slight and meagre: often even a joke, a lighthearted remark, a laugh, a nod of assent, and so on and so forth, provoke anger. For example, when Helen addressed her niece as 'Electra, long-time spinster', she incited her remark, 'You have taken your time to see sense; in the past you left your home in disgrace.'[4] And Callisthenes irritated Alexander by saying, when the large bowl was being passed around, 'I don't want to drink     E
Alexander and then need Asclepius.'[5]

1. At the battle of Leuctra, 371 BC.
2. No such statement from Aristotle survives, but cf. *De Partibus Animalium* 651A and Ps.-Aristotle, *Problemata* 898A.
3. For example, *Iliad* 23.598, 600; *Odyssey* 6.156. Plutarch expounds this piece of Homeric scholarship again in *The Primary Cold* 947D and in *Table Talk* 735F.
4. Euripides, *Orestes* 72, 99.
5. The anecdote on Alexander's excessive drinking recurs in *Table Talk* 623F–624A. Dionysus was the god of wine, and Alexander claimed divinity.

[4] Therefore, just as it is easy to control a flame which is starting to catch in hare's fur or on a wick or in a pile of rubbish[1] (whereas if it catches in a solid object with depth, it quickly destroys and devastates 'with lively zest the lofty work of builders', as Aeschylus puts it),[2] so anyone who pays attention to the early stages of anger and is aware of it gradually starting to smoulder and ignite as a result of some remark or rubbishy sarcasm doesn't need to exert himself a great deal, but often puts an end to it simply by keeping quiet and ignoring the remark.

F    Anyone who doesn't fuel a fire puts it out, and anyone who doesn't feed anger in the early stages and doesn't get into a huff[3] is being prudent and is eliminating anger.

I was accordingly not happy with Hieronymus, despite his useful comments and advice elsewhere, when he claims that because of its speed, anger is not perceptible when it is arising, but only when it has arisen and already exists.[4] I mean, all the emotions go through the phase of gaining mass and movement, but in none of them is this arising and growth so obvious. So
455A    Homer's teaching on this is skilful: when he says, 'So he spoke; and dark clouds of anguish overshadowed Achilles',[5] he is portraying Achilles as feeling sudden pain, when word reached him, with no lapse of time in between; but he portrays his anger at Agamemnon as slowly building up, and as gradually being ignited while a great number of words were being spoken.[6] But if any of the people involved had withdrawn their words at the

---

Asclepius was the god of healing, urgently required on the morning after Alexander's massive loving-cup had been circulating. Callisthenes was Alexander's nephew, and a historian of his exploits (FGrH 124).
1. This must be some kind of cliché, since a similar trio, including the hare's fur, is cited in Marital Advice 138F, as a simile for sexual desire: it catches fire easily, but goes out just as easily.
2. Aeschylus F357 Nauck and Radt.
3. The phrase is literally 'doesn't distend himself', but there is a triple pun: the verb can mean 'to get angry', 'to puff oneself up' (so as to be the equivalent of the solid object mentioned above), or 'to apply bellows to a fire'. It proved quite impossible to capture all this with a single English word.
4. Hieronymus F22 Wehrli.
5. Iliad 18.22.
6. Iliad 1.101 ff.

beginning and had resisted speaking them, their quarrel would not have escalated to such a degree and got so big. That is why whenever Socrates realized that he was getting too nasty to one of his friends, then because he was being driven 'as it were before a storm on the crest of an ocean wave',[1] he used to lower his voice, smile and stop looking stern – and so keep himself upright and in control by counterbalancing the emotion and by moving instead in the opposite direction.

[5] You see, my friend, there is a first-rate way to bring down our tyrant-like temper, which is not to listen or obey when it is ordering us to raise our voices, look fierce and beat our breasts, but to keep quiet and, as if the emotion were a disease, not aggravate it by thrashing and yelling. It may be that partying, singing and decorating doors[2] – typical lovers' behaviour – do somehow afford an alleviation which is not unpleasing or inelegant ('I came, but did not call your name: I kissed your door. If this is a crime, I am a criminal');[3] and it may be that mourners eliminate a lot of their grief as well as their tears in the release of crying and weeping; but anger is made considerably more intense by the behaviour and speech of people in an angry state.

It is best, therefore, to keep calm, or alternatively to run away and hide and find refuge in silence, as though we realized that we were about to have a fit, and wanted to avoid falling, or rather falling on someone – and it is friends above all whom we most often fall on. We do not feel love or jealousy or fear for everyone, but anger leaves nothing alone, nothing in peace: we get angry at enemies and friends, at children and parents, and even at gods and animals and inanimate objects. For example, there is Thamyris, 'breaking the gilded frame, breaking the structure of the strung lyre';[4] and Pandarus swearing harm against himself, if he failed to burn his bow 'after shattering it with his bare hands'.[5] And Xerxes even tried to brand and flog the sea, and sent a letter

---

1. *Chor. Adesp.* 20 Diehl, 1000 Page.
2. Love-sick swains hung garlands on the loved one's door, and serenaded outside it; on these and other practices, see *Dialogue on Love* 753B.
3. Callimachus, *Epigram* 43 Schneider, 42 Pfeiffer.
4. Sophocles F223 Nauck, F244 Radt. The story is in *Iliad* 2.594–600.
5. Homer, *Iliad* 5.216.

E    addressed to the mountain:[1] 'Great Athos high as heaven, don't
make huge, intractable rocks interfere with my actions, or else I
will tear you to pieces and hurl you into the sea.' Anger can
often be terrifying – but often ridiculous: that is why it is the
most hated and despised of the emotions; and it is useful to be
aware of both of these aspects.

[6] In my case, at any rate – I don't know whether or not this
is the correct way to go about it – I started my treatment as
follows: just as the Spartans tried to understand drunkenness by
watching their helots,[2] I tried to understand anger by watching
others. Hippocrates says that the severity of an illness is propor-
F    tionate to the degree to which the patient's features become
abnormal,[3] and the first thing I noticed was a similar proportion
between the degree of distraction by anger and the degree to
which appearance, complexion, gait and voice change. This impressed upon me a kind of image of the emotion, and I was very
upset to think that I might ever look so terrifying and unhinged to
my friends, wife and daughters[4] – not only fierce and unrecogniz-
able in appearance, but also speaking in as rough and harsh a tone
as I encountered in others of my acquaintance, when anger made
them incapable of preserving their usual nature, appearance, pleasant conversation and persuasiveness and courtesy in company.

456A    The orator Gaius Gracchus had a brusque personality and used
to speak rather too passionately, so he had one of those little
pipes made for himself which musicians use to guide their voices
gradually note by note in either direction. His slave used to hold
this and stand behind him while he was speaking, and sound a
moderate, gentle keynote which enabled Gracchus to revoke his
stridency and get rid of the harshness and anger of his tone. Just

1. See Herodotus 7.35 and 7.22–4. To prepare for his great invasion of Greece in
480 BC, the Persian king Xerxes bridged the Hellespont, but a storm wrecked
the first attempt, which led to his reaction. The passage around Mount Athos
was extremely treacherous for ships, so he dug a canal through the isthmus.
Herodotus has no mention of epistolary communication with the mountain.
2. The custom stuck in Plutarch's mind as a piece of practical ethics. He uses it
again in Customs of the Spartans 239A and in Life of Demetrius 1. The helots
were a serf population in Laconia and Messenia, subservient to the Spartans
and owned by the state.
3. Prognostic 2.
4. See p. 175 on the importance of this statement for dating the essay.

as the cowherd's 'wax-joined reed pipes in clear tones a sleep-inducing tune',[1] so Gracchus' slave mollified and allayed the orator's anger.[2]

If *I* had an ingenious attendant who was attuned to me, however, I would not be displeased if he employed a mirror during my outbursts of anger[3] – as is occasionally done, though for no useful purpose, for people who have just bathed – since to see oneself in an unnatural state, all discomposed, plays a not unimportant part in discrediting the emotion. Indeed, there is an amusing story that once when Athena was playing the pipes, a satyr told her off by saying, 'This expression doesn't suit you. Put down your pipes, take up your weapons and compose your cheeks.'[4] She paid no attention, however, but when she saw in a river how her face looked, she got upset and threw away the pipes.[5]

At least art is tasteful, and this distracts one's attention from the ugliness. (Marsyas apparently used a kind of halter and a mouthpiece to channel the force of his breath, and to rectify and conceal the irregularity of his features – 'gleaming gold joined the hair of one temple to the other and thongs, bound behind, he attached to his hard-working mouth'.)[6] Anger, on the other hand, not only disfigures the features by inflating and distending them, but also makes one's voice even more ugly and unpleasant, and 'moves the unmoved strings of the heart'.[7] I mean, when

1. Aeschylus, *Prometheus Bound* 574 f.
2. This fine anecdote recurs at length in *Life of the Gracchi* 2, where the skilled accompanist rightly makes the titles as Licinius.
3. The mirror theme recurs in Seneca, *De Ira* 2.36.1–3, but he attributes it to Q. Sextius, who was operating a philosophical school in Rome about the time of Augustus.
4. *TGF Adesp.* 381 Nauck.
5. The story of Athena and the pipes seems another commonplace in this theme. It recurs, for instance, in Ovid (*Ars Amatoria* 3.505 f.), where the context is also of facial distortions due to anger, and includes the mirror theme too.
6. The verses were attributed to Simonides by Tzetzes, *Chiliades* 1.372, but to Simmias of Rhodes (*c.* 300 BC) by Schneidewin (see J. Powell, *Collectanea Alexandrina* F3, p. 111). The reference is to a leather mouthpiece whereby the player could regulate the sound of his oboe(s), which were usually played in pairs. The supposed inventor, the satyr Marsyas, was flayed alive by Apollo after losing his musical challenge.
7. *TGF Adesp.* 361 Nauck, Kannicht and Snell. Plutarch liked the line: 43D, 501A, 505C, 657C.

the sea has been whipped up by winds and disgorges kelp and seaweed, people say that it is being purified; but the undisciplined, harsh and snide remarks which anger casts ashore from a mind in turmoil pollute primarily the speakers, and contaminate

D   them with the opprobrium of having always had these remarks inside them, bursting to get out, and of being exposed by their anger. That is why, as Plato says,[1] they pay the heaviest of penalties for the lightest of things – a word – since they give the impression of being antisocial, slanderous and malicious.

[7] So when I observe and notice all this, I end up committing to memory and reminding myself pretty constantly of the fact that although when feverish it is good to have a soft, smooth tongue, it is even better when angry. I mean, if the tongue of someone with a fever is unnatural, it is a bad sign, but it does not cause any further problems; but if the tongue of someone in a temper has become rough and offensive and inclined towards

E   abnormal language, then it manifests an insolence which causes an incurable breakdown of relationships and which betrays festering unsociability. Anger is worse than undiluted wine at producing undisciplined and disagreeable results: wine's results are blended with laughter, jokes and singing,* while anger's results are blended with bitter gall; and anyone who is silent while drinking is irritating and annoying to his companions, whereas there is nothing more dignified than silence while angry, as Sappho recommends: 'When anger takes over your heart, guard your babbling tongue.'[2]

[8] However, constant attention to people who have been trapped by anger affords more than these reflections: it allows

F   one to understand the nature of anger in other respects too, to see that it is not magnificent or manly, and that it has neither dignity nor grandeur. Nevertheless, most people mistake its turmoil for effectiveness, its menace for courage, its inflexibility for strength; and some people even call its callousness prowess, its

1. The phrase of Plato's which Plutarch recalls is most probably from *Laws* 717d1, but the passage and context at the back of his mind is probably *Laws* 935a. Such combinations of memory are not at all uncommon.
2. F27 Bergk, F158 Lobel-Page.

stubbornness energy and its asperity righteous indignation. But this is wrong, because the actions, behaviour and conduct it prompts betray its pettiness and weakness. It is not just that angry people viciously assault little children, treat women harshly and think they should punish dogs, horses and mules (as Ctesiphon the pancratiast[1] felt obliged to return his mule's kick);[2] it is also that the narrow intolerance of tyrants is obvious in their cruelty, and their state is betrayed by their behaviour, so that their bloodthirstiness resembles the bite of a snake which, when enraged and in agony, directs its extreme inflammation at anyone who has hurt it. When flesh is hit hard, a swelling occurs; likewise, the most infirm minds are most liable to pain, and consequently their anger is greater because their weakness is greater.[3]

457A

B

This is also why women are more irascible than men, and sick, old or unlucky people are more irascible than healthy, middle-aged or successful people. An avaricious person is very likely to get angry with his business manager, a glutton with his cook, a jealous man with his wife, a vain person when something bad has been said about him; but the worst of all are, as Pindar says, 'political men who court ambition too much: they stir up open grief'.[4] So it is from mental pain and suffering that anger arises, thanks above all to weakness; and whoever said[5] that anger is, as it were, the mind's sinews was wrong: it is the straining and spraining of a mind being unduly dislocated in the course of its defensive impulses.

C

[9] Anyway, observing these despicable cases was not pleasant, but simply necessary. But because I regard people who cope with fits of anger in a calm and composed manner as outstanding both to hear about and to witness, my starting-point is to despise

1. The pancration was a kind of vicious all-in wrestling.
2. And the dog's bite, Seneca scathingly suggests (De Ira 3.27.1).
3. The same image and assessment of the source of anger are used by Plutarch in a historical personalized context in Life of Coriolanus 15.4.
4. Pindar F210 Bergk, Maehler.
5. It was Plato, in Republic 411b. Philodemus, De Ira 31.24, attributed the phrase to Peripatetics, but Plutarch knew perfectly well that it came from Plato, and says so in On Moral Virtue 449F. He possibly omits Plato's name here out of deference, since he is disagreeing with him.

those who say, 'You wronged a man: should a man put up with this?',[1] and 'Tread him underfoot, tread on his neck, force him to the ground!',[2] and so on: these are provocative things to say, and some use them improperly to transpose anger from the women's quarters to the men's.[3] I think that manly courage is compatible with morality in all other respects, but incompatible only where gentleness is concerned, because gentleness is more self-contained.[4] It is possible for worse men to overcome better men, but to set up in one's mind a trophy of victory over anger (which Heraclitus claims makes 'a difficult opponent, since it purchases whatever it wants at the expense of the mind')[5] is a sign of great, overwhelming strength – a strength based on the faculties of rational judgement, which are the real sinews and muscles in the fight against the emotions.

That is why I constantly try to get hold of and read this kind of case, and not only when they are provided by philosophers (whom intelligent★ people regard as not being liable to gall), but even more when they are provided by kings and tyrants. For example, there is Antigonus' behaviour towards some of his soldiers who were cursing him near his tent, and didn't know he could hear them: 'Oh dear,' he said, poking his staff out of the tent and on to the ground, 'can't you go somewhere further away to criticize me?'[6]

Arcadion the Achaean[7] was always criticizing Philip and recommending escaping 'to a place whose inhabitants are ignorant of Philip'.[8] Then he happened to turn up in Macedonia, and Philip's

1. *TGF Adesp*. 382 Nauck, Kannicht and Snell.
2. *PLG* III, p. 694 Bergk.
3. The imagery of anger lodged in the men's rooms rather than the women's rooms in a house recurs in Ps.-Longinus, *De Sublimitate* 32.5, who is recalling Plato, *Timaeus* 69e.
4. Compare Plato, *Republic* 410d ff.
5. Heraclitus F85 DK. Plutarch uses it again in *Life of Coriolanus* 22.
6. This had become a stock anecdote in the context (Seneca, *De Ira* 3.22.2). Editors argue whether the reference is to the first, second or third King Antigonus. For the purposes of the anecdote, it does not matter in the slightest.
7. Another version of this fine story turns up in Athenaeus 249c–d.
8. A witty adaptation of Homer, *Odyssey* 11.122. The Homeric line finished with 'the sea' instead of 'Philip'.

friends thought that he should punish him and not let him get away with it. Philip dealt with him kindly, however, and sent him presents and gifts; later he told his people to find out what report Arcadion had given to the Greeks. They all vouched for    F
the fact that he had become an outstanding advocate of Philip, and Philip remarked, 'So I am a better doctor than you!' And once in Olympia some slander was being spread about him, and some people suggested that the Greeks ought to be made to suffer, since they were criticizing him despite his good treatment of them. 'What will they do, then,' he asked, 'if I treat them badly?'[1]

Also fine was Pisistratus' behaviour towards Thrasybulus, Porsenna's towards Mucius[2] and Magas' towards Philemon. Philemon    458A
made fun of Magas in one of his comedies, publicly in the theatre, with the lines: 'Here's a letter from the king for you to read, Magas . . . Poor Magas, what a pity you can't read!'[3] Later, Philemon was forced into Paraetonium by a storm, and fell into Magas' hands. Magas told a soldier to unsheathe a sword and simply touch Philemon on the neck with it, and then politely leave; and he sent him dice and a ball, as if he were a witless child, and then let him go.

Ptolemy was once mocking a scholar for his ignorance and asked him who Peleus' father was; the scholar replied that he would tell him, if Ptolemy told him first who Lagus' father was.[4] His remark was a mocking reference to the king's low-    B

1. Plutarch used this *mot* twice elsewhere: 143F, 179A.
2. The anecdotes now tumble out of Plutarch's notebooks so fast that there is no time even for elucidation. Thrasybulus kissed Pisistratus' daughter. The dictator's scandalized wife wanted revenge, but Pisistratus replied, 'If we hate those who love us, what shall we do to those who hate us?' (*Sayings of Kings and Commanders* 189C). The Roman youth Mucius killed the wrong man while attempting to assassinate the Etruscan King Porsenna. On being arrested, to show he was impervious to whatever the angry king could do to him, he held his right hand in fire until it was incinerated. Porsenna was so impressed that he let Mucius (henceforth Scaevola or Left-handed) go and made peace with the Romans. There are various versions of this famous tale (*Life of Publicola* 17), but the one most apposite for Plutarch's point is in Livy 2.12.
3. Philemon F144 Kock, F132 Kassel, Austin; Magas' response recurs in *On Moral Virtue* 449E–F.
4. A superficial academic conundrum of Homeric scholarship relating to Achilles' father Peleus is countered by a scarcely veiled personal insult concerning

class birth, and everyone was offended, feeling that the remark jarred and was uncalled for. Ptolemy said, 'If a king can't take mockery, then he shouldn't mock either.'

Alexander had been more harsh than usual in the affairs involving Callisthenes and Clitus.[1] So when Porus was taken prisoner by Alexander he entreated him to deal with him as a king should. 'Is that all?' asked Alexander. '"As a king should" covers everything,' replied Porus.[2] That is why 'the benevolent' is an epithet of the king of the gods (though the Athenians call him C 'the tempestuous', I think): punishment is the work of the Furies and demigods – it is not divine and Olympian.

[10] When Philip had levelled Olynthus, someone remarked,[3] 'But rebuilding an equivalent city will be beyond *his* capabilities'; likewise one might say to anger, 'You're good at demolition and destruction and ruination, but construction, preservation, mercy and patience require gentleness, forgiveness and moderation of passion: they require Camillus, Metellus, Aristides and Socrates, whereas plaguing and biting are what ants and mice do.'*

Moreover, when I also consider vindictiveness, I find that D anger's version of it is ineffective, by and large: it exhausts itself in lip-chewing,[4] tooth-grinding, empty assaults and curses consisting of mindless threats, and the result is as ridiculous as when children in a race fall down before they reach the goal for which they are striving, because they are not in control of themselves. It follows that the Rhodian put it nicely when he said to the Roman general's servant, who was yelling and coming on strong, 'I'm not bothered by your words, but by his silence.' And once

---

Ptolemy's father. The latter was an obscure Macedonian, Lagus, but persistent rumour had it that Ptolemy's mother was a mistress of King Philip II, and that he was a royal bastard. Which would Ptolemy prefer?

1. Common examples again. Clitus is in Seneca, *De Ira* 3.17.1, and Plutarch's *Life of Alexander* 51 and *On Moral Virtue* 449E (where Magas occurred, suggesting a notebook grouping); Callisthenes is in *Life of Alexander* 55.

2. The Porus story was too good to waste: 181E, 332E, *Life of Alexander* 60.

3. King Agesipolus of Sparta, according to *Sayings of Spartans* 215B; the story is used again in *On Listening* 40E.

4. This lip-chewing is also in Seneca (*De Ira* 1.19.3), who in turn refers it to Hieronymus' monograph *On Avoidance of Anger* (F21 Wehrli).

Sophocles has Neoptolemus and Eurypylus equipped with weapons, he says, 'Without making boasts, without hurling insults, the two of them smashed into the massed bronze weaponry.'[1]

The point is that although some savages treat their weapons with poison, courage has no need of bitter gall, since it is imbued with reason, whereas anger and rage are brittle and unsound. At any rate, the Spartans play pipes to quell anger in their men while they are fighting,[2] and before a battle they sacrifice to the Muses to ensure the stable presence of reason; and if they rout the enemy, they do not set off in pursuit, but revoke their passion, which is like those handy-sized knives in that it is retractable and manageable. Anger, however, has caused many, many people to die before exacting their revenge: Cyrus and Pelopidas of Thebes are just two examples.[3] Agathocles, on the other hand, good-temperedly put up with insults being hurled at him by the inhabitants of a city he was besieging, and when one of them asked, 'Potter, where will you get the money to pay your mercenaries?', he replied with a laugh, 'Here, if I raze your city!' Once some people mocked Antigonus for his deformity from their city walls, and he said to them, 'But I thought I was good-looking!' But when he had taken the city, he sold the mockers into slavery, and swore that he would keep in touch with their masters, to see if they ever insulted him again.[4]

I also notice that anger makes lawyers and orators commit great mistakes; and Aristotle records[5] that the friends of Satyrus

1. *TGF* Sophocles F768 Nauck, F210.9 Radt.
2. This novel idea would astonish the pipers of the Scottish Highland regiments. A more realistic view is conveyed in *Life of Lycurgus* 22.3 and in *Customs of the Spartans* 238B.
3. Cyrus the Younger, by madly rushing at the Persian King Artaxerxes in the battle of Cunaxa in 401 BC (Xenophon, *Anabasis* 1.8.26 f.); Pelopidas at the battle of Cynoscephalae (364 BC), by trying to pursue his enemy Alexander single-handed (*Life of Pelopidas* 32).
4. In the collection *Sayings of Kings and Commanders* 176F, this last remark is attributed to Agathocles and added to the Agathocles anecdote given above. Seneca (*De Ira* 3.22.4 f.) has his own more elaborate version of the Antigonus story. Agathocles, tyrant of Syracuse in the latter part of the fourth century BC, was reputedly the son of a potter. Antigonus, one of Alexander's generals, known as One-eyed or The Blind, was also supposed to be small and pugnosed.
5. Ps.-Aristotle, *Problemata* 875a34 ff.

459A  of Samos blocked his ears with wax when he was in court, in case he messed things up by getting angry at being abused by his opponents. As for ourselves, don't we often bungle the punishment of a slave who is misbehaving, because they get frightened at our threats and at what we are saying, and run away? Nurses say to children, 'Stop crying and you can have it', and we could usefully address anger in the same way: 'Simmer down, shut up, slow down, and you will improve the chances and the probability of getting what you want.' I mean, if a father sees his child trying to cut or carve something with a knife, he takes the knife himself and does it; and if the rational mind takes over from anger the job of retribution, then the person who deserves it receives the punishment, and the rational mind remains safe and

B  sound and valuable, instead of being punished itself, which is what often happens thanks to anger.[1]

[11] All the emotions need schooling, to tame (so to speak)[2] and discipline by training the part of oneself that is irrational and recalcitrant; but one's servants provide a better training ground for anger than for any other emotion. The point is that our dealings with servants contain no element of envy, fear or rivalry, and constantly getting angry with them causes a lot of conflict and error and, because we have power over them, our anger puts us on a slippery downward slope, as it were, with no one to stand in our way and restrain us. I mean, absolute control cannot fail to be liable to error when emotion is involved: the only solution is to use considerable restraint to restrict your power

C  and to resist the frequent complaints of wife and friends, as they accuse you of being weak and feeble.

I myself used to get very needled at my servants because of these accusations, and used to believe that by not punishing them I was spoiling them. But eventually I realized, first, that it is better to make them worse by patiently tolerating their badness than to concentrate on correcting others while allowing harshness and anger to corrupt oneself. And second, I saw plenty of cases

---

1. Similar sentiments had been expressed much earlier by Xenophon musing on the fate of Teleutias (*Hellenica* 5.3.7).

2. Plutarch apologizes not only for the metaphor, but also for the poetic verb he uses.

where, precisely because they were not being punished, they were ashamed of being bad, let forbearance rather than retaliation initiate change in them and, I assure you, more enthusiastically served those who quietly sanctioned their actions than those who D used flogging and branding: all this convinced me that reason is more authoritative than passion. The poet got it wrong when he said, 'Where there is fear, respect follows too.'[1] It is actually the other way round: respect engenders in people the kind of fear which entails self-restraint, while non-stop, relentless flogging does not instil remorse for past misdeeds, but rather the intention to get away with it in the future.

In the third place, I constantly remind myself and bear in mind that when we were learning archery, we were not told not to shoot, but not to miss;[2] likewise, learning how to punish in a well-timed, moderate, beneficial and appropriate way will not stop one punishing altogether. So I try to quell my anger above all by not denying the defendants the right to justify themselves, E but by listening to what they have to say. This helps because time checks emotion and gives it space to dissolve,[3] and also because rationality finds what method of punishment is appropriate, and how much is fitting. Moreover, the person who gets his just deserts has no excuse left for resisting correction, given that he is being punished not in anger, but because he has been convicted; and the most shameful factor is excluded, which is when the servant has a more just case than the master.

After Alexander's death, Phocion tried to stop the Athenians revolting too soon, or too readily trusting the news, by saying, 'If he is dead today, citizens of Athens, then he will be dead F tomorrow and the day after tomorrow.'[4] In the same way, in my opinion, anyone being driven headlong towards retaliation

1. The Homeric *Cypria* F20. Plato too had disagreed with the poet's sentiment (*Euthyphro* 12a ff.). In *Life of Cleomenes* 30, Plutarch approves of the line: such tags are not offered for detached elucidation, but are tools of context.
2. An archery model was used by the Stoics to explain their interpretation of the moral end (Cicero, *De Finibus* 3.22).
3. The philosophical importance of time diminishing emotion was argued by the Stoic Posidonius (F165 EK).
4. Also used, naturally, in *Life of Phocion* 22, and in the collection *Sayings of Kings and Commanders* 188D.

by anger ought to whisper to himself, 'If he is guilty today, then he will be guilty tomorrow and the day after tomorrow; and no harm will be done if he gets his just deserts later rather than sooner, but if he goes through it quickly, there will always – it has often happened in the past – be uncertainty as to his guilt.' I mean, which of us is horrible enough to flog and punish a slave for having five or ten days ago burned a savoury or knocked over a table or been rather slow to obey an order? But these are the things which make us upset and harsh and pitiless when they have just occurred and when they are still in the recent past. Solid objects seem bigger when it is misty,[1] and the same happens to things when one is angry.

Our first reaction, therefore, should be to remember facts like this; and if in the clear, steady light of reason the deed still seems bad, when there is no doubt that we are free of the emotion, then we should attend to it: we should not at this later date neglect or abandon the punishment, as we do food when we have lost our appetite. Nothing is so conducive to doling out punishment when anger is upon us as having failed to punish, having let the issue drop, when anger had left us: the experience is identical to that of lazy rowers, who lie at anchor when the weather is calm and then run the risks of a voyage when the wind is up. We too accuse rationality of being weak and feeble when it comes to punishment, and so rush on recklessly before the wind of anger when it comes.

The point is that it is proper for someone who is hungry to engage in eating, but it is proper for someone who is neither hungry nor thirsty for it to engage in retribution. He should not need anger in order to punish, as he might need a savoury, but it is essential that he waits until he has greatly distanced himself from the appetite for punishment and introduced rationality instead. Aristotle records that in his time servants were flogged in Tyrrhenia to the accompaniment of pipes;[2] but we should not follow suit and, for the sake of personal pleasure, be driven by a desire for satisfaction, as it were, to gorge ourselves with retalia-

460A

B

C

---

1. This was a scientific theory expounded by Posidonius (Frs. 114, 119 EK).
2. *Customs of the Tyrrhenians* F705, 2 Gigon; F608 Rose.

tion – to enjoy punishing (which is to behave like an animal), and then regret it later (which is to behave like a woman).[1] Rather, we should wait until there is no trace of either pleasure or distress, and rationality is present, and then take reprisal without being motivated at all by anger.

[12] Anyway, as may be obvious, this is not a cure for anger, but a means of postponing and protecting oneself against making mistakes while angry (despite the fact that, as Hieronymus says,[2] although a swollen spleen is a symptom of fever, reducing the swelling alleviates the fever). But when I was trying to see how anger actually starts, I noticed that although different factors trigger its onset in different people, there is almost always present a belief that they are being slighted and ignored.[3] It follows that we should help people who are trying to evade anger by putting the greatest possible distance between any given action and contempt or arrogance, by attributing the action instead to ignorance or necessity or emotion or accident. As Sophocles says, 'My lord, unfortunate people find that even their innate intelligence has no stability, but deserts them.'[4] And Agamemnon attributes his theft of Briseis to his being possessed, but still says, 'I want to make amends and give you vast gifts of recompense.'[5]

The point of this quote is that no one can make an appeal to someone if he despises him; and by being demonstrably humble, the offender gets rid of any impression of contempt. But anyone who is angry should not just wait for this to happen, but should of his own accord cling to what Diogenes said: 'Those people are laughing at you, Diogenes,' someone said; 'But I don't feel laughed at,' he replied.[6] So anyone who is angry should not

---

1. Plutarch returned to this theme, and indeed in much the same language (551A), in relation to delayed divine retribution (*On God's Slowness to Punish* 550E ff.); Seneca's version is in *De Ira* 1.17–18.
2. F23 Wehrli.
3. Already noted astutely by Aristotle, *Rhetoric* 1380a8 ff.
4. Sophocles, *Antigone* 563 f. When Plutarch used this quotation again at the beginning of *Life of Phocion*, precisely the same variations from our text of *Antigone* are reproduced. So Plutarch must have entered it into his notebooks in this form.
5. Homer, *Iliad* 19.138.
6. Again in *Life of Fabius Maximus* 10. But good anecdotes like this often change clothes in the telling: Seneca (*De Ira* 2.32.2) uses a very similar one for Cato.

think that he is being despised, but should rather despise the
other person, on the grounds that his offence was caused by
weakness, impetuosity, laziness, meanness, old age or youth.

However, our dealings with servants and friends must be completely free of this impression, since contempt for us as powerless
F  or as ineffective plays no part in their attitude towards us: our
servants regard us as good, on the assumption that we are fair to
them, and our friends regard us as their friends, on the assumption
that we are affectionate towards them. In fact, however, it is not
only wife, servants and friends that we behave harshly towards
because we think we are despised by them, but the same idea
often brings us into angry conflict with innkeepers, sailors and
drunken muleteers, and makes us get cross with dogs for barking
461A  at us and donkeys for bumping into us. We are just like the man
who wanted to hit a donkey driver, and then when he shouted,
'I'm an Athenian citizen', he said to the donkey, 'Well, *you*
aren't', and began hitting it and raining blows on it.

[13] Now, those continuous, constant feelings of anger which
gradually gather in the mind like a swarm of bees or wasps
are engendered in us above all by self-regard and discontent,
coupled with a luxurious and enervating way of life. It follows
that there is no more important means of promoting kind behaviour towards one's servants, wife and friends than being easy to
please and having a simple lifestyle, as a result of the ability to
adapt oneself to immediate circumstances and not to need a lot
B  of extras. On the other hand, 'anyone whose discontent makes
him critical, if his food is over-baked or over-boiled, or under-
or over- or medium-seasoned',[1] and who can't have a drink
without ice, or eat shop-bought bread, or take a morsel of food
served on plain or earthenware dishes, or sleep on a mattress
unless it billows like the sea in a deep swell, and who flogs and
beats his table servants, forcing them to hurry, making them
rush about, create a hubbub and work up a sweat as if they were
bringing poultices for boils – anyone like this is enslaved to a
feeble, nit-picking, complaining way of life, and fails to realize
that he is creating for his temper the kind of raw and oozing

1. *CAF Adesp*. F343 Kock, Edmonds.

condition which a chronic cough or* constantly bumping into   C
things causes. So we must train the body, by means of frugality,
to be self-sufficient and hence easily pleased, because people who
want little are seldom disappointed.

Food should be our starting-point: it is no great hardship
quietly to make do with what is to hand, and not worry* and
fuss about a considerable proportion of our food, which imposes
upon ourselves and our companions the most disagreeable flavour-
ing of all − anger. 'It is impossible to conceive of a less pleasant
meal'[1] than when servants are beaten and wife is cursed because
something is burned or smoky or has insufficient salt, or because
the bread is too cold.[2] Arcesilaus once had some visitors staying   D
and he invited friends over to dinner, but when the meal was
served, there was no bread, because the servants had forgotten to
buy any − which would make anyone scream loud enough to
crack the walls! But Arcesilaus smiled and said, 'It's a good thing
that intellectuals like a drinks party!'

Socrates once brought Euthydemus home from the wrestling-
school, and Xanthippe laid into them angrily, hurled insults at
them and eventually overturned the table.[3] Euthydemus was
very upset, and got up to go, but Socrates said, 'When we were
at your house the other day, a hen flew in and did exactly the
same, but we didn't get cross, did we?'

We should welcome friends gladly, with smiles and affection −   E
without scowling and without instilling fear and trepidation in
our servants. And we should also condition ourselves to be happy
to use any utensils, and not to have preferences: some people
(including Marius, we hear), having once chosen one particular
goblet or cup, refuse to drink out of any other, even when they
have plenty available; others are the same way about oil-flasks
and strigils, and love one set above all others; and then, when

1. Homer, *Odyssey* 20.392, of the feast of death which Odysseus prepares for the
   suitors of his wife.
2. Cf. Seneca, *De Ira* 2.25.1. Hot bread was a test of freshness, apparently: Ps.-
   Aristotle, *Problemata* 927a27.
3. Not all Greek wives were doormats, it seems. Plutarch tells a similar story of
   Pittacus' wife in *On Contentment* 471B. But perhaps philosophers' wives had
   more to put up with.

any of these special things gets broken or lost, they can hardly bear it and they resort to punishment. So anyone whose weakness is anger should get rid of rare and unusual things like cups, rings and precious stones, since their loss is more unsettling than the loss of common, everyday things. That is why, when Nero had an amazingly beautiful and lavish octagonal tent made, Seneca said, 'You are a self-convicted pauper, because this tent is irreplaceable if lost.' And in fact the tent *was* lost, as it happened, when its ship went down; but Nero remembered what Seneca had said, and did not get too upset.

Being unfussy about mundane things makes one unfussy and gentle with one's servants; and if one is gentle with one's servants, then obviously one will also be gentle with one's friends and dependants. It is noticeable that the first thing slaves try to find out about their new owner, after they have been bought, is not whether he is liable to superstition or envy, but whether he has a temper. In fact, it is generally true that where anger is present, husbands cannot tolerate their wives' impassivity, or wives their husbands' passion, or friends one another's familiarity. So when anger is present, neither marriage nor friendship is endurable; but when anger is absent, even drunkenness is no burden. Dionysus' wand provides punishment enough for anyone who gets drunk,[1] unless anger intrudes and imbues the wine with the god of cruelty and madness, rather than of ecstasy and dance.[2] Anticyra[3] cures straightforward insanity, but the combination of madness and anger is the stuff of tragedy and myth.

[14] We should eliminate anger from our lighter moments, because it imposes enmity on affability; from our discussions, because it turns love of debating into love of disputing; from our

---

1. *Narthēx* was a word for the thyrsus or sacred wand of Dionysus, which bore his power; but it was also the Greek for a schoolmaster's cane (Xenophon, *Cyropaedia* 2.3.19). So if you abused the wine god's gifts and got drunk, his cane in the form of a hangover would punish you. In fact, in an inscription setting out the rules for a Dionysiac society in Athens of the second century AD (the Iobacchi, *SIG* 1109.137 ff.), the *narthēx* is 'applied' to anyone who misbehaves himself, and he is thrown out of the banquet.

2. All these terms were cult epithets of Dionysus.

3. A Phocian town on the Corinthian Gulf celebrated for the production and preparation of the best hellebore in Greece, which was believed to be the chief remedy for madness.

decision-making, because it tinges authority with arrogance; when we are teaching, because it instils lack of confidence and a distaste for rationality; when we are doing well, because it promotes envy; when we are doing badly, because it deters sympathy by making people fight irritably with anyone commiserating with them. Priam is an example of this, with his 'Go away, you vile wretches! Haven't you got problems of your own? Why have you come to bother me?'[1]

Being easy to please, on the other hand, is either a help or an embellishment or a delight, and its gentleness overcomes anger and discontent of all kinds. Consider Euclides,[2] for instance: when his brother ended an argument by saying, 'I'll get my own back on you, if it's the last thing I do', Euclides replied, 'I'll win you over, if it's the last thing *I* do', and immediately made him alter course and change his mind. And Polemon was once being cursed by a man who was fond of precious stones and obsessed with costly rings; Polemon did not respond at all, but began to study one of the man's rings closely. So the man felt pleased and said, 'You'll get a far better impression of it, Polemon, if you examine it in sunlight rather than here.'

Once Aristippus was angry with Aeschines, and someone asked, 'What's happened to Aeschines' and your friendship, Aristippus?' He replied, 'It's sleeping, but I'll wake it up.' He went to Aeschines and said, 'Do you think there's absolutely no chance for me, no hope at all? Is that why you don't tell me off?' And Aeschines' response was: 'Given that you're inherently better than me in all respects, it's not at all surprising that you were the first to see what to do.'

It has been said that 'A new-born child, stroking a bristle-maned boar with his young hand, may – and so may a woman – bring him down more easily than any wrestler.'[3] We, however, domesticate and tame wild creatures, and carry wolf and lion cubs around in our arms, but then under the influence of anger

---

1. Homer, *Iliad* 24.239 f. The king of Troy, raging with grief at the death of his son Hector, drives off would-be sympathizers.
2. We know from *On Brotherly Love* 489D that this is Euclid of Megara, the follower of Socrates, not the famous mathematician.
3. *TGF Adesp.* F383 Nauck, Kannicht and Snell.

we reject children, friends and acquaintances; and we use our anger like a wild beast to assault our servants and fellow citizens, and misguidedly gloss over it as 'righteous indignation'. There is no difference, in my opinion, between this and calling other mental affections and afflictions 'foresight' or 'independence' or 'respect': it cannot free us from any of them.[1]

[15] Now, Zeno used to say[2] that seed is a compound, a mixture of extracts from all the faculties which make up a person's nature; and analogously, anger seems to be a kind of conglomerate of emotional seeds. It contains elements extracted from pain and pleasure and arrogance; it has the gloating pleasure of spite, and also gets its method of grappling from spite,* in the sense that the avoidance of its own suffering is not the purpose of its efforts, but it accepts harm to itself while destroying the other person; and one of its ingredients is the form of desire which is the most disagreeable of all, the longing to hurt someone else. When we approach reprobates' houses, we hear a pipe-girl playing at dawn and the sights that greet our eyes are, to quote, 'sediment of wine and shreds of garlands'[3] and inebriated servants at the door; but the fact that the longing to hurt others is an aspect of anger explains why you will see the manifest signs of cruel and irascible people on the faces and in the identification tattoos and chains of their servants; and 'wailing is the only constant refrain to arise in the house'[4] of an angry man – the wailing of estate-managers being flogged and serving-women having their arms twisted inside the house; and the consequence of all this is that anger is pitiful to anyone who can see that its desires and its pleasures involve pain.[5]

[16] Despite what has been said, anyone who is commonly susceptible to anger because of genuine righteous indignation must rid himself of the excessive, unmitigated part of his anger, along with his overconfidence in the people he comes across.[6]

1. See p. 124, n. 2, on *pathos* meaning both 'passion' and 'disease'.
2. *SVF* 1.128.
3. The origin of this quotation is unknown.
4. Sophocles F852 Radt; *TGF Adesp.* 387 Nauck.
5. A view that goes back to Plato, *Philebus* 31b–50d.
6. How misanthropy arises according to Plato, *Phaedo* 89d.

This overconfidence is one of the chief causes of the aggravation of anger, which is what happens when someone assumed to be good turns out to be bad, or when a supposed friend gets cross or critical. In my own case, I'm sure you know how much I am    C
naturally inclined towards thinking well of people and trusting them. It is like when you take a step, but there is nothing there to tread on: the more I commit myself to being friendly, the more I go wrong and get hurt by my mistakes. I might well not be able at this late stage to lessen this excessive susceptibility to and enthusiasm for friendship; but I can use Plato's words of warning to bridle my overconfidence. Plato says that his praise for the mathematician Helicon is couched the way it is because Helicon is a member of an inherently inconstant species;[1] and he claims to be right to be wary of people brought up in his city, because since they are human and the offspring of humans,[2] they    D
might at any time reveal the weakness inherent in their nature.

However, Sophocles' assertion that 'Most aspects of humanity will be found on investigation to be contemptible'[3] seems excessively harsh and restrictive. Still, the pessimistic, carping tone of this judgement does make us less liable to anger and its consequent disruptiveness; I mean, it is what is unexpected and unforeseen that throws us.[4] We should (as Panaetius said at one point) make use of the attitude summed up in Anaxagoras' dictum: when his son died, he said, 'I knew that I had fathered a mortal.'[5] Likewise, whenever we get irritated by someone's mistakes, we should    E

1. Plato, *Thirteenth Letter* 360c. Plutarch makes use of this tag again in *On Contentment* 474E, and in *On Compliancy* 533B–C, in such a way that it is clear that he had read the *Letter* and believed it to be by Plato, although he tends to quote from memory.
2. The phrase comes from Plato, *Laws* 853c. The city is the ideal city he is framing in that dialogue.
3. *TGF* Sophocles F769 Nauck, F853 Radt.
4. So too Seneca, *De Ira* 2.31.1. But it was an assumption behind much of Hellenistic philosophy, which accordingly stressed habituation and training to blunt and anticipate the unexpected.
5. Perhaps the Stoic Panaetius (F115 van Straaten) was the first to spotlight this *mot* of Anaxagoras (A33 DK). Posidonius (F165.33 EK) took it up, Cicero uses it twice in *Tusculanae Disputationes* (3.30 and 3.58), and by the time of Valerius Maximus (V.10.ext.1) it was in the quiver of every rhetorician and philosopher. Plutarch produced it again in *On Contentment* 474D (and cf. Ps.-Plutarch, *Consolation to Apollonius* 118D).

comment, 'I knew that the slave I bought was unintelligent', or 'I knew that my friend was not flawless', or 'I knew that my wife was a woman.'[1] And if one also keeps reiterating Plato's saying, 'Am I not like that too?',[2] he will turn his thinking inward instead of outward, and will interrupt his complaining with caution, and will consequently not employ a great deal of righteous indignation towards others when he sees that he himself requires a lot of forbearance. But as it is, every one of us gets angry and lashes out, and sounds like Aristides and Cato: 'Stop stealing!', 'Don't tell lies!', 'Why are you slacking?' And the most despicable thing of all is that we angrily reprimand others for being angry, and we furiously punish others for mistakes made because they were infuriated: we do not behave like doctors who 'use bitter medicine to flush out bitter bile',[3] but we aggravate and exacerbate the condition.

At the same time as bearing in mind these considerations, I also try to cut back a bit on my nosiness. I mean, knowing every single detail about everything, investigating and eliciting a slave's every occupation, a friend's every action, a son's every pastime, a wife's every whisper – this leads to many outbursts of anger, one after another every day, and these in turn add up to habitual discontent and surliness. Although Euripides is right to say that it is when things get out of hand that God 'intervenes, while leaving minor matters to chance',[4] I still think that a sensible person ought to entrust nothing to chance, and ought to ignore nothing: he should trust and make use of his wife for some matters, his servants for others and his friends for others (just as a ruler trusts and makes use of overseers, accountants and managers), while being himself, by virtue of his rationality, in charge of the most far-reaching and important matters. For just as tiny writing irritates the eyes, so the extra strain of trivial matters

---

1. The Greek is very neat, since 'wife' and 'woman' are the same word in Greek.
2. This must come from the oral anecdotal tradition, since it is not in our Plato. It caught Plutarch's fancy: 40D, 88E, 129D. See also p. 33, n. 2.
3. *TGF* Sophocles F770 Nauck, F854 Radt. When Plutarch quoted this line again in *On Contentment* 468B, his memory produced a different order of words.
4. *TGF* Euripides F974 Nauck. It is trotted out again in *Advice on Public Life* 811D.

chafes and unsettles one's temper, and it acquires a habit which is detrimental when more important matters are at stake.

All in all, therefore, I began to think that Empedocles' dictum 'Observe a fast from evil'[1] is crucial and inspired; furthermore, not just because they are agreeable, but also because they are not irrelevant to the practice of philosophy, I began to commend those familiar pacts, pledged with devotion, such as to honour God with one's self-control, by keeping oneself for a year untainted by sex and alcohol; or again to refrain from lying for a prescribed period of time, by paying attention to oneself to make sure that one always tells the truth, in both unguarded and serious moments.

And then I compared my own pledge with these, and found it just as pleasing to God and just as sacred. My pledge was to begin by spending a few days doing the equivalent of going without drinking and alcohol – avoiding anger, and doing so as if I were pouring ritual libations of water and of honey, but not of wine;[2] and then to spend a month, two months, doing this . . . In this way, by experimenting on myself, the period of time gradually got longer and I progressed towards increased tolerance, by using self-control to pay attention to myself and to keep myself composed and imperturbable – maintaining a holy silence – and to remain untainted by pernicious speech, unnatural actions and emotion. Emotion leads, for the sake of a form of pleasure which is small in quantity and disagreeable in quality, to enormous mental confusion and the most despicable remorse. And this, I think, is why (with God's assistance too) my experience tends to clarify the meaning of the well-known view that this composure, calmness and charity is nowhere near as kind and considerate and inoffensive to those who come across it as it is to those who possess it.

1. Empedocles F144 DK.
2. The normal Greek libation was of wine. Fundanus' offering to the gods will not be wine (anger), but the wine-free honey (sweetness of relationship) such as was offered to the Eumenides (Aeschylus, *Eumenides* 107); or rather, as Plutarch suggested in *Banquet of the Seven Sages* 156D, a wineless libation is suitable for amicable learned discussion.

# ON CONTENTMENT

## INTRODUCTION

One of the more difficult problems concerning Plutarch's essay *On Contentment* is the translation of the title. The Greek word *euthymia* means something like 'good spirits', 'cheerfulness'. It is translated into Latin by both Cicero (*De Finibus* 5.23) and Seneca as *tranquillitas animi*, which seems more like peace of mind or contentment. But Seneca (*De Tranquillitate Animi* 2.3) enlarges on the force of his translation thus: 'how the mind may always pursue a uniform and unimpeded course, at peace with itself, viewing its circumstances with a light heart and a joy that is unbroken, so that it stays steady and calm, never raised or depressed'. This indicates a positive quality of mental reaction, and does not spring from a negative description like the comparable but much more popular term in Hellenistic moral philosophy, *ataraxia*, lack of mental disturbance or turmoil. The Greek verb *euthymein* in Aristotle's *Rhetoric* (1379b18) denotes being cheerful in misfortune, and the opposite (*dysthymia*) means despondency and, in medical contexts (Hippocrates, *Traditional Medicine* 10), depression. The term was established in philosophical jargon by a famous fifth-century-BC monograph, still available in Plutarch's day, from the philosopher Democritus, who elevated the state of mind implied to a principal aim for moral behaviour. Surviving fragments of this work also stress the cheerfulness of contentment, which all later generations were to regard as the main characteristic of Democritus. Thus Seneca in his essay *De Tranquillitate Animi* (15) says that we must not descend into depression and a hatred of the whole human race but rather, like Democritus, we should be able to laugh at its follies.

Partly no doubt through Democritus, the tranquillity of cheerful contentment came to prominence in Epicureanism as a sort of pleasure, or rather the pleasant state of mind of the happy person.[1] In early Stoic philosophy, on the other hand, the concept occupied a minor and insignificant role, as a subdivision of the species 'joy' (*chara*, in Latin *gaudium*) of what the Stoics called 'good emotions' (*eupatheiai*), those experienced by the good man, and of course very different from the distorting passions which the Stoics wished to eliminate. But Panaetius, the leading Stoic of the later second century BC, wrote a monograph *On Contentment* (Diogenes Laertius 9.20), thereby rekindling interest in the subject in the first centuries BC and AD.

Because of this history, determined attempts have been made to derive Plutarch's essay either from an Epicurean source[2] or from a Stoic one, and in particular from Panaetius himself.[3] This won't do. In the first place we know nothing about Panaetius' monograph, except that he wrote it. And Plutarch never mentions it. Nor does Seneca for that matter. Secondly, the topic had become a commonplace for all the Schools of philosophy. Cicero in the fifth book of *De Finibus*, dealing with contemporary Platonic and Peripatetic views, simply equates contentment with the happy life itself without explanation (5.23). And the Cynic diatribe, or popular sermon, and the tendency to popular moralizing in general also had their leavening effect. Lastly, Plutarch's essay at some points favours attitudes congruent with Epicureanism but opposed to Stoicism, at others Stoic-coloured views alien to Epicureans. As usual, Plutarch has taken from his palette all the colours available to him, mixed them up and painted his own picture.

The introduction (§1) sets the contextual form, as a letter responding to Paccius, a Roman highly connected in public affairs and with a reputation as a political speaker. He had asked for some observations on contentment. Plutarch apologizes for a hasty compilation rushed to catch the post with their friend Eros, resulting in a practical guide culled from his own notebooks, but without the polish of literary form. The essay is certainly intended as practical moral counselling, but the denial of literary embellishment is specious. The essay is in fact carefully structured, and justly admired for its literary imagery and effects. For example, already in the opening chapter there are mingled linguistic echoes:

in a sentence at 465B the words describing the emotional and irrational part of the mind recall a favourite phrase of the Stoic Posidonius (Frs.31, 168 EK; but it also has Platonic notes), as does the verb applied to it of 'racing away' (Posidonius' disobedient horse, Frs.166, 31 EK), while on the other hand, what it runs away from, namely 'what is actually there' rings strongly of Democritus' *On Contentment* (F191 DK). And such subtle linguistic flavourings are typical of the whole essay. Again, at the end of the section Plutarch conjures up an animal metaphor for the passionate irrational element of the mind. The metaphor in general was widespread: for example, Plato's horses in *Phaedrus* 246a ff.; the 'bestial' part in *Republic* 571c, 591b; Posidonius' 'animal' aspect of mind (F161.5 EK). But Plutarch stamps his own coin, of savage Greek sheepdogs responsive and controlled only by the voice of their master (i.e. reason). They can still be met on the hills of modern Greece, and Plutarch, the Boeotian countryman, was no doubt familiar with this more homely and vivid example.

Section 2 is also highly characteristic. The theme is that contentment does not require inactivity and withdrawal from affairs, and it is plucked out first not only because Plutarch himself patently believed this, as evidenced from his own life, but also because he is addressing Paccius, a public figure, and so personalizing his message to the recipient. The presentation is choice. He starts with a text from the beginning of Democritus' *On Contentment*, although he does not name it and chooses to misunderstand it. In a literal translation, Democritus' assertion is that 'A man aiming at contentment should not "do many things" in private or public affairs.' Plutarch takes this to advocate inactivity, and spends the rest of the section contesting it. Inertia and laziness are no remedy for either physical or mental malaise. Also, it is not true that anyone inactive is content; if it were so, women would be less distressed and discontented than men! Famous literary examples fix mental images: the pining, retired Laertes reduced to the dower cottage in Ithaca; sulking, fretting Achilles withdrawn from the battle at Troy. Even Epicurus[4] permits limited engagement, although in Plutarch's view for the wrong reasons. This is good vigorous stuff. But Plutarch misinterprets

Democritus. John of Stobi quotes more of the passage (Democritus F3 DK), which shows that Democritus was not championing inactivity, but warning against *over*-involvement in affairs, where over-reaching oneself would inevitably end in distress (a position developed later in Plutarch's essay). Democritus' 'doing many things' is the equivalent of the Greek slogan, *polypragmonein*, 'much involvement', which in fifth- and fourth-century Greek came to have a bad sense of meddlesomeness, over-involvement. So Plato in *Republic* 433a recommends the popular maxim, as well as his own, that just and right action consisted of doing one's own thing, rather than *polypragmonein*. Now it is true that Democritus is misinterpreted in this elsewhere, for example in Marcus Aurelius 4.24. But Seneca (*De Tranquillitate Animi* 13.1) understands him correctly, and Plutarch himself twice in essays opposed to Epicurus (1100C and 1126A) takes the opposite view of Democritus. Indeed anyone reading on in Democritus could hardly fail to understand. And as this was the most famous work on the subject (Seneca, *De Tranquillitate Animi* 2.3), Plutarch had certainly read it. It is just possible that in over-hasty consultation of the famous notebooks (464F) he misinterpreted a sentence recorded out of context, but it is much more likely that Plutarch was unblushingly using a quotation out of context to enliven his own argument, which is his common practice elsewhere. It should be remembered that the ancients in general had no conscience or commitment to fidelity towards original sources.

The next three sections set the stage for the main development. Contentment is not a property of a way of life, nor is discontent cured by changing your lifestyle, for example by replacing poverty with riches. It is the illness which needs a cure, not the circumstances in which it is experienced (§3). Intelligence effects the cure. It should mould our circumstances, not vice versa (§4).[5] We do not choose our circumstances, nor are we in control of them, but we can accommodate ourselves to what fortune throws for us (§5). The simile of a game of dice (we can't control the throw, but what we do with the result is up to us) is referred to Plato (presumably *Republic* 604c5 ff.), but the language ('up to us') is technically Stoic, and Epictetus uses the same image (2.5.3).

These sections have brought out the two main factors on which contentment according to Plutarch depends: our external circumstances and our internal rationality. Plutarch first concentrates on the bearing of external circumstances (§§6–11). He starts by voicing a general principle, to make the best of one's circumstances, and establishes it typically by famous historical examples, pithy anecdotes (*chreiai*) and in general the popular diatribe form of practical moral advice (§6). But he breaks off once more (§7) for a particular personal application of this to Paccius himself, who is exposed in public affairs to provocation from other people. He must not react in kind, for his motives would be suspect and based on self-regard. Restraint and calm are necessary. But (returning now to the general point, §8) how do we make the best of our situation? First by counting the blessings we have, and enjoying them when we have them, instead of pining for what we do not have (§9); and secondly, by eliminating envy of what other people have (§§10–11). The maxim that contentment lies simply in enjoying what you have began with Democritus (F191 DK), and elements of the envy presentation are similar to passages surviving from the third-century-BC Cynic Teles (p. 43 Hense/470B; p. 12 f. Hense/470F).

But the real key lies in ourselves rather than in our circumstances, or rather in recognizing the relationship between self and circumstances (§§12–14). We must consider our own capabilities, for distress can occur through overestimation of these. We tend to think we are capable of anything, especially of what we are not (§12). Positive and appropriate choices for ourselves have to be made, because different ways of life clash, and we may be suited to one and not to the other. Hence the importance of the motto 'Know thyself' (§13). This famous Delphic maxim, made philosophically momentous by Socrates and Plato, is thus activated into a somewhat watered-down pragmatic guide of recognizing one's own practical capabilities and limitations. And in this sense, concludes Plutarch, the resource for our contentment or distress lies primarily within us, in our own minds, and not in fate or fortune (§14).

Now Plutarch should not be criticized for not doing what is irrelevant to his purpose. He is not writing a philosophical treatise, but sending thoughtful and useful advice to a Roman public figure in terms and presentation which will retain his interest and forcibly impress his mind. But he now reaches a position which engaged concentrated professional debate in the philosophical Schools: the ethical status of misfortune and its relation to happiness. But Plutarch must remain on his own level. So he posits that the human condition is a blend of good and bad, in which we achieve the best blend by making the most of the good (§15). He does not argue this, but drives it home with packed imagery, looping from vulgar instances of flies skidding off smooth surfaces and topical marvel lore to sophisticated comparisons from painting, language and music, interspaced with quotations from Heraclitus, Euripides, Menander and Empedocles. So the problem remains, how to deal with the bad. Well, by preparing yourself through anticipating it; hope for the best, but expect the worst (§16). This is made relevant by practical common instances: to come to terms with the fact that people will die, that you may lose your money or your job, that your wife may be unfaithful. This after all is part of the human situation. If you remove the unexpectedness of such possible eventualities, you will be better prepared to meet them with equanimity. A broad church of philosophers is mentioned here for quotation or anecdote, but this is not philosophical theory but social psychiatric therapy, only applied *before* the event as a prophylactic, not after as an attempted cure.

But for his last and most telling point, Plutarch has to use more obviously the philosophical underlay. He categorizes (§17) what brings distress as (*a*) what does so by its very nature and (*b*) what is not in itself distressing, but merely so because we wrongly think that something terrible has happened to us. Examples of the latter are lowly origins, an unfaithful wife, the failure to win a prize or the loss of a privilege. These are as it were self-inflicted wounds, false and unnecessary, since they should not affect the good condition of body or mind. On the other hand, category (*a*), instanced by illness, pain, death of one's child or friend, really *is* distressing. Nevertheless we have to recognize that such misfortunes are part of the human condition, but only a very minor part, which we must put into perspective, for the major and most important part of ourselves, our moral goodness, we control ourselves, and that is not subject to fortune. Fortune can make you ill, poor or unpopular, but it can't make a good man bad.

This classification was familiar and the subject of much philosophical debate. It was a position accepted in their own distinctive ways by Epicureans, Platonists and Peripatetics, and indeed even by Sceptics (Timon in Sextus Empiricus, *Adversus Mathematicos* 11.141–3). They all recognized this distinction between different categories of external circumstantial ills (as indeed of external goods), and so addressed themselves to the limiting of Fortune's blows. The Stoics, on the other hand, while of course recognizing the existence and the fact of pain and the like, held that all external advantages and ills had only relative value or disvalue compared with the absolute value of moral goodness, and so while it was preferable not to experience such ills, they could not in any case affect the actual happiness of the good man who had achieved a mental immunity to Fortune. Plutarch in his enthusiasm teeters towards Stoic absolutism, especially in his emphasis on the complete security of the good man qua good man (475E ff.), and in his immunity to loss (the Stilpo anecdote, 475C) and to harm (Socrates to the jurors, 475E). Both these examples had in fact become stock Stoic texts in the first century AD (Seneca, *De Constantia* 5.6; Epictetus 1.29.18 and elsewhere). But in the end Plutarch sides firmly with the natural reality of category (*a*) distress, and therefore is concerned with the aim of limiting, not eliminating, the attacks of fortune.

So the remainder of the essay (§§18–19) is concerned with mental training to this end. A person has to train his mind to face up to such distressful situations as illness, pain, exile and death, see their horrors as comparatively unimportant and so alleviate them. More positively, by recognizing what *is* in his power, he can train himself by repeating what he will *not* do (lie, mislead, steal). For externals cannot create a calm and contented mind; only the mind itself can do this.

The closing note (§20) is a kind of religious paean to the divine organization of the universe to which we can contribute by celebrating it with our resource of contentment, joy and happiness, in coming to terms with the present, remembering the past with gratitude and looking forward cheerfully and without apprehension to the future. The initial reference is to Plato's *Timaeus*, but there is a strong odour of Stoicism and indeed whiffs from the other Schools as well. But any reader of Plutarch will recognize that his own contribution is the most important of all.

Philemon Holland wrote of *On Contentment* that it was 'a treatise where a man may see the excellent discourses and most sound arguments of moral philosophy'. But that is nonsense, at least in any strict view of philosophy. The reader is not convinced through logical argument that *x* is the case. Rather in section after section he is brought to see, to recognize through compelling illustration and example that, yes, he does agree that this is so. This is literary skill used for a moral purpose, and the climaxes are created, not by a tightening or inevitability of argument, but by a crescendo of imagery, simile and metaphor, as in section 19. Plutarch is not attempting a subtle philosophical analysis of a problem, he is engaged with what Paccius or any other interested individual is going to *do* about it. This of course is concerned with philosophy, in the way that Epictetus claimed that his lecture room was a surgery (3.23.30). But Plutarch's wide range of philosophical ingredients are merely part of the mixture moulded by his common sense, vast reading, practical experience and insight, humanity, character and literary power. The essay has been much admired, and rightly; in the ancient world, for example, by St Basil and St John Chrysostom, and extracts appear in John of Stobi's collection. But Plutarch should not be praised for the wrong reasons, any more than he should be falsely criticized for not being a historian in the *Lives*.

The two essays *On Contentment* and *On the Avoidance of Anger* may form a pair, because they are linked by the prominent Roman statesman C. Minucius Fundanus and his friend Eros, for whom see the Introduction to *On the Avoidance of Anger*. At the beginning of *On Contentment* (464E), it is Fundanus' brittle temper and characteristic impatience for the return of Eros which will not allow Plutarch more time for his composition. But in *On the Avoidance of Anger* Fundanus claims, and is clearly given, some credit for the taming of this notorious temper. So did *On*

*Contentment* come first? Both were probably written in the late nineties (see Introduction to *On the Avoidance of Anger*). At any rate, the two essays do to some extent complement each other, *Anger* attempting to eliminate a destructive passion, *Contentment* being concerned with the establishment of a positive state of mind which distress cannot unbalance.

1. See, e.g., Gisela Striker, '*Ataraxia*: Happiness as Tranquillity', *The Monist* 73 (1990), pp. 97–110.
2. M. Pohlenz, *Hermes* 40 (1905), pp. 275 ff.; later partly recanted.
3. G. Siefert, *Plutarchs Schrift* Π. εὐθυμίας, Progr. Pforta, 1908; exclusively so indeed in the opinion of H. Broecker, *Animadversiones ad Plutarchi Libellum,* Περὶ εὐθυμίας, Bonn, 1954.
4. Epicurus was notoriously opposed to public involvement, e.g. Long and Sedley, *The Hellenistic Philosophers* 1.134.
5. Three bad examples of this adage are given: Alexander, Agamemnon and Phaethon; and three good ones: Crates, Diogenes and Socrates; the Cynic contribution is noticeable.

# ON CONTENTMENT

[1] FROM PLUTARCH TO PACCIUS. I hope this finds you well.[1]
Not long ago, I got your letter, in which you suggested that I
write down for you something about contentment, and about
those passages in *Timaeus*[2] which need rather careful interpretation. At pretty much the same time, our friend Eros suddenly
found he had to sail to Rome, since he had received a letter from
the illustrious Fundanus; typically, Fundanus told him to hurry.[3]   F
On the one hand, I didn't have as much time as I wanted to get
to grips with the topics you were asking me to address; but on
the other hand, I couldn't bear the idea of Eros leaving here,
going to you and being found to be completely empty-handed.
So I read those bits of my notebooks, written in fact for myself,
which covered the topic of contentment. I imagined that what
you too wanted from this discourse was practical help, not a
lecture whose aim was elegant composition; and I share your   465A
pleasure in the fact that although you have friends in positions of
authority, and although you have a pre-eminent reputation as a
political speaker, you have not experienced what Merops did in
the tragedy: it is not the case, as it was with him, that 'the
adulation of the masses has driven you mad'[4] and into abnormal
behaviour. No, you have taken to heart what you have often

1. See p. 365, n. 1.
2. Plutarch did write an essay *On the Generation of Soul in Timaeus*, but addressed
   it to his sons, not to Paccius (on whom see Introduction, p. 203).
3. The Roman Fundanus was the principal speaker in *On the Avoidance of Anger*,
   and had a temper. See the Introduction to that essay.
4. From Euripides' *Phaethon* (*TGF* F778 Nauck, F1 Diggle). Merops was
   Phaethon's putative father and king of Ethiopia.

been told: gout is not alleviated by a patrician shoe,★ nor a whitlow by an expensive ring nor a migraine by a crown.'[1] How on earth can assets or a reputation or power at court contribute towards having a mind that is free of distress and a life that is as calm as a millpond,[2] unless their possession and use are pleasant, but at the same time they are never missed if they are lacking? And what else guarantees this except rationality which has become accustomed to quickly restraining – and taking care to do so – the emotional, irrational part of the mind on the many occasions when it tries to exceed its bounds, and not conniving at its flooding and racing away from what is actually there?★

Xenophon[3] recommends that we remember and acknowledge the gods particularly in times of prosperity, so that when we are in need, we can confidently petition them in the knowledge that they are predisposed to be charitable and friendly. It is no different in the case of rational arguments which help us combat the emotions: anyone with any sense should pay attention to them before emotion arises, so as to widen his defensive preparations and thereby increase the benefit he gains. You know how aggressive dogs get thoroughly agitated at any and every loud voice and are calmed down only by the one with which they are familiar; so the mind's emotions too are hard to restrain when they are overexcited, unless rational arguments are already there, ingrained and familiar, to check the agitation.

[2] Whoever it was who said that 'Contentment is impossible for anyone who busies himself with personal or public affairs' makes contentment, in the first place, an expensive commodity if

1. The Roman formal shoe (*calceus*) was a sign of status as well as wealth: Cicero, *Milo* 28, *Philippics* 13.28; Horace, *Satires* 1.6.27; cf. Plutarch, *Life of Pompey* 24.12; Seneca, *De Tranquillitate Animi* 11.9. Gout (Hippocrates, *Aphorisms* 6.28–30; Horace, *Epistle* 1.2.47 ff.; Posidonius T33, T38 EK), whitlows (Hippocrates, *Epidemics* 2.6.27; Plutarch 43A–B, 73B, 440B) and migraine (Hippocrates, *Aphorisms* 5.64; Epictetus 3.22.73) were among the commonest, most painful and most fashionable ailments among the upper classes.

2. The metaphor for the good life of a sea calm and untossed by waves is a favourite with Plutarch, especially in relation to contentment: 8A, 101A, 602C, *Life of Galba* 10.7.

3. *Cyropaedia* 1.6.3.

its price is inactivity.[1] It is as though his prescription for every invalid is to say, '"You poor thing, stay perfectly still in your bed"',[2] whereas inertia is in fact no good as a treatment for a    D body suffering from numbness★ and, as psychiatry, it is equally ineffective to try to remove agitation and distress from the mind by means of laziness, weakness and betrayal of friends, household and country.

Moreover, in the second place, it is not true that anyone who is not busy is content. It would follow that women are more content than men, since they generally deal only with domestic matters; but in fact, although (in Hesiod's words) the north wind 'does not reach a young woman's tender body',[3] nevertheless distress, disturbance and depression trickle into the women's quarters through the agency of jealousy, superstition, ambition and innumerable empty beliefs. Laertes spent twenty years by himself    E away from civilization, 'with an old woman to look after him, who served his food and drink',[4] and although he shunned his country, home and kingdom, nevertheless his inactivity and ennui had distress as a constant close companion. Even absolute inactivity is likely to induce discontent in some cases: for example, 'But swift-footed Achilles, Peleus' son, descended from Zeus, stayed sitting by his sharp-prowed ships and never went to assembly, which brings men prestige, or to battle, but stayed there with his heart pining in longing for the war cry and for battle.'[5] The depth of his feeling and his grief caused him to say to himself, 'I    F sit by my ships, a pointless burden to the world.'[6]

This is why not even Epicurus thinks that a quiet life is desir-

1. The quotation is from Democritus' On Contentment (F3 DK), and was possibly the start of the work (Seneca, De Tranquillitate Animi 13.1). John of Stobi, in his Anthology (5, pp. 907 f. Hense) reproduces more, enough to show that Plutarch chooses to misrepresent Democritus, who did not propose inactivity, but the importance of staying within the limits of one's own natural ability.
2. Euripides, Orestes 258: Electra to her brother Orestes, who was seeing visions after murdering their mother.
3. Hesiod, Works and Days 519.
4. Homer, Odyssey 1.191 f., of the aged father of Odysseus, now retired from active life in the equivalent of a dower cottage in the country.
5. Homer, Iliad 1.488 ff.: Achilles sulking and withdrawn from the Greek battle lines after his quarrel with Agamemnon.
6. Homer, Iliad 18.104.

able; he says that people who want status and fame should go along with this aspect of their nature and engage in politics and public life, because they are inherently more likely to be thrown 466A off balance and to be harmed by inactivity – by failing to fulfil their desires.[1] But it is ridiculous for him to recommend public life, not to those with talent, but to those who are incapable of living peacefully. Contentment and discontent should be defined not by the frequency or rarity of one's actions, but by their goodness or badness: the omission of good deeds is – and this has been said before – just as annoying and disturbing as the commission of bad deeds.

[3] There are people who think that freedom from distress resides in one way of life in particular – for instance, in farming or bachelorhood or kingship. What Menander said can act as a B reminder for them: 'Phanias, I used to think that rich people, because they have no debts, don't sigh at night, or toss and turn, or moan "Poor me!"; I used to think they slept a pleasant, peaceful sleep.' He goes on to explain that, in his experience, even the rich suffer exactly as the poor do, and then says, 'Is grief related in some way to life? It consorts with a life of luxury, is inseparable from a life of fame, grows old with a life of poverty.'[2]

Consider people who are scared of sailing or who get seasick:[3] they imagine that the voyage will pass more easily if they exchange a skiff for a merchant ship, and then the merchant ship C for a trireme; but this gets them nowhere, because they take their sickness and fears with them. This is an analogy for exchanging one way of life for another; it does not eradicate from the mind the factors which make it distressed and disturbed, which are unworldliness, lack of discrimination and not being able, or not knowing how, to make proper use of one's present circumstances. These are the storm winds that vex both rich and poor, trouble

---

1. But compare A. A. Long and D. N. Sedley, *The Hellenistic Philosophers* 1.134, 136.
2. Menander, *The Cithara-player* F1 Körte and Sandbach. John of Stobi (5, p. 800 Hense) gives two and a half more lines.
3. This passage caught the fancy: it was collected by John of Stobi (3, p. 249 Hense) and imitated by St Basil, *Epistle* 2. But the simile was already in Ariston (John of Stobi 2, p. 218.7 ff. Wachsmuth).

both married and single; they make men shun public life and then find a quiet life intolerable; they make men pursue promotion at court and be miserable as soon as they get it. 'Helplessness makes sick people a peevish lot':[1] their wives irritate them, they complain about their doctors, grumble about their beds and 'for a friend to come is a nuisance, to leave is an offence', as Ion says.[2]   D But when the illness has dissolved and the humours are differently blended, health comes and makes everything nice and pleasant, in the sense that someone who yesterday detested eggs and cakes and bread made from fresh wheat, today is even glad* to eat coarse bread with olives or mustard seeds.

[4] The engendering of rationality within us causes this kind of satisfaction with, and change of attitude towards, any way of life. Alexander once shed tears while listening to Anaxarchus lecture on the existence of an infinite number of worlds. His friends asked him what the matter was, and he replied, 'Don't you think tears are called for, if there are an infinite number of worlds, and I've not yet gained control of just one?' On the other hand, Crates, with   E his bag and threadbare cloak, spent his whole life joking and laughing as though he were on holiday. Moreover, Agamemnon was troubled by his extensive responsibilities as king – 'You will recognize Agamemnon, son of Atreus, whom Zeus has singled out for constant hard work'[3] – but when Diogenes was up for sale, he lay on the ground and teased the auctioneer by refusing to get up when told to, but joking and saying with a laugh, 'Imagine it's a fish you're trying to sell!' Or again, Socrates went on discussing philosophy with his companions while he was in prison, but Phaethon used to weep when he had scaled the heights of   F heaven, if no one gave him his father's horses and chariot.

It is the shoe that bends along with the foot, not the other way around; and likewise, an implication of what we have been saying is that disposition moulds life. I mean, the notion that familiarity makes the best life pleasant for anyone who has chosen it[4] is wrong: it is rational intelligence which makes the life one

1. Euripides, *Orestes* 232.
2. Ion of Chios, F56 Nauck.
3. Homer, *Iliad* 10.88 f.
4. *On Exile* 602C gives this principle as a Pythagorean dictum.

already has both the best one and the most pleasant one. It
467A    follows that we should purify our innate well of contentment
and then external things will be in harmony with us too, provided
we don't maltreat them, and will seem congruent and congenial.
'There's no point in getting angry with one's situation, because it
is utterly indifferent; but success will accrue to anyone who treats
the situations he encounters correctly.'[1]

[5] Plato compared life to a game of dice in which it is not just
important to throw something appropriate, but also to make
good use of it however the throw turns out.[2] And where our
situations are concerned, it may be true that we do not control[3]
the throw of the dice, but it is our job, if we are sensible, to
B    accommodate ourselves to whatever fortune deals us and to allo-
cate everything to a place where, as each situation arises, if it is
congruent, we can maximize its benefit, and if it is unwelcome,
we can minimize its harm. A physical illness can make people
incapable of enduring either heat or cold, and those who muddle
unintelligently through life are like that, in the sense that they
get ecstatic at good fortune and depressed at bad fortune – which
is to say that both good and bad fortune knock them off balance,
or rather that they knock themselves off balance when they
encounter either of them; and it is the same story when they
encounter anything that one might term good. Theodorus the
Atheist (as he was called) used to say that although he delivered
his lectures with his right hand, the audience caught them in
C    their left hands; and uneducated people, faced with a favourable
or right-handed opportunity, often take it up* awkwardly or
left-handedly and make fools of themselves. Thyme, the most
acrid and dry of plants, provides bees with honey; and likewise
intelligent people can invariably find something congruent with
and useful to themselves from the most forbidding of situations.

[6] The chief thing, then, to practise and pursue is the attitude
exemplified by the man whose stone missed his dog and hit his

---

1. Euripides F287 Nauck, from the play *Bellerophon*.
2. Plato, *Republic* 604c5 ff. But contemporary with Plutarch, Epictetus the Stoic
   used the very same comparison (2.5.3).
3. The language is technically Stoic.

stepmother: 'That's not bad either!' he said. It is possible to change opportunities so that they are no longer unwelcome. Diogenes was exiled; 'That's not bad either', because he subsequently took up philosophy. Zeno of Citium had just one ship **D** left from his merchant fleet; when he was told that this one too★ was lost, sunk with all its cargo, he said, 'Thank you, fortune, for helping to drive me into a threadbare cloak.'[1]

Why can't the rest of us behave in the same way? Have you failed to capture some public position you were after? You can live in the country, minding your *own* business. Have you been spurned while courting the affection of someone in authority? You can now live a life free of risk and bother. Is your time again taken up with worldly business and worries? Well, to quote Pindar, 'the extent to which warm water relaxes a body is nothing'[2] compared to how fame and respect, conjoined with power, make 'work pleasant and labour non-laborious'.[3] Are you faced with misery and insults because lies or malicious tales **E** are being spread about you? This is a following wind, blowing you towards the Muses and the Academy, as Plato was driven by the storm winds of his friendship for Dionysius.[4]

It follows that another thing that is important for contentment is to reflect on famous men, and how they have not been affected at all by circumstances identical to one's own. Is childlessness your problem, for example? Look at the kings of Rome, none of whom had a son to whom he could bequeath his kingdom. Are you weighed down by poverty at the moment? But is there any Boeotian you would rather be than Epaminondas, any Roman rather than Fabricius?[5] 'But my wife has been seduced!' Well,

1. The stories of Diogenes and Zeno recur together in *How to Profit from One's Enemies* 87A, so it looks as if they were together in the notebooks. A threadbare cloak was the proverbial uniform of philosophers.
2. Pindar, *Nemean Odes* 4.4.
3. Euripides, *Bacchae* 66.
4. The association founded by Plato and named after the park on the outskirts of Athens where it was situated was dedicated to the Muses. Plato was supposed to have founded the Academy shortly after returning to Athens following his first unsuccessful visit to Syracuse to try to turn the tyrant Dionysius into a philosopher-king.
5. Parallel examples (as in Plutarch's *Lives*) – Greek (from Plutarch's own Boeotia) and Roman – of great leaders of slender means.

haven't you read the inscription at Delphi which goes 'Erected

F by Agis, lord of water and of earth'? And haven't you heard that
this is the man whose wife Timaea was seduced by Alcibiades,
and that in an undertone to her serving-women she used to call
her child Alcibiades? Yet this did not stop Agis from being the
most famous and important Greek of his day. Nor, for example,
did the promiscuity of Stilpo's daughter stop him living a more

468A carefree life than any of his philosophical contemporaries. In fact,
when Metrocles told him off for his daughter's behaviour, Stilpo's
response was, 'Is it my fault or hers?' Metrocles said, 'Her fault,
but your misfortune.' 'What do you mean?' asked Stilpo. 'Isn't a
fault a mistake?' 'Certainly,' said Metrocles. 'And isn't anyone
making a mistake also suffering a setback?' continued Stilpo.
Metrocles agreed. 'And isn't anyone suffering a setback also suffering a misfortune?' Stilpo concluded. This calm, philosophical
argument showed the Cynic's aspersion to be empty barking.[1]

B    [7] Still, most people *are* hurt and provoked, by their enemies'
flaws, as well as by those of their friends and relatives. I mean,
being inclined towards insolence, anger, spite, malice, jealousy
and hostility not only plagues those people who have these weaknesses, but also annoys and irritates foolish people – as, of course,
do a neighbour's short temper, an acquaintance's grumpiness and
a public administrator's iniquity. And I think that you too are
very far from failing to get upset at these flaws; like the doctors
in Sophocles who 'use bitter medicine to flush out bitter bile',[2]
you react to these affections and afflictions with rage and bitter-

C ness. But this is unreasonable,[3] because the public business which
has been entrusted to you and which you conduct is managed by
people whose characters are not straightforward and good, as
well-made tools should be, but are invariably jagged and warped;
and you should not, therefore, consider it to be your job – or at
any rate you should not consider it to be an easy job – to

1. The name Cynic was derived from the Greek word for 'dog', a nickname
   applied to Diogenes of Sinope, the founder of the school.
2. Sophocles *TGF* F770 Nauck, F854 Radt; also used in *On the Avoidance of
   Anger* 463F.
3. And therefore, by definition, Paccius' action is not 'appropriate' in the Stoic
   sense.

straighten them out. However, if you use them as a doctor uses tooth extractors and wound clamps – that is, as being made just the way they are – and if you show yourself to be as lenient and moderate as circumstances permit, then your pleasure in your own attitude will outweigh your distress at others' unsatisfying and iniquitous behaviour, you will regard them as doing what comes naturally to them (as dogs are when they bark) and you will stop unwittingly being infected by others' flaws, which is to let plenty of distressing factors seep into the sunken and low-lying land of this pettiness and weakness of yours.

Some philosophers find fault even with compassion, when it is felt for people who are out of luck, on the grounds that while helping people one comes across is a good thing, sharing their troubles and giving in to them is not. More importantly, they forbid us to be discontented or depressed even when we realize that we ourselves have flawed and defective characters; they tell us instead not to get distressed, but just to try to cure the problem, as is right and proper. You should consider, then, how utterly illogical it is for us to connive at ourselves getting cross and irritated because not everyone with whom we have dealings and who crosses our paths is fair and congenial.

No, my dear Paccius, you must make sure that we are not deceiving ourselves by denouncing and being worried about the iniquity of people we come across only in so far as it affects us, rather than in general – that is, you must make sure that we are not being motivated by selfishness, but by hatred of badness. The point is that if we are unduly discomposed by public life and if we have unwarranted impulses and aims, or alternatively unwarranted aversions and antipathies, then this makes us suspicious of people and irritated by them, because we think that they are the causes of our losses and accidents. A high degree of contentment and calmness in relating to people is an attribute of someone who has trained himself to cope with public life without fuss and bother.

[8] Bearing this in mind, let us return to the matter of one's situation. When we have a fever, everything tastes bitter and unpleasant, but once we have seen other people taking the same food without revulsion, we stop blaming the food and drink,

and start to blame ourselves and our illness. In the same way, we will stop blaming and being disgruntled at circumstances if we see other people cheerfully accepting identical situations without getting upset. So when unwelcome incidents occur, it is also good for contentment not to ignore all the gratifying and nice things we have, but to use a process of blending to make the better aspects of our lives obscure the glare of the worse ones. But what happens at the moment is that, although when our eyes are harmed by excessively brilliant things we look away and soothe them with the colours that flowers and grasses provide,[1] we treat the mind differently: we strain it to glimpse the aspects that hurt it, and we force it to occupy itself with thoughts of the things that irritate it, by tearing it almost violently away from the better aspects. And yet the question addressed to the busybody can be transferred to this context and fit in nicely: 'You spiteful man, why are you so quick to spot someone else's weakness, but overlook your own?'[2] So we might ask: why, my friend, do you obsessively contemplate your own weakness and constantly clarify it and revivify it, but fail to apply your mind to the good things you have? Cupping-glasses extract from flesh anything particularly bad, and likewise you are attracting to yourself the very worst of your attributes. You are making yourself no better at all than the Chian who used to sell plenty of ★ quality wine to other people,[3] but for his own meal used to taste wines until he found a vinegary one; and when someone asked one of his servants what he had left his master doing, the servant replied, 'Looking for bad when surrounded by good.'

As a matter of fact, most people do bypass what is good and refreshing in their lives, and make straight for the unpleasant, bad elements. Aristippus was different, however: he was good at lightening himself and raising himself up (imagine him on a pair of scales) towards the better aspects of his situation. At any rate, he once lost a fine estate, and people were insincerely saying how sorry and sympathetic they felt. He asked one of them, 'Haven't

1. Plutarch repeats this simile several times: 490C, 543F, 854B, *Life of Demosthenes* 22. It is likely that he himself suffered from eye fatigue.
2. *CAF Adesp*. F359 Kock and Edmonds.
3. Chian wines were famous in the ancient world for their outstanding quality.

you got just one little plot of land, while I have still got three farms?' The fellow said yes, and Aristippus said, 'Why, then, am I not feeling sorry for you, rather than the other way round?' D The point is that it is crazy to be upset about what one has lost and not feel happy about what one has kept; otherwise, we are behaving like little children who, when deprived of just one of their many toys, wail and scream and throw all the rest of their toys away. In the same way, if we let fortune distress us just once, then our whining and resentment deprives everything else as well of any benefit for us.

[9] Someone might ask, 'But what can we be said to have or not to have?' Fame, property, married status, a good friend – these are the things people have. When Antipater of Tarsus was close to death, he added up the good things that had happened to him, and included even the easy voyage he had had from Cilicia to Athens. And we must not overlook even things we share with E others, but take them into account, and be thankful that we have life and health and that we walk the earth; that there is no war, either foreign or civil, but that we may, if we so choose, farm the land and sail the seas without fear; that the full range of possibilities is open to us, from oratory and politics to a quiet, inactive life. When we have these shared things, we will increase our contentment with them if we imagine that we do not have them, and frequently remind ourselves how desirable health is to sick people, peace to people at war, and the acquisition of fame F and friends to an obscure stranger in a city as big as yours, and also remind ourselves how distressing it is to lose these things if they have been ours in the past. If we do this, then we will not rate and value any of these things highly only once it has been lost, while discounting it altogether as long as it is in our keeping. I mean, the fact that we do not own something does not increase its value; and we should not be acquisitive as if these things were important, and be constantly trembling in fear of losing them as if they were important, but ignore them and belittle them, while we have them, as if they were worthless. Instead, while we have 470A them, we should above all use them for our enjoyment and profit from them, so that, in the event of their loss, we can endure this too with greater equanimity. Arcesilaus used to point

out that although most people think it their duty to use their minds to explore and their eyes to examine other people's poems, paintings and statues in precise and minute detail, yet they forget their own lives, which could provide plenty of areas for pleasurable reflection: they constantly look outwards and are impressed by other people's fame and fortune, just as adulterers are by other men's wives, but belittle themselves and what they already have.

B
[10] Nevertheless, another thing that is important for contentment is to restrict one's inspection as much as possible to oneself and those things which are relevant to oneself, or else to consider people who are less well off than oneself. What one should avoid is lining oneself up against people who are better off, despite the fact that this is the usual practice: prisoners, for instance, envy those who have been freed, who envy people who have always been free, who envy those with citizen status, who in turn envy rich people, who envy province commanders, who envy kings, who – because they almost aspire to making thunder and lightning – envy the gods.[1] Consequently, since they never attain things which are out of their reach, they are never thankful for the things that are relevant to them. 'Gold-laden Gyges' possessions are of no interest to me; I have never yet been gripped by envy, nor do I seek to emulate what the gods do, nor do I desire a great kingdom. I do not set my sights on such distant views.'[2]

C

Someone might say, 'That's because this is a Thasian speaking.'[3] But there are other provincials – from Chios, Galatia or Bithynia – who are dissatisfied with having obtained a portion of status or power among their compatriots, and who weep because they do not wear patrician robes; and if they do, then because they have not yet held military command at Rome; and if they have, then because they are not consuls; and if they are, then

---

1. A similar catalogue of ascension was given by the Cynic Teles (p. 43 Hense, p. 45 O'Neil).
2. Archilochus F15 Lasserre-Bonnard, F22 Tarditi, F25 Bergk.
3. According to Aristotle (*Rhetoric* 1418b30 f.), the speaker in Archilochus' poem was a Thasian carpenter called Charon. Aristotle suggests, however, that this was a cloak for the sentiment of Archilochus himself, who lived in Thasos although he was born in Paros.

because when the announcement was made, they did not head the list. The only possible description of this is self-mortification and self-inflicted punishment, as a result of scrabbling for reasons to be ungrateful to fortune. On the other hand, anyone whose mind sanely reflects that the sun sees countless thousands of humans – 'all we who enjoy the broad land's produce'[1] – does not slump into depression and despondency if there are people more famous and rich than himself; there are so many human beings that his life is a thousand times more perfect than thousands of people's, so he continues on his path, celebrating his own destiny and life.

It may be impossible to choose one's opponents in the Olympic Games and so gain victory that way, but life's situations do often present one with opportunities for appreciating one's better position – for being envied rather than envying others – unless, of course, it is Briareus or Heracles one pits oneself against![2] So when you find yourself overawed by the apparent superiority of a man who is being carried in a sedan chair, make sure you look down and also see those who are keeping him off the ground; and when you find yourself envying Xerxes, as the Hellespontian did, on the famous occasion of Xerxes' pontoon crossing, make sure you also see the men being driven by whips to excavate Mount Athos and the men with faces mutilated when the bridge was destroyed by the waves;[3] if you take *their* thoughts into consideration as well, you find that they are envying your life and your situation.

Socrates once heard one of his acquaintances remarking how expensive Athens was:[4] 'A mina for Chian wine, three minae for a purple-dyed robe, five drachmae for a *kotyle* of honey.' Socrates

---

1. Simonides, *PMG* 542.24 f. Page, F5.17 Bergk. It was a famous poem. Protagoras expounds it in Plato, *Protagoras* 339a ff.
2. Since Briareus was a monster with a hundred arms, and Heracles was the archetypal strong-man hero, they had certain unfair advantages.
3. Xerxes, the Persian king, preparing to invade Greece in 480 BC, bridged the Hellespont, but when a storm wrecked the first attempt at a pontoon, he brutally punished the builders. The passage round Mount Athos was extremely dangerous for ships, so he had a canal dug through the isthmus. See Herodotus 7.22–4, 7.35. For the Hellespontian's comment, see Herodotus 7.56.
4. A similar anecdote had already been used of Diogenes by Teles, the Cynic of the second half of the third century BC (Teles, pp. 12 f. Hense, p. 12 O'Neil; cf.

grabbed hold of him and showed him some grain – 'An obol for
half a *hekteus* – Athens is cheap'; and then some olives – 'Two
bronze coins for a *choinix* – Athens is cheap';\* and then some
simple cloaks – 'Ten drachmae – Athens is cheap.' So when we
too hear someone remarking on how trivial and terribly distressing our personal situations are, because we are not consuls or
471A  governors, we can reply, 'Our situations are not at all unprepos-
sessing, and our lives are to be envied, because we are not beggars
or porters or flatterers.'

[11] Despite all this we habitually live, out of stupidity, with
our attention on others rather than on ourselves. So since human
nature contains plenty of malicious envy and spite, with the
result that the degree of pleasure we feel in what is ours is less
than the degree of irritation we feel at others' successes, then you
must not only notice the splendid and pre-eminent features of
the people you envy and admire, but you must also remove and
draw aside the florid veil, so to speak, of their reputation and
their façade, and get inside, where you will notice that they
B  contain plenty of unsavoury features and plenty of unpleasantness.
At any rate, something Pittacus said is instructive, since he is
outstandingly famous for courage, wisdom and morality: he once
had some friends round for dinner, and his wife burst in angrily
and overturned the table; his friends were astounded, but he said,
'No one's life is perfect; anyone with only my troubles is very
well off.'[1]

'In public this man is an object of envy, but as soon as he
opens the door of his home, he's in a pitiful state: his wife is in
complete control, she bosses him about and argues all the time.
He's got rather a lot of reasons to be miserable, whereas I've got

Diogenes Laertius 6.35). As is normal in anecdotal tradition, the point of the
story and the structure remain the same, while the details vary ad lib. The
monetary relationships are: 8 bronze coins = 1 obol; 6 obols = 1 drachma; 100
drachmae = 1 mina. The measures varied in different areas, but the Attic
relationships were: 4 *kotylae* = 1 *choinix*; 8 *choinikes* = 1 *hekteus*; 6 *hekteis* = 1
*medimnus*. A *kotyle* was roughly equivalent to half a pint. A *choinix* or quart of
meal was recognized as a minimum daily ration (Herodotus 7.187; Thucydides
4.16; Diogenes Laertius 8.18).

1. Even Plutarch ad-libs his anecdotes: this story had a different cast in *On the
Avoidance of Anger* 461D.

none.'[1] Plenty of these kinds of troubles accompany wealth, fame and kingship, but most people fail to notice them under the showy veneer. 'Son of Atreus, you are fortunate – your birth was favoured by fate and your destiny is to prosper':[2] this kind of accolade is given for weaponry, horses and an extensive army, for external possessions, but from within come the contradictory emotional cries, bearing witness against this hollow fame – 'Zeus the son of Cronus has thoroughly imprisoned me in deep madness'[3] and 'I envy you, old man, and I envy anyone whose life is at an end, if he has kept himself safe by avoiding recognition and fame.'[4] Here is another point we should bear in mind, then, to enable us to carp less against fortune and to decrease the extent to which, by admiring our acquaintances' attributes, we belittle and denigrate our own.

[12] Now, a major impediment to contentment is the failure to keep our desires furled or unfurled, so to speak, in a way which is commensurate with the prevailing potential. Instead, we give them too much slack through our hopes, and then when we fail, we blame fate and fortune, but not our own stupidity. We wouldn't describe as unfortunate anyone who wanted to shoot with his plough and hunt hares with his cow, nor would we say that anyone who fails to capture deer or boar with fishing-baskets or seines is being opposed by bad luck: it is stupidity and silliness which are setting him to impossible endeavours. The chief cause is in fact self-love, which makes people ambitious and competitive whatever the situation, and makes them greedily take on everything: they not only expect to be rich, erudite, strong, outgoing, pleasant and intimate with kings and leaders of nations, but they are discontented if their dogs, horses, quails and cocks[5] are not the best at what they do.

Dionysius the Elder was not satisfied with being the most

1. Menander F251 Körte and Sandbach.
2. Homer, *Iliad* 3.182, of Agamemnon.
3. Agamemnon at *Iliad* 2.111 (and 9.18).
4. Still Agamemnon, speaking to his old servant in Euripides, *Iphigenia in Aulis* 16 ff.; a popular passage, referred to by Cicero, *Tusculanae Disputationes* 3.57.
5. The most important animals for sport: Plato, *Lysis* 211e, *Hippias Major* 295c–d.

important tyrant of the time, but because his verse was worse
than that of Philoxenus the poet, and he failed to do better than
Plato at philosophical discussion, he got furiously angry – he
imprisoned Philoxenus in the quarries, and he sent Plato to
Aegina to be sold into slavery. Alexander was different: when
the sprinter Crison was racing with him and gave the impression
of deliberately slowing down, Alexander was very cross.[1] And
F    Achilles in the poem does well too: he starts off saying, 'None of
the bronze-clad Achaeans is my equal', but goes on, 'in war; but
there are those who are better in assembly.'[2] On the other hand,
472A  when Megabyzus the Persian visited Apelles' studio[3] and tried to
start a conversation about art, Apelles shut him up by saying, 'As
long as you kept quiet, you seemed to be someone because of
your golden jewellery and purple-dyed clothes, but now even
these lads here who grind the pigment are laughing at you for
talking nonsense.'

Now, although people might think, when they hear the Stoic
description of the sage not only as wise, moral and courageous,
but also as an orator, poet and military commander, as possessing
wealth and as a king, that they are joking,[4] nevertheless they
expect all these descriptions for themselves and are annoyed if
they don't get them. Yet even different gods have different
B    functions – one being called the god of battle, another the god of
prophecy, another the god of profit;[5] and Aphrodite is ordained
by Zeus to preside over marriage and sex, precisely because her
domain does not include military matters.[6]

[13] The point is that some pursuits inherently do not go
together, but rather tend in opposite directions. For instance,
rhetorical training and the acquisition of intellectual disciplines
need freedom and no pressure, but political power and intimacy
with kings do not accrue without one being busy and using up
one's time. Moreover, 'drinking wine and overeating meat may

1. See p. 81, n. 1.
2. Homer, Iliad 18.105 f.
3. See p. 80, n. 1.
4. See p. 80.
5. The three gods are Ares, Apollo and Hermes.
6. See Zeus' words in Homer, Iliad 5.428 ff.

make the body strong and robust, but they weaken the mind';[1] and whereas constant concern and care for money increase affluence, yet disdain and scorn for money constitute an important resource for philosophy. So not everything is for everyone: one should follow the Delphic inscription and know oneself,[2] and then engage in the single activity for which one is naturally suited; and one should avoid forcibly and unnaturally compelling oneself to envy alternative ways of life – and different ones at different times. 'A horse is harnessed to a cart, an ox to a plough; a dolphin darts with great rapidity by a ship; and whoever plans death for a boar must find a courageous dog.'[3]

Anyone, however, who is upset and distressed because he is not simultaneously a lion, 'mountain-reared, confident in his might',[4] and a little Maltese dog protected in the lap of a widow,[5] is crazy – but no crazier than anyone who wants to be Empedocles, Plato or Democritus, writing about the universe and the way things really are, and at the same time a Euphorion, with a rich older woman for a lover, or a Medius, hobnobbing with Alexander as one of his drinking companions, and gets irritated and distressed if he isn't an Ismenias, admired for his affluence, and an Epaminondas, admired for his goodness. I mean, runners aren't discontented because they don't win the wrestling competition: they find pride and satisfaction in their own prizes. 'You have obtained Sparta, so do it credit.'[6] And, as Solon says, 'We will not exchange our virtue for their wealth, since the one is stable, but different people have money at different times.'[7]

When Strato, the natural philosopher, was told that Menedemus' students far outnumbered his, he said, 'What else would you

---

1. Clement of Alexandria, *Stromateis* 7.33.7, assigned this statement to a physician called Androcydes.
2. See p. 61, n. 6.
3. Pindar F234 Maehler.
4. Homer, *Odyssey* 6.130, of the naked shipwrecked Odysseus startling the princess Nausicaa!
5. Pampered Maltese lap-dogs were famous: Strabo 6.2.11; Athenaeus 518F; Lucian, *De Parasito* 34; Theophrastus, *Characters* 21.9.
6. From Euripides' *Telephus*, F723 Nauck. The phrase is still used in the ordination of professors at St Andrews University.
7. See p. 129, n. 1.

expect? There are bound to be more people who want to bathe than want to put oil on their bodies.'[1] And Aristotle wrote to Antipater, 'The fact that Alexander rules over a lot of people does not make him the only one who can legitimately feel proud: anyone whose thinking about the gods is correct has just as much right.'[2] The point is that people who value what they have, as in these stories, are not upset by whatever anyone else they come across has. But what happens at the moment is that

F  although we do not expect a vine to produce figs or an olive to produce grapes,[3] yet if we don't have the advantages of both plutocrats and scholars, military commanders and philosophers, flatterers and those who speak their minds, misers and big spenders, all at once, we bully ourselves, are dissatisfied with ourselves, and despise ourselves as living deficient and unfulfilled★ lives.

473A      In addition, there are also clear reminders from nature. Different animals have been differently equipped by nature to provide for themselves: they have not all been made carnivores or seed-peckers or root-diggers. In the same way, nature has granted a wide variety of means of living to human beings – 'to shepherd, ploughman, bird-catcher and to the man whose livelihood comes from the sea'.[4] What we should do, then, is choose what suits our specific natures, work at it and forget others' occupations; in other words, we should not show up any deficiency in Hesiod's assertion that 'Potter is jealous of potter, builder of builder.'[5] I mean, people do not try to emulate only others with the same profession and same

B  way of life; instead, rich men envy scholars and are in turn envied by famous people, while lawyers envy professional orators and – strange though it may seem – free men and aristocrats are utterly in awe of what they see as the happiness of comic actors in successful plays, and of dancers and servants in the royal courts. The result is that they distress and discompose themselves a great deal.

1. The Greeks put oil on their bodies before exercise, while baths were for relaxation.
2. Aristotle's quip on Alexander recurs in *On Being Aware of Moral Progress* 78D, coupled again with an anecdote of rival numbers of student attendances, but then between Zeno and Theophrastus; the point is the same, the details differ.
3. A cliché of the time? Compare Luke 6.44.
4. Pindar, *Isthmian Odes* 1.48.
5. *Works and Days* 25. This for Hesiod was constructive conflict.

[14] It is clear from the differences between people's experiences that everyone has within himself the resources which may lead to contentment or discontent – the jars of good and bad do not sit 'on Zeus' threshold',[1] but lie in our minds. Foolish people overlook and ignore good things even when they are present, because their thoughts are always straining towards the future; intelligent people, on the other hand, use their memories to keep them vivid for themselves even when they are no longer present. Anything present is accessible for the minutest fraction of time and then escapes perception, and consequently foolish people think that it ceases to be relevant to us, or ceases to be ours. There is a painting of a man in Hades weaving a rope, who lets it out to a donkey at pasture, which eats up what he is weaving;[2] in exactly the same way, most people succumb to blind, ungrateful oblivion, which consumes them and leaves no trace of any event, any moment of success, pleasant relaxation, interaction or delight.

This oblivion prevents life being a unity of past events woven with present ones: it divides yesterday from today, as if they were distinct, and likewise treats tomorrow as different from today, and it immediately consigns every occurrence to non-existence by never making use of memory. The school of thought which eliminates growth on the assumption that being is in constant flux makes each person, in theory, different from himself, and then different again;[3] similarly, those who don't use memory to protect or recover what has gone before, but let it trickle away, day by day, make themselves in fact incomplete and empty and in suspense for the day to follow, as if the events of last year, the recent past and yesterday had no bearing on them or, in short, didn't happen to them.

1. As in Homer, *Iliad* 24.527. But Plutarch probably had in mind the use of this quotation in Plato, *Republic* 379d, since he echoes Plato's word 'resources'.
2. The painting was by Polygnotus in the Lesche hall at Delphi (Pausanias 10.29.1). The man's name was Oknos (Sloth), and he was supposed to have an extravagant wife. Oknos' rope became proverbial.
3. According to Plutarch (*On Common Conceptions* 1083A–B), the argument goes back to the comic dramatist Epicharmus (see also Plato, *Theaetetus* 152e), of the fifth century BC, but was debated in all the Schools of philosophy. Plutarch himself seemed fascinated by it (*On God's Slowness to Punish* 559A–B; *Life of Theseus* 23.1), but unfortunately his own discussion of it in *Table Talk* 741C has not survived.

[15] So this is another thing that unsettles contentment, but not as much as the next factor we must consider. You know how when flies settle on mirrors, they skid off the smooth parts but cling on to places which are rough and scratched; this is an analogy for how people slide away from happy, congenial matters and get caught up in their memories of unpleasant things. An even better analogy might be based on the story that in Olynthus there is a place (called 'Beetle-death') which beetles fall into and are unable to get out of: they go round and round in circles until they die there.[1] Likewise, without noticing it, people slip into recalling their bad times and are unwilling to revive or resuscitate themselves.

What we should do is treat the mind like a painting, and the events the mind recalls like the colours, and so give prominence to what is bright and vivid, and push anything gloomy into the obscurity of the background. I mean, it is impossible to eradicate and exclude the gloomy aspects altogether: 'The world is fitted together by interchange between opposites, as are a lyre and a bow',[2] and nothing in human life is pure and unalloyed. In music there are low notes and high notes, and in grammar there are vowels and consonants, and musicianship and literacy do not come from disliking and avoiding one or the other extreme, but from knowing how to make use of them all, and how to blend them into an appropriate mixture.[3] Events too contain polarity: as Euripides says, 'Good and bad are inseparable, but blending is possible, to make things fine.'[4] So, to continue our simile, we should not get discontented or give up when faced with discrepancy, but should behave like expert musicians: if someone plays bad music, they lessen its impact by playing better music, and they enclose wrong notes within right ones. So we should make our life's mixture harmonious and congruent with ourselves.

I mean, Menander is wrong when he says, 'From the moment of birth onwards, everyone is attended by a deity, who is an

---

1. This is popular 'marvel' lore going the rounds at the time: Pliny, *Naturalis Historia* 11.34; Ps.-Aristotle, *Mirabilia* 842a5 ff.
2. Heraclitus F51 DK.
3. Compare Plato, *Philebus* 17b ff.
4. From Euripides' *Aeolus*, F21 Nauck.

excellent guide through the mysteries of life.'[1] Empedocles is more likely to be right with his view that each of us has two destinies or deities, which take us in hand and into their power when we are born: 'Earth was there, and far-seeing Sun, bloody Discord and tranquil Harmony, Beauty and Ugliness, Speed and Slowness, fair Truth and dark-locked Doubt.'[2] [16] Consequently, since at birth we admitted, all together, the potential for each of these experiences, and since we therefore inherently contain plenty of inconsistencies, anyone with any sense prays for the better things, but expects the others as well, and copes with both sets by never behaving excessively. For, in the first place, as Epicurus says, 'Increased pleasure in approaching the future depends on decreased need of it';[3] and in the second place, increased enjoyment of wealth, fame, power and status depends on decreased dread of their opposites, in the sense that a strong desire for each of them instils a very strong fear of their departure, and so weakens and destabilizes the pleasure, as if it were a candle flame in a draught. Anyone whom rationality allows to stand up to fortune fearlessly and unflinchingly, and say, '"You are welcome if you bring a gift, and no great ordeal if you leave"',[4] is enabled by his courage and fearlessness (because he knows that its departure would not be unbearable) thoroughly to enjoy whatever his present situation is. When Anaxagoras' son died, he declared, 'I knew that I had fathered a mortal'; and it is possible not to stop at admiring his character, which enabled him to say this, but also to mirror him by saying, whenever fortune intrudes, 'I know that the wealth I have is transitory and unstable'; 'I know that I owe my position to people who have the power to remove it'; 'I know that although my wife is good, she is a woman, and that my friend is human − a member of an inherently inconstant species, as Plato remarked.'[5]

1. Menander F714.1−3 Körte and Sandbach.
2. F122 DK.
3. F490 Usener.
4. The origin of the quotation is unknown; it has sometimes been attributed to Callimachus.
5. Plutarch used the Anaxagoras anecdote and the Platonic remark (from *Thirteenth Letter* 360d) together again in *On the Avoidance of Anger* 463C−E; see notes on that passage.

The point is that, if anything happens which may be unwelcome, but is not unexpected, this kind of preparedness and character leaves no room for 'I couldn't have imagined it' and 'This isn't what I'd hoped for' and 'I didn't expect this', and so stops the heart lurching and beating fast and so on, and quickly settles derangement and disturbance back on to a foundation. Carneades used to remind people who were involved in important affairs

F that unexpectedness is the be-all and end-all of distress and discontent. Consider, for example, how much smaller the Macedonian kingdom was than the Roman empire. Nevertheless, when Perseus lost Macedonia, not only did he complain bitterly about his own destiny, but it was universally held that his misfortune and

475A fate were worse than absolutely everyone else's; but when Aemilius (who had defeated Perseus) resigned from his position of controlling more or less all the lands and seas in the world, he was fêted and he performed sacrifices to the gods for his acknowledged happiness. There was a good reason for this: Aemilius had accepted a position knowing that he would one day pass it on, whereas Perseus had lost his position unexpectedly. Homer too makes some good points about what happens when things are unexpected: Odysseus wept when his dog greeted him, but sat down impassively next to his sobbing wife;[1] the reason is that he reached his wife with his emotions tamed and controlled by rational foresight, but he fell into the other situation without anticipating it – its surprising nature made it come out of the blue.

B    [17] To express the matter generally, while some unwelcome events do by their very nature entail distress and pain, nevertheless, where the majority of such events are concerned, it is our minds that condition and teach us to resent them.[2] Therefore, when faced with this latter category of unwelcome events, it is useful always to have available Menander's line, which says, 'No experience is terrible unless you make it so.'[3] He is implicitly

---

1. Homer, *Odyssey* 17.302 ff. (dog); 19.209 ff. (wife).
2. Cicero has this same classification in *Tusculanae Disputationes* 3.31.
3. Menander F9 Körte and Sandbach, from *The Arbitration*.

asking the question: Unless your body or mind are actually affected, what difference does it make to you if, for example, your father was not an aristocrat, your wife is having an affair, you fail to win some prize or you lose your right to the front seats in the theatre? For these occurrences do not stop a man being in excellent physical or mental condition. And where the former events are concerned, the ones which do seem by their very nature to cause distress – such as illness, stress and a friend's   C
or child's death – then there is Euripides' famous line: 'I say "Poor me!" – but why? I am only experiencing what it is to be human.'[1] You see, no rational argument checks the downward slide of our emotions as well as one which reminds us that, in common with others and thanks to our nature, there are things which we cannot avoid; this necessity, which is due to corporeality, affords fortune its only hold on human beings; but corporeality is just one part of man's mixed nature, and in his most authoritative and important aspects he remains secure and stable.

When Demetrius had captured Megara, he asked Stilpo whether anything of his had been looted; Stilpo replied that he had seen nothing being carried off about which he would want to say 'mine'.[2] So, if fortune steals and removes from us everything else, we still have something in us which is such that 'the   D
Achaeans cannot carry or take it away'.[3] It follows that we should not completely belittle and denigrate our nature as being weak, unstable and entirely subject to fortune; on the contrary, we know that the part of man which is flawed and unsound (and so liable to fortune) is small, and that we ourselves control the better part, which safely contains the most important of our benefits – correct beliefs, things we have learned and arguments conducive to goodness – which therefore subsist indelibly and indestructibly. If we are aware of this, the future doesn't dismay or terrify us and, where fortune is concerned, we say what   E
Socrates said to the jurors (though he was apparently addressing

1. From *Bellerophon*, F300 Nauck.
2. Stilpo's reply is differently cast in *Life of Demetrius* 9, and again differently in *On the Education of Children* 5F. The anecdote recurs in Seneca, *De Constantia* 5.6.
3. A reminiscence of Homer, *Iliad* 5.484.

his prosecutors) – that Anytus and Meletus can kill him, but not harm him.[1]

The point is that fortune can make us fall ill, can deprive us of our wealth, can ruin our relationship with the people or the king, but it cannot make someone who is good, brave and high-minded into a bad, cowardly, mean-spirited, petty and spiteful person, and it cannot deprive us of the permanent presence of an attitude towards life which is a more helpful guide in this sphere

F than a helmsman is on a sea voyage. A helmsman is incapable of quelling a rough sea or the wind, and he cannot at will happen upon a safe harbour when he needs one, and he cannot endure whatever happens confidently and without flinching: as long as he doesn't give up, and relies on his skill, 'he escapes the hell-dark sea by reefing the mainsail right down to* the bottom of

476A the mast',[2] but when the waves loom over him, he sits there quaking and trembling. On the other hand, a wise person's attitude calms the majority of physical matters, since his self-control, responsible regimen and moderate exercise get rid of the preconditions of illness; and if some external source of infection crops up, like the onset of a squall, then, in Asclepiades' words, 'he furls and lightens the sail, and rides it out'; and if some major unpredictable event overtakes and overwhelms him, the harbour is close by – he can swim away from the uncaulked hull of his body.[3]

[18] You see, it is not desire for life, but fear of death which makes an unintelligent person depend on his body and grasp on

B to it (one is reminded of how Odysseus' fear of Charybdis below him made him grasp on to the fig tree),[4] 'when winds make both stopping and sailing impossible',[5] and he is dissatisfied with one option and afraid of the other. However, anyone who has

---

1. This is a rather garbled version of Plato, *Apology* 30c–d. Plato has Socrates refer to the jurors first, and then to Anytus and Meletus. But Plutarch's wording recurs almost exactly in Epictetus 1.29.18, 2.2.15, 3.23.21, *Encheiridion* 53.4. So this was the standard first-century reference.
2. Origin unknown (*TGF Adesp.* 377 Nauck); Plutarch quotes it again in a more abbreviated form in *On Superstition* 169B.
3. By committing suicide.
4. Homer, *Odyssey* 12.432 ff.
5. From Aeschylus' *Philoctetes*, F250 Nauck and Radt.

come, by whatever route, to understand the nature of the mind, and who appreciates that at death the change the mind undergoes is either for the better or at least not for the worse,[1] is well equipped by this lack of fear of death to be content about his life. Anyone who can not only enjoy life when the pleasant and congenial aspect of it is uppermost, but who, when faced with an excess of events which are antipathetic and incongruent with his nature, can also depart without fear and with the words, 'The god himself will free me, when *I* will it'[2] – well, it is inconceivable that such a man could be annoyed or angry or upset by anything that happened to him.

C

Whoever it was who said, 'Fortune, I have made a pre-emptive strike against you, and I have deprived you of every single loophole',[3] was not basing his confidence on bolts, locks and fortifications, but on principles and arguments which are available to anyone who wants them. And this kind of argument should not induce any degree of resignation or disbelief, but admiration, emulation, enthusiasm, and investigation and observation of oneself in relatively trivial circumstances, to prepare oneself for the more important matters, so that one does not avoid them or divert one's mind from attention to them or take refuge in excuses like 'That's probably the most difficult thing I'll ever come across.' For if the mind is self-indulgent, and takes the easiest courses all the time, and retreats from unwelcome matters to what maximizes its pleasure, the consequence is weakness and feebleness born of lack of exertion; but a mind which trains and strains itself to use rationality to conceive an image of illness and pain and exile will find that there is plenty of unreality, superficiality and unsoundness in the apparent problems and horrors each of them has to offer, as detailed rational argument demonstrates.

D

[19] Nevertheless, even the line of Menander which goes 'It is impossible for anyone still living to say, "That won't happen to me"'[4] produces a shiver of fear in many people; but this is

---

1. Cf. Plato, *Apology* 40c ff.
2. Euripides, *Bacchae* 498, translated and explained by Horace, *Epistle* 1.16.78 f.
3. It was Metrodorus of Lampsacus (F49 Körte), according to Cicero, *Tusculanae Disputationes* 5.27.
4. F295.1 Körte.

because they are unaware to what extent distress can be avoided by the beneficial practice of training oneself to gain the ability to look straight at fortune with open eyes, and not to form in oneself images which are 'soft and unweathered',[1] like someone who has been brought up away from sunlight,[2] in the shade of numerous hopes which constantly give way and provide no resistance against anything. However, we can also say the same thing as Menander – 'It is impossible for anyone still living to say, "That won't happen to me"' – but add that it is possible for anyone still living to say, 'Here's what I will not do: I will not lie, I will not mislead, I will not steal, I will not intrigue.' For this lies ready to hand, within our power, and its contribution towards contentment is not inconsiderable, but huge, since the alternative is for 'the realization of knowing that I have committed crimes'[3] to mark the mind with remorse, which continually bleeds and stings like a bodily wound.

You see, while all other discomforts are eradicated by reason, it is reason itself which creates remorse, when the mind with its conscience is pricked and punished by itself. People who shiver from a chill or feel hot from a fever are more troubled and worse off than people who have the same sensations because of external heat or cold; likewise, chance events entail distress which is easier to endure, because it comes from an external source; but when 'What has happened to me is no one else's fault but my own'[4] is the lament over one's mistakes, then because it comes from an internal source, from oneself, the result is a pain which one's sense of shame makes harder to bear. This is why a magnificent house, massive wealth, a splendid genealogy and high office, eloquence and fluency, are all incapable of giving life the degree of fair and calm weather that is afforded by a mind which is untainted by bad actions and intentions, and which bases life on a character that is calm and clear. A character like this is a

---

1. A tag from Homer, *Odyssey* 21.151.
2. Like women, instead of exercising in the open air.
3. Euripides, *Orestes* 396.
4. This line of verse also appears in *On Self-sufficiency*, by Teles, the Cynic of the third century BC (p. 8 Hense), who attributes it to Diogenes of Sinope.

fountain-head of fine achievements[1] which entail not only present activity that is exuberant and happy and a source of pride, but also past memories that are more rewarding and secure than hopes which, as Pindar says, 'sustain one in old age'.[2] Carneades said, 'Even if thuribles have been cleared out, they emit their scent for a long time.' And is it not the case that fine deeds leave behind in an intelligent person's mind an impression which remains pleasant and fresh, and thanks to which happiness is irrigated and thrives and he is enabled to rise above the level of those who moan and complain about life as being a vale of tears or a place designated for our soul's exile down here?

[20] I like Diogenes' quip: once when he was visiting Sparta, he saw his host zealously getting ready for a festival day, and he said, 'Isn't it the mark of a good man to regard every day as a festival day?' And a particularly glorious festival too, if we see things aright. The world is a temple of the highest sacredness, and nowhere could be more suitable for divinity; and man is introduced into this world by means of his birth not to view manufactured, immobile images, but to gaze upon what Plato describes[3] as the perceptible likenesses of intelligible things which divine intelligence has manifested as containers of an inherent principle of life and movement – the sun, moon and stars, the rivers with their continuous discharge of renewed water, and the earth with its supply of means of nourishment for plants and creatures. Life is an initiation into these things and there is no more perfect way to celebrate them; life, therefore, should be full of contentment and joy, and we should not make the usual mistake of waiting for occasional days like the holidays sacred to Cronus, Zeus or Athena for the opportunity to enjoy and revivify ourselves by paying mimes and dancers for bought entertainment.

Moreover, although we sit quietly and in good order on these occasions – for no one complains while he is being initiated or whinges while he is watching the Pythian Games or is drinking

---

1. A Stoic phrase, according to John of Stobi (*SVF* 1.203).
2. Pindar F214 Snell. Plato had quoted it in *Republic* 331a.
3. He is probably thinking of *Timaeus* 92c; cf. also *Epinomis* 984a.

during the festival of Cronus[1] – nevertheless, people bring shame
E on the festivals, which are arranged and conducted by God, by
spending most of the rest of their time in complaints, despondency and exhausting worry. And although people enjoy listening
to the delightful sounds of musical instruments and the singing
of birds, and enjoy watching the play and frolics of animals, and
conversely get perturbed when they growl and roar and look
threatening, nevertheless when they see that their own lives are
unsmiling, depressed and constantly constrained and restricted by
disagreeable experiences and events and innumerable anxieties,
F they are unwilling to find some means of supplying themselves
with recuperation and relaxation.* But even when other people
try to assist, they resist any argument which could help them
come to terms with their current situation without finding fault
with it, remember the past without ingratitude and approach
the future happily and optimistically, without fear and without
apprehension.

---

1. Since Cronus is the Greek equivalent of the Roman god Saturn, Plutarch is
probably alluding to his festival, the Saturnalia, in Rome, where Paccius is.

# ON GOD'S SLOWNESS TO PUNISH

## INTRODUCTION

As the title indicates, this essay is concerned with a religious problem, and one which can be traced in Greek literature from at least the sixth century BC until Plutarch's day, and indeed well beyond. It was a question which engaged both philosophy and religious thought, but Plutarch makes clear from the start that his main approach will be theological. The scene is set at Delphi, the most holy shrine of Apollo, and clearly at a time when Plutarch himself was in a position of importance and influence there (558B), where he had a second residence and was dignified with a priesthood of Apollo.

Moreover, as so often happens in Plutarch, the essay begins abruptly, in this case with the announcement of the precipitous departure of an Epicurean acquaintance, who had been lecturing the group on the subject of providence as an ungrounded and fictitious doctrine. This was a live and much-argued philosophical issue; Platonists and Stoics held that the world was governed by divine providence, while Epicureans derided the idea. But the debate on providence itself is dismissed with the Epicurean. The remaining characters comprise an intimate and like-minded group consisting of Plutarch himself, his much-loved brother (or more probably half-brother) Timon, a relation by marriage called Patrocleas and a friend, Olympichus, who all firmly believe in providence, and address themselves rather to a particular difficulty with respect to it, namely the apparent slowness of the deity to punish crime and injustice. Patrocleas at once points out that this seems to clash with our idea of gods and that it would appear to encourage rather than deter wickedness (§2). Olympichus, it is true, raises the more usual *topos* of contemporary writing,[1] that this tardiness of God might destroy belief in providence itself in

that the wicked would assume that later misfortune was the
result of chance, not providence (§3). But the rest of the essay is
devoted not to this challenge to providence, but to attempted
explanation of the justice and purpose of divinely delayed retribution. Thus the initial worries of Patrocleas and Olympichus, and
an impending more serious objection to providence from Timon
(549E), are hijacked by our priest of Apollo, Plutarch himself,
who takes over and dominates the whole exposition (§§4-33).

The problem of the late dispensation of justice by the gods
came to the fore when the old amoral Olympic gods began to
yield to a concept of god as good and the dispenser and guardian
of the moral law. Given then the contradiction between (a) good
and just gods acting through pervasive providence on the one
hand and (b) the evidence on the other that the wicked flourish
and that crime at least sometimes pays, the following solutions
were put forward by the Greeks: in the first place, a straight
denial or rejection of either (a), with the argument that there is
no such thing as providence (the Epicurean answer, dismissed in
this essay), or of (b) namely, it is not true that crime *ever* pays
(the proposition of Plato and of the Stoics). These were the main
philosophical answers. The religious and popular reactions were
to accept both (a) and (b), but with the rider that although
wickedness may flourish for a time, nevertheless justice catches
up with the criminal eventually. But in that case, reasons for the
divine delay had to be produced, and so they were. When,
however, it was then pointed out that, even so, some criminals
and sinners patently died before paying for their misdeeds, two
final and highly influential solutions were offered: (i) in that case
the children or descendants of the guilty man paid for his crime;
or (ii) the wicked person did in fact receive retribution after
death in another existence. Plutarch in this essay reviews all of
these proposals except the rejection of (a). In all this there is an
ethical content of course, but the orientation and form of the
presentation is theological.

There is an initial difficulty of approach (§4). As with human
law, it would seem to be necessary, if we are to interpret divine
legislation, to understand the intention of the divine legislator. But
how is this possible for mere mannikins? Plutarch compromises.

On the one hand he recognizes the dogmatic intellectual confidence of Plato, that unless you have learnt and acquired sure knowledge, success is not possible (550B); but on the other hand he acknowledges the tendency of the New Academy to withhold judgement,[2] for he decries Solon's law which insisted that people must vote one way or the other (550C). The result is a very personal middle course of religious humility combined with lack of scepticism, and insatiable curiosity in the religious problem with limited confidence in approaching it. His procedure is marked by the Academic formula of plausibility ('reasonable', 'plausibility', 550B–C), which is all that can be sought. Two other important points are made at the start. In any practical art or science such as medicine or law the particularization of application of the general technical rule is an essential feature (549F); and Plutarch at this point assumes that the prime purpose of divine punishment is remedial, for the care of the soul (550A).

The next sections (§§5–8) put forward some suggestions to explain the delay. God's slowness to punish may be intended as an example or pattern for human virtue, to school by delay the passion for immediate retribution (§5). This springs from a very Platonic root, that the divine was an ideal pattern and virtue an assimilation to God; and Plutarch starts with reminiscences of *Theaetetus*, quickly passing to *Timaeus*, one of the most widely read dialogues of the later Hellenistic period. But his stress on the corrupting distortion of emotions is more characteristic of Hellenistic Stoicism, and of Plutarch himself. And indeed to characterize God as the supreme exemplifier is to foist on to religion his own favourite practice of arguing by example.

God may be allowing time for improvement (§6). Here Plutarch assesses human justice unfavourably as no more than the imposition of instant suffering in return for suffering caused, and contrasts it with the divine purpose of healing the psychic turmoil of emotions in the mind of the transgressor. In other words God distinguishes between those capable of reform (because they are merely ignorant of what is right) and those who are not (shown by their deliberate choice and intention for evil), and gives the former time to redeem themselves. This seems an unhappy argument, since every instance of late punishment would then mark a mistake on God's part, who would have judged as capable of redeeming himself someone who in fact failed to do so. Plutarch is also opposing a theory of *human* retribution long outmoded in Greek law and moral theory, by making a very contemporary distinction between knowledge and intention. Perhaps he had in mind the Stoic theory that each human being has a form of the divine ruling principle within him, through which he has the responsibility of working with and aiding the divine organization of the universe.[3]

The next suggestion is that God may be using bad men as tools for producing good (§7), a version of the problem of evil, where evil is excused as an instrument of good. This is supported by a wealth of impressive examples from history, poetry and nature; but apart from being a somewhat cynical view of the deity, the argument itself is becoming topsy-turvy. For certain human examples are now taken as patterns for God's behaviour. But the original assumption claimed that it was God who was a pattern or example for human behaviour. The danger of basing argument on human examples is that you can always produce counter-examples in the other direction. Plutarch then raises the view (§8) that delay occurs in order that punishment should be adequate and take place at a fitting time and manner. Examples of cases where this seems to have happened are inclined to strike the unguarded mind with awe; but on the whole, to make the punishment fit the crime suits Gilbert and Sullivan's Mikado better than a benevolent deity; and besides, what has happened to the therapeutic theory of punishment? No doubt all these suggestions are put forward hesitantly, as no more than interesting possibilities for consideration, and certainly no single one of them, nor indeed all of them together, were considered by Plutarch as the likely explanation for the problem.

He now turns to a different kind of answer, that their original assumption of deferred punishment by God is wrong. In fact, the suffering of punishment by the wicked man is always coeval with injustice, springing from the same soil and root (§§9–11): the penalty of injustice is never delayed. This is a philosophical solution, the answer of Plato and the Stoics. But Plutarch does not treat it as a philosophical argument in context or in origin. He actually assigns it to the poet Hesiod and *contrasts* his position with a Platonic reference (§9, 553F), which he takes out of context. Plato, in *Laws* 728b–c, makes the distinction between mere punishment, which must come after the crime, and the just penalty, which takes effect immediately – the damage done by his wicked action to his soul, causing him to be wretchedly unhappy until 'cured' by punishment. The theory of Plato (e.g. *Theaetetus* 176d ff.) and the Stoics was the deeper philosophical view that vice imperils, distorts, corrupts the most precious part of a human being, his essential self, his soul; therefore the wicked are bound to be fundamentally unhappy. Plutarch's development is more immediately recognizable and comprehensible for the ordinary man: that the wicked are subject to continual terrors, regrets, anxieties, emotions, dreams, fancies and delusions, like the prolonged terrors of anticipation of the condemned man (§10). His approach is pathological rather than ontological. It is presented not by argument but by aphorisms: vice creates from itself the instrument of its own punishment; criminals have not been punished on growing old, but have grown old in punishment; evil-doers need neither god nor man to punish them, their own life suffices. Also the picture of guilty terror suits Plutarch's vivid powers of illustration.

The next topic is that delayed punishment of the guilty may be effected through their descendants (§§12–21). The importance of this view is marked not only by the length of the treatment Plutarch accords to it, but also by the literary device of having Timon forcibly introduce the injustice of innocent children suffering for the sins of parents (§12), so that Plutarch himself can argue its plausibility as an act of divine justice.

This belief was indeed widespread and influential, with a long history behind it. It is traceable to the earliest Greek poets for cases of oath-breaking, an offence against the gods,[4] and becomes more urgent and explicit in the poetry of the sixth century BC.[5] The religious-minded historian Herodotus makes it the core of his accounts of Croesus, king of Lydia, who inherited the guilt of his ancestor Gyges (1.91.1–2) and of the Spartan Glaucus, who reneged on his oath by misappropriating a trust deposited with him (6.86γ2–δ). Pindar alludes to the belief (F213 Snell,

Maehler), and it is pervasive in fifth-century-BC Attic drama.[6] The orators recognize it, especially in cases of perjury and impiety.[7] Plato records it with some scorn as a popular belief (*Republic* 364b2–c2, 366a4–7; *Theaetetus* 173d6–e1), but even he appears to countenance it in exceptional cases, or in inherited religious guilt (*Laws* 856c8–d2, 854b; 759c; *Phaedrus* 244e). Cicero (*De Natura Deorum* 3.90) shows that it is still alive and potent in the later Graeco-Roman world. There are parallels in other societies too. West[8] noted occurrences in Indian and Babylonian thought; and we may compare Joshua 7.24 and the apostle John 9.1–3. Protest in literature was not lacking.[9] It was, however, mainly countered by the development of the legal responsibility of the individual in Greek law, and by the emphasis on the moral responsibility of the individual in philosophy. But it is noticeable that its origins and continued persistence in popular belief lay in religious backgrounds connected with sacrilege and offences against the gods,[10] which is no doubt why it interested Plutarch himself, and led him to give it so much prominence in this essay.

Plutarch begins his support (§13) with the mild observation that many so-called examples of children paying for their fathers' sins are fables; which is somewhat brazen on his part considering his own common practice. He also points out that if we approve of continued honours and gratitude for descendants of earlier revered patriots, we should also accept hereditary obloquy. This can be no more than suggestive, as it has nothing to do with either gods or justice. But Plutarch thinks there may be something in the theory, and proceeds with a medical analogy (§14). As diseases are contagious, even seemingly over intervals of space, so injustice and crime may be forces which can be transmitted from one human being to another by a method we cannot explain, and so children may need the cure of justice. But this is a strange argument. We might think of a hereditary disease, but Plutarch is talking in terms of *contagion* over an interval of *time* (558E).

He moves (§§15–16) to the traditional explanation based on the continuum of responsibility founded on the strong Greek belief in the unity of identity of the family. But that could only lead to group responsibility and group justice, which cannot be put on the same plane as the responsibility of the individual. A country may be held responsible for a Prime Minister's signature, but not the PM's son. Plutarch does not appear to see the difference.

But we seem to be moving away from the original criminal and his punishment, so Olympichus objects (§17) that if *he* is to be punished *through* his descendants, survival after death must be granted. Plutarch naturally retorts tartly that his concept of religion demands this anyway; but the interruption permits him to create a clever new framework. The discussion has been leading in two divergent directions, the punishment (and cure) of the sinner, and the cure (by punishment) of the descendant. Plutarch, by setting up an interworldly existence, can now (§18) suggest both punishment for the dead father through observing (in the other world) what is meted out to his living children (in this), and that a living child with a hereditary disease now incurable in the dead father can be given prophylactic treatment by punishment (§19). This is imaginative religion and should not be confused with rational argument. But confusion does seem to be growing between different kinds of punishment: therapeutic, retributive and deterrent; or perhaps Plutarch simply holds that all three types are necessary.

This passage concludes (§§20–21) with further justification of punishment of children as a preventative cure for a latent inherited tendency. Here one simply has to assume that God knows what he is doing. Heredity plays funny tricks, and although the erratic nature of specific examples is beyond our discerning, it is the result of God keeping a close eye on the working out of the genes.

The essay now takes a final turn, moving from attempted explanation to imaginative illustration in the form of a myth or cautionary tale (§§22–34). It is the story of Aridaeus of Soli who had led a shameful life, died, but recovered, a reformed character, on the day of his funeral. In the meantime his disembodied intelligence, still anchored to the rest of his soul below, had benefited from a guided tour of part of the other world. He had thus seen the souls of the dead rise like bubbles of airy fire to the moon, which was their natural area of congregation. Their condition was betrayed by their regular or irregular motion, and by the purity of their luminosity or by the mottled and scarred markings left by their crimes when incarnate. Punishment is meted out lightly for those already punished in life, more drastically if they died without atoning and most cruelly and with eternal banishment if incurable. The punishment is to purge the irrational passions that cloud the soul.

Two features relevant to Plutarch's theme are dwelt on. One is the imagery of interworldly contact and communication, which works both ways: not only with souls rising after death, but also, should a soul fail to gain the liberation of pure luminosity, the residual irrationalities and injustice are revived through the charms of the chasm of Lethe reaching up from the earth. Such souls are condemned to fall back into reincarnation. In addition, there are daimons which govern communication through oracles and dreams, both true and delusory.

The second feature is allowance for interaction within generations of a family. A new bad soul is shown to its parents, who first receive punishment themselves and must then watch while their offspring's soul is subjected to torment. Most pitiful of all were the souls who thought that their punishment was over, only to be attacked by the souls of descendants punished because of them and now hauled off together with these souls to suffer once more. In other words Plutarch is reiterating in imaginative painting his religious belief that the wicked always do atone after death for vicious behaviour, both in themselves and through their tainted descendants.

Plutarch wrote two other eschatological myths besides this one (P), in *On Socrates' Personal Deity* (S) 589F–592E, and in *On the Face on the Moon* (M) 940F–945D. The three are complementary, and contain Plutarch's beliefs about the so-called other world, our relationship to it and its relation to this one; about what happens when we die in a continuity of existence; about what 'we' are and where we 'go'; about the purpose and function of a moral progression through reward, punishment and purification within what he believes to be the rational providential organization of the continuum of the universe. His myths, like his other writing, were fashioned within a tradition; indeed they were modelled on Plato's three great eschatological myths on ultimate reward and punishment, immortality, justice and moral responsibility in *Gorgias* 523a ff., *Phaedo* 107d ff. and *Republic* 614b ff.

Some of the links are obvious and intended, such as the introduction, which distinguishes a preceding explanatory account (*logos*) from a complementary fictional myth (*mythos*): *P* 22, *S* 21, *M* 26; *Gorgias* 523a. Still more deliberate is the device of having Aridaeus of Soli (*P* 23) and Timarchus of Chaeronea (*S* 21) return from the dead; it is a clear and respectful reminiscence of the supposed experience of Er the Pamphylian in *Republic* 614b. Also, a kind of map of the other world peopled by regular denizens developed, to which Plutarch pays some passing literary reference. The Elysian Plain turns up in *M* 29, and the famous Meadows, which started in *Odyssey* 11.539 (and appear in *Gorgias* 524a, *Republic* 616b), in *M* 26, as the 'gentlest part of the air'. The groves of Persephone (*Odyssey* 10.509) become the portion of Persephone in *S* 22 (cf. *M* 27). Chasms, a feature of *Iliad* 8.14 and *Phaedo* 112a, reappear in strength in *S* 22 and disguised as Lethe in *P* 27. Colours, a striking characteristic in *Phaedo* 110c and *Republic* 616c, shine undiminished in *P* 28 and *S* 22. The Daughter of Necessity and her attendants (*P* 25) echo *Republic* 616c and 617c; and not unnaturally, the triple Fates of *Republic* 617c are used again in *S* 22 (cf. *M* 30).

But these are no more than reminiscence of familiar landmarks for readers. In fact Plutarch introduces a quite novel eschatological topography of his own. Earlier accounts placed Hades (the Unseen World) far across Ocean (Homer), or deep in the earth or on the highest peaks of earth (*Phaedo*). Plutarch puts it up in the air round the moon. This is not merely the recession of the legendary before the advances of knowledge, but a linking of theology to contemporary natural philosophy. Psychic substance was held to be an airy fire, like the upward shooting bubbles of *P* 23. Since this was also believed to be the physical composition of the moon, it becomes the natural level of souls freed from the earthy body. In *M*, Plutarch takes this a stage further, with a second death on the moon freeing intellectual fire to rise to the level of the sun. It looks as if Plutarch by his selenic eschatology has integrated his religious psychology within the cosmic framework of Stoic natural philosophy. The astronomical and stellar imagery not only gives an impression of reality, but Plutarch can now use the unity of the continuum of the natural universe to illustrate a continuum of psychic experience.

In the content too of reward and punishment, purification and rebirth, traditional elements reappear: the betraying movements of the souls (P 23; S 22; Phaedo 108a–b); their naked exposure (P 26; Gorgias 523e); the markings on them (P 24; Gorgias 524c ff.); the recognition of historical individuals (P 32, 29; Republic 615c); judgement and purification (cf. Gorgias 525a ff., Phaedo 113d ff., Republic 615b ff.); rebirth (P 32, S 22, M 30; cf. Republic 617d ff.). Even Plutarch's vivid dwelling on the severity of punishments, with torment and torture, no doubt for the alarmed persuasion of the reader, has a forerunner in Gorgias 525c ff. But his repeated emphasis on the cauterization of the passions as the aim of the cure is based on the moral orientation of contemporary moral philosophy. And the two quite distinctive features in On God's Slowness to Punish of interworldly influence, and generation interaction in family punishment have been mentioned above. There are also further developments in the other two myths of psychic demonology, stellar imagery and the possible continued progression to the pure limits of the cosmos, for which the reader is referred to the Introduction to On Socrates' Personal Deity.

One last aspect deserves mention. The description of the sensations of Aridaeus in On God's Slowness to Punish and of Timarchus in On Socrates' Personal Deity strongly suggests that Plutarch was familiar with the psychic phenomenon of 'out-of-body' experience or bilocation. One feature is the impression of a cable or cord by which the wandering soul is attached to the lower soul in the body below (564C), which keeps a pull on him (566D), and may pull him back into his body (568A); so also On Socrates' Personal Deity 592D. Modern accounts of bilocation such as Broad's[11] also report this sensation. The feeling of a blow on the head (590B) and a violent pain in the head as if forcibly compressed (592E) are recorded in Broad (pp. 179, 183, 184, 186); also the impression of the sutures of the skull parting for the release of the soul (590B; Broad, p. 182). Again the metaphors of the sea, and shooting up (563E–F) find echoes in Broad (p. 182). Shamanism was a recognized cult in the Greek world, and shamans are cited in their literature;[12] in *On Socrates' Personal Deity* 592C–D Plutarch tells of one, Hermodorus (he probably meant Hermotimus) of Clazomenae. But it looks as if Plutarch was not only aware of the phenomenon, but actually conversant with its sensations.

The essay is dedicated to T. Avidius Quietus, a man of some importance in the Roman world, suffect consul in 93, legate of Britain in 98 and, like his brother C. Avidius Nigrinus, a governor of Achaea. He was also a friend of Pliny (Pliny, *Letter* 6.29.1), like Fundanus, to whom Plutarch dedicated *On the Avoidance of Anger*. Plutarch was acquainted with both brothers, as his essay *On Brotherly Love* is for them. The dedication indicates a latish date of composition. On internal evidence, the essay was certainly written after the eruption of Vesuvius in 79 (566E), and probably after the death of the emperor Titus in 81 (566E); but the dedication to Avidius should place it in the late nineties, or even in the early second century. The maturity and power of the composition would fit with this rich period of Plutarch's writing. It was much admired in antiquity; Proclus in his work *De Providentia* simply purloined considerable swatches of it; and it has remained one of Plutarch's most read pieces.

1. E.g. Seneca, *De Providentia 1*.
2. E.g. Cicero, *Academica* 2.59.
3. E.g. Posidonius Frs. 186, 187 EK; but also cf. Plato, *Timaeus* 90a–d.
4. Homer, *Iliad* 4.158–65; Hesiod, *Works and Days* 282–5.
5. Solon F13.25–32 West; Theognis, 203–8.
6. E.g. Aeschylus, *Choephori* 61–5, 1065–75; *Eumenides* 266–75; Sophocles, *Oedipus at Colonus* 964–8; Euripides, *Hippolytus* 820, 831 f., 1378–83.
7. Ps.-Lysias 6.20; Isocrates 11.25; Lycurgus, *Against Leocrates* 79; Demosthenes 57.27.
8. Hesiod, *Works and Days* 228.
9. Theognis 731–52; Bion of Borysthenes, F27 Kindstrand (Plutarch 561C); Cicero, *loc.cit.*; Jeremiah 31.29 f., Ezekiel 18.
10. It was legally built into the oath-curse itself: Antiphon 5.11, Andocides 1.98.
11. C. D. Broad, *Lectures on Psychical Research*, pp. 184 f.
12. E. R. Dodds, *The Greeks and the Irrational*, pp. 140 ff.

# ON GOD'S SLOWNESS TO PUNISH

548A [1] Once our Epicurus[1] had finished speaking, Quietus,[2] he
B didn't give anyone a chance to respond, but since we happened
to be at the end of the stoa, he hurried away. We stood still and
looked at one another in amazement at his odd behaviour, and
then turned and resumed our walk. A little later, Patrocleas
broke the silence by saying, 'Well, do you think we should
discontinue the inquiry, or respond to the argument as if its
proponent were here, even though he isn't?'

'But if he had shot us,' replied Timon, 'and then run away, it
certainly wouldn't be right to ignore the missile sticking in us.
C Brasidas apparently pulled the spear out of his body and used this
very weapon to strike and kill the person who had thrown it. In
our case, however, if people fire an outrageous or false argument
against us, we needn't bother to repay them in kind, surely: all
we need do is deflect the idea before it gets through to us.'

'Well,' I said, 'what was the most effective thing he said, in
your opinion? I mean, a lot of it was a confused mishmash, and it
was completely disorganized and eclectic: he was coming down
hard on the notion of providence as if he were hacking at it in a
fit of abusive rage.'

[2] Patrocleas said, 'I think the slowness and lateness of divinity
D in retaliating against sinners is particularly awkward. In fact, the
points he made about this have renewed and reawakened that
idea in me right now: I used to get disturbed a long time ago by
Euripides' line "He is slow – but the gods are by nature like

1. An Epicurean acquaintance. Following a common idiom, Plutarch refers to
   him by the name of the founder of the School of which he was an adherent
   (cf. Posidonius F47.45 EK; Plutarch 928E).
2. See Introduction, p. 249.

that."[1] And yet God should be sluggish about nothing,[2] and least of all about sinners, who are not themselves sluggish or "work-shy"[3] in transgressing, but in fact are driven towards immoral behaviour by their emotions at a furious pace. Moreover, to quote Thucydides, "When reprisal comes as soon as possible after the event",[4] it immediately bars the way against                          E people who are strongly inclining towards making use of their badness while it is in full flow. For deferment of the debt of punishment is not only more debilitating to the injured party's hopes and more depressing than deferment of any other kind of debt, but it is also the best boost to the wrongdoer's daring and audacity; on the other hand, retaliation which wastes no time in challenging audacity not only deters future crimes, but is inherently the greatest possible consolation to the victim. So, for my part, I am also often troubled by Bias' statement, when I recall what he said to a certain bad man – which was, apparently, that                 F he had no doubt that he would pay a penalty, but he was worried that he, Bias, would not be around to witness it.

'I mean, how did the Messenians who had been killed long before gain by Aristocrates being punished? Aristocrates betrayed them at the battle of Boar's Cairn and got away with it for over twenty years, and all this while he continued to rule over Arcadia;[5] later he was found out and punished, but they were long gone. Or again, Lyciscus betrayed the Orchomenians;[6] much later he was afflicted by a disease which ravaged his body, because      549A he spent his whole time washing and immersing himself in the

1. Euripides, *Orestes* 420. Orestes is referring to Apollo.
2. As Plato had said (*Laws* 901e4 ff.).
3. A word probably coined by Hesiod, *Works and Days* 413.
4. Thucydides 3.38.1. The Athenian politician Cleon urged strong reprisals against the Mytileneans, who had revolted.
5. Plutarch has confused the treachery of Aristocrates, king of the Arcadians in the mid seventh century BC, at the battle of the Trench (Polybius 4.33.5 f.; Pausanias 4.17.2), with Aristomenes, the traditional hero of the Messenian resistance to Sparta of the same period, and his victory at the battle of Boar's Cairn (Pausanias 4.19.3).
6. This probably refers to the destruction of Orchomenus by the Thebans and the Boeotian Federation in 364 BC, when treachery occurred (Diodorus 15.79.5). But Lyciscus is mentioned nowhere else. This may be a case of Plutarch's more intimate knowledge of Boeotian local history.

river, and he swore that his body should rot and called down
curses on it, since he was a traitor and a criminal. But what
consolation was this to those Orchomenians who had lost children, friends and relatives? At Athens, the bodies of people polluted by bloodshed were once cast out – their corpses banished
beyond the frontiers – but not even the grandchildren of the
people originally murdered were in a position to witness this.[1]

'It follows that it is strange for Euripides to use the following
argument for putting someone off iniquitous behaviour:[2] "Don't
be alarmed: justice won't come up to you or any other unjust
person and stab you in the guts. No, it comes with silent and
B    steady tread and grabs* criminals when they don't expect it." I
mean, this is exactly the same argument that criminals probably
use to urge and induce themselves to undertake illegal activities,
claiming that immorality yields a crop that comes to instantaneous fruition and is plain to see, whereas retribution arrives later –
much later than the enjoyment.'

[3] When Patrocleas had had his say, Olympichus took up the
theme: 'Patrocleas, there is another outstandingly odd consequence of divine tardiness and slowness in this respect, which is
that this delay destroys belief in providence: when trouble does
C    not ensue for bad people immediately after any given crime, but
comes later, they classify it as a piece of bad luck, and call it an
accident, not retribution, and so derive no benefit from it, in the
sense that although what happens might hurt them, they do not
repent of their actions. Consider the case of a horse: a blow or a
jab immediately following a slip or a mistake improves a horse,
and shows it the way to an alternative, proper mode; but if you
lay into it and jerk on the bit and yell at it later, after an interval
of some time, it assumes that the purpose of all this happening is

---

1. The polluted dead of Athens were the bones of the killers of Cylon's force
   who had taken sanctuary in the Acropolis in 612 BC. Plutarch, in *Life of Solon*
   12.3, implies that the purificatory expulsion took place in Solon's time, about
   594, which would make nonsense of a period beyond the grandchildren of the
   victims. But Herodotus records (5.70) the expulsion as taking place at the
   request of Cleomenes at the end of the sixth century, which suits Plutarch's
   point here. Thucydides (1.126.12) implies an earlier and a later expulsion.
   Perhaps the living were expelled first, and the bones of the dead later.

2. *TGF* Euripides F979 Nauck.

not instruction, but something else, which involves pain but has nothing to do with training. In the same way, if vice is lashed and bridled by being punished every time it slips and falls, it might eventually become cowed and humble, and it might appreciate, with fear, that God, in overseeing human affairs and passions, is not dilatory when it comes to meting out justice; but this justice of Euripides', with its gradual and steady pace, which assails wrongdoers when they don't expect it, looks more like an accidental than a providential phenomenon, because of its inconsistency, tardiness and irregularity. Consequently, I don't see how those proverbial slow-grinding mills of the gods are any use at all:[1] they make justice dim and smother hesitancy about performing evil deeds.'

[4] I was poised to address what he'd said, when Timon asked, 'Shall I, for my part, now impose the crowning difficulty on our discussion, or shall I leave it to grapple first with what's already come up?'

'Why must we bring on the third wave[2] and overwhelm the discussion even more,' I asked, 'if it turns out to be incapable of repelling or avoiding the first challenges? But first things first: just as it is traditional to make the ancestral hearth one's starting-point,[3] so we should start with the caution evinced by Academic philosophers about divine matters, and forswear speaking about these things as if we actually knew anything. Being human and investigating the affairs of the gods is an extreme version of being tone-deaf and talking about music, or having never served in the army and talking about warfare: we resemble amateurs trying to use arguments from probability based on opinions and conjecture to unearth the ideas of experts. Given that it is hard for a layman to interpret the thought processes that led a doctor

1. The proverb is quoted fully in Sextus Empiricus, *Adversus Mathematicos* 1.287: the mills of God grind slowly, but they grind exceedingly small.
2. In popular lore, it was the third wave which was huge and swamped everything before it. Plutarch probably remembers the metaphor from Plato, *Republic* 472a; but its use was embedded in classical literature (e.g. Aeschylus, *Seven Against Thebes* 760, *Prometheus Bound* 1015; Euripides, *Hippolytus* 1213).
3. The phrase was proverbial already in Plato, *Euthyphro* 3a; as the hearth was the central focus of the house, so we should set out from what is of prime importance and central. Plutarch used it several times: 93E, 920F, 948B, 1074E.

to operate sooner rather than later or to cauterize today rather than yesterday, it cannot be easy or secure for a human being to say anything about the gods except that God is the best judge of the timing required for remedying vice, and dispenses punishment to each individual as if it were a medicinal drug – there is no universal dosage and the timing of the punishment is not identical in all cases.

'The point is that the art of curing the mind – otherwise known as justice and morality[1] – is the most important of all the arts, as is affirmed by thousands of writers, including Pindar when he calls the god who has power and authority over everything "of unsurpassed skill",[2] because what he crafts is justice, whose job is to define the timing, means and quantity of each sinner's punishment. And this is the art of which, according to Plato,[3] Minos became a student, despite being a son of Zeus, because in matters of justice study and acquisition of the technical knowledge are essential prerequisites of the ability either to succeed or to appreciate success. I mean, even laws instituted by humans are not invariably and always reasonable at first sight, and some moral principles[4] even seem absolutely ridiculous. For instance, in Sparta the first thing the ephors do once they have taken up office is issue an injunction against the growing of moustaches and enjoining obedience to the laws for anyone wanting to avoid legal penalties.[5] And in Rome the process of emanci-

---

1. Reminiscent of Plato, *Gorgias* 464b–c.
2. Pindar F57 Snell and Maehler. Again at 807C and 1065E, and quoted by Plutarch's contemporary, Dio Chrysostom 12.81.
3. Plutarch must have been thinking of *Minos* 319b–e, from the details of his repetition at 776E. Minos was originally king of Cnossus in Crete (Homer, *Odyssey* 19.178), son of Zeus and lawgiver through his father's guidance (Plato, *Laws* 624a–b, *Minos* 319b–c), and eventually one of the judges of the dead (Homer, *Odyssey* 11.568 ff.; Plato, *Minos* 319d).
4. Plutarch is using terms which were also philosophically technical. 'Reasonable' (*eulogon*) was a criterion for the Academic Arcesilaus, and also for the Stoics with respect to their class of morally appropriate actions. 'Principle' (*prostagma*) was used for an absolute injunction or principle of the moral law.
5. Recorded by Aristotle F539 Rose, F545 Gigon. According to Plutarch's *Lives of Agis and Cleomenes* 30.3, the intention was to accustom the young to obedience in even the most trifling matters. It survives again in the *Commentary on Hesiod* F90 Sandbach.

pating a slave involves striking him on the body with a light stalk,[1] and wills establish some people as the future heirs, but sell the estate to quite different people – which is absurd, on the face of it.[2] But the most absurd law of all is the one of Solon's which disenfranchises anyone who, in times of civil strife, fails to side with one faction or the other and join in the divisiveness.[3] In short, anyone who doesn't know the lawgiver's reasoning or doesn't understand the rationale for any given decree could come up with plenty of legal oddities. So, given that human laws are opaque to us in this way, is it surprising that it is not easy to say, where the gods are concerned, why they punish some wrong-doers later, and some sooner? [5] This is not meant to be evasive, but it is an appeal for leniency, so that the argument can, so to speak, keep its gaze fixed on a harbour, a place of safety, and so use plausibility to weather the storm of these difficulties.

'The first point to bear in mind is that, as Plato says, God has established himself as a manifest paradigm of everything commendable and so makes possible, for anyone capable of following him, human virtue, which is in some sense an assimilation to God.[4] In fact, this is how the underlying nature of things, despite being chaotic, gained its starting-point for changing and evolving into the ordered universe – by assimilation to and a kind of participation in divine identity and goodness.[5] And Plato also says that nature ignited vision in us for our minds to gaze in awe on the movements of the heavenly bodies,[6] and so become

1. The Roman jurist Gaius (second century AD) records this ceremony of manumission (*Institutes* 4.16).
2. Gaius (*Institutes* 2.102) explains this procedure. By the 'selling' of the estate, the 'buyer' acquires the legal rights of an executor, which he uses for future heirs.
3. Aristotle records this law of Solon against neutrality (*Athenian Constitution* 8.5). Plutarch expresses astonishment again in *Life of Solon* 20.1.
4. For assimilation to God: Plato, *Theaetetus* 176b (cf. *Republic* 500c–d). For God as pattern: Plato, *Phaedrus* 253a, *Theaetetus* 176e. For 'following God': Plato, *Phaedrus* 248a, *Laws* 715e ff. Arius Didymus (first century BC), the philosophy teacher of Augustus, assigned 'follow God' to Pythagoras (John of Stobi, *Ecloguae* 2.49.16 Wachsmuth).
5. Compare Plato, *Timaeus* 29e ff.
6. Compare Plato, *Timaeus* 47b; but closer in language is the paraphrase of *Timaeus*, dating from the first century AD and known as *Timaeus Locrus*, section 11. These were all subjects of contemporary discussion. On igniting vision, see the Stoic philosopher Posidonius F193 EK, and Plutarch himself at

accustomed to welcome and appreciate elegance and organiza-
E     tion, and loathe the disharmony and inconsistency of the emotions and avoid random purposelessness as the origin of all vice
and discord.[1] For the most important way in which human
beings can, by their nature, profit from God is to imitate and
pursue the goodness and perfection which he contains, and
thereby make virtue their stable state.

'It follows that, if God takes time and is in no hurry to impose
punishment on sinners, this is not because he is worried about
making a mistake or changing his mind if he punishes quickly; it
is because he is freeing us of the bestial savagery we employ
F     when punishing, and is teaching us to avoid anger and to avoid
the time when "our temper is leaping higher than our intelligence",[2] and is burning and seething – in other words, to avoid
assaulting people who have hurt us as if we were slaking thirst or
satisfying hunger.[3] Instead, he is teaching us to imitate his gentleness and procrastination, and to turn to punishment in an orderly
and concordant fashion, with time assisting our decisions rather
than involving us in the slightest regret. As Socrates said,[4] it is
better for lack of self-control to make a person hurl himself on to
unsettled water and drink it, than it is for him to gorge himself
551A    on retaliation[5] against the body of a member of his own species
and race while his rational mind is muddied and filled with anger
and rage, before it has become steady and clear. The point is that
Thucydides was wrong to talk about "reprisal as soon as possible
after the event"[6] receiving an appropriate reward: it is when it
comes as long as possible after the event that it does so. Melanthius
says that anger "displaces intelligence and then commits criminal

---

958E. And Arius Didymus had an entry on assimilation to God (John of Stobi,
   *Eclogues* 2.49.8 Wachsmuth).
1. This is still reminiscent of Plato, *Timaeus* 47a–c, but the emphasis on emotions
   transposes the argument to contemporary Hellenistic philosophy.
2. *TGF Adesp.* 390 Nauck.
3. The rest of section 5 raises topics common to contemporary debate on anger.
   See especially *On the Avoidance of Anger* 459B–460C.
4. There were collections of such 'Sayings of Socrates' available in Plutarch's
   time (e.g. Hibeh Papyrus 182).
5. The very words used in *On the Avoidance of Anger* 453E.
6. See p. 251, n. 4.

acts";[1] likewise, rationality too first sets anger and rage aside, and then commits acts of justice and fairness.

'This is why people are calmed down even by human exemplars, if they are told that when Plato had his staff raised against his slave, he stood for a long time "remonstrating with his anger", as he tells us himself.[2] Or again, they can hear how when Archytas found out that the slaves on his estate had behaved offensively and disobediently, and then realized that he was feeling too wound up and violent towards them, he stopped himself doing anything except saying, as he was leaving, "You're lucky I'm angry with you."[3] So if recalling what *people* have said, and talking about what they have done, can decrease the violence and extremity of anger, it is considerably more likely that when we see God, who has nothing to fear and no regrets, still deferring retaliation to the future and allowing time to pass, we will become circumspect in similar circumstances, and will regard the patient magnanimity which God displays as a godlike aspect of virtue, because although it doesn't commonly use punishment to improve people, yet it does benefit and chastise a lot of people by taking its time over punishment.

[6] 'Second, then, we should realize that human-instigated punishments serve only to repay hurt with hurt,[4] and* stop when the original perpetrator has suffered, but have no further purpose. They are rather like dogs, therefore: they bark at and harry wrongdoers, and follow hard on the heels of actions. It is reasonable to assume, however, that God takes a careful look at the emotions of the sick minds to which he is dispensing punishment, to see if they have the slightest possible tendency and inclination towards remorse, and that he determines how much time should elapse for those people whose nature is not absolutely and incorrigibly evil.

1. See p. 178, n. 2.
2. But not in our Plato. This story had become common coin in the topic: other versions occur in Seneca, *De Ira* 3.12.5, Diogenes Laertius 3.38 and again in Plutarch 1108A.
3. Another commonplace: versions in Cicero, *Tusculanae Disputationes* 4.78 and *De Re Publica* 1.59, from where it spawned in later literature (e.g. Lactantius, *De Ira Dei* 18.4).
4. But also religious law at the centre of much Greek tragedy, and proverbialized as 'the doer must suffer' (e.g. Aeschylus, *The Libation Bearers* 313).

'You see, God knows the amount of goodness which the minds bore when they left him and proceeded to birth, and he knows how solid and substantial their innate nobility is: this nobility does not naturally erupt into evil, except when it is corrupted by being cultivated badly and in the wrong company – and even then, if it is subsequently well tended, there are occasions when it regains its proper condition. So, because he knows all this, he doesn't hastily impose the same punishment on everyone: he wastes no time in mowing down and removing from life anything which is irredeemable, because although constant association with wrong is certainly harmful to others, it is above all the wrongdoer himself who is harmed; but he gives time, the chance to change, to people whose sinfulness has probably taken root because they didn't know what was right, rather than because they deliberately chose what was wrong; but if they don't change, he metes out punishment to them too – I mean, he certainly doesn't worry about them escaping!

'The thing to bear in mind is that people's characters and ways of life do change a lot. This is why our changeable part is called "temperament" – and also "character", because nothing goes in deeper than conditioning and nothing clings more potently.[1] Anyway, in my opinion, people long ago called Cecrops two-sided not because he started off as a good king and became a savage, serpentine tyrant,[2] although this is the reason some people give, but for quite the opposite reason: he was initially sinuous and terrifying, and then later was a humane, kind ruler. Certainty may be impossible in that instance, but we do know that Gelon of Sicily, Hieron of Sicily and Pisistratus the son of Hippocrates used improper means to become tyrants and then used their power for good; although they gained their authority illegally, they became fair rulers, who benefited their people. Under Pisis-

1. The root of the Greek word for 'temperament' (*tropos*) is a verb meaning 'change'; here Plutarch also relates 'character' (*ēthos*) with 'conditioning' (*ethos*), as others had done before him: e.g. Aristotle, *Nicomachean Ethics* 1103a17–18. In fact, there was a Greek proverb, 'All character comes from conditioning' (Plato, *Laws* 792e2).

2. Cecrops, a mythical king of Athens, was portrayed as a serpent below the waist.

tratus and Hieron, a high degree of law and order flourished, and
so did agriculture, and the populace shed their extravagance* and
gossiping in favour of responsibility and industriousness; Gelon
was also an outstanding protector of his country at war, and after
defeating the Carthaginians in a major engagement, when they
sued for peace he made it a precondition that the terms should
include a guarantee that they would stop sacrificing their children
to Cronus. Lydiadas, the tyrant of Megalopolis, changed actually
during his tyranny: his hatred of injustice led him to hand legal      B
authority back to the populace, and he later died a splendid
death, fighting for his country against her enemies. If someone
had killed Miltiades prematurely, when he was the tyrant in the
Chersonese, or had successfully prosecuted Cimon for sleeping
with his sister, or had indicted Themistocles on the charges later
brought against Alcibiades for coarse and criminal public sprees,[1]
and got him exiled from Athens, then would we not have lost
our Marathons, our Eurymedons and the glory of Artemisium,
"where sons of Athens laid the gleaming foundation of freedom"?[2]

'The point is that the accomplishments of great natures are      C
never small, and their intensity stimulates their energy and dyna-
mism into activity, which tosses them hither and thither until
they eventually reach the stable haven of a settled character.
Someone inexperienced in farming would not welcome the sight
of land covered in dense undergrowth and wild plants, teeming
with animals, and streaming with rivulets and mud; but exactly
the same features show anyone who has acquired discrimination
and discernment that the soil is rich, extensive and friable. Likewise, great natures often bloom in odd and undesirable ways,      D
and our initial reaction is to find their rough and prickly aspects
intolerable, and to think we ought to cut them down and prune

1. According to Athenaeus (533D, 576C), Themistocles yoked four prostitutes to
   a chariot and drove them through the crowded streets of Athens. This, adds
   the helpful Athenaeus, was before the Athenians became addicted to boozing
   with prostitutes.
2. See p. 164, n. 4. The line refers to the battle of Artemisium (480 BC); Artemisium, Marathon (490) and Eurymedon (c. 467) were three of the most famous
   battles of the Persian Wars, and were won respectively by Themistocles,
   Miltiades and Cimon.

them; but a better judge recognizes even in these aspects the signs of stock which is good and valuable, and he waits for the time when they cooperate with reason and virtue, and the moment when their nature produces its particular fruit.

[7] 'So much for that. Now, don't you think that the Egyptian law which some Greeks have copied is a reasonable one – the one that a pregnant woman who has been sentenced to death is to be kept in prison until she gives birth?'[1]

'Of course,' they replied.

'And,' I went on, 'if someone is not pregnant with actual
E  children, but has the potential to manifest and bring into the world, in due course, some latent action or design, by exposing an unnoticed crime or by helping to formulate life-saving advice or by discovering an essential function, then isn't it better to postpone retaliation until he has performed this service rather than kill him prematurely? *I* think so, anyway,' I added.

'So do we,' said Patrocleas.

'And you're right,' I said. 'I mean, if Dionysius had been punished at the outset of his tyranny, then you can see that no Greeks would be living in Sicily, because it would have been devastated by the Carthaginians. Similarly, Greeks would not have settled in Apollonia or Anactorium or the Leucadian penin-
F  sula if Periander's punishment had not been postponed for a long time. And in my opinion the purpose of Cassander's punishment being delayed was for Thebes to be repopulated.[2]

'Most of the foul mercenaries who took part in the capture of this sanctuary here[3] accompanied Timoleon on his voyage to Sicily, where they defeated the Carthaginians[4] and deposed the tyrants, and subsequently died a foul death in their turn. You see, on occasion divinity has actually used sinners to punish other sinners – used them as executioners, as it were – and then crushed them: this is what has happened, I think, in the case of a great

---

1. A common law in the ancient world (Diodorus 1.77.9 f.; Aelian, *Varia Historia* 5.18); and for Rome, Ulpian, *Digesta Iustiniani Augusti* xlviii.19.3.
2. The Macedonian Cassander rebuilt Thebes in 316 BC, after it had been destroyed by Alexander.
3. The dialogue is set in Delphi: see also 553E, 556F and 560C.
4. In 341 BC; see Plutarch, *Life of Timoleon* 30.

many tyrants. A hyena's gall-bladder and whey from a seal have some use in the context of illness, even though the creatures are in all other respects noxious;[1] on the same principle, God has occasionally imposed on countries which need to suffer and be punished a tyrant's unrelenting savagery and a ruler's oppressive cruelty, and has not relieved them of the cause of the pain and tribulation until it has removed and decontaminated the disease. Phalaris was this kind of medicine for the Agrigentines, and so was Marius for the Romans.

'God even explicitly announced to the Sicyonians that the country needed a flagellator,[2] when they dismembered the young man Teletias, who had won at the Pythian Games, while trying to take him away from the Cleonaeans on the grounds that he was a citizen of their country. Orthagoras' tyranny and then the oligarchies centred on Myron and Cleisthenes put paid to the Sicyonians' unruly ways; but the Cleonaeans have come to nothing, because they did not get the same medicinal treatment.

'You are all well aware of Homer's words, "He fathered a son who was considerably better than him at everything."[3] In fact, Copreus' son, to whom he is referring, achieved nothing brilliant or outstanding. However, the descendants of Sisyphus, Autolycus and Phlegyas dwarfed great kings with their prowess and goodness;[4] in Athens, Pericles was a scion of a family which was under a curse;[5] and in Rome, Pompey the Great's father was

553A

B

C

---

1. The general idea is in Aristotle (F370 Rose, F276 Gigon). Plutarch used hyena's bile again in *On Common Conceptions* 1065B, and seals' rennet as a cure for epilepsy occurs in Theophrastus, *Historia Plantarum* 9.11.3, and in Aelian, *De Natura Animalium* 3.19.

2. The word was part of a Pythian oracle (Diodorus 8.24), which explains Plutarch's interest in the story. There is no other trace of Teletias. The Sicyonian tyranny was in the seventh and sixth centuries BC.

3. Homer, *Iliad* 15.641 f.: Periphetes of Mycenae, killed by Hector.

4. Sisyphus, 'the craftiest of men' (*Iliad* 15.153) and condemned to torture in Hades (*Odyssey* 11.593), was the ancestor of the heroes Bellerophon, Glaucus and Sarpedon (*Iliad* 6.155 ff.), and according to one story (Plutarch, *Greek Questions* 301D; see *On the Use of Reason by 'Irrational' Animals* 992E) the true father of Odysseus. Autolycus, the prince of thieves and perjury (*Odyssey* 19.394 ff.) was the grandfather of Odysseus. Phlegyas, who burned the temple of Apollo at Delphi (Pausanias 9.36.2 f.) and joined Sisyphus in Hades (Virgil, *Aeneid* 6.618 ff.), was the grandfather of Asclepius.

5. The Alcmeonidae, who had been implicated in the killing of Cylon's force: see p. 252, n. 1.

Strabo, who was so detested by the Roman people that they cast his corpse out and trampled it underfoot.

'What follows from this? There is nothing odd in a farmer not cutting down the prickly asparagus plant unless he has gathered the edible root, or in the Libyans not burning their shrubs until they have collected the ladanum from them. So why should there be anything odd in God not destroying the root of a famous royal line, even though the root may in itself be useless and offputting, until it has produced its proper fruit? It is preferable for the Phocians to have lost ten thousand of Iphitus' cows and horses, and for even more gold and silver to have been taken

D from Delphi, than for Odysseus, Asclepius and all the other men of virtue and vast altruism who came from bad and useless stock not to have been born.

[8] 'Don't you think it better for punishment to occur at exactly the right moment and in an appropriate manner, than quickly and instantaneously? For instance, for Callippus, who feigned closeness to Dion and murdered him with a dagger, to have been dispatched in turn with the identical dagger by people close to him?[1] Or for the bronze statue of Mitys of Argos, who was killed in a period of civil strife, to fall during a show in the agora on to Mitys' slayer and kill him?[2] And I'm sure you are familiar, Patrocleas, with what happened to Bessus of Paeonia and Ariston, the mercenary commander from Oeta.'

E 'No, I can't say I am,' he said, 'but do please tell me.'

'Well,' I said, 'the tyrants gave Ariston Eriphyle's jewellery, which had been deposited here,[3] and he took it and gave it to his wife as a present; his son set the house on fire because he was furious with his mother for some reason, and burned everyone in it to death. And Bessus apparently killed his own father and wasn't found out for ages, and then, when he was out at dinner

1. This is Academic lore, and so of interest to Plutarch (also *Life of Dion* 58); Dion was the Syracusan friend of Plato.
2. This is the kind of anecdote that found its way into collections of remarkable happenings, as in the Ps.-Aristotelian collection, *Mirabilia* (846a22 ff.); but it also turns up in Aristotle, *Poetics* 1452a7 ff.
3. In the temple at Delphi. Eriphyle, bribed by the necklace, sent her husband Amphiaraus to his death, and was killed in revenge by her son. The necklace thus bore this curse (Diodorus 16.64.2).

with friends, he jabbed a swallow's nest with his spear, knocked it to the ground and killed the baby birds. Of course, the people who were there said, "What's the matter? What a peculiar thing to do! What made you do that?" He replied, "Because they've been telling lies about me for hours, screaming that I killed my father, haven't they?" The people there were amazed; they told the king what he'd said, the truth of the matter came to light and Bessus got his just deserts.

[9] 'But so far,' I went on, 'our arguments have assumed as axiomatic the notion that retaliation against sinners is delayed. That is not the whole story, however: we must also imagine that we hear Hesiod's words. Hesiod disagrees with Plato's view that punishment is a painful consequence of crime;[1] he says instead that it is crime's correlate, growing at the same time, out of the same soil, the same root. "The schemer himself is the one who suffers worst from an evil scheme," he says, and, "Anyone who contrives evil for someone else is contriving evil personally for himself."[2] We are told that the blister beetle carries within itself a kind of remedial antidote, mixed in with the poison; wrongdoing, however, generates pain and punishment along with itself, and so pays the penalty for injustice not at some later date, but concurrent with the actual crime. On the way to the place of punishment, every criminal shoulders his own cross; and every instrument of punishment is fashioned by vice for itself and by itself, because it is a rather skilful craftsman of a life of misery and involves not only dishonour, but also plenty of terror, remorse, harsh emotions and endless anxiety.

'Some people, however, behave exactly like children: they gaze at criminals in the theatre, who may well be dressed in robes shot with gold and in purple cloaks, wearing garlands and dancing victory dances, and they are so impressed and amazed that they think they are happy – until they see them being

---

1. Plato, *Laws* 728c, but the context is different: see p. 243.
2. The first line is *Works and Days* 266. Plutarch misremembered the second line, which is similar to *Works and Days* 265, but is instead Callimachus, *Aetia* I, F2.5 Pfeiffer, which is repeated again in Lucillius, the epigrammatist of the time of Nero (*Palatine Anthology* XI.183.5) and became proverbial (Aelian, *Varia Historia* 8.9).

stabbed and lashed, and see those florid, expensive clothes burst-
C ing into flames.[1] I mean, in most cases, people don't realize that
criminals who have the trappings of huge mansions, high office
and conspicuous power are being punished, until they suddenly
have their throats slit or are thrown off a cliff – and one wouldn't
say that this constituted their punishment, but rather that it was the
culmination and conclusion of their punishment. Plato says of
Herodicus of Selymbria, who contracted consumption, an incurable disease, and became the first person to combine medicine
and exercise, that he devised for himself and others with the
same ailment a protracted death;[2] likewise all those criminals who
seem to have avoided instantaneous catastrophe are in fact paying
D a more protracted, not more delayed, penalty: they are not
punished *after* a longer time, but *for* a longer time; they have not
been punished on growing old, but have grown old in punishment.

'When I talk about a long time, I mean long relative to us: to
the gods the whole period of a human life is nothing, and the
racking or crucifixion of a criminal now, rather than thirty years
previously, is like doing it in the afternoon rather than in the
morning. This is especially so given that life for the criminal is as
confining as a prison from which there is no release or escape,
even though it allows the time to be filled with plenty of ban-
quets, business transactions, presents and gratuities – and indeed
games, as when prisoners play dice or backgammon with the
rope hanging above their heads.

[10] 'It is obvious, surely, that those who are in prison awaiting
E execution are being punished right up to the time when their
heads are cut off, or that someone who has drunk hemlock[3] and
is walking around, waiting for his legs to get heavy, is being
punished before he is gripped by the numbness and rigidity
which between them constitute unconsciousness. But there is
nothing to prevent us denying this, if we consider only the final
moment of punishment as punishment, and disregard the feelings,

---

1. Known as the *tunica molesta*, a fine robe soaked or smeared with inflammable
   material, in which a criminal was burned to death.
2. Plato, *Republic* 406a–b.
3. A method of execution in Athens: see Plato, *Phaedo* 117a–118a on Socrates'
   execution.

F

fears, apprehensions and regrets to which every criminal is liable, by virtue of the fact that he has done wrong – which is like denying that a fish which has swallowed the hook has been caught, until we see it being baked or cut up by a cook. As soon as anyone has committed a crime, he has been caught by justice; he has gobbled up the tasty bait of his crime,[1] but his conscience is lurking inside and it makes him pay, and "like a darting tunny he churns the sea".[2]

'The point is that the notorious impetuosity and defiance of evil is strong and pervasive up to the moment when the crime is committed; but then the gusts of passion die down, and evil falls a weak and timid victim to fear and superstition. Consequently Stesichorus' fictional dream of Clytemnestra is very true to life. Stesichorus' lines go somewhat as follows: "She imagined that a snake approached, with the top of its head all bloody; and then from the snake appeared the royal offspring of Pleisthenes."[3] In fact dreams and daydreams, the utterances of seers, the striking of lightning – in short, anything which is supposed to be achieved by the agency of God – induce floods of fear in people who are in this state. For example, we are told that Apollodorus once dreamed that he was being skinned and then boiled by the Scythians, and that his heart spoke from the pot and said, "This is my fault."[4] And apparently, on another occasion, he dreamed that his daughters were running in a circle around him with their bodies ablaze and on fire. And we hear that Hipparchus, the son of Pisistratus, dreamed just before his death that Aphrodite threw blood at his face from a cup. Ptolemy Ceraunus[5] once summoned

555A

B

---

1. The metaphor comes from Plato, *Timaeus* 69d1. It caught on: Cicero also quotes it in *De Senectute* 44.
2. *TGF Adesp.* 391 Nauck, Kannicht and Snell.
3. Stesichorus F42 Bergk, F219 Page. The royal offspring was Orestes, who would kill his mother Clytemnestra in revenge for her murder of his father Agamemnon.
4. Apollodorus was a tyrant of Cassandreia (i.e. Potidea in Chalcidice) in the early third century BC, who was noted for his cruelty (see 556D below). He served up a murdered boy as a stew for his court to eat; hence the dream. His story is in Polyaenus, a rhetorician of the second century AD (6.7).
5. A son of Ptolemy I Soter. He retreated to the court of Lysimachus, king of Thrace, and in 281 BC murdered Seleucus, a Macedonian associate of Alexander, who had acquired Babylonia after Alexander's death.

C his friends, and they arrived to find him imagining that he was being tried by Seleucus – with a jury of vultures and wolves, who were distributing chunks of meat to his enemies.★ When he was in Byzantium, Pausanias' criminal nature led him to send for Cleonice, a young woman who was not a slave, with a view to making her spend the night with him;[1] but when she came, he became deranged and paranoid, and he killed her. Later, he had a recurrent dream in which she said to him, "Draw closer to justice: criminality spells certain doom for men." The dreams went on and on, apparently, and so he sailed to the Psychopompeion[2] at Heracleia and used certain expiatory offerings and libations to summon the girl's spirit; when she appeared before his eyes, she told him that his misery would end when he was in Sparta. And as soon as he got there, he died.

D    [11] 'It follows from all this that if death signals the start of non-existence for the soul – if death marks the end of all kinds of reward and punishment – then one would be more inclined to say that it is those sinners who are punished and killed quickly who are treated leniently and casually by divinity. For even if one were to claim that a sinner, living out his life, was supplied with only one source of misery, it would have to be that when he assesses his immorality, the realization that it is an unsatisfying, unrewarding business, which for all its enormous struggles yields no benefit, nothing worth the expenditure of effort – this realization unhinges his mind. It is like the story about Lysimachus (you know the one), that when lack of water forced him to surrender himself and his army to the Getae, he said, when he
E had been taken prisoner and had quenched his thirst, "I have done wrong! I have traded a vast kingdom for a fleeting pleasure!"[3] Still, when the compulsion of a feeling is instinctive,[4] it is

---

1. This famous story (Pausanias 3.17.8 f.) was told by Plutarch in greater detail in his *Life of Cimon* 6.4–7.
2. A place where departed souls are conjured up: see 560E–F below.
3. Plutarch used the story again in *Advice on Health* 126E. Lysimachus was one of the successors of Alexander the Great in command of Thrace. He was captured in 294/3 BC.
4. See the distinction made in *On Socrates' Personal Deity* 584E.

extremely hard to resist; but when an illegal and terrible act is committed on account of monetary greed, or because of coveting political fame and power, or for the sake of some sexual gratification, and when subsequently the raging thirst of the emotion dies down and the person eventually sees that the permanent conse- F quences of his immorality are feelings of shame and fear, not anything useful or necessary or valuable, then the conclusion is bound to occur to him often that hollow fame, or a demeaning, disgusting form of gratification, has led him to undo all that is best and most important in human morality, and has filled his life with shame and turmoil.

'Simonides used to say, wryly, that while he always found his fee box full, his gratitude box was always empty.[1] Similarly, once wrongdoers clearly see the iniquity within themselves, they find it empty of gratifying pleasure and devoid of worthwhile hope,* but ever full of fear, distress, unhappy memories, and 556A both apprehension about the future and mistrust of the present. Consequently, just as we hear Ino in the play, when she has come to regret her actions, saying, "Dear women, I wish I could make a fresh start, and live in Athamas' house with what I have done undone",[2] so every sinner's mind ponders and reflects how it can get rid of the memory of its crimes, eradicate its conscience, B cleanse itself and make a fresh start with a different life. You see, iniquity is not confident or undeluded or stable and secure in its choices (otherwise we would of course have to say that immoral people are wise); but when the furious pursuit of wealth or pleasure and unbridled envy coexist in a person along with hostility and vindictiveness, then if you look you will find underlying superstition, a lazy attitude towards work, a cowardly attitude towards death, a tendency to be pulled abruptly in different directions and a pretentiousness that makes them vainly consider other people's opinions. They fear not only their critics, but also C their supporters – because their supporters are being wronged by

1. Simonides of Ceos was a professional writer of panegyrics. When a customer offered gratitude, Simonides replied that he kept his fee box full, and the gratitude box empty. The full story is given in John of Stobi 3.417 f. Hense. Plutarch used the conceit again in 520A.
2. From Euripides' lost play *Ino*, F399 Nauck.

their deceit and are shown to be staunch opponents of bad people by the very fact that they enthusiastically support people who appear to be good.

'The point is that in so far as evil is strong, it is the strength of inferior iron: it is brittle and offers little resistance before snapping. And so when they ultimately gain some insight into their own natures, they are troubled and dissatisfied, and denounce their own lives. When a bad person repays a loan, acts as a financial guarantor for an acquaintance, or makes a voluntary or taxed contribution to his country, with consequent fame and respect, then because his will is utterly wayward and erratic, he is immediately plunged into regret and he deplores what he has done; when some people are applauded in the theatre, their love of fame deteriorates into love of money, and their first reaction is to groan. It is unthinkable that this could happen, but that those who slaughter people with a view to becoming tyrants or forming factions, as Apollodorus did, or who steal money from friends, as Glaucus the son of Epicydes did,[1] do not suffer pangs of regret or hate themselves or deplore what they have done. Anyway, if a mere mortal may legitimately express an opinion on this, I think that sinners need no external agent, divine or human, to punish them: their lives do the job adequately, by being utterly ruined and thrown into disarray by their evil. [12] But be careful: my argument may be going on too long.'

'It probably is,' said Timon, 'given how much is still facing it and remains to be said. I mean, I am now going to produce the final difficulty, as if it were an athlete which had been waiting its turn, since you have competed pretty well against the first ones.

'Euripides frankly denounces the gods for diverting "the parents' mistakes on to the children",[2] and although the rest of us may not voice it, you should regard us as agreeing with this denunciation. The point is that either the actual perpetrators have been punished, in which case there is no need for the gods to punish innocent people, since it is unfair for even perpetrators to

---

1. The cautionary tale of the Spartan Glaucus, who tried to renege on a trust left in his care by a Milesian, is in Herodotus 6.86.
2. *TGF* Euripides F980 Nauck.

be punished twice for the same crimes; or the gods have been slack and have wasted the chance of punishing the wrongdoers, and then at a later date they exact it from the innocent, in which case they are making up for their slowness by injustice, which is not on.

'Here's an illustration. I'm sure you know the story of how Aesop came here bringing gold from Croesus.[1] He meant to make a magnificent offering to the god, and also to give every inhabitant of Delphi four minas, but apparently he got angry and fell out with the locals; so he made the ritual offering, but sent the money back to Sardis, because he didn't think that the people deserved a windfall. They then engineered a charge against him of temple robbery and executed him by pushing him from the famous cliff called Hyampeia.[2] Subsequently, the story goes on, divine wrath afflicted them with failed harvests and with all kinds of strange diseases, and as a result they used to visit all the festivals where Greeks were assembled and make an announcement inviting anyone who so wished to claim compensation from them for Aesop. Two generations later Idmon of Samos arrived at Delphi;[3] not only was he not a relative of Aesop, but he was in fact a descendant of the people who had bought Aesop as a slave in Samos. It was only when the Delphians had compensated him that their troubles ceased. (We are also told that this incident was the reason for moving the place of punishment for temple robbers from Hyampeia to Aulia.)

'And not even Alexander's devoted admirers, of whom I am one, commend his levelling of the city of Branchidae and his slaughter of all the inhabitants, whatever their ages, because their great-grandfathers had betrayed Apollo's temple near Miletus.[4]

557A

B

1. Another version in Aristophanes, *Wasps* 1446 ff., with the scholiast's note, and in *Life of Aesop* G, 124 ff. Perry.
2. One of the thousand-foot limestone cliffs known as the Phaedriadae dominating the north of Delphi.
3. This part of the story is in Herodotus 2.134, who calls him Iadmon.
4. The full story is given by the Alexander historian of the first century AD, Quintus Curtius (7.5.28–35). The Branchidians had betrayed the Milesian temple to the Persians (Strabo 14.1.5), who in turn had granted them safe refuge in far-off Sogdiana, across the Oxus, north of Afghanistan, where Alexander eventually found them (Strabo 11.11.4).

Once the inhabitants of Corcyra asked Agathocles, the tyrant of Syracuse, why he was devastating their island, and he said with a mocking laugh, "Because your ancestors took Odysseus in, of

C course";[1] and when the Ithacans similarly objected that his troops were taking their sheep, he said, "When your king came to our land, he blinded the shepherd as well."[2]

'Apollo's behaviour is even more odd, wouldn't you say? He makes the present-day inhabitants of Pheneus suffer, by blocking up the gorge and so flooding all their land,[3] because (as we are told) a thousand years earlier Heracles tore the seer's tripod out of the ground and took it to Pheneus.[4] And he tells the Sybarites that their troubles will end when they have appeased the wrath of Hera of Leucadia by being annihilated three times.[5]

D 'Moreover, the Locrians have only recently stopped paying for Ajax's lechery by sending young women to Troy,[6] "who like slaves – half-naked, barefoot, bareheaded – spent every morning of their lives, even when old age came and weighed them down, sweeping around Athena's altar".[7] Does this make sense? Is it fair? I mean, we don't approve of the Thracians branding their

---

1. Corcyra was thought by the ancients (e.g. Thucydides 1.25) to be the Homeric island of Scheria, the home of the Phaeacians who welcomed the shipwrecked Odysseus in *Odyssey* 6. See the next note for why a Syracusan should hold a grudge against Odysseus.

2. The shepherd was the Cyclops Polyphemus, blinded by Odysseus in *Odyssey* 9. One tradition put the country of the Cyclopes in Sicily, where Syracuse is.

3. Pheneus in Arcadia was geographically prone to flooding. Pausanias (8.14) noted the supposed high-water marks.

4. The reference is to a particularly notorious and undignified legendary tussle between Heracles and Apollo for the holy tripod of Delphi; Cicero, *De Natura Deorum* 3.42, is unwilling to believe it. Plutarch mentions it again at 387D and 413A, for it was stock Delphic lore; see also Pausanias 3.21.8, 10.13.7.

5. Sybaris in the south of Italy was destroyed in war by its neighbour Croton, and finally replaced by the colony Thurii.

6. In the Trojan legend, the Locrian Ajax assaulted the priestess Cassandra in the temple of Athena during the sack of Troy, for which the Locrians had to send a constant supply of girls there for temple service: Lycophron, *Alexandra* 1141 ff.; Polybius 12.5.7; Strabo 13.1.40.

7. Of uncertain origin; assigned to Euphorion by Powell, *Collectanea Alexandrina* 40 f.; and see *EGF Adesp.* 9 Davies.

own wives to this day in retaliation for Orpheus,[1] or of the natives who live near the Eridanus wearing black (we hear) in mourning for Phaethon.[2] And it would be even more absurd, in my opinion, if the people who were alive at the time of Phaethon's death did nothing, and then people born five or ten generations later started to mourn him and wear different clothes because of him. All the same, this is merely silly, not terrifying or irreversible; but is there any rational explanation for why the anger of the gods should at the time go underground, as some rivers do, and then later re-emerge and afflict other people, and culminate in disasters of the worst kind?'

[13] He paused for the first time, and because I was afraid that he would start up again and introduce further, more problematic dilemmas, I seized the opportunity to put a question to him. 'Very well, then,' I said. 'So you think that all these tales are true, do you?'

'Even if only some of them are,' he replied, 'that doesn't alter the difficulty your argument faces, does it? What do you think?'

'Well,' I said, 'possibly my argument is like someone with a very strong fever, in the sense that whether he happens to be wearing one item of clothing or a lot, he feels more or less just as hot; but all the same, when the number of garments is reduced to one, he feels better. But unless you insist, never mind that – despite the fact that most of what you said does smack of fictional invention. Instead, remember the recent festival of Theoxenia, and how impressive and satisfying you found that aspect of the proceedings which involves the announcement that a special portion was being reserved as a gift for Pindar's descendants.'[3]

'No one could fail to be pleased by the elegance of this traditional accolade,' he said, 'which is so typically Greek in its straight-

---

1. Herodotus (5.6) knew of Thracian tattooing, and naturally stories grew around this, to Greeks, unnatural practice. Plutarch's version is that it was a mark of shame for the dismembering of Orpheus by Thracian women. Athenaeus (524D) has a different version.

2. Polybius has the story (2.16.13 ff.). Phaethon, while driving the chariot of the sun, was hurled to his death by Zeus' thunderbolt, his sisters were turned into poplars and their tears into amber. The Eridanus is the River Po.

3. Pindar's Sixth Paean was composed for this Delphic festival held in March/April, at which Apollo was imagined as a guest.

forwardness – unless, to quote Pindar himself, "his black heart has been forged in an icy flame".'[1]

'I won't, then, bother to go into a similar announcement which is made at Sparta,' I said, 'the one which honours and commemorates the ancient poet Terpander with the words "in the train of the bard of Lesbos",[2] because the principle is the same. But I am sure that your family expects to be more highly regarded in Boeotia than other people because you are of the lineage of Opheltas, and likewise in Phocis because of Daiphan-

B    tus.[3] And you were with me recently, and helped me, when I was playing a part in keeping for the petitioners, the Lycormae and Satilaei, the right to wear a chaplet, which is a patrimonial privilege for the descendants of Heracles, and I was claiming that it was particularly important that the descendants of Heracles should securely possess the privileges and rewards for the good their ancestor had done Greece, given that he himself had been insufficiently thanked and compensated.'

'Thank you for the reminder,' he said. 'That was a fine contest, and very germane to philosophy.'

'So don't get all worked up and condemnatory, Timon,' I said, 'and don't become embittered if certain people are punished

C    because they have bad men or criminals for ancestors; or alterna- tively, don't be pleased and approbatory when good lineage is honoured. If we allow lineage to retain the rewards for virtue, then it necessarily and logically follows that we should not sup- pose that punishment will default and fail prematurely in the case of crimes, but rather that it is bound to keep up with rewards in matching repayment with deserts. Anyone who is pleased to see Cimon's descendants honoured at Athens, but deplores and disap- proves of the expulsion of Lachares' or Aristion's descendants,[4] is

---

1. Pindar F123.5 f. Snell and Maehler.
2. A fragment of Aristotle (F545 Rose, F551 Gigon) explains that the phrase proclaimed that any descendants of the poet Terpander (who originally came from Lesbos) were invited to perform first.
3. This sentence raises the problem whether Timon was Plutarch's full brother or half-brother: see p. 6.
4. All three were Athenians. Cimon (first half of the fifth century BC) was the traditional example of a much-respected general and statesman. The other two were hated brief dictators of Athens, Lachares in 297–295, Aristion in 88–86 BC.

far too fickle and casual – or rather, he is thoroughly peevish and difficult to please where God is concerned, since he complains if the grandchildren of an immoral, iniquitous person seem to do well, but he also complains if a bad person's line is checked and elimin-  D ated, and his criticism of God is just as strong whether failure is experienced by the children of a good father or those of a bad one.

[14] 'You should consider what I've been saying as a kind of barricade against people who overdo harsh criticism and condem- nation. But let's go back and try, so to speak, to pick up the beginning of the thread in the darkness, circuitousness and impre- cision of discussing God, and gradually and carefully steer our- selves towards a probable, plausible conclusion. That is the best we can hope for, since we cannot talk of certainty and truth even where our own human actions are concerned. For example, why do we tell the children of those who have died of consumption or dropsy to sit and soak their feet in water until the corpse has  E been cremated? It seems that this prevents the transfer or onset of infection. Or again, when a goat takes eryngo into its mouth, why does the whole herd stay still until the goatherd has come and taken it out?[1] And these are not the only influences whose contagiousness and infectiousness are unbelievably fast and far- reaching, and which reach one object through the intermediacy of another. It is not spatial intervals which are puzzling us,  F however, but temporal intervals. But it is more surprising for a disease which started in Ethiopia to have infected Athens, killed Pericles and made Thucydides ill,[2] than for justice to have come and seized the children of the evil inhabitants of Delphi and Sybaris. I mean, influences reverberate, as it were, and link up from their ends to their beginnings, and even if the cause of this is unclear to us, it performs its proper function.

[15] 'Moreover, wrath directed comprehensively against a whole city is easy to justify. A city is like a living creature: it is a

1. This is popular lore, signalled by Plutarch's inclusion of the tale in *Table Talk* 700D, and his attempted explanation by a spread of emanations of fiery pungency in *Philosophers and Princes* 776F. A different version started in Aris- totle, *Historia Animalium* 610b29 ff.; and Pliny, *Naturalis Historia* 8.203 f. is still giving both versions.
2. This was the famous plague which hit Athens in 430 BC during the Pelopon- nesian War.

559A single, continuous entity, which changes as it ages, but does not therefore dispense with itself or become something else, and then something else again, over time. Such an entity always has coherence of experience and self-affinity,[1] and accepts whatever criticism and gratitude may be due for the things which it as a whole does or has done, as long as the coalition which forms it and combines it out of various strands preserves its singleness. To divide it over time, and say that there are many cities – an infinite number of cities, rather – is like saying that a single person is in fact many people, because he is currently old, was formerly young and even further back was a teenager – or

B rather, it is absolutely identical to Epicharmus' argument which generated the sophism about a person growing.[2] I mean, one might just as well say that someone who borrowed money in the past does not owe a thing, since he has become a different person; and that someone who was yesterday invited to dinner is a gatecrasher today, because he is not the same person.

'In fact, ageing makes an individual change more than it does a city as a whole. Anyone who hadn't seen Athens for thirty years would still recognize it, and the current characteristics and motivations of its inhabitants, their pastimes and occupations, and the sources of their pleasure and anger, are very similar to what they were a long time ago. But a relative or friend who met a person after a long interval would scarcely recognize him,

C and the changes in one's characteristics, as they are effortlessly modified by every argument, task, emotion and convention, are incredibly odd and peculiar even to a constant companion. Nevertheless, a person is described as a single unit from birth to death;[3] and my claim is that a city, which likewise remains self-identical, ought to be liable for the faults of its ancestors, just as it shares in their fame and authority. Otherwise, we will implicitly be throwing everything into Heraclitus' river, which cannot be entered

---

1. The terms are particularly associated with Stoic technical nomenclature.
2. That he was someone else with each change. For the argument, see Diogenes Laertius 3.10 f., and Plutarch, *On Contentment* 473D and *On Common Conceptions* 1083A.
3. For the argument, see Plato, *Symposium* 207d ff.; Plutarch, *On the E at Delphi* 392A ff.

twice, he says,[1] because its nature is transitional as a result of total change and alteration.

[16] 'If a city is a single, consistent entity, then a lineage is too, of course, since it stems from a single source which gives it a D certain quality and pervasive coherence. Nothing which is born is separate from its creator, in the sense that a work of craft is: anything which is born arises out of its creator, rather than merely thanks to its creator, and consequently contains and carries some portion of his attributes in itself, and is punished and rewarded in conformity with these attributes. At the risk of sounding frivolous, I would say that when Cassander's statue was melted down by the Athenians, and when Dionysius' body was cast out after his death by the Syracusans, there was less justice in their treatment than there was in their descendants being penalized. I mean, the statue had nothing of Cassander's nature in it, E and Dionysius' soul had left his body already; but Nysaeus and Apollocrates, Antipater and Philip, and likewise all the other children of bad men, inherently contain the most authoritative portion of their forebears, and not in a dormant or passive condition – it gives them life and growth, and guides their actions and thoughts. No, it is not awful or odd in the slightest for descendants to be heirs.

'To generalize, the beneficial thing to do is also the right thing to do. This is the case in medicine, where it is absurd to claim F that it is not right to cauterize the thumbs of people with hip trouble, to excoriate the abdomen when the liver is abscessed or to rub ointment on the tips of cows' horns when they have hoof-rot.[2] It is no different where punishment is concerned. Anyone who thinks that the right course of action is anything other than what cures iniquity, and who is distressed if some people are used as the means of applying the cure to others (as when venesection is used to alleviate ophthalmia),[3] is apparently seeing no further

1. Heraclitus F91 DK.
2. This traditional farming tip had a long history, from Aristotle, *Historia Animalium* 595b13 ff., 604a14 ff., to Cato, *De Re Rustica* 72, and Pliny, *Naturalis Historia* 28.266. But there is ambiguity as to whether cow's horns or the horny parts of the hoof are meant.
3. Hippocrates, *Epidemics* 2.6.12.

560A than what is right before his eyes: he is forgetting that when a
schoolteacher beats one pupil, the effect of the punishment is
wider, and when a military commander kills every tenth man,
he makes all the rest obedient.[1] So not only can one part of the
body be put into a particular state, whether better or worse,
through the intermediacy of another part, but the same also happens at the mental level, even more readily than it does at the bodily
level. At the bodily level, apparently, it is necessarily the same
condition or change that is engendered; but at the mental level,
the mind has the capacity to be induced, by whether its imagination arouses confidence or fear, to live a better or worse life.'

[17] Olympichus interrupted me in mid-speech and said, 'You
seem to be implicitly underpinning your argument with a huge
B    assumption – that the soul persists.'

'Yes,' I said, 'and I do so with your permission – or at least
you granted the assumption earlier, in the sense that our argument
has consistently assumed, from the beginning right up to the
point we've reached now, that God deals with each of us according to his deserts.'

'So,' he said, 'you think the idea that our souls are either
completely indestructible or last for some time after death[2] is a
logical consequence of the idea that the gods take us into consideration and assign every detail of our lives, do you?'

'Isn't it, my friend?' I asked. 'Does God stoop so low and
concern himself so much with trivia that he would take account
of us to the extent that he does if we did not carry something
divine within ourselves,[3] something which somehow resembles
C    him and is lasting and stable? If we were as transient as leaves, as
Homer says,[4] and withered and faded away to nothing within a
short space of time? Would he behave like those women who
tend and care for their gardens of Adonis in terracotta pots,[5] and

---

1. For the Roman practice of decimation, see Livy 2.59 and Suetonius, *Augustus* 24.
2. The alternatives were put in Plato's *Phaedo* 87a–88a. Plato argued for the first
   alternative, the Stoics for the second.
3. Both Plato and the Stoics held that we do.
4. *Iliad* 6.146 ff.
5. Women grew plants in pots or window-boxes which would sprout in a week
   or so, for the festival of Adonis, when they were scattered in springs (Theocri-

concern himself with transient souls which grow in a vessel of flesh too delicate to allow life to take root strongly, and which are then obliterated at the first opportunity? Perhaps you'd rather leave all the other gods be, and concentrate on our local god here,[1] and consider whether, in your opinion, while he knows that the souls of the dead perish straight away, evaporating from their bodies like mist or smoke, he still insists not only on the dead being often propitiated, but also on them receiving magnificent gifts and privileges. If this is the case, he is deceiving and deluding those who trust him. I, at any rate, would not abandon the persistence of the soul, unless the Pythia's tripod were stolen by another Heracles and destroyed,[2] and the oracular shrine effaced. But as long as there are plenty of oracular pronouncements, as there are even in modern times, of the kind that we are told was given to Crow of Naxos, then it is irreligious to sentence the soul to death.'

'What was this pronouncement,' asked Patrocleas, 'and who was this Crow? I am not familiar with either what happened, or to whom or to what the name refers.'

'No, it's my fault,' I said, 'for using a nickname rather than a name.[3] The person who killed Archilochus in battle was called Callondes, apparently, but was nicknamed Crow. Although his approach to the Pythia was initially rejected, on the grounds that he had killed a man who was under the Muses' tutelage, later – as a result of his begging and pleading and explaining himself – he was told to go to the "residence of Tettix" and propitiate Archilochus' soul. The place in question was Taenarum, because that is where Tettix of Crete is said to have gone with an expeditionary force, settled in the area around the Psychopompeion[4] and founded a city. And the Spartans were given a similar

---

tus 15.113). Plutarch may have had in mind Plato's similar use of the 'gardens of Adonis' in *Phaedrus* 276b.

1. Apollo.
2. See p. 270, n. 4. The Pythian priestess sat on Apollo's tripod to deliver oracles.
3. It was a famous story, given fully in Aelian F80 Hercher.
4. See p. 266, n. 2. Taenarus is on the tip of the central peninsula of the southern Peloponnese, where traditionally Heracles dragged up Cerberus from Hades, and so a channel with the underworld was thought to exist there.

instruction by the oracle, to propitiate Pausanias' soul, so they summoned exorcists from Italy, who performed a ritual and drew the ghost away from the temple.[1]

[18] 'The argument which confirms God's providence,' I went on, 'is therefore simultaneously the same one which confirms the persistence of the human soul: do away with one and you do away with the other. But if the soul survives,★ it is more plausible for it to be rewarded and punished after bodily death, because it is like an athlete in the competition of life:[2] it is only when the competition is over that it gets repaid. However, the rewards and punishments it gains after death, when it is on its own, for its past life are non-existent as far as we living beings are concerned: we don't realize that they exist, and we don't believe they do. On the other hand, the rewards and punishments which are transmitted through their children and descendants are obvious to people here on earth, and so serve to deter and restrain plenty of criminals.

'No punishment is more shaming or painful, as you can imagine, than seeing one's offspring in trouble because of oneself. And once the soul of a man who has transgressed both divine and human law, and has died, sees children or friends or family involved in overwhelming disasters because of him and paying the price of his misdeeds – and this is quite different from seeing mere statues torn down or privileges revoked – then even if he were to be offered Zeus' throne, he would not be induced a second time to become immoral or criminal. I could demonstrate that this is so by repeating an account I recently heard, but I hesitate because you might think it just a fictional tale.[3] That is why I am making use only of plausible arguments.'

561A

B

---

1. The victorious Spartan general of the Persian Wars was suspected of intriguing with the helots and was starved to death in Sparta in the temple of Athena (Thucydides 1.132–4). See also p. 266, n.1.
2. The simile stems from Plato (*Republic* 613b ff., 621d); Plutarch used it again in 1105C, and compare 593D ff., 943D.
3. The distinction between an account (*logos*) and a story (*mythos*) is Platonic (*Protagoras* 320c) and was used by him to move from argument to myth (*Phaedo* 108d, 114d; *Gorgias* 523a, 527a), and so Plutarch used it too in connection with his myths (see p. 247).

'No, don't do that,' protested Olympichus. 'Tell us the story too.'

Everyone else insisted as well, so I said, 'Let me demonstrate the plausibility of what I've been saying first, and then we'll come to the fictional tale, if you want to – though "fiction" may not be the right word. [19] The point is that Bion says that for God to punish the offspring of bad men is more absurd than for a doctor to give medical treatment to a grandchild or child for the illness of their grandfather or father.[1] But the situations are not precisely analogous: treating one person does not stop another person being ill – no one with ophthalmia or a fever has got better as a result of seeing ointment or a poultice being applied on someone else – but criminals are punished for all to see because it is the function of justice, when it is implemented rationally, to punish some people in order to curb others.

'However, Bion didn't notice the respect in which the situation he adduced for comparison actually resembles the issue in question. Sometimes, when someone has already caught a virulent but not incurable disease and, because of lack of resolution and determination, has then given in to it and died, and when he has a son who does not appear actually to be ill, but is simply liable to the same disease, then if someone like a doctor, a relative, a coach or a good master understands the son's condition, he imposes a strict diet on him, bans savouries, desserts, alcohol and women, applies constant medication, puts him on a tough course of exercises, and stops the illness getting serious by dissipating and banishing it at source, while it is still negligible. I mean, isn't this what we recommend to people born of chronically ill fathers or mothers – to resolve to give themselves consideration and care and attention, and to waste no time in expelling the spore which has been blended into their constitution by catching it before it has become fixed and immobile?'

'Of course,' they said.

'So,' I continued, 'when we introduce exercise, diet and medication for the children of epileptics, depressives and arthritics, even though these children are not actually ill, this is not odd, but

1. Bion F27 Kindstrand. The same comparison is in Philo, *De Providentia* 2.7.

necessary behaviour, and not an absurd practice, but a helpful one. We do it to prevent them getting ill. A body generated by a bad body deserves treatment and care, not punishment, and anyone whose cowardice and weakness is such that he describes the treatment as punishment, because he is being deprived of pleasures and given pain and hard work, is to be ignored. So, if a body generated by a bad body deserves treatment and care, should one ignore a hereditary trait of iniquity as it grows and tries to flourish in a youthful character? Should one delay and procrastinate until it has spread and erupted under the influence of the emotions, "and the mind produces rotten fruit", to quote Pindar?[1]

[20] 'Surely God is in this respect at least as wise as Hesiod? Hesiod's injunction and advice is "not to procreate on returning from the misery of a funeral, but after a sacred festival", because at the moment of conception a human life is open not only to vice and virtue, but also to pain, pleasure and every emotion, and that is why he recommends people to procreate when they are happy, joyful and relaxed.[2] But there is something which is beyond Hesiod – it is not within the domain of human wisdom, but is up to God – and that is to distinguish and discern similar and dissimilar traits before they have erupted under the influence of the emotions into the committing of great crimes.

'The point is that whereas bear-cubs, wolf-cubs and young apes directly reveal their inherited character in a totally unsuppressed and undisguised fashion, yet a human being gets involved in customs and rules and regulations, which might well enable him to conceal the bad sides of his nature by imitating goodness. There are two possible results of this: either his nature completely obliterates and avoids the hereditary blemish of iniquity, or it deceptively conceals its wickedness for a long time in a sheath, as it were. And we are the objects of the deception: we eventually recognize his iniquity only when we have been, so to speak, physically struck or hurt by any of his crimes. Or rather, we

562A

B

C

---

1. F211 Snell and Maehler.
2. But what Hesiod (*Works and Days* 375 f.) probably had in mind was that death and the dead tainted ritual purity and were thus inauspicious for conception.

usually assume that it is the committing of a crime that makes a person criminal, and the act of rape that makes a person immoral, and running away that makes a person a coward – which is equivalent to thinking that scorpions grow a sting only when they strike and that vipers gain their poison only when they bite. This is stupid. The beginning of badness and the eruption of badness are not simultaneous, but any bad person carries his iniquity with him from the start: once a thief obtains the opportunity and the ability, he puts his thieving into practice, and the same goes for a tyrant and his lawlessness.

'Given God's nature, however, our minds are clearer to him   D than our bodies; it follows, of course, that he is well aware of every person's attitudes and nature, and that he doesn't postpone punishment until violence manifests physically, or disrespect is verbally expressed, or lechery reaches the genitals. It is not because he has been wronged that he retaliates against a wrongdoer, it is not because he has been a victim that he gets angry with a robber, it is not because his wife has been seduced that he hates an adulterer: it is quite usual for him to punish someone with an adulterous or greedy or immoral nature in order to cure him, by eradicating his iniquity before it has taken hold, as one would arrest epilepsy before a fit.[1]

[21] 'Not long ago, we were irritated at the fact that wrongdoers are punished after a considerable delay; if we now accuse God   E of sometimes coming down hard on some people for their traits* and dispositions, even before any crime has been committed, we do so because we are ignorant of the fact that often the future is worse and more terrifying than the past, the hidden than the overt, and because we are incapable of realizing the reasons why it is preferable to ignore some people even though they have already done wrong, but to nip others in the bud even though they have only the intention to do wrong. This is precisely analogous to why medicines too do not suit some people who are ill, but are good for others who, even though they are not ill, are in a more precarious situation than those who are.

1. It looks as if Plutarch developed similar views in his *Commentary on Hesiod*: see F42 Sandbach.

F     'It follows that "the gods divert the parents' mistakes on to the children"[1] is not a universal truth. If a bad parent has produced a good child (just as a diseased parent can produce a healthy child), then the child is absolved from the hereditary guilt – it is as if iniquity has adopted another family's child. On the other hand, it is of course perfectly appropriate for someone diseased who revives the family trait of wickedness to inherit the debt of the penalty for that iniquity. I mean, Antigonus wasn't punished on account of Demetrius, nor (to go further back in history) was Phyleus punished because of Augeas or Nestor because of

563A  Neleus,[2] since they were all good men, although their fathers had been bad. It is only when people have embraced and welcomed their heredity into their nature that justice pursues and thoroughly accounts for the trait of iniquity.

'Sometimes a father's warts, freckles and moles do not appear on his children, but recur later on his sons' and daughters' children; once a Greek woman gave birth to a black child, and then, during the course of her trial for adultery, she discovered that her great-grandfather had been Ethiopian;[3] one of the children of Python of Thisbe (who died not long ago, and was said to be related to the Sown Men) bore on his body a spear-shaped mark, which was the family trait emerging and surfacing from the

B     depths, so to speak, after so much time.[4] Likewise, it is not uncommon for early generations to conceal and smother mental characteristics and emotions, and for the inherent nature to blossom forth at some later time, using other generations as its vehicle, and resurrect the native vice or virtue.'

---

1. See p. 268, n. 2.
2. Demetrius Poliorcetes was a crueller king of Macedon than his son Antigonus Gonatas. Heracles cleaned the stables of Augeas but was refused payment; when the matter was adjudicated, Phyleus decided against his father. Neleus, king of Pylos, refused to give Heracles purification for the murder of Iphitus; so Heracles killed him and all his sons except Nestor, who became the grand old man of the Greeks at Troy.
3. This story started in Aristotle (*Historia Animalium* 586a), passed into collections of strange events and blossomed in another version in Pliny, *Naturalis Historia* 7.51.
4. The Sown Men were the descendants of the legendary warriors who sprang from the earth when Cadmus sowed the dragon's teeth. Dio Chrysostom (4.23) also mentions this spear-shaped birthmark.

[22] I stopped talking at this point, but Olympichus said with a smile, 'We are not congratulating you, because we don't want you to get the impression that we are forgetting about the fictional tale and are assuming that the argument has sufficiently established the point. We'll wait until we've heard the tale as well, before making up our minds.'

This, then, is how I came to tell them about a certain relative and friend of Protogenes, whom they knew because he had once  C visited us here.[1] This man, a native of Soli, had denied himself no sensual indulgence in his youth; then, having swiftly used up all his money, he was compelled for some time to turn to crime. In a complete volte-face, he made wealth his goal – so he behaved just like those depraved people who don't look after their wives while they are married to them, but let them leave, and then, when their wives are married to other people, immorally try once again to seduce them.★ He never stopped himself doing anything, however despicable, as long as the consequence was profit and gain. What he acquired from this was no great fortune, but, quite soon, a very extensive reputation for iniquity. The chief source of his notoriety, however, was a response  D which the oracle of Amphilochus gave him.[2] Apparently, he had sent to ask the god whether he would live a better life in the future: the god replied that he would be better off when he died.

Now, in a sense, this is exactly what happened to him a short while later. He fell from a height on to his head, and although there was no wound, only a bruise, he seemed to be dead; and then two days later, when he was actually just about to be buried, he came to.[3] Once he was well and normal again, which didn't take long, he transformed his life beyond recognition: in fact, he is acknowledged by the Cilicians to have been the most honest businessman of his times, and they know of no one who was more religious or who caused his enemies more distress or  E

---

1. A friend of Plutarch (749B, 750A ff.) who turns up in *Table Talk* as a speaker. He seems to have been rather like his friend from Soli.
2. At Mallos in Cilicia. The oracle was still operating in Plutarch's time (*On the Obsolescence of Oracles* 434D).
3. This *mise en scène* is modelled on Plato, *Republic* 614b.

was a truer friend.[1] The upshot was that everyone who met him wanted to hear the reason for the change, since they imagined that so thorough a reorganization of character could not be due to any banal circumstances. And they were quite right, as he himself explained to Protogenes and other equally good friends of his.

[23] When his intelligence was expelled from his body, at first (he said) the transformation made him feel like a helmsman might feel if he were thrown overboard from his ship into the depths of the sea.[2] Next, he rose upwards a little way, and seemed then to be breathing as a whole and to be seeing in all directions around himself, as if his soul were a single open eye. What he was seeing, however, was not what he had been seeing before, except for the stars – but they were huge, and at immense distances from one another, and were emitting light which was not only an amazing colour, but also had energy, which allowed his soul to ride the light as evenly as a ship on calm water, and to travel everywhere easily and swiftly.

He omitted a great deal of what he saw, and went on to say that when the souls of the dead come up from below, they form a fiery bubble as they cleave the air; then, when the bubble gently bursts, the souls emerge in human form,[3] but in miniature. They do not all move uniformly: some of the souls leap out of the bubble with incredible lightness and shoot upwards in a straight line; others behave like spindles and whirl around in a circle while at the same time tending sometimes in a downward direction and sometimes in an upward direction, and so move in an untidy and chaotic spiral and take a very long time before eventually quietening down.[4]

The majority of the souls were strangers, but he saw two or

1. It was a popular and traditional view that justice lay in doing good to friends and harm to enemies.
2. An apposite comparison, as Plato had said (*Phaedrus* 247c) that intellect is the helmsman of the soul. The eschatological myth which follows is discussed in the Introduction, pp. 245–8.
3. A common belief. Plutarch gives it his own twist in *On the Face on the Moon* 945A, by saying that the body is given its form by the imprint of the soul (which in turn is moulded by the mind).
4. For the different motions of the souls, compare *On Socrates' Personal Deity* 592A, and Plato, *Phaedo* 108a ff.

three of his acquaintances, and tried to communicate with them
and talk to them. They didn't hear him, however, and were
behaving unusually: they were frantically and frenetically trying      B
to avoid being seen or touched. At first they darted about here
and there on their own, but later they met plenty of other souls
in the same state and clung to them, and the whole mass moved
all over the place aimlessly, making meaningless noises mixed up
with sounds like exclamations of grief and terror. There was
another set of souls, high up in the pure part of the ambient,[1]
who looked radiant, and when they approached one another,
which they did often, it was out of affection; however, they kept
away from the other, distracted souls. Apparently, they indicated
their repugnance by contracting into themselves, and their pleas-     C
ure and approval by expanding and spreading out.

[24] He said that he recognized one of these souls as that of a
relative, but only just recognized him, since he'd died when he
was a child. This soul came up close to him and said, 'Hello,
Thespesius.' He was astonished, and said that he wasn't Thespesius, but Aridaeus.[2] 'You may have been Aridaeus before,' replied
his relative, 'but from now on you are Thespesius, "godlike".
You see, you haven't actually died: the gods have allowed you to
come here with your intelligence, but with the rest of your soul
left behind in your body like an anchor. If now or at any time in
the future you need evidence of this, here it is: the souls of the
dead do not cast a shadow, and they do not blink their eyes.'[3]       D

These words stimulated Thespesius to use his rational mind to
pull himself together to a greater degree, and he looked and saw
that whereas he had a vague, shadowy line, which swayed in
time with him, they were surrounded by an aura of light and

1. Compare *On the Face on the Moon* 943D.
2. Aridaeus was a well-known Macedonian name (e.g. the half-brother of Alexander the Great). But we are surely meant to recall Ardiaeus the tyrant mentioned
   in Plato's Myth of Er in *Republic* 615c. The new 'real' name is a common
   feature of all magical belief, as the secret essential feature of one's true being;
   cf. T. S. Eliot, *Old Possum's Book of Practical Cats*, 'The Naming of Cats'.
3. These are Pythagorean notions, according to Plutarch in *Greek Questions*
   300C. But in fact it is a pervasive belief of folklore that the shadow is part of
   the living personality. It was because of his shadow that the souls in Purgatory
   recognized that Dante was a living man (*Purgatorio* III.25 f., 94 ff.).

were transparent. They weren't all identical, however. Some emitted light of a single, even, constant, uniform intensity, as the full moon does when it is at its most pure; others had intermittent patches or occasional welts; others were extraordinary to look at,

E  since they were blotchy all over, marked with freckles like vipers; and others had faint scratchmarks.[1]

[25] Thespesius' relative (there is no reason not to refer to people's souls by name in this way) proceeded to give a detailed account of everything. He said that the role of chief punisher of wrongdoing of every kind has been given to Inevitability, the daughter of Necessity and Zeus,[2] and that no criminal, however grand or insignificant, can use anonymity or dominance to escape her. There are three kinds of punishment, and each has its own custodian and agent. Swift Reprisal takes care of those who are punished without delay and whose punishment is entirely physi-

F  cal: she acts gently, in a sense, and leaves a lot of residual impurities. People whose iniquity is more difficult to heal are handed over to Retribution after their death by their deity.[3] The third and most savage of the assistants of Inevitability is Revenge, who takes on those who are altogether incurable, once Retribution has rejected them: she hounds them as they wander here and there, trying to hide; she exterminates them all, in a variety of brutal and cruel ways, and imprisons them in the place which has no identity or form.

565A  'As for the first two types of punishment,' he went on, 'the one administered by Reprisal, which takes place while the criminal is still alive, resembles certain punishments employed by foreigners. In Persia, for instance, one form of punishment entails the depilation and whipping of the clothes and headgear of people who are being punished, who weep and beg for the punishment to end;[4] analogously, punishments which involve

---

1. Compare Plato, *Gorgias* 524d–525a for the marks on the soul.
2. Compare Plato, *Phaedrus* 248c, *Republic* 616c, 617c.
3. For this function of one's individual deity, compare Plato, *Phaedo* 107d and 113d.
4. According to Ammianus Marcellinus (a historian of the fourth century AD), it was Artaxerxes Longarm, king of Persia in the fifth century BC; so also Ps.-Plutarch 173D. Plutarch used the story again at 35E.

people's property or bodies make no telling contact and fail to address the actual iniquity, but are usually aimed at people's reputations and how they are perceived.

[26] 'Anyone who gets from there to here without having been punished and purified falls into the hands of Retribution. His soul is exposed and naked;[1] there is nowhere for him to slink away to; he is incapable of covering up and concealing his wicked- B ness, but everything about him is utterly plain for all to see. If either of his parents or any of his ancestors were good, she shows him first to them, so that they can see how contemptible and despicable he is; if they were bad, he watches them being pun- ished (and they can see him watching), before his own extensive punishment, in which each of his emotions is stripped from him. This ordeal involves agony which is so overwhelming and excruci- ating that it exceeds the pain of corporal punishment to the same extent that actual pain would be more real than dreaming about it.

'The scars and welts which each of the emotions entail are more permanent in some cases than in others. And,' he continued, C 'have a look at the variety and diversity of ways in which the souls are coloured. One is drab and dirty, smeared with stinginess and cupidity; another is the red of blood or fire, thanks to his viciousness and cruelty; grey always signifies that hedonistic self- indulgence has proved difficult to eradicate; just as blackness is what squid discharge, the presence of spite and malice produces the venomous, pus-like green you see over there.

'These colours are the result of iniquity down there on earth, when the soul is modified by the emotions and in turn modifies what the body does. Here, on the other hand, the complete obliteration of these colours, and the soul's gaining a single, lucid hue, are the culmination of purification and punishment. But as D long as the colours are there, then the emotions recur with all their turbulence and excitation, which is faint and quickly extin- guished in some souls, but in others has a vigorous intensity. After repeated doses of chastisement, some of these souls regain their proper condition and state, but others are returned to the

1. So Plato, *Gorgias* 523e.

bodies of living creatures by the violence of their incomprehension and indiscriminate hedonism.* One soul, because its rational faculty is weak and it has never practised the contemplation of truth, is pulled towards incarnation by its need for action; another
E  needs an instrument for indulgence and longs to weave together its desires with their gratification, and to satisfy them with the help of the body, since here all that is available is an incomplete shadow, a phantom pleasure which can never be fulfilled.'[1]

[27] Here he stopped talking, and Thespesius was guided by him easily and unerringly over what seemed to be a vast region, although he didn't take long to cross it: he was borne aloft, as if he had wings, by the beams of light, until he reached the mouth of an enormous tunnel which stretched on downwards, and the force that had carried him there abandoned him. He noticed that the place had the same effect on every other soul: they tucked
F  themselves up as birds do, landed and walked around the mouth – they didn't dare to go straight in. The inside looked like a Bacchic cave,[2] in that it held a rich variety of plants and greenery and flowers of every colour; and it exuded a mild, gentle, scented breeze which induced exquisite rapture. The effect on the state of mind was like the effect of wine on people who are getting drunk: as the souls revelled in the delightful scents, they began to expand and to become affable with one another; and all around the place was filled with merrymaking, laughter and every kind of song sung by people having fun and enjoying themselves.
566A  Thespesius' guide said that this was where Dionysus had ascended from the world, and subsequently brought Semele;[3] and he said that the place was called the place of oblivion.[4] And that is why,

1. Compare *On the Face on the Moon* 945B, and Plato, *Phaedo* 81b–e, 108a–b.
2. There were Bacchic caves on Parnassus above Delphi (Macrobius, *Saturnalia* 1.18.3); but Plutarch is thinking of grottoes decked and equipped for Bacchic revels. Antony constructed one for his own entertainment in Athens itself (Athenaeus 148C).
3. Semele, the mortal mother of Dionysus, was consumed by the divine force of her lover Zeus, whose wife, the goddess Hera, tricked her into persuading Zeus to appear before her in the majesty of his godhead. But Dionysus brought her up from Hades and made her immortal (Diodorus 4.25.4).
4. Compare Plato, *Republic* 621a. Plutarch has his own quite individual version of this section of eschatological topography, moulded by the philosophical opposition of reason and emotion, intelligence and the senses.

although Thespesius wanted to spend some time there, he didn't let him, but forcibly pulled him away, and gave him an explanation while he was doing so: he said that pleasure dissolves and saturates intelligence, but irrigates and plumps up one's irrational and physical aspects, and so makes one remember corporality. The consequence of remembering this is a craving and a longing that pulls one towards birth, which is so called because it is the inclination of a soul weighed down by liquidity to *be* on *earth*.[1]

[28] He travelled the same distance again, and then he saw something which looked like a huge mixing-bowl with streams flowing into it; one stream was whiter than sea foam or snow, another was the purple of iris blossom, and so on – each coloured differently, with its own unique lustre when viewed from a distance.* When they got close, however, the mixing-bowl turned out to be a deep hole in the ambient, the colours faded and only the whiteness remained bright. And he saw three deities sitting close together, facing one another in a triangle, and mixing the streams together in particular proportions.[2] Thespesius' guide said that this was as far as Orpheus had come when he was searching for his wife's soul, and that he had incorrectly perpetuated and spread in the world a false notion, that the Delphic oracle was shared by Apollo and Night; this was wrong, he said, because Apollo and Night have nothing in common. 'In fact,' he said, 'what you're seeing now is an oracle shared by Night and Moon. It doesn't reach anywhere on earth at all, and it doesn't have a single location: it travels all over the place and reaches mankind in dreams and fantasies. For this is where dreams come from and, as you can see, they take in and then disseminate straightforward truth blended with complex delusion.[3]

---

1. Plutarch here playfully derives *genesis* ('birth') from *gē* ('earth') and *neusis* ('inclination'). We have done what we can to capture the pun – as it were, *b-irth*.

2. For the imagery of three deities and of the mixing of colours, compare Plato, *Republic* 616e f., 617c, *Phaedo* 110b f. But again Plutarch's presentation is entirely his own, with a characteristic attack on the tale that at Delphi there was an oracle shared by Apollo and Night. Clearly this arose from some Orphic source.

3. The ancients believed dreams to be oracular, but dangerously so. In Plutarch's imagery white represents truth, the other colours the deceptiveness of delusions.

D    [29] 'I am no longer sure,' he continued, 'whether you will be
able to see Apollo's oracle. Your soul's cable is stretched taut
down to your body, to which it is anchored, and allows no
further upward slack or play.'[1] While he was saying this, however, he tried to take Thespesius to where he could show him the
light which emanated from the tripod, he said, and which passed
through the bosom of Themis before settling on Parnassus.[2] But
although Thespesius longed to see all this, the brilliance of the
light blinded him. As he skirted by, however, he did hear a high
female voice announcing in verse, among other things, what
seemed to be the time of his death; and the deity told him that
this was the Sibyl's voice,[3] and that she sang about the future as
E    she journeyed here and there on the face of the moon. Thespesius
wanted to hear more of what the Sibyl was singing, but he was
repulsed by the centrifugal force of the moon's motion, as if he
were on the edge of a tornado,[4] and he overheard only brief
snatches. These included something about Mount Vesuvius and
about Dicaearcheia coming under a fiery blast in the future,[5] and
a scrap of verse about the emperor contemporary with these
events: 'Though good, illness will put an end to his rule.'[6]

[30] Their next stop was to see people being punished.[7] At
first, this was simply a distressing and pitiful sight, but then
Thespesius started to come across friends, relatives and acquaint-
F    ances being punished; and this was a shock. They were suffering
terribly, and being punished in demeaning and agonizing ways;
they cried out pitifully and mournfully to him. Finally, he saw
his own father emerging out of a pit, marked and scarred all

----

1. On the cable, see 564C, 564D and *On Socrates' Personal Deity* 591F–592B. See
   Introduction, p. 248, for its similarity to modern recorded accounts of bilocation.
2. In legend, the goddess Themis occupied the oracle at Delphi before Apollo.
3. Sibyl was a generic name for various oracular priestesses (see *The Pythia's
   Prophecies* 398C ff.). One Sibyl was connected with Delphi.
4. For the imagery, compare *On the Face on the Moon* 943D.
5. The reference is to the famous eruption of Vesuvius in AD 79. Dicaearcheia is
   modern Pozzuoli. In fact, Dicaearcheia was not affected by the eruption, but
   Plutarch mentions it because, as the busiest international port in the area, his
   readers would definitely have heard of it.
6. The emperor Titus.
7. Compare Plato, *Gorgias* 525a ff. for the punishment of souls.

over, and reaching for him with his hands. The overseers of his
father's punishments allowed him no secrets: they forced him to
admit that he had foully poisoned some visitors for their money.
On earth, no one had suspected him, but here he had been found
out; he had already suffered, and now was being taken away for
more.

Thespesius was so scared and terrified that he didn't dare beg    567A
or plead for mercy for his father, but just wanted to turn and run
away. But he couldn't see the gentle relative who had been his
guide; instead, other deities, who were frightening to look at,
were pushing him forward, as if to say that he had no choice but
to continue exploring everything. He noticed that anyone whose
crimes had been immediately detected and punished was not
now having to endure severe torment here* or be oppressed to
the same degree, since all that remained to be dealt with was his
irrational, emotional aspect. However, those who had spent their
lives without their iniquity being detected, because they covered
themselves with a screen and a semblance of goodness, were      B
hemmed in by guards of a different kind, who harassed and
tormented them until they forced them to turn their souls inside
out, with ghastly wriggles and convolutions which were reminiscent of how lugworms turn themselves inside out when they
swallow a hook.[1]

The guards flayed and cut open some of them, who were
carrying their wickedness in their rational, authoritative part, to
reveal them as infected and spotty. And he said that he saw other
souls entwined, snake-like, in groups of two or three or more,
who were eating one another because they held a grudge or felt
vindictive about things which had been done to them, or which
they had done, during their lifetimes. There was also a row of    C
pools, one of boiling gold, another of freezing lead, and a third
of rough iron. The deities in charge of these pools used imple-

1. It is uncertain which marine animal this 'sea-scolopendra' is (though in this
respect, at least, its behaviour is identical to that of a lugworm). Aristotle
(*Historia Animalium* 621a6 ff.) started this story about it, which recurs in
Oppian, *Halieutica* 2.424, and in Aelian, *De Natura Animalium* 7.35. In *Are
Land or Sea Animals More Intelligent?* 977B, Plutarch, from a confused memory
of the Aristotelian passage, assigned the story to the fox-shark.

ments, like blacksmiths, alternately to lift souls up and then lower them – these were the souls of people whose criminality stemmed from greed and avarice. When the souls had been heated up in the golden pool until they became transparent from the heat, the deities dropped them into the pool of lead for tempering; they immediately froze as hard as hailstones, and then the deities transferred them to the iron pool; here they became

D  hideously black, and they were so hard that bits of them were chipped and broken off, and their shapes became distorted; and then they were taken back to the gold pool again. These metamorphoses caused them excruciating pain, Thespesius said.

[31] The souls whose suffering aroused the most pity, he said, were those whose debt had been inherited by descendants or children, because they were under the impression that they had been absolved from repayment, but were then apprehended at a later date. What happened was that whenever any of their descendants or children arrived there and came across the soul of their forebear, they assaulted him furiously, yelling and scream- ing; they showed him the evidence of their suffering, and cursed

E  him and chased him around – and he couldn't escape and hide, however much he wanted to. Before long, the avenging deities were hunting him down and rushing him off for his original punishment, and he would go off wailing, because he already knew what penalty he was facing. And Thespesius said that some of these souls were swarming with descendants, who clung to them exactly like bees or bats, and emitted piercing cries[1] in anger at the memory of the pain they had endured because of them.

[32] The last thing he saw was the souls being modified for

F  rebirth.[2] They were being wrenched and reshaped into all kinds of living creatures by specialist artisans, who were using a combi- nation of tools and blows to join and force together some parts, twist others back, and obliterate and eliminate others altogether, so as to make the souls fit different characteristics and ways of

---

1. The image and the language are intended to recall the famous Homeric simile (*Odyssey* 24.6–10) of the souls of Penelope's suitors being led shrieking like bats by Hermes to the place of the dead.
2. For Plato's version of the rebirth process, see *Republic* 617d–621b.

life. And he saw among the others Nero's soul, which was in a bad way, not least because it had been run through with red-hot nails.[1] The artisans had a form already prepared for him – that of the Indian viper,* in which he would live once, as a foetus, he had eaten his way out of his mother;[2] but suddenly, he said, an intense light blazed forth, and a voice arose from the light, ordering them to transfer Nero's soul to another, more inoffensive species by fashioning the form of a musical animal which could live near marshes and ponds.[3] For, the voice announced, he had already been punished for his crimes, and moreover the gods owed him a favour for freeing the nation which, of all those he ruled, was the best and the most favoured by the gods.[4]

568A

[33] Up to this point, he had been a spectator; but he was poised to turn back when he became paralysed with fear.* A woman of incredible beauty and size had grabbed hold of him, and she said, 'Come here, you. This will help you remember everything better.' And she was bringing a red-hot stick, like painters use,[5] up close to him. Another woman stopped her, however, and he was jerked away, as suddenly as if he had been fired from a bowstring, by an extremely tempestuous and strong wind; he landed on his body and looked up almost from his actual grave.[6]

1. The image comes from Plato, *Phaedo* 83d.
2. The legend that the young of the viper ate their way out of their mother's womb goes back to Herodotus (3.109), and remained popular as a natural marvel, e.g. in the poet Nicander's *Theriaca* 133 f. (second century BC) and in Pliny, *Naturalis Historia* 10.170. Nero had his mother murdered in AD 59.
3. Nero had musical pretensions; he was to be reborn as a frog.
4. Nero had proclaimed the independence of the Greek cities at the Isthmian Games of AD 67.
5. In encaustic painting, and so make an indelible mark on his memory. Compare *Life of Cato* 1.7, which is itself an echo of Plato, *Timaeus* 26c.
6. For the violence of rebirth, compare Plato, *Republic* 621b.

# ON SOCRATES' PERSONAL DEITY

## INTRODUCTION

This is a strange and adventurous piece, complex and innovative in form and structure. It turns out to be a curious combination of historical novel and philosophical discussion; but the effect is gained not by a juxtaposition of two features, but by an interlacing of the two themes for the greater effect of each.

The setting and framework is a famous historical tale of adventure and derring-do close to Plutarch's loyal Boeotian heart: the liberation of Thebes in December 379 BC, by a daring *coup d'état*, from Spartan occupation and their Theban collaborators. Here are the historical bones of the story: in 382 BC, when Sparta was establishing dominance over Greece, a Spartan army on its way north to Olynthus under General Phoebidas was encouraged by an oligarchic group in Thebes to install and support their government with a garrison in their acropolis, the Cadmeia. A number of Theban democrats escaped to Athens, and Thebes became a kind of puppet dictatorship ruled by the Theban magistrates Archias, Leontiades, Philippus and Hypates, and enforced by their bodyguard and 1,500 Spartans in the Cadmeia. A plot was hatched in December 379 between the exiles in Athens and a small group of local patriots whereby a dozen of the former, led by Pelopidas and Melon, crossed into Theban territory disguised as farmers on a hunt, slipped into Thebes itself with the evening influx of returning labourers, and so united with the small band of conspirators in the safe house of Charon. The plan was simple, not to say hare-brained. Archias' secretary Phyllidas, who was in the plot, was to lay on a celebratory party (it was the Festival of Aphrodisia) where Archias and his cronies were to be rendered as drunk as possible and lustful with the promise of well-born Theban women for their night's entertainment. Some conspirators disguised as the women would finish them off, a second party would deal with the other two main magistrates in their houses, free their compatriots from the prison and invite the citizens to join them in liberating Thebes. After a day and night of alarms, excursions and near disaster, astonishingly the plan worked, and most incredible of all, 1,500 intimidated Spartans sitting on the Cadmeia tamely withdrew under truce. Not surprisingly, their commander was later executed by the Spartan government. And that was not all, for from this colourful episode the whole balance of power in Greece began to change through the rise of Thebes and Boeotia under Epaminondas and the decline of Sparta.

Other accounts of the stirring exploit survive in Xenophon (*Hellenica* 5.4.1–13; the events occurred during his lifetime), Nepos (*Pelopidas* 2.1–4.1), Diodorus Siculus (15.25–27) and in Plutarch's works again in *Life of Pelopidas* (6–13). There are minor discrepancies and differences of emphasis. Xenophon and Diodorus give more prominence to Athenian support. Xenophon does not mention Pelopidas at all, but writes of Melon; nor does he mention Epaminondas, the subsequent hero of the rise of liberated Thebes. But Epaminondas did not take part in the coup, as Nepos informs us, and Plutarch has to explain why, as well as making his brother Caphisias, of whom there is no other mention, a leading character. Xenophon also has a different number for the returning exiles, and the details of the conspirators' groups vary. But as Xenophon himself said (5.4.7), there were already at his time different versions, and they would grow with elaboration. Plutarch himself would grow up in Boeotia with a variety of embroideries. In fact his own two accounts contain minor discrepancies (see notes on pp. 352, 354, 357). But this could well be due to the desire for dramatic effect in the essay. For example, the fatally wounded Cephisodorus is still alive (dead in the *Life*) between Leontiades and Pelopidas in the final sword fight (597F). Again Plutarch in the essay sets the whole exploit, from the first contact with the returning exiles to the *coup d'état*, within the space of a single day and night, while Xenophon (5.4.3) places a day's interval between the return of the exiles and the attack, and the *Life* puts the contact plans earlier.

The essay has certainly over-compressed for dramatic effect, because Archias' warning letter from Athens could not on that programme have named the house in Thebes which was to hide the exiles.

None of this matters. There is no disagreement about the main elements of the account. No one in Plutarch's day could possibly have known the intimate details of the famous coup as Plutarch relates them. But then he is writing a historical romance, and the sequence of events is superbly painted with vivid detail, doing justice to a famous historical canvas of Boeotian history. So no serious historical problem arises. But the actual presentation is not so simple.

In the first place the story is not told straight, but as a play within a play, retailed on request, after the liberation had taken place, by a participant, Caphisias, the brother of Epaminondas. He tells it in Athens, where he was on an embassy (§1, 575D), to an Athenian friend Archedamus and a group of eminent Athenians. These were real people; and Archedamus was probably Archedemus of Pelex, a well-known Theban sympathizer and campaigner mentioned by Aeschines (2.139; cf. 575D); Caphisias was probably addressing him with the Boeotian form of his name. So this part is historical faction.

This device is not original of course, but recalls a similar employment of narrative dialogue by Plato, most obviously in *Phaedo*, where Phaedo recounts to a friend Socrates' last day in prison, his conversation with his friends there and finally his execution. The form has the advantage of reporting a historical event in full with the benefit of hindsight, and yet also with the sense of immediacy from the person who was there. For such a narrator can slip into the dialogue and discussion as if it was taking place.

In fact there are grounds for thinking that Plutarch was deliberately recalling *Phaedo* for the reader. He makes the headquarters of the conspirators in Thebes the house of Simmias (§2, 576B–C), where they met under the disguise of a discussion group, and Simmias is a major participant in the talk before the action. This is the Simmias who was Socrates' Theban friend, and one of the intimate group with him in the last hours (Plato, *Phaedo* 59c); and Plutarch seems to go out of his way to point a connection between

Simmias and Plato at 578F. Again, one of the main discussions concerns the puzzling feature of Socrates' deity or divine sign. In form, the Plutarchan essay, like *Phaedo*, involves discussions which took place while those involved were waiting, and both Plutarch and Plato include myths and culminate with memorable narrative descriptions of the final action, the *coup d'état* in Thebes, and the execution of Socrates in Athens. But if *Phaedo* is recalled, it is not imitated; the similarity is superficial, the differences are characteristic, and highlight interpretational problems in Plutarch. In Plato the dialogue is dominated by the central philosophical discussion, which is completed by the simple but superb final narrative; the formal unity of the dialogue is achieved through the organic relationship between the argument on immortality and the action of the death of Socrates. In Plutarch, the tension between and within action and discussion is heightened by the storyteller's art of continual interlacing interruption of one to the other. But it is not immediately clear what relationship the topics of conversation have to the events, nor whether there is an internal coherence of direction within the discussion itself. Any solution to this problem should emerge from a brief analysis of structure.

Section 1 sets the preliminary scene at Athens, and underlines the aim of delivering an account of real events (575C). But for this Caphisias is to recount both the action (*praxis*) and the talk (*logos*) (575D). Both were always important to Plutarch. Usually for him they must not only be consistent, but action should be the culmination and embodiment of argument. In addition, at Athens above all, Plutarch is concerned to counter the old jibe of boorish backwood Boeotian impatience with philosophical talk (575E).

Since the rest of the essay turns on the interweaving of action and discussion, it will be convenient to classify the former as category A, and the latter as category B. We naturally begin with A: the conspirators' cover as a philosophical discussion society and their first contact with the exiles who are on the move from Athens (§2). But immediately there is a historical problem (A), the non-participation of Epaminondas, which provokes moral reasons (B) (§3). The first alarm (A) now occurs in §4 with the Theban puppet leader Archias interviewing a conspirator, the

seer Theocritus; but it merely concerns omens and prophecies
disturbing to Sparta, and meanwhile the plot to get Archias
drunk that evening is hatched with secretary Phyllidas.

Meanwhile (B) at Simmias' house a discussion opens on the
desecration of Alcmene's tomb by the Spartans (§5), but this topic
is immediately left in the air by news of mysterious goings-on at
the tomb of the Pythagorean Lysis at Haliartus (§6). This is a
new element which I propose to label C. This new theme in turn
is only clarified piecemeal after interruptions, in §8 and §13, as a
visit by a Pythagorean Theanor. Almost certainly Plutarch invented this whole incident (Theanor simply means Man of God)
which he develops as a device linking A and B. Theanor and the
tomb incidents are represented as part of the action, and have a
particular relationship to Epaminondas, but also Theanor and his
views become germane to the debate. Section 7 returns to B
with further talk about the interpretation of the puzzling inscription from Alcmene's tomb sent by King Agesilaus of Sparta to
Egypt for decipherment. It appears to have been a kind of oracle
from God. This is once more interrupted by C (§8) with more
news and details of the Pythagorean's actions at Lysis' tomb. The
stranger performed appropriate rites required for piety and purification, which were initiated by dreams and apparitions. He would
remove the body unless some divine power (the first mention of
the Greek word *daimonion* of the essay's title) opposed it. The
context is being steered towards divine contact and instruction.

The next sections (§§9–12) settle down to a discussion (B)
arising out of the reported happenings at the tomb. Galaxidorus
(§9) attacks them as examples of superstition, a kind of retreat
from the rational procedures of philosophy to oracles, divination
and dream visions. To this Pythagorean mumbo-jumbo Galaxidorus opposes his ideal philosopher Socrates, who pursued truth
with cold logic. This is in effect an attempted opposition of
philosophy and religion, and is in turn counterattacked by the
seer Theocritus. Socrates himself had a guiding deity, a divine
sign, here related to a kind of divination (580C); it is concerned
with prophecy in matters opaque and unfathomable to human
intelligence (580D). Galaxidorus is willing to admit that Socrates
had some kind of sign (§11), but he retains doubts about what

kind of divinatory sign it was, and what its contributory value was compared with other accompanying reasons held by Socrates. He suggests (§12) that 'signs' may be trivial in themselves, like a sneeze, or a pimple in a medical diagnosis; the important aspect is the interpretation put upon them. This is the characteristic of all prognosticating arts and sciences. In other words, Galaxidorus recognizes only technical divination, a human art operating on divine signs, and thus would reconcile philosophy and 'scientific' divination. But this is to ignore 'natural' divination, where there is allegedly a direct contact between god and individual, and of which Socrates' sign was supposed to be an instance.

At this point theme C breaks in again (§13) with the introduction at Simmias' house by Epaminondas of the Pythagorean stranger Theanor, who is said to be confirming noble principles by noble acts (582E). He is trying to repay Epaminondas for his kindness in performing final duties to his dead mentor Lysis. A different discussion (B) (§§14–15) is thus triggered on the morality of kindness and its repayment.[1] Epaminondas rejects Theanor's repayment for philosophical reasons. He values his poverty, as Lysis had taught him, as an antidote to the dangers of wealth; as such it should be kept tempered by continually experiencing it and refusing offers of wealth. Epaminondas widens the theme (§15) to an examination of the moral status of poverty and wealth and our proper attitude to them, and sets up the argument through an analysis of desire designed to justify the moral practice of training to eliminate destructive desires. The philosophical colour of this argument, which is Plutarch's of course, will be raised later. For the moment we must ask what is the contextual reference of this episode. It seems to be related to the character of Epaminondas. He is explicitly contrasted (583F–584A) with the tyrant Jason of Pherae, whose bribe he had indignantly refused. But the widening of the argument to corrupting desires in general clearly sets the young Epaminondas against the Theban tyrant Archias, who is about to destroy himself by drunkenness and lust. The focus on Epaminondas is confirmed by section 16, where Simmias voices approval for Epaminondas' *argument*, said to be due to his *philosophical* upbringing by his father Polymnis. But then the essay reverts to the Lysis theme, recording divine

warnings from the tomb not to move the body, because Epaminondas had done all the religiously correct things. There is mention of Lysis' deity; and then mysteriously we are told that
Epaminondas had the same deity for his life (586A); that is,
presumably, he enjoyed the same *divine* guidance that Lysis had.

The action (A) boils up again (§§17–19). Hipposthenidas loses
his nerve and tries to call off the plot (§17). He believes he is
acting rationally (586D), and tries to justify himself by rational
arguments (586D–F), but in fact his real reasons are superstitious,
through divination and a dream (586F–587A). The seer Theocritus reinterprets the signs in the opposite way. But it is too late,
for the messenger sent by Hipposthenidas to turn back the exiles
will have gone. But no. The messenger appears. He had been
prevented – by what? Sheer luck or coincidence? Or was it by a
sign (587F)? The reaction of the conspirators, lapsing through
sudden anticlimax into anxiety and fear instead of relief, is psycho-
logically correct as well as maintaining tension.

So they return to the final conversation (B), which now concentrates on Socrates' deity or divine guidance (§§20–23). Simmias
first tries to give a rational or philosophical account of the phenomenon. He suggests that it may be a voiceless communication
from a daimon, or deity, making direct contact with the intellect
without the medium of the senses (588E). He reminds his friends
that they accept this kind of thing happening in dreams, when
the usual bodily senses are not operative. In this way, a higher
intellect or mind can impinge directly on a lower responsive
intellect (588E), and so guide it. Simmias argues by illustration
on the level of familiar models (588F–589D): a receptiveness to
peculiar pulses of energy; illumination through reflected light.
The extraordinary thing about Socrates was that this happened
when he was wide awake with all his wits and senses about him.
But that was precisely the special thing about him: he had his
own guide in him, tuned in presumably to his higher deity when
the latter decided to help (589E–F).

This philosophical approach leaves the picture incomplete, and
(as Plutarch did also in *On God's Slowness to Punish*) Simmias fills
out his presentation (§§21–2) with the myth of Timarchus of
Chaeronea, which represents religious belief and a theological

account. He tells of how the soul after death shoots up like a star and becomes a daimon, or deity, and eventually through purification may escape the wheel of reincarnation and remain a deity up in the region of the moon or beyond. But some of these soul deities retain an interest in incarnate souls, which they try to help if permitted, and such a soul deity may even be assigned to a particular person. In incarnate souls themselves a deity may remain, the intellect itself, which is distinct not only from the body, but also from the lower soul. *This* daimon, if not sunk, immersed and so blunted in the bodily functions and passions of the lower soul, floats on top like a buoy, and so is free to direct, and also to respond to higher divine communication. In these two sections Plutarch appears to be trying to unite philosophy and religion in a marriage of equals.

The opinion and comments of Epaminondas are hoped for (592F); but we get Theanor instead, who, we are told, draws on the same sources as Epaminondas (592F). Epaminondas, we recall, was brought up in philosophy. Is Theanor presented as his religious *Doppelgänger*?

Theanor (§24) comments that Timarchus' story should simply be accepted as holy and inviolable, and that it should not be difficult to accept Simmias' argument as well (593A). After all, it is observably common to all species that some favoured individuals are more responsive to higher command than others (593B). He accepts (unlike Galaxidorus in §12) two species of divination: technical and direct (593C). The former has been developed because the latter is rare (593D). It is rare because few are singled out as real men of God. He also suggests that the supervisionary deities only help directly when an incarnate soul is nearing the end of the struggle for purified liberation (593F–594A). Such a truly exceptional one was Socrates. Are we to understand that the young Epaminondas is making some progress at least (cf. 586A)?

At any rate, Epaminondas is kept in the picture until the last possible moment (§25), with a final request for participation, rejected once more on moral and, it also must be said, on prudential grounds (594C). The actors take their positions for the final act, Archias and his cronies going off to their debauch and the conspirators assembling with the exiles in Charon's house (§26). The stage is set.

So the remaining sections (§§27–34) are devoted to the action (A). They are a fine example of Plutarch's complete mastery of narrative storytelling. But as the suspense throughout has been built through interruptions interlacing the historical account and the conversational themes, even now, when we are left with the former on its own, Plutarch contrives internal disruptions and uncertainties. First, the unexplained summoning of Charon to Archias (§§27–8). Is this betrayal? No, all is well (§29); just vague rumours of returned exiles which Archias is too involved in his carousal to pursue. Then next (§30), a warning letter to Archias from his namesake in Athens with incriminating details. But Archias is by now too far gone in his cups and lustful expectation to bother opening it. '"Urgent business will keep until tomorrow."' At long last the coup unwinds in swift detail: the killing of Archias, Philippus and Cabirichus (§31); the killing of Leontiades by Pelopidas with the dying Cephisodorus sprawled between them, and Hypates caught on the roof (§32); the freeing of prisoners (§33); and the final capture of the whole of Thebes (§34).

This analysis has at least brought out Plutarch's technique of narrative suspense through the complex interweaving of quite varied strands of activity and talk. But what of the problem raised earlier of the relevance of the discussions to the action? The conversations focus for the most part in their development on the question of divine communication and guidance, culminating in an attempted interpretation of the most notorious historical example of this in Socrates' divine sign, from which the essay even takes its title. But what has this to do with the coup and liberation of Thebes? Plutarch is surely not choosing any chance topic to defend the intellectual curiosity of his countrymen when under stress. In any case there is not even an internal coherence of conversational topic. For the section on kindness, repayment, poverty, wealth and the schooling of corrupting desires has nothing to do with the main theme of divination; but it certainly relates to Epaminondas, who leads this discussion and who was famous in Theban tradition for his defence of poverty and for the nobility of his character. And further, the structure of the essay also shows that the main divination and divine-guidance

theme itself arises from and peaks in the Pythagorean strand of
Lysis and Theanor, our theme C; and the Theban bud from that
stem is again Epaminondas. So it turns out that Epaminondas is
the one character in the essay who unites and personifies the
discussion themes, combining philosophy and religion in the
moral stature of his character and in his Pythagorean training.
Indeed he is the only character in the essay who is said to enjoy
divine guidance, through the same daimon/deity that Lysis had
(586A). Now this is not only ingenious; it is a highly audacious
stroke. For Epaminondas, whom Plutarch greatly admired, by
deliberate choice took no historical part in the great national
exploit of the *coup d'état*. But he is a pervasive character in this
essay, hovering in the wings as a kind of *éminence rose*, represented
as the moral core of the liberation, with the virtual prophecy
that he will step forward after the bloodshed and lead democratic
Thebes to greatness.

Greek ethical philosophy, apart from radical Cynicism, assumed that man was a social animal and placed him in society
and politics. So in Plato's *Republic* the microcosm of the individual is related to the macrocosm of the state. Aristotle's *Politics*
naturally follows his *Ethics*, and Plato's ideal philosopher-king of
the *Republic* had a continued history in Hellenistic philosophy. So
perhaps Epaminondas is seen here, not in this anti-tyrannical
context as the philosopher-king, but as the philosopher-
democrat.

Most of the discussion relates to religious and theological
themes, but the one purely philosophical argument, that on the
moral standing of poverty and wealth and the classification of
desire, is very characteristic of Plutarch. It is stitched to the
historical Epaminondas (584D–F), but Plutarch used the analysis
of desire again in much the same language in *On the Use of
Reason by 'Irrational' Animals* 989B ff. There is the Platonic distinction between necessary and unnecessary desires (*Republic* 558d ff.,
571b ff.) with which Plutarch would of course have been familiar;
but Plutarch's treatment cannot be traced to a single philosopher
or school; it has elements which one might associate with Epicurean, Stoic, Peripatetic and Cynic sources. The original analysis is
quite Epicurean,[2] but the term *emphytos*, translated 'instinctive',

is more Stoic, while the Greek word used for 'extraneous' (*epēlydes*) was connected with Aristotle's pupil Aristoxenus,[3] who was also influenced by Pythagoreans. The suggested cure by habituation and practice (584E) is Peripatetic, but the suppression of corrupting desires is strongly Stoic; while the emphasis on training (*askēsis* with its accompanying terms), whereby you abstain from what is allowed as practice for abstaining from what is forbidden (585A), thereby facing temptation continuously in order to conquer it, is undoubtedly Cynic. This is a glorious hotchpotch which yet contains little which any Hellenistic school of philosophy would seriously take exception to. It displays beautifully that one of Plutarch's main skills was to create a kind of philosophical koine. In the matter of poverty and wealth, since the context is tailored to the historical Epaminondas' famous championship of poverty, Plutarch's final weighting goes to the Cynic rejection of wealth as unnatural, rather than to the Stoic view that wealth was preferable to poverty, but had no moral value in itself. This was different again from the Peripatetic/Academic position, where adequate affluence could positively add to happiness.

The main discussion, however, leads to an examination and interpretation of Socrates' divine guiding sign. This was a notorious puzzle which never ceased to fascinate the Greeks. According to his contemporaries Plato and Xenophon, it was a divine sign received by Socrates in the form of a voice. So it was a kind of divinatory influence, which according to Plato was inhibitory, stopping a false move, although its absence was interpreted by Socrates as approval. Xenophon allowed it a more positive role. Both recognized it as a kind of divination, but clearly quite different from any accepted form. In the first place their uncertainty is signalled by the vague term by which they refer to it, the divine thing (*daimonion*); they never personify it as Socrates' deity, or daimon. Secondly, it belonged to neither recognized class of divination: it was not an external sign open for interpretation by technical divination, since it was a personal phenomenon not available to others. Nor was it in the accepted form of direct natural communication from a god, which took the form of possession when you were out of your mind, or of dreams and the like when asleep or unconscious. Socrates was awake with all his wits about him when it occurred. Plato rightly said that it was unique (*Republic* 496c); indeed dangerously so in a democracy, since it sounded as if Socrates claimed a personal line to God. It produced uproar in court at Socrates' trial (Xenophon, *Apology* 14).

Plutarch's answer is indicated in his myth of Timarchus, one of the three eschatological myths[4] he wrote, probably about the same period. They concern the function, fate and progress of souls after death, and their continued relationships with incarnate souls. For a general introduction to the form, presentation and topography of these myths, see the Introduction to *On God's Slowness to Punish*.

In this essay the framework imagery is astronomical (for explanation of details, see footnotes, pp. 340–43). Souls when they die are represented as stars shooting up from earth towards the moon, or sinking back down again to earth. They are also referred to as daimons, or deities. The history of the daimon model in philosophy is long and complex, and can only briefly be traced here with a few relevant earlier examples, principally from Plato. The word daimon in Homer was simply another word for god; but it soon became commoner to regard daimons as intermediate deities or spirits between gods and men, and with strong relationships with humans. One such role was as ruler, director or guide (Hesiod, *Works and Days* 109 ff.), which Plato used in his myths (*Phaedo* 107d ff.; *Republic* 617d ff.) in the form of personal guardian spirits linked to our destiny. Another story was that good men may *become* daimons when they die (Hesiod, *Works and Days* 121 ff.), used by Plato as an illustration, not to be taken literally, of his Guardians when dead (*Republic* 469a). So Empedocles (F115) used daimon for our occult self after death. But Plato also in different contexts internalized the image. The go-between characteristic of daimons was used as a model for love (*eros*), at *Symposium* 202d13 ff., as an aspect of us which links human to divine ideals. And Plato even once (*Timaeus* 90a) applied the term to our rational directing capacity situated at the top of our body (i.e. the head; cf. Plutarch 591E). Differently again, in *Epinomis* 984–5, daimons are an actual constituent of the intelligible cosmic structure, up in the air below the gods of the visible stars and acting as go-betweens for humans below.

Now, even from this selection, earlier ingredients for Plutarch's daimonology are apparent. But basically there were two different concepts, not conflated: (i) daimons are independent of us, but form some kind of guiding or linking function between ourselves and the gods; and (ii) daimons in some way or other *are* us or a part or aspect of us. The connection between the two was not apparent and created confusion, in the question of responsibility, for example. In Plato's *Republic* our spirit guide controls us, but *we* are ourselves responsible.

Plutarch's solution was to retain both main types of daimon, but to claim that they were basically the same thing. Human beings are not a composite of body and soul, but tripartite: body, soul (*psyche*) and intellect (*nous*).[5] So in the *On the Face on the Moon* myth there can be two deaths, of body on earth, of psyche on the moon, after which intellect rises pure to the highest region. But it is the intellect alone which is the daimon, whether incarnate or discarnate. So Plutarch can say that in a sense the different uses of daimon are simply of the same kind of daimon at different stages. Since the intellect-daimon remains substantively identical and only varies in purity or quality, so divine guidance or communication is possible through the contact of a purer or higher intellect on a lower one, because the medium is the same. It is, however, difficult because the incarnate intellect-daimon is impeded not only by the body but also by the psyche, and can only respond in circumstances when they are both lulled. It is only in the rarest cases, where a man like Socrates has already virtually freed his intellect-daimon from body and psyche, that response can occur in everyday situations.

How typical of Plutarch to take and put together ingredients already there and culled from his vast reading, and fashion something new and ingenious. It should be added that the topic of psychological daimonology was extremely popular through the first century BC to the second century AD, and produced a number of different and fascinating versions. One still more direct unification of daimon problems was provided by the synthesis of the Stoic Posidonius (F187 EK), that the daimon within us, which we must follow to achieve our happiness, is precisely our moral intelligence, the ruling aspect of our mind. But this daimonic aspect or part is, by Stoic natural philosophy, actually a concentration of the active rational principle which directs the universe by being physically immanent through it. So Marcus Aurelius put it (5.27) that our daimon *was* a fragment of God.

1. A contemporary theme of debate; e.g. Seneca, *De Beneficiis*.
2. *Letter to Menoeceus* 127 ff.; *Vatican Sayings* 21, 25.
3. John of Stobi 3.424.15 ff. Hense.
4. Cf. also *On God's Slowness to Punish*, *On the Face on the Moon*.
5. *On Socrates' Personal Deity* 22, 591D ff.; *On the Face on the Moon* 28.

# ON SOCRATES' PERSONAL DEITY[1]

575B [1] 'Once, Caphisias,[2] I remember, I heard from an artist an excellent description, cast as a simile, of people who look at pictures. He said that amateur, unskilled viewers are like those who greet a large crowd *en masse*, whereas skilled professionals are like those who address everyone they meet individually and in personal terms, in the sense that the first group get an impression of the finished products which is not precise, but only hazy, whereas professionals have the discrimination to take each aspect of the work separately, and they don't overlook or fail to comment on anything, whether good or bad. Now, in my opinion, we can extend the analogy to real events too: when faced with history, lazier minds are satisfied if they gather just the gist and the conclusion of a situation, whereas anyone who appreciates honour and nobility, and who views the products of the master art, as it were, of virtue, finds the details more enjoyable, on the grounds that although the result has a lot in common with chance, yet by virtue of their causes the particular contests of virtue against chance occurrences and the acts of intelligent bravery in the face of fearful conditions ⟨become clear cases of⟩ rationality suitably blended with opportunity and emotion.* You can assume that we too belong to this category of viewer, and

1. We have only two manuscripts of this essay. The weakness of the manuscript tradition means, among other things, that there are places where actual gaps occur in the text. Sometimes plausible guesses can be made as to the Greek text which originally filled the gap; sometimes only the general sense can be divined; sometimes a gap simply has to be left blank. In any case, such places are indicated in the following translation by the use of triangular brackets.

2. The Athenian Archedamus is talking to Caphisias, the brother of the Theban patriot Epaminondas, in Athens. See the Introduction, pp. 296 ff., for the characters and the setting.

therefore please tell us in detail exactly what happened, from start to finish, and ⟨share⟩ with us the discussion which, ⟨we hear⟩, took place ⟨. . .⟩ in your presence. You should know that I wouldn't have hesitated, but would have gone to Thebes just for this, if I didn't already have the reputation in Athens of being excessively pro-Boeotian.'

'No, Archedamus. Given that your affection makes you so enthusiastic and eager to learn what happened, I should have made coming here to give you an account "a higher priority than any occupation", as Pindar puts it.[1] As it is, since an embassy has brought us here, and since we have time to spare while waiting for the Assembly to give us its response, to resist and to be rude to a cordial and true friend would probably revive the slur which used to be brought against the Boeotians – of being averse to discussions[2] – but is now fading, ⟨since Simmias and Cebes⟩ have demonstrated their enthusiasm in the presence of your Socrates, and we have done so in the presence of Lysis the priest.★ But you should check whether the people here are inclined to listen to an account which combines action and discussion at such length. I mean, it will take quite a while to get through it, since you insist that the account incorporates the discussion as well.'

'Caphisias, you don't know these men. But I tell you, they are worth knowing: their fathers were good men, and were well disposed towards Thebes. Let me introduce them to you: Lysithides, the nephew of Thrasybulus; Timotheus, the son of Conon; these are the sons of Archinus;[3] and the rest are all members of our circle ⟨as well⟩. Consequently, your account has a friendly and sympathetic audience.'★

'That's good to hear. But what would be a reasonable place for

---

1. *Isthmian Odes* 1.2. It was a common tag (e.g. Plato, *Phaedrus* 227b9), but with typical learned wit, Plutarch here inverts its context, because the original ode says that Thebes, where Caphisias has come from, is a higher priority than any occupation.

2. Plutarch was naturally sensitive to this gibe, and rose to it regularly (e.g. *On the Spite of Herodotus* 864D).

3. These were famous Athenian families who had been involved in the restoration of democracy at Athens and in the revival of her fortunes after her defeat and occupation by Sparta at the end of the Peloponnesian War. They were therefore a sympathetic audience to hear the details of the liberation of Thebes from oligarchic dictatorship and a Spartan garrison.

me to start my account, given what you already know of the events?'

'Well, Caphisias, we are pretty clear on the situation in Thebes before the exiles returned.[1] We know that Archias and Leontiades and their companions prevailed upon Phoebidas to seize the Cadmeia while the treaty[2] was in force, and then banished some citizens and used fear to keep the rest in check, while they themselves took control illegally and by force. We found all that out here because, as you know, we became friendly with Melon, Pelopidas and their people,[3] and we were constantly in their company all the time they were in exile. Furthermore, we have heard that although the Spartans fined Phoebidas for his seizure of the Cadmeia, and stripped him of his command of the expedition against Olynthus, they still sent Lysanoridas and two others to replace him and strengthened the garrison in the acropolis. And we also know that Hismenias[4] met an ignoble death immediately after his trial, since Gorgidas sent letters to the exiles here, telling them all about it. So what we need from your account are the circumstances of the actual return of your comrades and the defeat of the tyrants.'

[2] 'Well then, Archedamus, in those days the routine was for all the conspirators to get together in Simmias' house,[5] because he was recuperating from a hurt leg. Although we used to meet one another to see what needed doing, ostensibly we were busy discussing philosophy, and since Archias and Leontiades[6] were in fact not utterly unfamiliar with this kind of activity, so as not to arouse suspicion, we often used to induce them to come along. And anyway, Simmias had only recently returned to Thebes after a long period abroad travelling among foreign peoples, and he was well stocked with all kinds of stories and ideas from other

1. In 382 BC, Theban oligarchs persuaded the Spartan general Phoebidas, who was heading for Olynthus with an army, to seize and garrison their citadel, the Cadmeia. They tyrannized Thebes until returning exiles restored democracy in 379 by the famous exploit which is the subject of this essay.
2. The Peace of Antalcidas of 386 BC.
3. That is, the Theban anti-oligarchic exiles.
4. The Theban leader of the opposition party to the oligarchs and Sparta.
5. According to Plato's *Phaedo*, Simmias was one of Socrates' companions in his last hours in prison before execution. See the Introduction, pp. 296–7, for the links between this essay and *Phaedo*.
6. Two of the leaders of the oligarchic dictatorship.

countries, which Archias loved to listen to when he had the time: he would make himself comfortable among the young men and voice a preference for us passing the time in philosophical discussion rather than concentrating on his party's plans.

'The day came when the exiles were supposed to make their way secretly to the city walls when night fell. A man arrived from here[1] – Pherenicus had sent him – who was a stranger to all of us except Charon. He told us that the twelve youngest exiles had gone hunting with their dogs near Mount Cithaeron,[2] with the intention of arriving some time in the evening, and that he had been sent to give us advance warning of this and to find out who would supply the house in which they would be hidden when they came, so that armed with this knowledge they could go there without delay. We didn't know what to do. We were thinking about it, when Charon said that he had no objection to providing the house himself. The man therefore decided to return post haste to the exiles.

[3] 'Theocritus the seer squeezed my hand tightly, looked at Charon who was walking in front of us, and said, "He may be no philosopher, Caphisias, and he hasn't had the benefit of a particularly outstanding education, like your brother Epaminondas, but, as you can see, a code of conduct steers him naturally towards right action and of his own accord he takes on a highly dangerous job for his country's sake. Epaminondas, however, despite his claim to have been better schooled for goodness than any other Boeotian, is unenthusiastic and reluctant ⟨...⟩ in making use of his excellent natural and nurtured talents ⟨for⟩ this or some better occasion."

'"Don't get carried away, Theocritus," I replied. "We are doing what we think right, whereas Epaminondas thinks it better for us not to follow this course of action; he is failing to persuade us of this, but it is reasonable for him to resist when he is invited to participate in something which both his nature and his judgement rebel against. I mean, if a doctor guarantees to get rid of a disease without operating and without cauterizing, it wouldn't

1. Athens, where the essay is set.
2. A mountain ridge bordering Attica and Boeotia.

be fair of you, in my opinion, to force him to operate on the body★ or to cauterize it."

⟨'"No, I suppose it wouldn't," he said.⟩

'"So the same goes for him," ⟨I said. "He himself insists⟩, as you know, that ⟨only dire necessity will induce him to kill⟩ any of his compatriots without a trial, but that he will be the first to side with people who are trying to liberate his country without spilling the blood of kinsmen and without slaughter. But since he was outvoted, and since we have instead embarked on this course, he is asking us to let him avoid the taint and guilt of murder, and to be in a position to seize opportunities as they arise, so that both justice and expediency attend his conduct. For, he claims, it will be an indiscriminate business: it may be that Pherenicus and Pelopidas will move against those who most deserve it, who are evil, but Eumolpidas and Samidas are so inflamed and passionate in their fury that once they have been given the go-ahead in the dark of night, they will not lay down their swords until they have filled the whole city with death and have killed plenty of their own personal enemies."

577A

[4] 'Galaxidorus interrupted★ my conversation with Theocritus ⟨to tell us that Archias⟩ and Lysanoridas the Spartan were near by, hurrying from the Cadmeia as if to meet us. So we stopped talking. Archias called Theocritus over, took him to Lysanoridas and, once he had made them duck off the road a little way to the foot of the Amphion,[1] carried on a private conversation with them for a long time. This made us very anxious, in case they had heard some rumour or received some information and were questioning Theocritus about it.

B

'While all this was going on, Phyllidas (whom you know, Archedamus), who was at that time secretary to Archias and his fellow polemarchs[2] – he was in on the plot ⟨and knew that the exiles were on the point of⟩ returning – took hold of my hand and ostensibly started joking with me in his usual fashion about my working out and wrestling; then, when he had separated me from the others, he asked whether the exiles were on schedule.

1. A hill in Thebes to the north of the Cadmeia.
2. A high office at Thebes with special military reference. The highest magistracy of Boeotarch had been abolished in the emergency.

'"Yes," I replied.                                                                                    C

'"So I've done well," he said. "I've arranged the reception for today, whose purpose is to get Archias into my house and make it easy for our men to overpower him, when he's under the influence of alcohol."

'"Yes, you've done very well indeed, Phyllidas," I said, "and you must try to get all or quite a few of our enemies together in one place."

'"That won't be easy," he said. "Well, in fact it'll be impossible. You see, Archias is expecting a certain highly regarded lady to come to him tonight, so he doesn't want Leontiades around. So you must divide yourselves between the two houses. I mean, I suppose that once both Archias and Leontiades have been cap-    D tured, all the rest will disappear into exile; or if they stay, an offer of amnesty will appeal to them so much that they won't make any trouble."

'"That's what we'll do," I said. "But can you tell me what's going on between them and Theocritus? What are they talking about?"

'"I'm not certain," he replied, "and I don't know for sure,★ but I did hear that awkward and ominous signs and portents have been foretold for Sparta."

'⟨Just then Theocritus rejoined us and we carried on to Simmias' house where⟩ we were met by Phidolaus of Haliartus, who said, "Simmias wants you to wait here for a short while. He's having a private meeting with Leontiades about Amphitheus,[1] to ask whether it is possible★ for the man's sentence to be commuted to exile rather than death."                                                    E

[5] '"You've appeared at just the right time," said Theocritus. "It couldn't have been planned better. I was wanting some information: when Alcmene's grave was opened up in your country,[2]

---

1. A leader of the democrats, in prison under sentence of death.
2. When Alcmene, the mortal mother of Heracles, died, legend had it that a stone was substituted for her body. Plutarch has the tale again in Life of Romulus 28.7, and it recurs in Pherecydes (FGrH 3.F84) and in Pausanias 9.16.7. Haliartus, the supposed location of the tomb, was roughly halfway between Thebes and Chaeronea, on the southern shore of Lake Copais.

what was found there, and what did it look like in general? That is, if you were actually there when Agesilaus had the remains collected and moved to Sparta."

'"No, I wasn't there, in fact," said Phidolaus. "I was very disenchanted and annoyed with my compatriots, so they excluded me. Anyway, ⟨no human remains⟩ were found ⟨in the interior, only a stone⟩, and a small bronze bracelet and two earthenware jars with earth inside which had become petrified and compacted over the years. ⟨But at the entrance⟩ of the tomb ⟨lay⟩ a bronze plate with a lengthy inscription of incredible antiquity; it was completely incomprehensible, even though when the bronze had been cleaned with water it was perfectly legible. The script could best be compared with Egyptian in the peculiar, alien way it was formed, and that is why Agesilaus, as I was told, sent copies to the king[1] and asked him to show them to his priests, to see if they could decipher it. But Simmias might be able to shed some light on the matter for us, since it coincided with his time in Egypt, when he had a lot of discussions with the priests for philosophical reasons. At Haliartus, people think that the extremely poor harvest and the incursion of the lake were not accidental, but that this manifestation of wrath was due to the grave and occurred because we allowed the excavation."

'There was a brief pause, and then Theocritus said, "It looks as though the Spartans have incurred divine wrath too, as is indicated by the omens which Lysanoridas was asking my advice about just now; in fact, he is off to Haliartus now, to block up the tomb again and to pour libations, on the instructions of some oracle, to Alcmene and Aleus, even though he has no idea who Aleus was.[2] And when he gets back from there, he means to try to find Dirce's grave, whose location no one here in Thebes knows except former hipparchs.[3] What happens is that one night

1. The Pharaoh to whom King Agesilaus of Sparta sent the script was Nectanebis I (cf. Diogenes Laertius 8.87).
2. Aleus was a Boeotian name for Rhadamanthus whom Alcmene was supposed to have lived with after the death of her husband Amphitryon.
3. Cavalry commanders – another Theban office. There is no other mention of the secret tomb of Dirce, but for a similar procedure, compare Oedipus' instructions for his secret tomb in Sophocles, *Oedipus at Colonus* 1530 ff.

the outgoing hipparch takes his successor and shows him the
grave – there are only the two of them there. They perform
certain rituals on the grave, but nothing which involves fire,
obliterate and eliminate any traces of the rituals and then separate
and return under cover of darkness. Now, although I ⟨approve
of taking the rites seriously like this⟩, Phidolaus, I don't think
they will easily find ⟨the grave's location⟩: most of the former
constitutional hipparchs are in exile, or rather, all of them are
except Gorgidas and Plato, and they won't even try to get the      C
information from them, because they are afraid of them; and the
current powers that be in the Cadmeia may have succeeded to
the spear and the seal,[1] but they are completely ignorant about
both ⟨the rituals and the grave⟩."

[6] 'Leontiades and his friends had departed while Theocritus
was talking, so we went in and greeted Simmias, who was sitting
on his couch in a very depressed and miserable state – presumably
because he had not got what he'd asked for. His gaze took us all
in, and he said, "God, what brutal and barbaric characters! Wasn't      D
Thales absolutely spot on all those years ago, when he came
home after some time abroad and his friends asked him what was
the oddest thing he had noticed, and he replied, 'An old tyrant'?[2]
I mean, even someone who has not personally been wronged in
the slightest loathes the oppressiveness and the difficulty of dealing with them, and this in itself turns him against power which
sets itself higher than law and is answerable to no one – unless
God takes care of it, which is probably the case. Anyway, Caphisias, this visitor who has come to see you – do you know
who he is?"

'"I don't know who you're talking about," I said.

'"Nevertheless," he said, "Leontiades tells me that a man was
seen getting to his feet by the tomb of Lysis during the night; he
had a large retinue and impressive trappings, and had apparently      E
camped there on pallets, since there were beds of willow and
tamarisk, and also the remains of burnt offerings and libations of

1. The badges of office in Thebes; cf. 597B.
2. Also reported by Diogenes Laertius 1.36. Thales probably meant that it was
extraordinary for a tyrant to survive to old age (cf. Plutarch in 147B).

milk. And this morning he was asking people he met whether he would find Polymnis' sons in town."

'"Who on earth could this visitor be?" I asked. "From what you say, he sounds like a man of distinction on public business."

[7] '"Yes, that's right," said Phidolaus, "and we'll make him welcome when he reaches us. But meanwhile, Simmias, there's an inscription we were puzzling about just now, and if you know more about it than we do, please tell us. It's the inscription on the plate which Agesilaus took from Haliartus when he ran-sacked Alcmene's grave, and it is said that the priests in Egypt deciphered it."

'Simmias remembered straight away. "I'm not aware of this plate," he said, "but Agetoridas the Spartan came to Memphis with a long letter from Agesilaus and visited Chonuphis the seer; and this coincided with the time when Plato, Ellopion of Peparethus and I ⟨were frequently in Chonuphis' company⟩, occupying ourselves with doing philosophy together. The king sent Agetoridas to Chonuphis with orders to decipher the writing if he could, translate it and get it back to him soon.* Chonuphis spent three days researching all kinds of scripts in ancient books, before writing back to the king. He told us too what the inscription said: it enjoins the institution of a competition in honour of the Muses. He also said that the style of the script dates it to the reign of Proteus – and that it is the type of script which Heracles the son of Amphitryon mastered – and yet the inscription is a way for God to direct and advise the Greeks to ease up, stop fighting and make philosophy their only means of competition, by relinquishing their weapons and deciding moral issues by relying on the Muses and on dialogue.

'"Even at the time we were of the opinion that Chonuphis was right, and this opinion was strengthened later, when on our journey back from Egypt some Delians met us in Caria with a request for Plato: they wanted him, as a geometer, to make sense of a peculiar oracle which Apollo had propounded for them. The oracle was that Delos and the rest of Greece would be free of the evil that is currently besetting them if they doubled the Delian altar. But they were incapable of understanding the oracle's meaning, and made fools of themselves in constructing

the altar: they doubled each of the four sides, and then found that, on this multiplication, they had unintentionally come up with a solid whose volume was eight times the original; they did this because they were unaware of the combination of ratios by which something which is three-dimensional is doubled.\* That is    C
why they asked Plato for his assistance with the problem.[1]

'"Plato remembered what the Egyptian had said, and asserted that Apollo was teasing the Greeks for their disregard of education, and was obliquely pouring scorn on our ignorance and telling us to tackle geometry, and to do so in a wholehearted fashion, since the comprehension\* of two mean proportionals, which is the essential prerequisite of doubling a cube by increasing it by an equal amount in all dimensions, is certainly out of the question for a paltry mind, but takes acuity of intellectual perception and a high degree of training in geometrical diagrams. Anyway, he went on, although Eudoxus of Cnidus or Helicon of Cyzicus would do the job for them,[2] they shouldn't suppose that this was what Apollo was demanding: rather, he was commanding the Greeks as a whole to abandon warfare and suffering,    D
and so attend the Muses; and to soothe the emotions by concentrating on discussion and study, and so associate with one another in a way from which no harm, but benefit, accrues."

[8] 'My father Polymnis had entered during Simmias' speech. He sat down next to Simmias and said to him, "Epaminondas asks you, and everyone here, to wait here, unless you have something more important to do with your time, because he wants you to meet someone who is in town – a man ⟨who is⟩

1. The duplication of the cube was one of the most famous and vexed problems in early Greek mathematics; it was sometimes known, because of this background, as the Delian problem. The reader will most conveniently find details and explication in I. Thomas, *Greek Mathematical Works*, vol. 1, pp. 256–308, and in Sir Thomas Heath, *History of Greek Mathematics*, vol. 1, pp. 244–70. Eutocius (in Thomas, ibid.) claims that Hippocrates first tackled the problem in the fifth century BC with the concept of mean proportionals, but Plato was certainly interested: cf. *Meno* 82b ff. for doubling a square; *Theaetetus* 147d ff. for irrational numbers; *Timaeus* 32b for mean proportionals. Plutarch was also fascinated: 386E, 718E–F, *Life of Marcellus* 14.9.

2. Elsewhere (718E–F), Plutarch maintains that Plato reproached Eudoxus, Archytas and Menaechmus for resorting to mechanical devices in approaching the problem, rather than sticking to pure mathematics.

not only impressive in himself, but has also come here for an impressive and excellent purpose ⟨as an emissary⟩ from the Pythagoreans in Italy. He has come, prompted by certain vivid

E    dreams and visions, he says, to pour libations to Lysis the Elder at his grave; he has also brought plenty of money, and thinks he ought to recompense Epaminondas for looking after Lysis in his old age – he is very keen to do so, despite the fact that we are not inviting him or wanting him to help us out in our poverty."

'Simmias was very pleased at the news. "He sounds wonderful," he said, "and well suited to philosophy. But what stopped him from coming to us straight away?"

F    '"I think he spent the night at Lysis' grave," he replied, "so Epaminondas took him to the Hismenus to bathe, and then they'll join us here. He camped at the grave before coming here to meet us because the primary purpose of his visit is to collect what's left of the body and take it to Italy, unless some deity were to have manifested during the night and opposed him."

'My father fell silent at this point, [9] but Galaxidorus said, "God, it's so hard to find anyone untarnished by affectation and superstition. Some people are accidentally caught by these emotions because of inexperience or weakness; others want to give the impression of being highly favoured by the gods or of being special people, so they claim that the gods sanction their actions, and they gloss any stray thoughts as dreams, visions and all that

580A    pretentious rubbish. Now, it is arguable that this serves a purpose for people who are involved in politics and have no choice but to live in relation to a wilful and undisciplined mob – the purpose of using superstition as a bridle, something to pull on to sidetrack and divert the masses towards what is good for them. But a façade of this kind seems not only inappropriate for philosophy, but also contradictory to its promise, in the sense that* it promises to use reason to teach everything that is good and beneficial for people, and then falls back on the gods to explain how actions are initiated, which is to belittle reason; and it devalues proof, which is supposed to be its main advantage, and relies on omens

B    and things seen in dreams – and in dreams bad people are just as likely to meet with success as good people. And this, in my opinion, Simmias, is why your teacher Socrates adopted a more philosophical stance in the way he approached education and argument: he chose his accessible and straightforward approach as being suited to an autonomous individual and fully compatible with the truth, and he treated affectation as mere smoke arising from the fire of philosophy, and dispersed it in the direction of the sophists."

'Theocritus responded with a question: "What are you saying, Galaxidorus? Has Meletus convinced you that Socrates had nothing but contempt for divine matters? I mean, that's what he accused Socrates of when he had him up before the Athenian court."[1]                                                                C

'"No, of course I'm not saying that he despised genuinely divine matters," he replied. "But whereas he inherited from Pythagoras ⟨and his disciples⟩ a philosophy ⟨that had become⟩ filled with apparitions and fiction and superstition, ⟨and⟩ Empedocles bequeathed him an absolutely intoxicated version, Socrates accustomed philosophy to face facts in full possession of its senses,[2] so to speak, and to make truth a goal to be pursued with sober reason."

[10] '"That's as may be," said Theocritus. "But, my dear friend, are we to call Socrates' personal deity[3] a lie, or what? I don't think that anything that Pythagoras is said to have done as a seer is as important or as divine. I mean, Homer in his poem has Odysseus 'attended in all his struggles' by Athena,[4] and exactly the same goes for Socrates: throughout his life his personal deity seems to have afforded him the kind of perceptiveness which, all by itself, 'leads the way and sheds light'[5] – to have          D given him this guide as a companion whenever he was in situa-

1. The indictment of Socrates as preserved in the state records (Diogenes Laertius 2.40) claimed that he was guilty of not believing in the gods the state believed in and of introducing different, new deities; also of corrupting the young.
2. The epic word used here is intended to recall the seer Teiresias (Homer, *Odyssey* 10.494 f.) who, although in the shadow world of the dead, was permitted to have all his wits about him.
3. See Introduction, pp. 300–301, 304–5, for the phenomenon.
4. *Odyssey* 13.301.
5. From Homer, *Iliad* 20.95, where it refers to Athena before Achilles.

tions which were opaque and unfathomable by human intelligence, in the course of which★ his personal deity invariably communicated with him and made his decisions inspired.

'"You should ask Simmias and the rest of Socrates' friends for more instances, and less trivial ones, but I myself was there on one occasion: I had gone to visit Euthyphro the seer. You'll remember this one, Simmias. Socrates happened to be climbing the hill up towards the Symbolon[1] and Andocides' house, and he was at the same time asking Euthyphro questions and lightheart-
E  edly testing him. Suddenly he stopped, went quiet and became withdrawn for quite a time; then he turned around and started to head down the box-makers' street. ⟨He recalled⟩ those of his friends who had already gone on ahead ⟨with the information⟩ that his personal deity had come ⟨to him⟩. So most of the group turned back with him, including myself, since I wasn't letting Euthyphro out of my sight; but some of the young ones carried straight on, with the intention of showing up Socrates' personal deity, and they persuaded Charillus the pipe-player to go along with them (he had accompanied me to Athens, to visit Cebes). As they were going along the statuaries' street, past the lawcourts,
F  they encountered a herd of pigs: the pigs were covered in mud and there were so many of them that they were jostling one another. There was no escape; the pigs bumped into some of them and knocked them to the ground, and the rest of them just got filthy. Even Charillus came home with his legs and clothes spattered with mud, and consequently, whenever ⟨we⟩ think of Socrates' personal deity, we chuckle, ⟨although at the same time⟩ we are impressed by how God never abandoned him or overlooked him under any circumstances."

[11] 'Galaxidorus said, "So what you're saying, Theocritus, is that, in your opinion, Socrates' personal deity had some particular, special character, aren't you? That what his experience confirmed, and what he allowed to tip the scales when he was surrounded by matters which were so opaque as to baffle the rational mind, was not an aspect of everyday divination? A single weight in isolation does not tip a beam: it needs to be

1. A square in Athens (W. Judeich, *Topographie von Athen*, p. 178).

added to weight in equilibrium, and then it inclines the beam as     581A
a whole in the direction of its own force. In the same way, a
sneeze or an incidental remark or any sign of that kind ⟨is too
trivial⟩ and light ⟨to be capable of⟩ pushing a weighty mind
towards action; but when it is added to one of two contradictory
considerations, it resolves indecision by removing equivalence,
with the consequence that movement and motivation occur."[1]

'"Nevertheless, Galaxidorus," my father replied, "I myself
was told by a Megarian, who had been told by Terpsion, that
Socrates' personal deity was a sneeze – his own and others'. If
someone else sneezed to his right, whether behind him or in     B
front of him, he was motivated to act, whereas a sneeze to his
left served as a deterrent; and as for his own sneezes, one when
he was poised to act confirmed his intention, whereas one when
he was already in the process of acting checked it and arrested it.
But what seems surprising to me is that, if it was sneezing that he
was relying on, he used to tell his friends that what prevented
him from acting or told him what to do was not sneezing, but a
personal deity. I mean, this certainly★ smacks of affectation and
vanity, my friend, not of the honesty and integrity which make
us regard the man as truly great and exceptional.

'"⟨No, it is inconceivable that a man like this could⟩★ be
deterred from acting and could discard a decision because he was
disturbed by an external voice or a random sneeze. In all walks     C
of life, Socrates' intentions used to display ⟨unswerving energy⟩
and intensity, as if they were missiles and the decision-making
that was their source was upright and strong. I mean, he chose to
stay poor throughout his life, when he could have had possessions
and people would have been glad and grateful to give them; and
he stuck with philosophy against overwhelming odds; and finally,
when his friends had worked hard and made it easy for him to
escape and save his life, he was not swayed by their pleas and he
did not capitulate at death's approach, but continued to rely on
his rationality, which never wavered in the face of danger. None     D

1. Plutarch probably took this image of scales for decision-making from the
   Stoic Chrysippus, where scales in equilibrium are finally tipped by the occurrence of some additional cause: Plutarch, *On Stoic Self-contradictions* 1045B–C.

of this is the behaviour of a man whose will could be deflected by random remarks or sneezes, but one who was being guided towards goodness by a higher authority and government.

'"I am also told that he predicted the destruction of the Athenian forces in Sicily to some of his companions.[1] And then there's the story of an earlier event that Pyrilampes, the son of Antiphon, used to tell. Pyrilampes was captured by us with a lance wound in the course of the rout at Delium and when he was told (by the envoys who had come here from Athens to sue for peace) that Socrates, along with Alcibiades and Laches, had reached the coast at Oropus and made it safely home,[2] he often spoke of Socrates, and also of how some of his own friends and troops who had fled with him towards Mount Parnes and had consequently been killed by our cavalry had ignored Socrates' personal deity and so, when retreating from the battle, had taken a different route from the one Socrates led his band along. I imagine Simmias has heard this story as well."

'"Often," said Simmias, "and from lots of people, because these events led to Socrates' personal deity being the talk of the town in Athens."

[12] '"Well then, Simmias," said Phidolaus, "are we going to let Galaxidorus get away with his trivialization and reduction of divination of this calibre to sneezes and chance remarks? These suffice for the masses and for ordinary people when unimportant issues are at stake and they can afford to be less serious, but when more severe dangers and more important events are occupying them, then what happens, to quote Euripides, is that 'no one indulges in these follies in the presence of weapons'."[3]

---

1. The brilliant armada against Syracuse, which set out with such high hopes in 415 BC, and was destroyed in 413 (Thucydides 6–7). Socrates' opposition through his personal deity is recorded in the Platonic *Theages* 129c–d, and mentioned again by Plutarch in *Life of Nicias* 13.9, and in *Life of Alcibiades* 17.5, where he seems to infer the influence of the personal deity.

2. The context is the Athenian defeat by the Boeotians at Delium in 424 BC (details in Thucydides 4.96). The story about Socrates was, as Plutarch says, one of the most famous in the collection, and admitted different embroidery of detail: Plato, *Apology* 28e, *Laches* 181a, *Symposium* 221a ff.; Cicero, *De Divinatione* 1.123; Plutarch, *Life of Alcibiades* 7.6. Athenaeus actually dismisses the whole story (215D).

3. From Euripides' *Autolycus*, F282.22 Nauck.

'Galaxidorus said, "Phidolaus, I am quite prepared to hear what Simmias has to say on these matters, if he personally heard Socrates discuss them, and to suspend disbelief along with all of you; but so far I've heard nothing from you and Polymnis which is not easy to demolish. In the field of medicine, a rapid heartbeat or a pustule may be trivial, but it is also a symptom of a non-trivial matter; for a helmsman, the cry of a sea bird or a scudding wisp of cirrus cloud presages wind and a rougher sea; and in the same way, although a sneeze or a chance remark may not be important in itself, ⟨yet it might indicate an important⟩ matter to a mind skilled in divination. The point is that no area of expertise underestimates the importance of using minor matters to foretell major ones, and rare matters to foretell common ones. Imagine someone who is unversed in what writing can do: an inscription might seem to him to be short and insignificant in appearance, and the fact that a literate person can glean from it details of major wars which occurred long ago, the founding of cities, what kings did and had done to them, would seem incredible to him. If he were then to claim that for our researcher into history to disclose and describe any of these events was a divine affair, you would be overcome by delighted laughter, my friend, at the man's innocence. By the same token, you must check whether it is not because we are ignorant about what any of the objects of divination can do and how they pertain to the future that in our naïvety we are annoyed when an intelligent person uses them to express something about obscure issues – and because he does so while claiming that it is no sneeze or voice that is directing his behaviour, but a personal deity.

'"I turn now to you, Polymnis, and your surprise that Socrates, who more than anyone else, thanks to his lack of affectation and his straightforwardness, brought philosophy down to a human level, should have called his sign not a sneeze or a chance remark, but in a very high-flown manner his personal deity. I mean, I would have found the opposite surprising, for a consummate conversationalist and master of words like Socrates to have said that what communicated with him was not his personal deity, but his sneezing. This would be like someone claiming to have been wounded by a weapon, not by the person who wielded the

582A

B

C

weapon, or again like someone saying that the weight was meas-
ured by the scales, rather than by the person who put the object
on the scales. The result is not due to the instrument, but to the
person who applies the instrument he employs for the result; and
the sign which the communicator uses is an instrument as well.
But as I said, we must listen to anything Simmias might have to
say, since his knowledge is more precise."

D
[13] '"Only when we've found out who these people are
coming into the house," said Theocritus. "But wait: it's Epaminondas – here he is – and he seems to be bringing the visitor to
meet us."

'We looked towards the door and saw Epaminondas come in
first, with some of our friends and fellow conspirators – Hismenodorus, Bacchyllidas and Melissus the pipe-player – and then behind
them came the stranger, who was aristocratic in appearance (although it was clear that his character was not cruel and haughty)
and impressively attired. He sat down next to Simmias, my
brother next to me and the others wherever they could. When
all the hubbub had died down, Simmias attracted my brother's
attention and said, "Well, Epaminondas, does your visitor have a
E
name? What do we call him? Where's he from? This is the way
that meeting someone and getting to know him usually begin."

'"He is called Theanor, Simmias," Epaminondas replied. "He
is a native of Croton, comes from the philosophical school there,
and is no disgrace to the great name of Pythagoras. And now he
has come all the way from Italy to validate excellent principles
by excellent acts."

'"Yes," the stranger responded, "and there is one particularly
excellent act that you are obstructing, Epaminondas. You see, if
F
it is excellent to do good to friends, it is also not contemptible to
have good done to one by friends. Kindness requires a recipient
just as much as it requires a donor: where its excellence is concerned, it is incomplete without both of them. Anyone who
refuses to accept kindness, when it is offered cleanly like a well-
thrown ball,[1] lets it fall to the ground incomplete and negates its

---

1. The comparison of throwing and catching a ball for giving and receiving
kindness had gained some popularity. Seneca uses it too in *De Beneficiis* 2.17.3

excellence. What target is so gratifying to shoot at and hit, and so disappointing to miss, as when one fires the shaft of kindness at a person who deserves to have good done to him? However, in the former case an unsuccessful shot is due to the shooter, since the target is unmoving; but in the latter case, it is the one who declines and evades the shot who wrongs the kindness, which fails to reach the person★ who was the target of the effort.

'"Anyway, I have already explained to you the reasons for my sailing here; but I want to tell these people too, and to use them       583A
as judges in your case. When the Pythagoreans were beaten in the uprising and their communities were expelled from one city after another, and when Cylon and his faction piled kindling all around a house in Metapontum while a surviving group was meeting, set fire to it and killed them all in one go, except Philolaus and Lysis,[1] who were young in those days and used their strength and agility to break through the conflagration, Philolaus escaped to Lucania and made it safely from there to other friends of his, who were already regrouping and were starting to beat the Cylonians, but Lysis' whereabouts were unknown for a long time, until Gorgias of Leontini sailed back       B
from Greece to Sicily and gave Aresas and his circle the reliable news that he had met Lysis, who was spending time in Thebes. Aresas missed him so much that he felt impelled to make the voyage himself, but he was altogether too old and weak; so he issued instructions that Lysis was to be brought back to Italy, alive if possible, or that his remains were to be fetched if he had died.

'"Aresas didn't live to see his friends complete the assignment: wars, uprisings and tyrannies intervened and prevented us from doing so. And then the now-dead Lysis' personal deity made it vividly clear to us that he had died, and people who knew the

---

ff., and claims to have found it in the Stoic Chrysippus (*SVF* 3.725). It recurs in Plutarch's *Commentary on Hesiod*, F52 Sandbach; and the same metaphor is used in the context of lecturing and listening at *On Listening* 45E.

1. The burning of the Pythagorean meeting place almost certainly occurred in Croton not Metapontum, and Lysis' fellow escapee was not the famous Philo-laus, but Archippus. See W. Burkert, *Lore and Science in Ancient Pythagorean-ism*, pp. 115 ff., p. 228 n. 48. Pythagorean tradition was oral, and Plutarch is not very reliable in it.

C facts told us how you, Polymnis, had taken care of the man and had installed him in your home – how his old age had been sumptuously catered for in an impoverished household and how his name had been entered in the public register as your sons' father,[1] so that he passed away happy. So despite my youth I was sent by my elders to be a single representative of the many who are offering money, which they have, to those who do not have it, to pay the debt incurred by your considerable kindness and affection. Moreover, Lysis received an excellent burial at your hands, and more important to him than an excellent burial is that the kindness of friends should be repaid by friends and relatives."

[14] 'The stranger's words started my father weeping for a long time at the memory of Lysis, but my brother smiled his
D usual smile at me and said, "What are we doing, Caphisias? Are we giving up our poverty for affluence without a word?"

'"No," I replied, "we must not give up our prized 'nurse who tended us well'.[2] You must protect her – I mean, it is up to you to speak."

'"All right," he began. "Father, I used to be afraid that there was only one way our household was going to be taken over by money, and that was through Caphisias' body! Not only does it require splendid clothes so that it can be paraded proudly in front of his admirers – and there are so many of them – but it also needs vast quantities of food so that it can keep on exercising and competing in the wrestling ring. But here he is refusing to
E surrender his ancestral poverty or to blunt its edge, so to speak. Although he is young, he prides himself on his economy and is content with his immediate circumstances. So what would we spend money on? What use would we have for it? Shall we gild our weapons and embellish our shields with a combination of purple and gold, as Nicias of Athens did?[3] Shall we buy for you, father, a Milesian coat, and for our mother a dress edged with purple? For we will not, of course, waste the windfall on our stomachs, by entertaining ourselves in increased luxury, as if

---

1. That is, their honorary father, or the father of their education.
2. Homer, *Odyssey* 9.27.
3. Nicias' shield was still displayed in a Syracusan temple according to *Life of Nicias* 28.6.

affluence were a rather demanding guest we had admitted into our home."

'"Perish the thought, son," said my father. "I hope I never see our lives transformed in that way."

F

'"On the other hand," said Epaminondas, "we are not going to sit at home and guard any wealth we have either, without making use of it: that would negate both the kindness and the value of the acquisition."

'"Of course it would," my father said.

'"Now," Epaminondas continued, "when Jason the Thessalian warlord recently dispatched a lot of money to us here and begged us to accept it,[1] I made no attempt to disguise my feelings, but behaved rather rudely: I replied that his offer was actually a case of unprovoked assault, because his desire for monarchy was leading him to try to bribe a member of an autonomous and independent city. My friend," he said, turning to the visitor, "I welcome your motives, and have no problem at all with them, since they are excellent and compatible with philosophy; but you have come bringing medicine for friends who are not sick. Suppose you had heard that we were at war, and had accordingly sailed here with the intention of helping us by military means, only to find a harmonious and peaceful situation: you would not have felt obliged to offer your weapons of war and to leave them where they weren't needed. This is a good analogy: you have come to support us in a putative struggle against poverty, on the assumption that she is harassing us, but in fact she is absolutely no burden for us and is a prized member of our household. There is no need for your financial weaponry against her, since she is not distressing us. Please tell your friends back in Italy that although there is not the slightest disgrace in the uses to which they put their wealth, they have friends here who make excellent use of poverty; and that Lysis has himself repaid us for looking after Lysis and seeing him buried, especially by teaching us not to find poverty distasteful."

584A

B

[15] 'At this Theanor said, "It may be a sign of mediocrity to

---

1. A Plutarchan anachronism, since Jason did not achieve power until some years after Thebes was liberated.

find poverty distasteful, but is it not odd to be afraid of affluence and to avoid it?"

⟨ "'Yes," replied Epaminondas, "it is odd,⟩ *if* it is not rationality that makes one reject it, but a posture prompted by bad taste or some affectation."

'"And what rational argument," he retorted, "would stop one acquiring it by excellent and moral methods, Epaminondas? Or here's a better question, since in answering me I want you to
C     present a gentler side of yourself than you did when answering the Thessalian. Do you think that although the giving of money may be right, accepting it never is, or that both the donors and the recipients are always wrong?"

'"No, you're on quite the wrong tack," Epaminondas replied. "I think that both granting and receiving anything, including wealth, may be either contemptible or gracious."

'"Well," asked Theanor, "isn't the voluntary and willing repayment of debt an example of excellent giving?"

'Epaminondas concurred.

'"And isn't accepting something excellently given an example
D     of excellent receiving? Could there be an example of receiving which is more moral than receiving from moral giving?"

'"No, there couldn't," he said.

'"It follows, Epaminondas," said Theanor, "that if one of two friends is obliged to give to the other, the other is obliged to receive, of course. Although in battles one has to get out of the way of an opponent who is a good shot, yet when a friend is trying to be kind it is not right to evade or rebuff him if his giving is excellent. The point is that even if poverty is not distasteful, nevertheless affluence is not so discreditable and objectionable."

'"No, it's not," said Epaminondas. "But it's possible for a gift excellently given to be increased in value and excellence by being refused. Let's investigate this together, as follows.[1] There are, of course, all sorts of desires with all sorts of causes: some are
E     called instinctive and they sprout up in the body and aim for

---

1. For the philosophical background of the rest of this section, see Introduction, pp. 303–4.

necessary gratification; others are extraneous, and although their source* is illusion, yet if someone is badly brought up, they eventually become so familiar that they acquire strength and vigour, become attractive to the mind and are more influential in debasing the mind than the necessary desires. And while the power of even the instinctive emotions can be considerably decreased by reason helped by habituation and practice, yet the full force of training, my friend, must be brought to bear on the extrinsic, superfluous desires: one must struggle to eradicate them by having one's rational mind discipline them by suppressing and checking them. I mean, if the rational mind can withstand the impulses towards food and drink, and so dispel thirst and hunger, it is surely much easier to restrain the impulses towards affluence and reputation, and ultimately to eliminate them, by refusing to partake of their goals and by suppressing them, isn't it?"

'The visitor agreed, and Epaminondas continued, "In your experience, is there a difference between training and the purpose which training aims for? You might say, for instance, that the purpose of athletic ability is to compete against a rival for a prize, but that the training is the preparation by means of exercise of the body for this purpose. So do you acknowledge that the same goes for virtue as well, that the purpose and the training are separate things?"

'When the visitor agreed, Epaminondas said, "Consider self-control first. Do you think that refraining from contemptible and lawless pleasures is training in self-control, or rather the purpose and proof of self-control?"*

'"I would say it is the purpose and proof," he replied.

'"And wouldn't you say that training and practice in self-control is the method you Pythagoreans universally employed and still employ today? You exercise and work up as strong an appetite as any animal's, then you sit for a long time at tables laden with outstanding food of various kinds, and then you let your servants feast on this while you yourselves supply your now-disciplined desires with ordinary, simple food. Don't you think this is training and practice, since refraining from pleasure when something is permissible is training the mind for when it cannot have things?"

' "Certainly," he said.

' "There is a method of training for morality too, my friend,
B to enable it to resist love of affluence and money. It is not
refraining from night-time forays to steal our neighbours' goods
or to mug them; and if someone refuses a bribe to betray his
country and his friends, he is not in training against avarice, since
in this instance it is probably the law and fear which prevent his
greed from leading him astray. No, it is anyone who regularly
abstains from making money when it is moral and sanctioned by
the law who is undertaking deliberate training and conditioning
to keep himself distant from all immoral and illegal gain. The
point is that it is impossible to retain equanimity in the midst of
pleasures which are not only intense, but also abnormal and
C harmful, unless one has often disdained permissible pleasure; and
it is equally hard to bypass nefarious proceeds and huge profits
when they become available if a person's avarice has not
withdrawn★ a long way and been disciplined, but has been acclimatized to acquisitiveness by lack of restraint where money-
making is permissible, and so gets excited at the prospect of
wrongdoing and refrains from greed only with considerable difficulty and effort. However, if someone has not betrayed himself
for favours from friends or for handouts from kings, but has
even refused an endowment from fortune and kept his avarice
from pouncing on a treasure trove, then avarice does not rear up
at the prospect of wrongdoing and discompose his mind: he has
D no difficulty in conducting himself by the standard of excellence,
with pride and full knowledge in his mind of the noblest truths.
These are the people Caphisias and I admire, my dear Simmias,
and so we beg our visitor to grant us the opportunity to reach a
point where poverty has adequately trained us for this state of
virtue."

[16] 'When my brother had given this explanation, Simmias
nodded★ two or three times and said, "Epaminondas is a great
man – yes, great. And Polymnis here is responsible for this,
because right from the start he provided the best philosophical
upbringing for his sons. However, you must resolve this issue
with them yourself, Theanor. Now, if you're allowed to tell me,
E I'd like to ask whether you are going to disinter Lysis and

transfer him to Italy, or are you going to let him stay here with us, so that he can dwell with his friends and comrades when we join him there?"

'Theanor smiled and said, "It turns out that Lysis is happy where he is, Simmias, since Epaminondas has served him well and fulfilled his every need. You see, there is a particular ritual which takes place at the burial of Pythagoreans, in the absence of which we do not think we fully attain the blissful end which is properly ours. So, when we discovered through our dreams that Lysis was dead – we can tell from a clue given in our dreams whether the vision is of a dead person or a living one[1] – lots of us were of the opinion that Lysis' burial had been incorrectly seen to in a foreign land and that we should move him so that he could come by the traditional rites back in Italy. I came here with that intention, and as soon as I got here, although it was already late in the day, I had some of the local inhabitants show me the way to his grave. I poured libations while calling on Lysis' soul to return to confirm the necessity of performing these rites. But as the night wore on, although I saw nothing, I seemed to hear a voice telling me to let sleeping dogs lie,[2] since Lysis' body had been properly seen to by his friends, and his soul had already been judged, assigned another deity and released into a fresh incarnation.[3] Furthermore, when I met Epaminondas the following morning, he told me the way in which he had buried Lysis, and I realized that Lysis had trained him well in everything, including the secret aspects, and that Epaminondas' life was governed by the same deity as Lysis' had been:[4] you can tell the helmsman by his voyage, and I don't think I'm mistaken in my

F

586A

---

1. The dead neither blink nor cast a shadow (see *On God's Slowness to Punish* 564C).
2. The phrase (literally 'Don't move what may not be moved') probably originated in religious taboo (Plutarch, *On Isis and Osiris* 359F; cf. Herodotus 6.134), but had long been proverbial (Plato, *Philebus* 15c, *Laws* 684d).
3. The Pythagorean doctrine of reincarnation featured a new spirit guide (daimon) for each reincarnation. The imagery is adopted by Plato in his Myth of Er (*Republic* 617d ff.). But Plato makes the returning soul choose its own new daimon or life: 'The responsibility lies with the chooser; God is not responsible.'
4. This is very obscure and mysterious, but is probably meant to be so.

assessment. I mean, there are countless routes through life, but not many on which deities guide us." Theanor finished and looked at Epaminondas as if he were reappraising his nature and appearance all over again.

B
[17] 'Meanwhile the doctor had approached and unwound Simmias' bandage prior to attending to his bodily needs. And then Phyllidas entered the house with Hipposthenidas and asked Charon, Theocritus and myself to leave the others; he took us to a corner of the colonnade with his features showing how extremely disturbed he was.

'"What news, Phyllidas?" I asked. "I hope nothing too surprising has happened."

'"It doesn't surprise me at all, Caphisias," he said. "I knew all along that Hipposthenidas was feeble, and I told you all so and asked you not to take him into your confidence or invite him to join the plot."[1]

'We were horrified at his words. Hipposthenidas said, "For God's sake, Phyllidas, don't say that – and don't mistake impetuosity for bravery and ruin us and our city. No, let the men return
C
safely, God willing."

'This provoked Phyllidas to retort angrily, "Tell me, Hipposthenidas, how many people do you think are privy to the secret of this business?"

'"I, at any rate, know of at least thirty," he replied.

'"Why, then," Phyllidas went on, "when so many people are involved, did you, all by yourself, ruin and undermine the decisions we had all made together? Why did you send a rider to the men, when they were already on their way, to tell them to turn back and not to press on today – today, when even chance has played a huge part in paving the way for their return?"

D
'We were appalled at what Phyllidas said, and Charon fixed Hipposthenidas with a fierce glare and exclaimed, "Damn you! What have you done to us?"

'"Nothing terrible," Hipposthenidas replied. "Why don't you stop shouting and let me share my thinking with you? After all, I

---

1. The beautifully told story of Hipposthenidas appears to have been a historical incident in the plot. Plutarch refers to it again in *Life of Pelopidas* 8.5–9.

am just as much of an elder statesman as you, with almost as many respectable white hairs. If our decision is to show our fellow citizens the kind of bravery that embraces danger and courage that disdains life, Phyllidas, the day is still young, and we needn't wait for evening: we can arm ourselves and set out against the tyrants now. We can kill and die and hold our lives cheap. Killing isn't hard, dying is easy. What is not easy is taking over Thebes when there are large quantities of hostile forces all   E around us and evicting the Spartan garrison while losing only two or three men. Phyllidas has a huge amount of wine ready and waiting for his parties and receptions – but it cannot be enough to get Archias' bodyguard of fifteen hundred men drunk; and even if we do overpower him, Herippidas and Arcesus are waiting, stone-cold sober, in the morning.[1] Why are we in such a hurry to let our friends and relatives return to certain death – and to do so when their return is not even a complete secret to our enemies? Why do you think the Thespians[2] were told two   F days ago to arm themselves and await our Spartan leaders' summons? And I've found out that they're planning to question Amphitheus today, and then to execute him when Archias gets back. Doesn't this strongly suggest that our plans are no secret? Isn't our best course to wait a while – it wouldn't be long, just long enough to seek divine approval? I mean, the seers say that the burnt offerings during the ritual ox sacrifice to Demeter indicated considerable public disturbance and danger.

' "And, Charon, there is something you should be particularly careful about. When I was travelling into town yesterday from the country, I had Hypatodorus the son of Erianthes as a companion. He's basically a good man, and a relative of mine, but despite the fact that he knows nothing of our plans, he said, 'I   587A don't know Charon very well, Hipposthenidas, but he's a friend of yours, so it's up to you to warn him of danger, if you think it appropriate, because of a very portentous and bizarre dream I had. The other night I imagined that his house was in labour, as

1. They were the two Spartan commanders left with the garrison: Lysanoridas had gone to Haliartus with Archias (578A, 594D).
2. The Thespians inhabited an area of south Boeotia to the east of Mount Helicon. Their town Thespiae was used as a base by Sparta after 382 BC.

if it were pregnant. He and his friends were anxiously praying and standing around it, while it bellowed and made inarticulate noises. Eventually, flames blazed up inside it and the fire was so great and terrible that it went on to consume most of the city, although the Cadmeia was only wreathed in smoke, since the
B   fire didn't spread upwards.' That was more or less what his vision was, Charon, as he described it to me, and it terrified me straight away, but I became even more worried when I heard today that it is your house that the exiles are intending to stay at. I am afraid that we might bring catastrophe down on our own heads, while achieving nothing significant against our enemies, except giving them a bit of a shock. I mean, I interpret the city as ours, and the Cadmeia as theirs, as indeed it is."

[18] 'Charon wanted to make some reply to Hipposthenidas, but Theocritus interrupted and stopped him, and said, "But from my point of view, Hipposthenidas, despite the fact that the ritual
C   inquiries I have made have always been auspicious for the exiles, nothing has ever inspired me with so much confidence about our project as this vision. What you're saying is that a great, blazing light sprang up in the city from a friendly house, while our enemies' residence was blackened by smoke, which never brings anything better than tears and chaos; and that meaningless sounds were emitted by us, which means that even if someone does try to inform against us, our project is liable only to vague rumour and blind suspicion, and its disclosure and its success will be simultaneous. And it is not surprising that the ritual sacrifice was inauspicious, since it is not the public but the ruling party who provide the impetus and the victim for the sacrifice."

'Even before Theocritus had finished, I started to ask Hippos-
D   thenidas, "Who did you send to intercept them? If you didn't do it too long ago, we'll try to catch him up."

'Hipposthenidas replied, "Caphisias, in all honesty, I doubt that you could catch him up: he has the best horse in Thebes. You all know him, since he is Melon's chief charioteer and thanks to Melon has been in on the plot since the beginning."

'I spotted the person he was talking about and said, "You mean Chlidon, don't you, Hipposthenidas, who won the horse-race at last year's festival of Heracles?"

' "Exactly," he said. "That's the man." '

' "And who is this," I asked, "who has been standing by the courtyard door for a long while watching us?" '

'Hipposthenidas turned and exclaimed, "Good God, it's Chlidon! Oh no, don't tell me something awful has happened!" '   E

'Chlidon saw that he was engaging our attention, so he quietly approached from the door. Hipposthenidas greeted him with a nod and asked him to tell all of us ⟨. . .⟩

' "I know all about these people, Hipposthenidas," he said, "so when I didn't find you at home or in the agora, I guessed that you had come here to them and I made my way straight here so   F that you wouldn't be in the dark about anything that has happened. After you told me to go all out to meet the men on the mountain, I went home to get my horse. When I asked my wife for my bridle, however, she couldn't lay her hands on it, but spent a lot of time in the storeroom pretending to look for it and rummaging through the contents. Once this game of hers had gone on long enough, she finally admitted that she had lent the bridle to a neighbour at his wife's request. When I got cross with her and started calling her names, she began to swear and curse and wish me plagued with disastrous journeys and equally disastrous return journeys. God, I hope the gods divert all of it on to   588A her own head! Eventually, my anger reached such a pitch that I started to hit her, and then a crowd of neighbours and their wives ran up, and after all the despicable things I did and had done to me, I only just made it here to you, so that you could send someone else out to the men, since I am in a thoroughly distracted and awful state at the moment." '

[19] 'We experienced a strange emotional readjustment. Although just a short while earlier frustration had been irking us, yet now we were nervous and worried because matters had reached an urgent crisis and were moving so fast: delay was no longer possible. Despite my anxiety, I spoke to Hipposthenidas; I   B took his hand and consoled him with the thought that even the gods were encouraging us in our venture. At this juncture, Phyllidas left to attend to his reception and to manoeuvre Archias straight to the drinks party, and Charon left to make his house ⟨ready for the arrival of the exiles⟩. Theocritus and I returned to

where Simmias was so as to talk with Epaminondas when the opportunity arose.

[20] 'By now, they were well advanced in a high-powered debate – the one which Galaxidorus and Phidolaus in particular had launched a little earlier by raising questions about the nature and character of what is known as Socrates' personal deity. We had missed Simmias' response to what Galaxidorus had said; but Simmias told us that he once asked Socrates about the matter, but didn't get a reply, and so never asked again. However, he said that during his time with Socrates he had often heard him express the opinion that anyone who claims visual contact with the gods is a fraud, but that on the other hand he had often seen him listen carefully to people who claimed to hear a voice, and grill them thoroughly and exhaustively.

' "We used to talk the matter over privately with one another," he said, "and as a result of what I've just told you, we came to the assumption that Socrates' personal deity was not a vision, but was either an actual auditory experience or a mental perception of something verbally communicated to him in some unusual fashion, along the lines of how in a dream there is no objective sound, but we imagine we hear people's voices by receiving impressions and mental perceptions of words. Other people, however, get this kind of perceptiveness when they are genuinely asleep, because the physical quietness and relaxation of lying down and sleeping improves their ⟨hearing, whereas when they are awake⟩ their minds can hardly hear higher beings and they are too congested with troubling emotions and distracting desires to be able to listen and be receptive to the meaning. Socrates, on the other hand, had an intellect which was clear and dispassionate, whose involvement with the body was minor and limited to necessities, and which was therefore sensitive and responsively alive to phenomena.[1] The phenomenon in this case was, at a guess, not sound but a deity's voiceless message, which impinged on his intellective faculty as sheer meaning.

1. Parts of the above passage reappear in Chalcidius, *On Plato's Timaeus* 255 (p. 288 Wrobel). For the comparison between oracular dreams and waking obtuseness, compare Cicero, *De Divinatione* 1.110; and for daimonic contact in dreams, see Posidonius F108 EK (*Commentary* pp. 428 ff.).

'"The point is that making a sound resembles striking a blow:[1] the ears are the means by which words forcibly gain admittance to the mind when we talk to one another. But the intellect of a higher being guides a sensitive mind, which does not need striking, by impinging on it with an idea; and the mind yields to the higher intellect, and allows it to take charge of decreasing or increasing the energy of its impulses to action, which are not violently influenced by conflicting emotions, but are as receptive to change and as pliable as loosened reins. This needn't strike us as odd: we can see the same principle in the fact that little rudders make huge ships change direction, and in the spinning of potters' wheels, which revolve smoothly at the touch of a fingertip. These objects have no minds, of course, but they are mobile in construction, and are delicate enough to yield to an active agent when influence is applied. The human mind, however, is a network of countless tensile impulses, and therefore, if handled rationally, it is far more receptive to change than any other instrument, and far more capable of being influenced and moved to fulfil an idea. The point is that in this situation the origins of the emotions and impulses extend into the intellective faculty, so that a vibration in the intellective faculty exerts force on the emotions and impulses, and consequently has a motivating and directional effect on the person.

'"This also enables us to understand, in particular, the great power of an idea: as soon as the mind lays the foundations of something in the intellect and initiates an impulse towards that object, then insentient bones and sinews and fluid-filled flesh, and the heavy body which is constituted out of these materials as an inert, sluggish mass – the whole of it gets to its feet, with energy in all its parts, and moves as though on wings towards action. Furthermore, the kind of movement, coercion and excitation which enables the mind, by conceiving an idea, to use its impulses to motivate the body is not difficult or altogether too obscure to understand.

'"But if the rational mind, by conceiving an idea, can so easily move the body without making a sound, we would not, I imag-

---

1. This had become a stock definition of sound: Plato, *Timaeus* 67b; Aristotle, *De Anima* 420b29; and for Stoicism, Diogenes Laertius 7.55.

ine, doubt that the intellect can be guided by a higher intellect, a more divine mind which impinges on it from elsewhere by making the kind of contact with it which is as natural between rational minds as reflection is to light. In fact, it is one another's ideas, expressed through the medium of sound, that we grope in the dark, so to speak, to make sense of, whereas the ideas of deities bring light with them, and so illuminate those who receive

C   them.★ The ideas of deities need no verbs and nouns: these are the tokens of human intercourse which allow people to see images and reflections of ideas, but the only people who understand ideas in themselves are those who – as I've said – admit a particular, divine light.[1]

'"Nevertheless, there is a sense in which what happens in the case of speech spoken out loud can allay doubts. I mean, air is stamped with the form of articulated speech and as a whole becomes words and speech, and so carries the idea towards the mind of the listener. So why should it seem implausible for air also to be modified by ⟨superior⟩ beings to conform to an idea alone, and thanks to its sensitivity to communicate to superhuman, special people the sense of the idea's conceiver? Just as the

D   digging of ⟨tunnellers⟩ is found out by its setting off a corresponding vibration in bronze shields when its vibration arises from underground and reaches the shields, while passing straight through everything else without any noticeable effect,[2] so deities' messages pass through everyone else and resonate only in people who are even-tempered and whose minds are calm – who are precisely the people we describe as holy and superhuman.

'"The usual view, however, is that the divine realm is revealed to people when they are asleep, and that the suggestion that the gods motivate people just as much when they are awake and fully conscious is implausible and dubious. This is like thinking that a musician plays his lyre when the strings have been loosened,

---

1. The above passage contains echoes (darkness and light, image and reality) for the reader from the famous Allegory of the Cave in Plato's *Republic* 514a ff.
2. Plutarch is not at all clear about this. The story comes from Herodotus 4.200 (repeated by Aeneas Tacticus 37.6–7) on the siege of Barce in 512 BC. Underground military tunnelling was detected by striking a metal shield on the ground; if this was done above a mine, the shield (supposedly) rang.

and then doesn't pick it up and play it when it has been tuned and adjusted. They fail to understand that their belief is prompted E by their own internal discord and cacophony, from which our friend Socrates was free, just as the oracle which was given to his father when Socrates was still young proclaimed. The oracle told his father to let him act on whim, and not to constrain or divert the boy's impulsiveness, but to let it be, and to pray for him to Zeus of the Agora and to the Muses, but not to interfere in any other respect where Socrates was concerned – which is to say, of course, that Socrates had his own internal guide in life, who was F better than any number of teachers and educators.

[21] '"That, Phidolaus, was the idea we came to about Socrates' personal deity while he was alive, and his death has made no difference; so we do not think highly of those who ⟨adduce⟩ chance remarks, sneezes and so on and so forth. We did, however, once hear Timarchus of Chaeronea's account of the matter, but perhaps I'd better keep quiet about that, since it ⟨sounds more like⟩ a fable ⟨and a piece of fiction than⟩ a rational argument."[1]

'"No," said Theocritus. "Please tell us it. In its rather imprecise way even fiction in a sense touches on truth. But first tell us who 590A this Timarchus was: I can't place him."

'"That's not surprising, Theocritus," replied Simmias, "since he ⟨died⟩ very young, after imploring Socrates to have him buried next to Socrates' son Lamprocles, who had died a few days earlier and had been a friend in his own age group.[2] Anyway, Timarchus longed to understand the nature of Socrates' personal deity – he was young, of course, and had recently made quite an impressive start in philosophy – and after telling no one except Cebes and myself, he went into the cave of Trophonius, once he had performed the traditional rituals at the place of the oracle.[3] He stayed down there for two nights and one day, and B

1. See p. 247.
2. This is indeed fiction, since Socrates' eldest son Lamprocles was still alive when his father was executed (Plato, *Apology* 34d, *Phaedo* 116b; cf. Kirchner, *Prosopographia Attica* 8993); but then Timarchus himself is almost certainly invented.
3. The oracle of Trophonius was near Lebadeia in Boeotia. Pausanias (9.39) describes the ritual and surroundings in detail. They were certainly of a nature likely to work strongly on the imagination.

then, when most people had given him up for dead and his relatives were starting to mourn him, he came back out early in the morning with a very radiant look on his face. He knelt at the shrine, and as soon as he had got away from the crowd, he began to tell us all the amazing things he had seen and been told.[1]

[22] '"He said that after he had gone down into the place of the oracle, at first he encountered deep darkness, and then, once he had prayed, he lay down for a long time without really knowing whether he was awake or dreaming. What was clear, however, was the impression he had of his head being struck, with an accompanying bang, and of the sutures of his skull opening up and releasing his soul.[2] His soul withdrew from his body and to its delight blended with air that was translucent and pure; it seemed at first, when that happened, as though his soul

C    had recovered after a long illness, and was flexing itself for a while and increasing in size, unfurling like a sail; and then next he could just make out the pleasant whistling sound of something whizzing around overhead. He looked up to find that the earth was nowhere to be seen, but instead there were islands of softly glowing fire which swapped colours between themselves: first one would have a particular colour, then another one would, as if they were being constantly bathed in different colours by a light which varied according to their changes. There appeared to be innumerable islands, of prodigious size; and although they were not all the same size, they were all equally spherical. It occurred to him that the ⟨high⟩ whistling of the ether was

D    caused by their revolution, since there was a correlation between the smoothness of their motion and the evenness of that sound, which was a harmony created by all of them together.[3]

---

1. The following myth should be compared with that in *On God's Slowness to Punish* 563C ff. and in *On the Face on the Moon* 942D ff. See in general the Introductions to this essay and to *On God's Slowness to Punish*, pp. 245–8, 305–6.

2. See p. 248 for this common feature of bilocation.

3. The imagery, with its literary reminiscences of the Islands of the Blessed of Homer, *Odyssey* 4.560, or of the islands in Plato's myth in *Phaedo* 111a, in fact represents the astronomical structure of the heavens. The islands are the heavenly bodies, and the sounds are the music of the spheres (cf. Plato, *Republic* 617a–b). For the stress on colour, see p. 247.

'"Between them was a sea or lake[1] whose blue expanse was shot through with the mingling colours. A few of the islands[2] sail out in a channel and cross the current,[3] but the others, the majority,[4] are carried ⟨along with the current⟩, as ⟨the sea itself smoothly and evenly⟩ moves around in a circle, so to speak. Here and there the sea is very deep, especially in the south; but elsewhere there are intermittent, brief shallows, and in many regions it floods and ebbs again, though without admitting major displacements of its volume.[5] In places, its colour is pure sea-dark, but elsewhere it is not pure, but as cloudy as a pond.[6] The islands complete their journey★ through the surging water and return,[7] but they do not finish precisely where they started or form perfect circles: they slightly alter their routes and each forms a single spiral in the course of a revolution.[8] The sea containing the islands slopes by a factor of a little less than eight parts of the whole (or so Timarchus thought) in relation to what is right in the middle of the ambient sphere and is greatest,[9] and it has two mouths, opposite each other, where rivers of fire enter

1. The celestial sphere and its movement.
2. The planets.
3. The current represents the celestial equator as the main stream of the celestial sphere.
4. The fixed stars.
5. The Greeks thought the south starless, and so in Plutarch's imagery too deep for islands. The shallows may represent the Milky Way, or nebulae, or groups of stars. Ebb and flow should indicate expansion and diminution in visible stellar phenomena. Phases of the moon? Eclipses? Variation in the visibility of the Milky Way? Haloes, parhelia, horizon distortion?
6. The outer regions of the heavens were thought to be pure ether, the sublunar area misty.
7. The planets 'turning back' from the tropics.
8. The spiral, first mentioned in Plato, *Timaeus* 39a, represents the planets' own movements in relation to the diurnal circular movement of the fixed stars. Plutarch uses this description again of the sun in his *Life of Phocion* 2.6.
9. The 'sea' of the planets (i.e. the zodiac or ecliptic) inclines at a fixed angle to the central celestial equator (referred to here as 'what is right in the middle of the ambient sphere and is greatest'). Plutarch seems confused, however. If the meridian is divided into sixty parts, then the ancients generally reckoned that the inclination of the ecliptic was four parts, or 24 degrees (Geminus 5.46). Plutarch gives eight parts, or 48 degrees, which is not the obliquity of the ecliptic, but the distance between the two tropics.

and discharge their contents, with the result that the sea is pushed seething back and its blue is churned into white.[1]

'"Timarchus enjoyed the sight of all this, but when he looked downwards, he saw a huge chasm[2] which was as round as if a sphere had been scooped out of it; it was horribly frightening and cavernous, and was filled with deep darkness which was not still, but was turbulent and often boiled up. From this pit he heard the howling and keening of countless creatures, the crying of innumerable babies, and the wailing of both men and women at once; and all sorts of other confused noises emerged faintly from far in the depths. He found all of this extremely disturbing.

'"After a while someone said to him, although there was no one in sight, 'Timarchus, what do you long to understand?' And he said, 'Everything, because it is all so incredible.'

'"'But,' came the reply, 'we have hardly any access to the upper levels, which are the province of others who are gods. However, if you like, you can investigate Persephone's domain,[3] which we manage, and is one of the four levels – the one defined by the river Styx.'

'"Timarchus asked what the Styx is. 'It is the channel into Hades,' was the reply. 'Its source is diametrically opposite from here, and at its apex it cuts into the light. As you can see, it stretches up from Hades down there, and where its circuit touches the light it delimits the last region of the universe. There are four sources of all things: the first is the source of life, the second of movement, the third of birth and the fourth of death. Unity connects the first to the second at the invisible point;[4] Intellect connects the second to the third at the sun; Nature connects the third to the fourth at the moon. Each of these connections is presided over by a custodial Fate, a daughter of Necessity: Atropos oversees the first, Clotho the second, and Lachesis the one at

---

1. This is obscure, but may refer to the Milky Way, at the intersection of the zodiacal and galactic circles.
2. For such chasms, see p. 247.
3. The groves of Persephone marked the approach to Hades in Homer, *Odyssey* 10.509.
4. The periphery of the celestial sphere.

591A

B

the moon,[1] which is where the critical turning-point of birth lies. You see, whereas all the other islands have gods, the moon is the domain of earthly deities; so although its route generally takes it slightly over the Styx, so that it avoids it, once every 177 secondary measures it is caught.[2] At the imminent presence of the Styx, the souls cry out in terror, since Hades sweeps many of them off and snatches them away.[3] But other souls swim close to the moon and are gathered up by it from below: these are the souls whose incarnation has ended at the opportune moment. However, the moon flashes lightning and thunders terrifyingly at any of them who are foul and impure, to keep them at bay; and they bemoan their lot as in their deficiency they are carried back down again to another incarnation, as you can see.'

'"'No, I can't see anything,' said Timarchus, 'except a lot of stars poised quivering at the chasm, others disappearing into its depths, and some darting up from below.'

'"'You don't realize it,' was the response, 'but you are actually seeing the deities. This is how it is: every soul has intelligence; none is irrational or unintelligent, but to some extent a soul becomes fused with flesh and emotions, and so is altered by pleasures and pains and is diverted towards irrationality. They don't all become fused to the same extent. Some sink wholly into the body and, once they have become entirely disordered, they go through life completely scattered by the emotions. Although other souls are absorbed to a degree, at the same time they leave the purest part of themselves outside, and this purest part is not sucked in, but is like the tip of a float: it rests lightly on the surface, arising from the head of the person who has, so to

1. The order of priority of the Fates is the same as that in *On the Face on the Moon* 945C, although their position is different. This is the order of Plato, *Laws* 960c, but not of *Republic* 617c.
2. The language is curiously technical, no doubt to weave a veil of mystery. There were two 'measures' of day (Geminus 6.1), the first from sunrise to sunset, the second from sunrise to the following sunrise; 177 days of the latter was the equivalent of six lunar months. It was believed that eclipses of the moon happened at such intervals (*On the Face on the Moon* 933E, 942E). In Plutarch's imagery the shadow of the earth (which causes an eclipse of the moon) is the Styx, leading to Hades (i.e. Earth) below.
3. Similar imagery in *On the Face on the Moon* 943D, 944B.

speak, sunk in the depths, and it keeps upright around it however much of the soul is under its command rather than dominated by the emotions. Now, the part which is drowned in the body is referred to as "soul", while the part which is immune to death is usually called "intelligence" and is thought to be an internal faculty, just as objects reflected in mirrors appear to be inside the mirrors. However, anyone who understands the matter correctly calls it a "deity" on the grounds that it is external.[1]

F    ' "So, Timarchus,' the voice continued, 'you should take the stars that you saw as being extinguished to be the souls which sink totally into the body, and the ones which are rekindled, so to speak, and reappear from below, shaking off murky mist as if it were mud, to be the souls which are rising to the surface out of their bodies after death. And the stars which are tossed about up at the top are the deities of people who are described as "possessing intelligence". Try to discern individual differences in how they are connected and united with souls.'

592A    ' "Timarchus accordingly looked more carefully and noticed that the stars were rocking – some more than others – like the corks we see floating on the sea and marking the lines of nets; some of the stars, however, described a spiral, as spindles do when they are being spun, but a chaotic and irregular spiral, since they were incapable of moving consistently in a straight line.[2] The voice explained that the deities with straight, orderly motion were dealing with souls which, thanks to a cultured upbringing and education, were amenable to the rein, since their irrational aspect was not too obstinate and unbroken.[3] On the other hand, those which frequently swerved here and there in an

B    irregular and chaotic fashion, as if they were being jerked by a halter, were paired with souls which they had to struggle against, because the souls' characters, thanks to lack of schooling, were disobedient and unmanageable: at one point a deity is in control and brings the soul round to the right; at another it is deflected

1. This is a reminiscence of Plato, *Timaeus* 90a. The tripartition of body, soul and intelligence is a central feature of the myth in *On the Face on the Moon* (943A ff.); and compare *On God's Slowness to Punish* 564C.
2. This is closely similar to *On God's Slowness to Punish* 564A.
3. The extended metaphor of controlling the soul as a horse is a clear reminiscence of Plato, *Phaedrus* 247b, 248a–b.

by emotion and caught up in the pull of sin; and then it resists
again and strains for control. When a deity pulls back on the
connection, which is like a bridle introduced into the irrational
part of the soul, this is the deity inducing what people call
'remorse' for sins and, in the case of lawless and indulgent pleasures, 'shame' – which is really pain and bruising caused when a
soul is curbed by its controlling and presiding deity. This punish-      C
ment goes on until the soul becomes obedient to the rein and as
domesticated as a gentle pet, so that it stops needing to be hurt
and hit, and quickly recognizes its deity by signs and signals.

'"'Now, it takes a long time,' said the voice, 'for these souls
to be guided and pointed towards their duty. But then there are
those souls which from the very beginning, from the moment of
their birth, are amenable to the rein and are submissive to their
innate deity: these are the souls which give rise to people who
are seers and are inspired by the gods. One of these souls was that
of Hermodorus of Clazomenae:[1] I'm sure you have heard how,
night and day, it used to leave his body altogether, travel considerable distances, encounter and witness a lot of conversations and      D
events at great length, and then return; this went on until his
wife betrayed him, and his enemies came to his house, took his
body – while his soul was elsewhere – and burned it. In fact, this
is not strictly accurate: his soul did not leave his body, but it
allowed his deity to travel and journey far and wide by keeping
its connection with the deity loose and slack, with the result that
the deity saw, heard and told him about a lot of things from
outside his normal range. As for those who did away with his
body while he was asleep, they are still paying the penalty in
Tartarus. You will understand all of this better within three      E
months,' the voice added, 'but now go.'

'"When the voice had finished speaking, Timarchus said, he
wanted to turn around and see who the speaker was. But he got
another intense pain in his head, as if his head had been violently
crushed, and he became unconscious and unaware of everything
relating to himself; but then he came round a short while later

1. Almost certainly a mistake for Hermotimus of Clazomenae (Tertullian, De
   Anima 44), who had Pythagorean connections (Diogenes Laertius 8.5) and was
   a legendary shaman.

and found himself in the cave of Trophonius, near the entrance, lying where he had originally lain down.

[23] '"That is Timarchus' story. Within three months he had gone to Athens and died, just as the voice had said. We were amazed at this and told Socrates the story, and he ticked us off for waiting until after Timarchus' death to tell him, because he would have liked to have found out more about it from the man himself and questioned him more closely. You have now been paid in full, Theocritus, with the story as well as the rational argument. But I wonder whether our visitor ought not to be invited to join in the debate as well, since the topic is highly suitable and appropriate for men of God."

'"Why doesn't Epaminondas share his views with us?" asked Theanor. "He can draw on the same sources as me."

'My father smiled and replied, "That's what he's like, Theanor – quiet and cautious when it comes to speaking, but with an insatiable appetite for learning and listening. That is why Spintharus of Tarentum, who spent quite a while with him here, goes on and on, as I'm sure you know, about how in the world today he has never met anyone who knew more or spoke less.[1] So please tell us what you yourself think about what's been said."

[24] '"All right, then," he said. "My view is that what Timarchus said should be treated as holy and inviolable, and should be dedicated to Trophonius.[2] As for what Simmias said, I doubt that anyone would find it hard to accept: we call swans, snakes, dogs and horses sacred, so the existence of men of God, of people dear to God, shouldn't be hard to accept, especially given the view that the human, not the avian, race is close to God's heart.[3] A man who loves horses does not care equally for every member of the species, but always selects a particular one as best and singles it out for special training and preparation and affection; and our superiors brand those of the human herd, so to speak, who are the best, and count them worthy of singular, special lessons, whose disciplinary effect is not conveyed by reins or

---

1. Again in *On Listening* 39B.
2. This merely follows the rule for all who had descended into the shrine, according to Pausanias 9.39.14.
3. Repeated in *Life of Numa* 4.4.

curbs but by communication by means of signs of which the
common herd is completely unaware. I mean, most dogs don't
understand hunting signals, and most horses don't understand
equestrian signals: only those who have been given lessons quickly
recognize what they are being commanded to do by a casual    C
whistle or tongue-click and set about their duty.

'"It seems clear that Homer too is aware of the distinction
we're talking about.[1] He calls some seers 'augurs' and 'diviners',[2]
but thinks that others base their predictions on an understanding
and recognition of what the gods communicate directly. For
instance, he says, 'Priam's son Helenus heeded in his heart the
plan which had pleased the gods in their deliberation' and 'That
is the message I received from the immortal gods.'[3] Beacons,
proclamations and trumpets allow outsiders to perceive and recognize the intentions of kings and military commanders, whereas
they speak in their own voices to their close and trusted friends;    D
analogously, the gods communicate directly with few people,
and do so infrequently, whereas most people receive only signs,
which is why divination has been developed.

'"So* the gods arrange the lives of few people, the ones they
have singled out for felicity and for really being men of God.
Then there are souls which have been released from incarnation
and are from then on free of corporality – like totally autonomous versions of unpenned animals – and they are, in Hesiod's
words, deities which look after people.[4] You know how athletes
who are too old for training never quite lose their enthusiasm for
winning and for physical exercise, but love watching others train
and give them advice and run beside them; in the same way    E
those who, thanks to their mental virtue, have finished with the

1. The distinction is between divination as a technical art of interpretation of
   signs, which can be learned and professionally practised, and 'natural' divination, by which certain persons by inspiration are receptacles for direct divine
   communication. The classification was especially connected with the Stoics
   (Cicero, De Divinatione 1.11 f.; Posidonius Frs. 106, 108 EK).
2. The first word occurs, for instance, in Iliad 1.69 and 6.76, the second in Iliad
   1.62 and 24.221.
3. The first quotation is Iliad 7.44 f.; the second Iliad 7.53.
4. Hesiod, Works and Days 122 ff.; they are the dead of Hesiod's golden race of
   men. Plutarch also uses this reference at 361B and 431E.

trials of life and have become deities do not altogether discount the affairs, debates and interests of this world, but look kindly on people who are exercising themselves for this same goal, share their aspiration towards virtue, encourage them and, when they see that the struggle has almost reached the objective, that they are within striking range, they assist their urgent strivings.

F        '"The point is that deities do not help just anyone. When men are trying to swim ashore, people standing on land just watch in silence while they are still out at sea, far from land; but when the swimmers get close, the people run along the shore and wade in to get beside them, help them verbally and physically, and get them out safely. This is ⟨also, my friends,⟩ how deities act: while the sea of circumstances overwhelms us and we are exchanging bodies like so many rafts,[1] ⟨they leave⟩ us to struggle on our own and keep at it, as we try to survive and reach a safe harbour by utilizing our innate virtue; but when a soul has endured challenge after challenge with grit and determination, through countless incarnations, and now that its tour is coming to an end draws near the inhabitants of the next higher realm, sweating
594A    profusely from the danger and the effort involved in its emergence,[2] God does not forbid its personal deity from helping it, but allows any deity which sets out to help to do so. Each deity sets about saving the soul in its charge by encouragement, and when the soul gets near enough it listens to the deity and is saved. However, any soul which does not do as it is told is deserted by its deity and abandoned to its own wretched fate."

[25] 'After this speech, Epaminondas looked at me and said, "Caphisias, it's just about time for you to go to the gymnasium
B        and keep your appointment with your friends. I'll look after Theanor when the rest of us decide to go our separate ways."

'"Yes," I said, "I'll do that. But first I think Theocritus here wants a quick conversation with you, with Galaxidorus and myself in attendance."

'"He's welcome to a conversation," Epaminondas said, and

1. In successive reincarnations.
2. The Greek word is an echo of Odysseus' 'emergence' from stormy seas on to the shore of the Phaeacians in *Odyssey* 5.410.

got up and took us to the side wing of the colonnade. We stood around him and tried to coax him into joining our enterprise. But he said that although he was well aware that today was the day of the exiles' return, and although he and Gorgidas had organized their friends to seize the opportunity,[1] only dire necessity would induce him to kill any of his compatriots without a trial; and he added that it was also appropriate for the Theban    C populace for there to be some people innocent of and untainted by any actions taken, because they would be less liable to be suspected by the people of making recommendations that diverged from the most moral course. We agreed.

'He returned to Simmias and the others, while I went down to the gymnasium and met my friends. By swapping partners during our wrestling, we received and passed on information and organized ourselves for the enterprise. We also saw Archias, Philippus and their friends anoint themselves and then leave for dinner: Phyllidas was afraid that they would kill Amphitheus first, so he    D got Archias into his house as soon as he returned from escorting Lysanoridas by leading him to expect that the ⟨married⟩ woman he fancied would be coming to the party, and so persuaded him to join his regular companions in revelry and to relax and unwind instead.[2]

[26] 'It was now late and a wind was making it bitterly cold. Most people had therefore retreated indoors rather sooner than usual. We met up with Damoclidas, Pelopidas, Theopompus and some others, and took charge of them, while others met up with the rest of the exiles: they had split up as soon as they began to    E cross Cithaeron. The wintry cold gave them a reason to cover their faces and so they passed through the city without having to worry. Just as some of them were entering the city gates, there was a flash of lightning on their right, but no thunder; this seemed to be a good omen for safety and fame, implying that their deeds would be both outstanding and unaccompanied by danger.

---

1. With the result reported at 598C–D, and at *Life of Pelopidas* 12.2.
2. For these details and the narrative in the next two sections, compare the account in *Life of Pelopidas* 9.

[27] 'When all forty-eight of us were in the house, and Theocritus was already performing the sacrifices all by himself in a side-room, there was a lot of hammering on the door, and a little later a servant came and announced that two of Archias' subordinates were knocking at the courtyard door, on an urgent mission to Charon, and were ordering it to be opened and getting cross at the somewhat slow response. Charon was very disturbed, but he told his servants to open the door immediately, and he himself went to meet them wearing a chaplet, as if he were drinking after performing rites, and asked the subordinates what they wanted.

F

'One of them said, "Archias and Philippus sent us with instructions for you to go to them as soon as possible."

'Charon asked what the urgency was in summoning him at that time of day and what news there was. The subordinate replied, "We don't know anything else. What are we to tell them?"

'"Please tell them," said Charon, "that once I have taken off my chaplet and put on my coat, I'll be right behind you. I mean, if I walked with you at this time of day, people would think I was going against my will and would be upset."

595A

'"That's all right with us," he said, "because we also have instructions from the authorities to take to the garrison at the base of the acropolis."

'So off they went. Charon came in to us and told us what had happened. We were all terrified at the thought that we had been informed on, and most people suspected Hipposthenidas: he had tried to use Chlidon to stop the exiles returning, and they imagined that, when that had failed and danger was imminent, his fear had made him betray the conspiracy – and he would be believed; the point was, he hadn't come to the house with the others, and all in all gave the impression of being an ambivalent rogue. Nevertheless, we all thought that Charon should go and obey the authorities' summons.

B

'Charon sent for his son, who was the best-looking boy in Thebes, Archedamus, and was very keen on physical exercise; he was about fifteen years old, but was far stronger and better built than others of his age. "This is my only child, my friends," said

Charon, "and I love him dearly, as you know. I am leaving him in your hands, and with gods and deities as witnesses I give you this directive: if it should turn out that I do you wrong, show no mercy – kill him. Then go on to face whatever happens like men of virtue: don't waste your bodies in a cowardly and inglorious     C
death at the hands of these monsters,* but fight back, and keep your minds undefeated[1] for our country."

'We were impressed by the dignity and true goodness Charon displayed with these words, but resented the idea that we could suspect him, and we told him to remove his son. Pelopidas added, "On the whole, Charon, we don't think it was a good idea for you not to transfer your son to another house. Why should he be exposed to danger by being confined in the same place as us? You should have him leave even now, so that if anything happens to us, he can be brought up with the noble aim of making the tyrants pay."

'"No," said Charon. "He will stay here and share any danger     D
you may face: it would be just as disgraceful for him as for you to fall into our enemies' hands. So, my son, have courage beyond your years in this, your first experience of unavoidable conflict, and join the substantial and excellent ranks of your compatriots who are facing danger for the sake of freedom and goodness. All is by no means lost yet; our cause is just, so some god somewhere is watching over us."

[28] 'Few eyes were dry, Archedamus, at the man's words, but he himself shed no tears: resolutely, he entrusted his son to Pelopidas' care and left the house, shaking each of us by the hand on the way and trying to raise our morale. And you would particularly have appreciated how the boy remained cheerful and didn't show any fear at the prospect of danger: like Neoptolemus,     E
he didn't grow pale or become scared,[2] but he drew Pelopidas' sword and examined it. Just then, Cephisodorus the son of Diogiton arrived. He was one of our comrades, and was wearing his sword and an iron cuirass under his clothes. When he found out

1. Perhaps an anachronistic echo of the technical Stoic definition of courage (*eupsychia*) as keeping one's mind undefeated (*SVF* 3.264).
2. Achilles' son, as described in *Odyssey* 11.528 ff.

that Archias had sent for Charon, he told us off for procrastinating and urged us to go straight away to our allocated houses, on the grounds that we would then either be in a position to attack them before they attacked us, or at least that it was preferable for us to have got out in the open and to come to grips with men★ who were just as disorganized and scattered, rather than to stay
F cooped up in a room where we would be wiped out like a swarm of bees by our opponents. Theocritus the seer also motivated us, because his sacrifices had been auspicious and favourable, and had guaranteed safety.

[29] 'While we were arming and organizing ourselves, Charon arrived back beaming and smiling.[1] He looked at us and told us not to worry, because nothing awful was happening, but in fact our enterprise was on its way. "By the time Archias and Philippus
596A were told that I had come in response to their summons," he said, "drink had already made them groggy, and their minds had relaxed along with their bodies. They could hardly get to their feet to leave the room and come to the door. Then Archias said, 'Charon, we hear that exiles have surreptitiously entered the city and gone to ground.'

'"I was extremely shaken by this, but I asked, 'Where have you heard that they are? Which exiles?'

'"'We don't know,' said Archias, 'and that is why we asked you to come, in case you've heard anything more definite.'

'"My head cleared a bit, as if I had been jolted.★ I reasoned that the information had reached them in an unreliable fashion
B and that our enterprise had not been given away by anyone who was in the know, since if anyone with accurate knowledge had given them the information, they would not be unaware of the location of the exiles; in other words, what had reached them was a rumour or some imprecise report which was going around the city. So I said to Archias, 'I know that there were floods of these sorts of empty rumours and irritating false stories when Androclidas was alive, but I've heard nothing recently, Archias.

1. For the following section of the narrative, compare *Life of Pelopidas* 10.1–5. There Charon tells what happened only to Pelopidas, keeping the others in the dark.

But I'll look into the report, if you want, and if I find out anything which warrants anxiety, you will not be kept in the dark.'

'"Yes, Charon,' said Phyllidas. 'Do everything you can to investigate and find out about this. There's no reason for us not to treat everything as important, and to take every precaution and care. Forethought and insurance are admirable qualities.' While saying this, he had taken hold of Archias, and he steered him back into the house, where their drinking continues. So let us not delay, my friends," Charon concluded. "Let us pray to the gods and then go."

'After Charon had finished, we began to say our prayers and to bolster one another's courage. [30] It was the time when most people are at dinner; the wind was getting stronger and sleet was now lashing down, so the streets we went along were almost deserted. Those – including Pelopidas, Damoclidas and Cephisodorus – who had been assigned to attack Leontiades and Hypates, who lived close to each other, left the house wrapped up in their cloaks, each with no weapon except a short-sword. Charon, Melon and their group were to attack Archias and his companions; they put on breastplates and wore bristling chaplets of fir or pine, and some were dressed in women's clothes, so they looked like party-going drunks along with some women.[1]

'Our luck, Archedamus, had never been particularly good: right from the start, bad luck punctuated our enterprise with danger, as scenes punctuate a play, and made our boldness and preparation no more effective than our enemies' impotence and ignorance; and now its course coincided with the actual execution of our plans and brought a critical exchange, terrifying for the unexpected reversal it could herald.[2] Just as Charon returned from his meeting with Archias, Philippus and the others, and was getting us ready for our enterprise, a letter arrived from Archias the high priest here in Athens to the Theban Archias –

1. These details are also in *Life of Pelopidas* 11.1–2.
2. A reversal (*peripeteia*) in the protagonist's life, often brought about through an exchange (*agōn*) with another character, was the standard climax in classical Greek tragedy; so Plutarch is typically extending his metaphor, this time of drama, beyond a mere two-dimensional reference.

the two of them were friends, apparently, and had stayed in each
other's houses. The letter divulged the return of the exiles, their
F    plans, the house they had gone to and their fellow conspirators.
But Archias was by now exorbitantly drunk and excited by his
continuing to expect the women to come; he received the letter,
but when the bearer told him that it contained an urgent message,
he said, "Urgent business will keep until tomorrow." He put the
letter under his pillow, called for his goblet and asked for it to be
filled, and kept sending Phyllidas outside to see if the women
were coming.[1]

[31] 'This atmosphere of expectancy occupied the party – but
it was we who arrived. We pushed straight through the servants
to the dining-room and paused in the doorway, looking at the
597A   occupants of the couches one by one. Our chaplets and costumes
disguised our presence, so there was no uproar.[2] But when Melon
made his way through the room – he was the first to do so –
with his hand clutching the hilt of his sword, Cabirichus, who
held the office which was subject to election by lot, pulled on his
arm as he was passing his couch and called out, "Isn't this Melon,
Phyllidas?" Melon shook himself free of his grip, drawing his
sword at the same time, and rushed over to Archias, who was
struggling to get to his feet, and stabbed him again and again
until he was dead.

'Charon wounded Philippus in the neck, but Philippus continued to fight back with the goblets that were within his reach,
B    until Lysitheus threw him off his couch on to the ground and
killed him. We tried to calm Cabirichus down by telling him
that he ought not to be helping the tyrants, but should play a
part in freeing his country, since he was a priest and had dedicated
himself to the gods for his country's sake. But, partly because

1. The story of the letter is also in *Life of Pelopidas* 10.6–10, where there is no
   mention of the house the exiles were to go to; nor should there be any
   mention, since Charon had only that morning sent a message to the exiles
   offering his house (576C–D). It seems unlikely that the intelligence could have
   reached Archias the high priest in time for his letter; Plutarch's sense of
   dramatic anecdote has led to inconsistent embroidery. Archias' aphorism on
   urgent business became proverbial.
2. In *Life of Pelopidas* 11.3, they are greeted uproariously as the arrival of the
   expected women.

he'd been drinking, he could not be persuaded by rationality of the expedient thing to do: in his distracted and confused state, he started to get up and to point the spear which our Theban leaders traditionally always carry. I grabbed the middle of the shaft, lifted the spear up in the air over his head, and yelled at him to let go of it and so save himself, or else be struck down. But Theopompus came up from our right and hit him with his sword. "Lie there," he said, "with those you fawned upon. You    C don't deserve to wear a chaplet in a free Thebes or perform any more sacrifices to the gods in whose names you have often damned your country by praying for her enemies." Cabirichus collapsed to the ground, and then Theocritus (who was near by) retrieved the sacred spear from the blood. We killed the few servants who dared to resist, and locked those who did not put up a fight in the dining-room, because we didn't want them to escape with news of what had happened until we knew whether    D the others had been successful.

[32] 'The others' business went as follows.[1] Pelopidas and his men made their stealthy way to Leontiades' courtyard door, knocked and told the servant who answered that they had come from Athens with a message for Leontiades from Callistratus. The servant told Leontiades, who ordered him to open the door. As soon as the servant had removed the bar and opened the door a fraction, they all dashed in at once, knocking the man to the ground, and sprinted through the courtyard towards the sleeping-quarters. Leontiades immediately guessed what was going on, drew his dagger and made to defend himself, because    E although he was a lawless, tyrannical man, he was mentally resolute and physically strong. However, he was not alert enough to hurl the lamp to the ground and engage his assailants in the dark: as soon as the door was open, they could clearly see him in the light. He stabbed Cephisodorus in the side and then, once he had taken on Pelopidas (who was the second into the room), he screamed out for his servants. But Samidas and the others blocked the way, and the servants were not prepared to risk a fight with the most renowned men in Thebes, who were also outstanding

1. Compare *Life of Pelopidas* 11.

F    warriors. The fiercely contested sword fight between Pelopidas and Leontiades was taking place in the doorway, which was narrow, and moreover Cephisodorus was lying in between the open doors with his life ebbing away, so the others could not go to help Pelopidas. But finally, although he received a superficial head wound, our man wounded Leontiades in many places, forced him to the ground and killed him. Cephisodorus was still warm with life at that point: he saw his enemy fall, stretched out his hand to touch Pelopidas and, with the others' names on his lips, died happy. Their work done there, they turned to Hypates: they got his doors open in a similar fashion, and killed him as he was trying to escape over a roof to his neighbours.

598A    [33] 'Then they hurried in our direction, and met us out on the street near the Colonnade. Once we had greeted one another and exchanged news, we went to the prison. Phyllidas called for ⟨the man⟩ in charge of the prison and said, "Orders from Archias and Philippus: you are to bring Amphitheus to them at once."

'But he realized that it was unusually late for this, and saw that Phyllidas was not in a calm state as he was talking to him, but was heated and churned up from his fight, so he suspected that he was lying. "Phyllidas," he said, "when have the polemarchs

B    ever sent for a prisoner at this time of day? And when have they ever used you? Have you brought any authorization?"

'⟨"Here is my authorization," said Phyllidas⟩ and simultaneously impaled him in the ribs with a cavalry lance he was holding. This was a bad man he slew, and on the following day quite a few women trampled and spat on the corpse.

'We smashed down the prison doors and called out first Amphitheus' name, and then those of anyone else any of us was acquainted with. When they recognized our voices, they leapt up from their beds in delight, dragging their chains with them, while those with their feet locked in the stocks reached out their hands and loudly implored us not to abandon them. By the time

C    the prisoners were free, a lot of the people who lived in the neighbourhood had realized what was happening and were joyfully approaching the prison. When the women were told about their relatives, they discarded the norms of Boeotian behaviour,

rushed out of their homes to meet one another, and asked
anyone they came across for information; and those who found
their fathers or husbands stayed with them, and no one stopped
them, because anyone who met them was greatly influenced by
their own compassion and by these decent women's tears and
prayers.

[34] 'At this juncture, I found out that Epaminondas and
Gorgidas were already congregating with their friends at the    D
temple of Athena, so I went to meet them.[1] Many of the best
citizens had already gathered there, and more were constantly
flooding in. I gave them a detailed report of what had happened
and advised them to go to the agora and lend a hand, and every
single one of them immediately began to tell their fellow citizens
that freedom was imminent. The porticoes, which were full of
all kinds of spoils taken in war, and any sword-smiths' workshops
which were in the vicinity, yielded up their weaponry to the
crowds that formed at this point. And Hipposthenidas arrived as
well, accompanied by some friends and servants, and bringing
the trumpeters who were coincidentally in town for the festival   E
of Heracles. They lost no time in sounding the alarm in the
agora, and others of them elsewhere, so that whichever way they
turned, our enemies were given the disquieting impression that
the uprising involved everyone.

'The pro-Spartans fled ⟨from the rest of the city to⟩ the
Cadmeia and took with them the so-called élite troops who
regularly spent the night on guard duty at the base of the acropolis. The troops at the top of the acropolis were faced with the
influx of this disorderly rabble and could see us in the agora: no
quarter of the city was undisturbed, but chaotic noises reached
them from all directions. So, even though there were about
fifteen hundred of them, they decided not to go down into the   F
city; they were especially terrified at the danger of the situation,
and they claimed that they were waiting for Lysanoridas,[2] since
⟨he had said that he would be with them⟩ that day – which is
why, we hear, Lysanoridas was subsequently given a heavy ⟨fine⟩

1. *Life of Pelopidas* 12 gives another version of the final scenes.
2. He had gone to Haliartus (578A).

by the Spartan senate, and Herippidas and Arcesus were apprehended in Corinth and executed on the spot.[1] The pro-Spartans
made a truce with us, surrendered the Cadmeia and began to
depart along with their troops.'

1. So also *Life of Pelopidas* 13.3.

# IN CONSOLATION TO HIS WIFE

## INTRODUCTION

Plutarch's baby daughter, a much loved two-year-old named Timoxena after her mother, and especially cherished since she came after four boys, died when he was away from home. His wife sent off a courier to Athens with the sad news, but the man missed Plutarch and Timoxena had to see to all the funeral arrangements herself. Plutarch first heard of what had happened from a granddaughter at Tanagra, and wrote to his wife this moving letter of consolation, which survived among his published works.

We are, however, well aware that 'Consolation' literature was an established and popular literary form of the time, and it can be shown that in Plutarch's letter to his wife the formality of presentation and the framework of illustration and argument contain a number of items that can be paralleled as stock themes from extant examples of the genre. So the question must be asked whether what we have is a personal document of mourning and solace to his wife or a literary composition arising from the loss of the child and intended ultimately for publication.

First of all, the external setting in which Plutarch places the letter raises some problems. What was Plutarch doing in Tanagra in north-east Boeotia? His wife clearly thought he was in Athens (608B). He was certainly not in Tanagra on his way to Athens from Chaeronea. Tanagra is less than fifty miles from Chaeronea, and the interval taken to reach there was not enough for the child's death and completed funeral arrangements to have taken place after he had left home; indeed the news of the funeral had preceded his arrival at Tanagra (608B). But if he was on his way home, he could have reached Chaeronea himself almost as soon as a letter, so why wait to compose such a thoughtful and polished epistle? But there are two possible answers to this: either it may not have been possible for Plutarch to return at once, for he could have had an engagement elsewhere to be fulfilled first; or he was on his way home, but as we well know, in times of extreme stress and emotion, it is often easier and more cathartic to write down and send one's thoughts before confronting a loved one in person.

At least one of the reasons Plutarch was in Tanagra was to see family. But who precisely this family was has roused fierce discussion. He was told of his baby's death by a granddaughter, and the Greek word used means literally a daughter's daughter. Most people, however, assume from the letter (608C, 609D), that Plutarch's family consisted of the four boys (who are named elsewhere too: Soclarus, Charon, Autobulus and Plutarchus) and little Timoxena, now dead. So it has been suggested hopefully that it was not a granddaughter but a niece, a daughter of one of Plutarch's brothers, that was intended.[1] That interpretation goes against the form of the Greek word, there is no clear instance of such a use of the word and it is contrary to Plutarch's own usage.[2] More inconveniently still, three young men turn up in Table Talk (Cranton, 620A; Firmus, 636A; Patrocleas, 642C, 700E) labelled by the word which normally means son-in-law (gambros), who then are downgraded to husbands of nieces.[3] So it has been suggested[4] that Timoxena may not have been Plutarch's first wife, and that he had been married before with children. This too has rightly raised unease, not only through lack of any mention of another wife, but because Plutarch specifically, in his Life of the Younger Cato 7.3, extols the good fortune of the man married to a single wife throughout a long life, and it is difficult not to see in this a reflection from his own happy marriage. There is a simple solution:[5] Plutarch and Timoxena had a lot of children (608C), and there is no reason why other girls could not have come before the four boys. They are not mentioned elsewhere, but Plutarch, while talkative about the male members of his family, is reticent about his close female relations: he never mentions his mother. The four sons are listed in the letter because they formed a row after which a late baby girl was much desired by their mother (608C). So the oldest child who died (609D) was not Soclarus, but the oldest girl – the sex is unspecified in the Greek. Thus the little girl who blurted out the news to Plutarch in Tanagra (608B) was a true granddaughter of Timoxena, and Plutarch mentions her, rather than her mother, for close family affectionate reasons.

The setting then seems not contrived, but real and personal. So too is the presentation, although it may strike a modern reader as rather formal. But we live in a very informal age; other times and societies, such as those of Jane Austen or of Plutarch, retained a formality of address and composition which was perfectly natural and in no way artificial or contrived in feeling and sensibility. His letter is undoubtedly laced with topical themes of consolation, but it would be extraordinary if it were not. Anyone who has had to write letters of sympathy at bereavement will be only too conscious of the slippery path to be traced between the allure and helpfulness of stock themes and expressions and the dangers and horrors of cliché. But Plutarch was also embedded in a scholastic and literary tradition, for consolation themes were a recognized exercise in rhetorical training, a central topic of debate in the Hellenistic philosophy schools, and a popular literary genre for publication.[6] Thus a whole tradition had built up which was not only impossible to ignore, but was part of contemporary education. Everyone had read the famous work *On Grief* by Crantor, Head of the Academy in the early third century BC (Cicero, *Academica* 2.135). There were repositories of suitable themes, allusions and quotations, such as were shown by the *Consolation to Apollonius*, found in Plutarch's works, but certainly not a product of his mature pen. Extant works such as Cicero's *Tusculanae Disputationes*, and Seneca's *Consolations to Marcia*, *to Helvia* and *to Polybius* reveal repeated common themes. Plutarch himself, according to the Lamprias Catalogue of his works, had written two such Consolations, to Asclepiades (111) and to Bestia (157). So it was to be expected that such themes would appear in Plutarch's letter to his wife, and they have been pointed out in the footnotes to the translation. He would need no research library to recall them, and the couple of quotations he used would be in his head. All this is simply the natural material he had at hand. What matters is how he used it.

What he did was to personalize it in the picture he gives us of his wife, her character, her behaviour and her love for her family. For example, the theme of inappropriateness of extravagant ostentation or display is traced through his wife's restraint at the funeral, and recalled, not vaguely but in specific personal detail, in her admired control on the death of her earlier children, especially her lovely boy Charon. Such self-control is treated in relation to family love (§4, 609A) and to their married relationship (§5, 609C). Or again, the topic of distressing intrusion from hordes of over-enthusiastic women 'sympathizers' is instanced by Timoxena's own action in keeping them off a friend's sister in mourning (§7, 610C). The natural subject of the dead person's character is raised by recalling the sweetness and touching unselfishness of the little girl at that age, but this is done to reflect and illuminate his wife's pure and intense love for and pleasure in her (§2, 608C). And in this way Plutarch can suggest that the great joys the child gave them can outweigh the distress at losing her (§3, 608D–F).

Section 6 (609E–610B) will serve as a good example of how Plutarch transforms stock themes. He begins with the *topos*: natural, instinctive grief is sharp and short, as animals show; humans prolong and exaggerate their grief through false opinions and beliefs on top of their natural instincts (cf. e.g. *Consolation to Apollonius* 102C–D; Seneca, *Consolation to Marcia* 7). This is followed by a stock fable about Grief benefiting from the handout of favours from Zeus (cf. *Consolation to Apollonius* 112A). Plutarch immediately personalizes this: mothers who howl the longest are those who play with their children as toys after others have changed their nappies: but Timoxena, who cared for her child lovingly herself, is restrained in her grief. Practical advice follows: grief must be consciously controlled from the beginning, otherwise it will establish a stronghold from which it is difficult to escape. Also, conventional mourning which neglects the body and physical needs simply transmits debilitating effects of pain and distress on the mind precisely when it needs strengthening through physical fitness and support. All this is expressed in very typical Plutarchan style with vivid language and imagery. But it is clearly no conventional offering; he meant it. One need only recall *On the Avoidance of Anger* §§3–4 (454C ff., 454E), where he stresses this very point, that an exaggerated emotion or passion must be attacked immediately if there is to be any hope of control.

This raises the other clear purpose of the letter. Besides the unmistakable expression of loving sympathy, Plutarch is attempting to produce practical advice on how to cope. This is expressly stated at 608F, where he hopes that 'the arguments we have often deployed on others will help us in our hour of need'. The 'us' is important; he includes himself as well as his wife. And, indeed, it is hard not to believe that he is writing for his own consolation and help as well, since his love for his baby girl is transparent (608E–F); his recollection of it provoked the statement.

But it is also clear how tied up it is with his love for his wife. The portrait we are given of her is strong and affectionate: of a woman of character, capable, straightforward, her own mistress, but bound up in close, loving relationship with her family. Plutarch treats her as an equal with admiring respect; she joins him on public occasions, plays hostess to his learned friends. She was clearly a highly intelligent and cultivated woman herself, as the letter addressed to her, with its typical Plutarchan allusions and literary and philosophical polish, shows. Almost certainly she was the Timoxena who wrote on the subject of *Love of Finery* for a friend, as Plutarch tells us in *Marital Advice* 145A. Above all, Plutarch's love for her is obvious. When he asks that they both must try to keep control of their emotions in the extremity of their misfortune, he expresses it beautifully through his love for her. Her distress, he says, would affect him more even than their child's death (608B–C). This haunting picture of a happy marriage has attracted and affected generations of readers of Plutarch. At the head of manuscript B of Plutarch (Parisinus gr. 1675) in the Bibliothèque Nationale in Paris, there is a charming drawing of Plutarch writing, with Timoxena sitting companionably by his side.

Plutarch's final review (§§ 9–11) of sources of help and comfort for his wife and himself is interesting in its presentation and balance. First, they must remember that it is reason which establishes a stable state of mind and equanimity of spirit, which can put their loss in proper proportion. This is the appeal to philosophy. But it only skirts in the briefest way the fringes of large philosophical issues, raising without comment the Stoic view that happiness does not depend on the mere totting up of good and bad events in men's lives, or again broaching philosophical attitudes to death by rejecting the Epicurean argument of the dissolution of the soul with the body. This is very much the territory of essays such as *On Contentment*, but Plutarch merely mentions the basic principle without embroidery. He ends rather with two more personal strengths for them both. One consists of the traditions and beliefs they have been brought up with, rooted in their families and society in their beloved Chaeronea; and the other is the faith of the religion of the Mysteries which proclaims the immortality of the soul and happiness in another world after death. Even here there is a remarkable and honest absence of dogma, and Plutarch will only allow that it is harder to reject such faith than to believe it. But they should take comfort that their child has gone to a better and more divine place, and so look to themselves to behave accordingly both in action and in thought.

The answer to our original question as to whether we have a personal letter or a literary composition for publication could be that the alternatives are not necessarily exclusive. There is nothing in the letter which suggests that it was not originally a message of grief and comfort sent at the time to his wife, and much, in particular its depth of feeling, which suggests that it was. On the other hand, there is no apparent reason which would prevent its later publication by Plutarch himself or a descendant, and contemporary custom would recommend it. It is in any case a remarkable document, which has rightly been much admired.

1. E.g. R. Volkmann, *Leben, Schriften und Philosophie des Plutarch von Chaeronea*, I, p. 29; K. Ziegler, *Plutarchos*, col. 15.
2. Cf. *On God's Slowness to Punish*, 563A; *Life of Aristides* 27.4.
3. Ziegler, *loc. cit.*
4. Cf. De Lacy and Einarson, Plutarch, *Moralia*, Loeb vol. VII, p. 576.
5. Cf. J. Hani, *Plutarque* VIII (Budé), p. 177.
6. See R. Kassel, *Untersuchungen zur griechischen und römischen Konsolationsliteratur* (*Zetemata* 18); J. Hani, *Plutarque, oeuvres morales* II. p. 14 ff. (Budé).

# IN CONSOLATION TO HIS WIFE

[1] FROM PLUTARCH TO HIS WIFE. I hope this finds you well.[1] The man you sent to give me the news of our child's death seems to have missed me during his overland journey to Athens, but I heard about it from my granddaughter when I got to Tanagra.[2] I imagine that the burial rites are over by now, and I hope they were conducted in a way that makes the chance of your feeling distress at the burial both now and in the future as remote as possible. But if there is something you haven't yet done, even though you want to, because you are waiting to hear what I intend to do, and it is something which you think would make things easier to bear, then it will happen too, with no fuss and superstitious nonsense – not that you are at all liable to these faults.

[2] All I ask, my dear, is that while reacting emotionally you make sure that both of us – me as well as you – remain in a stable state. I mean, the actual event is a known quantity and I can keep it within limits, but if I find your distress excessive, this will discompose me more than what has happened. Nevertheless, I was not born 'from oak or rock',[3] as you yourself know, given that you have been my partner in bringing up so many children – all brought up with no one else's help in our own home – and I know how overjoyed you were with the birth, after four sons,

1. Letters, whether real or literary, require the names of the recipient and of the sender. Plutarch adds his normal greeting – literally, 'do well' or 'prosper'.
2. Tanagra is the main town in north-east Boeotia, some fifty miles from Chaeronea. On the vexed question of this granddaughter, see Introduction, pp. 360–61.
3. A very ancient phrase of obscure origin, but much quoted from the earliest times (Homer, *Iliad* 22.126, *Odyssey* 19.163; Hesiod, *Theogony* 35). See M. L. West, *Hesiod, Theogony*, pp. 167–9.

of the daughter you longed for and with the fact that it gave me
the opportunity to name her after you. In addition, one's love
for children of that age is peculiarly acute, since the pleasure it
affords is absolutely unsullied and untainted by any element of
anger and criticism. Also, she was inherently wonderfully easy to
please and undemanding, and the way she repaid affection with
affection and was so charming was not only delightful, but also
made one realize how unselfish she was. She used to encourage
her wet-nurse to offer and present her breast not only to other
babies, but also to her favourite playthings and toys: she was
unselfishly trying to share the good things she had and the things
she most enjoyed with her favourites, as if they were guests at
her very own table.

[3] However, my dear, I fail to see any reason why, when this
and similar behaviour pleased us during her life, it should upset
and trouble us when we recall it now. I worry about the alternative, however – that we might consign the memory of her to
oblivion along with our distress. This would be to act like
Clymene, who said, 'I hate the curved cornel bow! I wish there
were no gymnasia!':[1] she was always nervous about recalling her
son, and avoided doing so, because distress was its companion,[2] and it is natural to avoid anything painful.[3] No, our daughter was the sweetest thing in the world to hug and watch and
listen to, and by the same token she must remain and live on in
our thoughts, and bring not just more, but a great deal more
pleasure than distress – if it is plausible to expect that the arguments we have often deployed on others will help us in our hour
of need – and we must not slump in dejection or shut ourselves
away and so pay for those pleasures with distress that vastly
outweighs it.

[4] People who were with you also tell me, with some surprise,

1. From Euripides' *Phaethon* F785 Nauck. Clymene's son was Phaethon, who
   perished when attempting to drive his father's (the sun's) chariot; he presumably
   also enjoyed archery and other sports in Euripides' play.
2. The theme is stock. Seneca, in his *Consolation to Marcia* 2–3, cites Octavia for
   this condition and opposes Livia to it.
3. An Epicurean position (Sextus Empiricus, *Adversus Mathematicos* 11.96, and the
   texts collected under Epicurus F398 Usener), but naturally entering Consolation literature (e.g. Seneca, *Consolation to Polybius* 18.7).

that you haven't adopted mourning clothes, that you didn't make yourself or your maids follow any ugly or harrowing practices[1] and that the paraphernalia of an expensive celebration was absent from the funeral – that instead everything was conducted with discretion and in silence, and with only the essential accoutrements. It was no surprise to me, however, that you who    609A
never tricked yourself out for the theatre or a public procession, and never saw any point in extravagance even where your pleasures were concerned, maintained unaffectedness★ and frugality in sad circumstances.

The point is that Bacchic rites are not the only circumstances which require a decent woman to remain uncorrupted:[2] she should equally assume that the instability and emotional disturbance which grief entails call for self-control, which is not, as is popularly supposed, the enemy of affection and love, but of mental indulgence. Affection is what we gratify by missing, valuing and remembering the dead, but the insatiable desire for    B
grief – a desire which makes us wail and howl – is just as contemptible as hedonistic indulgence, despite the notion that it is forgivable because, although it may be contemptible, it is accompanied not by any pleasure gained from the desire, but rather by distress and pain. Could there be anything more absurd than banishing excesses of laughter and mirth, and yet allowing the floodgates of tears and lamentation, which spring from the same source as merriment, to open to their fullest extent? Or – as some husbands do – quarrelling with their wives about extravagant hair perfume and gaudy clothing, and yet submitting when they cut off their hair in mourning, dye their clothes black and adopt ugly postures when sitting and uncomfortable ones when    C
reclining at table?[3] Or – and this is the most irritating of all – resisting and restraining their wives if they punish their servants of either sex excessively and unfairly, and yet ignoring the

1. It was common practice in funeral customs to display the extravagance of one's grief through the disfigurement of the body and appearance, such as shaving off hair, wearing black and adopting unrestrained and ugly postures; see also 609B, 609F.
2. A reminiscence of Euripides, *Bacchae* 317 f.
3. It is not clear what mourning practice is being referred to; for the general principle, see n.1 above.

vicious, harsh punishments they inflict upon themselves when they are under the influence of emotion and misfortunes which actually call for a relaxed and charitable attitude?

[5] Our relationship, however, my dear, is such that there never has been any occasion for us to quarrel on the one score, and there never will be any occasion for us to quarrel on the other, I am sure. On the one hand, every philosopher who has spent time with us and got to know us has been impressed with the inextravagance of your clothing and make-up, and with the modesty of your lifestyle, and every one of our fellow citizens has witnessed your unaffectedness during rituals and sacrifices and at the theatre. On the other hand, you have already demonstrated in the past that you can remain stable under these circumstances, when you lost your eldest child and again when our lovely Charon left us before his time. I remember that I brought visitors with me on my journey from the coast at the news of the child's death, and that they and everyone else gathered in our house. As they subsequently told others as well, when they saw how calm and peaceful it was, they thought that nothing terrible had happened and that a baseless rumour had got out, because you had behaved so responsibly in arranging the house at a time when disarray is normally excusable, despite the fact that you had nursed him at your own breast and had endured an operation when your nipple got inflamed,[1] which are noble acts stemming from motherly love.[2]

[6] It is noticeable that most mothers take their children into their arms as if they were playthings (after others have cleaned them and smartened them up), and then, if the children die, these mothers wallow in empty, indecent grief. They are not motivated by warmth of feeling, which is a reasonable and commendable emotion:[3] their strong inclination towards shallow beliefs, plus a

1. She probably suffered the agony of a breast abscess – the result of infection getting into the breast through a cracked nipple – which in pre-antibiotic days would have been cauterized.
2. Plutarch uses similar language in *Life of Demosthenes* 22.3, in contrasting the attitude of Demosthenes and Aeschines to bereavement; the story is repeated in *Consolation to Apollonius* 119B.
3. A Stoic definition (Diogenes Laertius 7.116), but approved of by Plutarch (*Life of Solon* 7.5).

dash of instinctive emotion, causes outbursts of grief which are   F
fierce, manic and unruly.[1] Aesop was apparently aware of this:
he said that when Zeus was distributing recognition among the
gods, Grief asked for some as well; so Zeus allowed Grief to be
acknowledged – but only by people who deliberately wanted to
acknowledge it.[2]

This is certainly what happens at the beginning: only an individual lets grief enter himself; but after a while it becomes a
permanent sibling, a habitual presence, and then it doesn't leave
however much one wants it to. That is why it is crucial to resist
it on the threshold and not to adopt special clothing or haircuts
or anything else like that, which allow it to establish a stronghold.   610A
These things challenge the mind day in and day out, make it
recoil, belittle it and constrict it and imprison it, and make it
unresponsive and apprehensive, as if the wearing of these clothes
and the adoption of these practices out of grief cut it off from
laughter and light and the sociability of the table. The conse-
quences of this affliction are physical neglect and an aversion to
oiling and bathing the body and to other aspects of the daily regimen, when exactly the opposite should happen: purely mental
suffering ought to be helped by physical fitness. Mental distress
abates and subsides to a great extent when it is dispersed in
physical calm, as waves subside in fair weather, but if as a result   B
of a bad regimen the body becomes sordid and foul and transmits
to the mind nothing benign or beneficial, but only the harsh and
unpleasant fumes of pain and distress, then even those who desire
it find that recovery becomes hard to achieve. These are the
kinds of disorders that take possession of the mind when it is
treated so badly.

[7] Nevertheless, I have no cause to worry about the worst
and most worrying disorder which occurs in such cases – 'the

1. It was a recurrent theme in Consolation literature that natural instinctive grief
is sharp and short, as with animals; it is humans who tend to prolong and
exaggerate grief through false beliefs on top of their natural instincts. Cf.
Seneca, *Consolation to Marcia* 7.1; *Consolation to Apollonius* 102C–D.
2. An old tale of unknown origin, but common stock for Consolations. The
*Consolation to Apollonius* 112A gives it to 'an ancient philosopher' speaking to
Queen Arsinoe. It turns up under Sotion in John of Stobi 3.972.7 Hense.

invasion of malignant women',[1] with the cries and expressions of sympathy which they use to polish and hone distress, and to prevent its being diminished either by external factors or of its own accord. For I know about the battles you recently had when you went to assist Theon's sister[2] and defended her against the incursions of the women who came with their weeping and wailing – behaviour which is exactly the same as fighting fire with fire.[3] I mean, when people see a friend's house on fire, then everyone contributes what he can to put it out as quickly as possible; but when that same friend's mind is on fire, they bring fuel! And although when someone has an eye infection, people don't let just anyone touch it or treat the inflammation, people who are grieving sit and let everyone who comes by prod at their running sore, so to speak, and aggravate the condition, until instead of being an insignificant itching irritation, it erupts into a seriously disagreeable affliction.[4] Anyway, I know that you will be on your guard against this.

[8] Please try, however, to use your mind as a vehicle for often returning to the time when this child of ours had not yet been born and we had no reason to blame fortune; and then connect that time with the present, and imagine that our circumstances are no different again.[5] You see, my dear, we will seem to regret that our child was ever born if we find more to complain about now than in the situation before her birth.[6] We must not erase the intervening two years from our memories, but since they brought happiness and joy, we must count them as pleasant. The good was brief, but should not therefore be

---

1. From Euripides' *Andromache* 930, used again by Plutarch at 143E. He also noted the exacerbating effect of enthusiastic 'sympathizers' in *On Exile* 599A–B.

2. Theon was one of Plutarch's close friends; he appears frequently in his dialogues.

3. A proverb much liked by Plutarch: 61A, 123E, 143F, 919D, *Life of Artaxerxes* 28.1. He may have got it from Plato, *Laws* 666a.

4. For the imagery in relation to provoking grief, compare *Consolation to Apollonius* 102A; Cicero, *Tusculanae Disputationes* 4.63 (from Chrysippus); and Seneca, *Consolation to Helvia* 1.2.

5. Teles, the Cynic of the third century BC, used this same device (p. 61.2–4 Hense; pp. 68 f. O'Neil).

6. The same point is made by Seneca, *Consolation to Helvia* 19.7.

regarded as a long-term bad influence; and we should not be ungrateful for what we received just because our further hopes were dashed by fortune.[1]

The point is that a reverential attitude towards the gods and being charitable and uncomplaining with regard to fortune always yield a dividend which is both fine and enjoyable, and anyone who, in a situation like ours, makes a particular point of highlighting the memory of good things and turning his mind away from the dark and disturbing aspects of his life towards the bright and brilliant ones instead either completely extinguishes    F whatever it is that is causing him pain, or at least decreases and obscures it by blending it with its opposite.[2] Perfume is always nice to smell, but it is also an antidote to unpleasant odours; likewise, bearing good things in mind serves the extra purpose of essential support, in times of trouble, for people who are not afraid to recall good times and do not critically hold fortune entirely responsible for every bad thing that happens. And that is a condition we should avoid – the syndrome of whingeing if    611A the book of our life has a single smudge while every other page is perfectly clean. [9] I mean, you have often been told that happiness is a consequence of correctly using the rational mind for the goal of a stable state, and that if it is a chance event which causes one to deviate, this does not constitute a major reversal and does not mean that the edifice of one's life has collapsed and been demolished.

Suppose that we too were to follow the usual practice of being guided by external circumstances, of keeping a tally of events due to fortune and of relying on any casual assessment of whether or not we are happy:[3] even so, you should not take into considera- tion the current weeping and wailing of your visitors, which is    B trotted out on each and every occasion, prompted by pointless

1. So too Seneca, *Consolation to Marcia* 12.1; and cf. Seneca, *Consolation to Polybius* 10.1 f.
2. Plutarch believed strongly in this principle; see *On Contentment* 469A. There he illustrated it by sight, here by smell.
3. It was the Stoics who held that happiness could not depend on a totting up or reckoning between external goods and evils, for they had only relative value in comparison with the absolute value of moral reason.

social customs. You would be better off bearing in mind that they continue to envy you for your children, your home and your way of life. As long as there are others who would gladly choose your fate, even including our present upset,[1] it is awful for you, as the bearer of the fate, to complain and grumble, instead of letting the very source of your pain bring you to the realization of how much we have to be grateful for in what we still have. Otherwise, you will resemble those people who pick out Homer's headless and tapering lines,[2] and ignore the many extensive passages of outstanding composition: if you do this, and nitpickingly whinge about the bad features of your life, and

C   gloss over the good points in a vague and sweeping fashion, you will be behaving like those mean and avaricious people who build up a considerable hoard and don't make use of what they get, but still moan and grumble when they lose it.

If you feel sorry about our daughter dying before she was able to marry and have children, then again you can find other reasons for cheering yourself up, in that you have known and experienced both these states: I mean, they cannot simultaneously* be significant and insignificant blessings, depending on whether or not one has been deprived of them![3] And the fact that she has gone to a place of no pain ought not to be a source of pain to us.[4] Why should she cause us to suffer, if there is nothing that can now cause her pain? Even huge losses cease

D   to be a source of distress when the point is reached at which the objects are no longer missed, and your Timoxena suffered only minor losses, since what she was familiar with and what she found pleasure in were not things of great importance. And as for things she was unaware of, which had never entered her mind or caught her fancy* – how could she be said to have lost them?

---

1. A point made by Plutarch again in *On Exile* 600A; so too Boethius, *The Consolation of Philosophy* 2.4.17.
2. 'Headless' lines began, and 'tapering' ones ended, with a short syllable where the metre required a long one; cf. Athenaeus 632D ff., and Plutarch again in *On Curiosity* 520A.
3. Again in *On Contentment* 469F.
4. The *Consolation to Apollonius* 114D develops this argument.

[10] Then there is that other idea you've come across, which is commonly accepted, that it is quite impossible for anything to harm or distress something which has been dissolved.[1] But I know that both the doctrine we've inherited from our ancestors[2] and the maxims of the Dionysian Mysteries (which those of us who are in the group are privy to)[3] prevent you believing this idea. So, since the soul cannot be destroyed, you can compare   E what happens to it to the behaviour of caged birds: if it has made a physical body its home for an extended period of time, and has allowed a plethora of material events and long familiarity to domesticate it to this way of life, then it resumes its perch inside a body and doesn't let go or stop its involvement, through rebirth after rebirth, with worldly conditions and fortunes. If old age is the butt of calumny and slurs, you should appreciate that this is not because of wrinkles, grey hair and physical enfeeble-ment: no, its most cruel feature is that it makes the soul lose touch with its memories of the other world,[4] attaches it to this   F one, wraps it and constricts it (since it retains the shape it gained while it was acted on★ by the body). On the other hand, a soul which, although captured, ⟨remains only a short while in a body before being released⟩★ by the gods and departing, springs back up to its natural state as if, although it had been bent, it retained its suppleness and malleability.[5] Just as fire is quickly rekindled again and returns to its former state if it is relit straight after being extinguished, ⟨but the longer the interval, the harder it is to relight, so too the most fortunate soul is the one which is able, in the poet's words,⟩ 'to pass as swiftly as possible through

---

1. The reference is to Epicurus, *Letter to Menoeceus* 124, and *Key Doctrines* 2, cited again by Plutarch in 1103D and 1105A; the Epicureans believed that a person's soul was a concatenation of atoms, like everything else, and was therefore liable to dissolution at death.

2. Plutarch proclaimed his own adherence to traditional faith again in *Dialogue on Love* 756B.

3. So Plutarch was an initiate. The Mysteries fostered belief in a happy afterlife and the immortality of the soul.

4. Plato too, in *Phaedrus* 250b–c, had used the imagery of the Mysteries for the vision of the soul when it is free from the imprisonment of the body.

5. Precisely the same point was made by Seneca, *Consolation to Marcia* 23.1. Plutarch used the imagery again in *On the Soul* F177 Sandbach.

Hades' portals',[1] before a strong love of the things of this world has been engendered in it and before it has become moulded to the body by being softened and melted as if by chemicals.

612A    [11] Our ancient ancestral customs and rules are a better guide to the truth in these matters. People do not pour libations for their infant children when they die or perform any of the other rites that in other cases one is expected to perform for the dead, because babies have not been pervaded by earth or any earthly things. Again, people do not linger over their★ burial or at their grave or in laying out their bodies, because the laws regarding death at that age★ do not allow it, on the grounds that it is irreligious to grieve for those who have exchanged this world for a fate, and a place too, that is better and more divine. Since mistrusting these laws is more problematic than trusting them,

B    let us make sure that our external actions conform to their injunctions, and that our internal state is even more untainted, pure and restrained than our external activity.

1. Theognis 427: one of the famous expressions of Greek pessimism. It is best not to have been born at all, but next best is 'to pass as swiftly as possible through Hades' portals'.

# ON THE USE OF REASON BY
## 'IRRATIONAL' ANIMALS

---

## INTRODUCTION

The scene is the tenth book of the *Odyssey*; or rather, Plutarch's version of the tenth book of the *Odyssey*. Troy has fallen after ten years' siege and Odysseus, one of the bravest, and by reputation the most sagacious of the Greek commanders, is trying to get home again to Ithaca and his wife Penelope, who with incredible patience, not to say stubbornness, is still virtuously fending off the unwelcome attentions of the local gentry. She will have to keep going for another ten years while Odysseus is blown halfway round the Mediterranean from one adventure to another. At this point he is on the island of the beautiful sorceress Circe, who has the unfortunate propensity of transmogrifying her human lovers into swine. A good number of Odysseus' company are already in the pigsty, but Odysseus not only holds out against Circe's advances and undoubted bewitching attractions, but pleads with her to turn his comrades back again to humans, so that they can be on their way. Circe treats this rather rude suggestion in kindly fashion (she is rather soft on Odysseus), but doubts whether her herd would have the slightest inclination to deswinify themselves. However, she is willing to humour the incredulous Odysseus by permitting him to attempt to persuade them. One is produced, introduced as Gryllus (a proper Greek name, but meaning Grunter) and given back his human speech, as Odysseus cannot cope with grunt language. This loquacious pig not only argues that life in Circe's pigsty is much to be preferred to Ithaca, but also that pigs and animals in general have a purer intelligence and moral character than humans, and so no animal in its right mind would ever wish to be a human. He knows because he has been both. Now in order to appreciate what is happening to the stunned Odysseus, and more generally the wit, ingenuity and sheer originality of Plutarch's presentation, the reader should know a little of the background against which this was written and which would be taken for granted by Plutarch's audience. It is a complex and rich one: a mixture of philosophical theory, zoological investigation, collections of animal stories and wonders, and rhetorical debating practice.

The philosophical issue centred on whether animals were irrational or could be said to display intelligence and reason. Plato, for example, in *Laches* 196e–197c, refused to call any animal brave, because he held that courage is a moral virtue controlled by reason, and animals are irrational; at most they could be said to be bold. The debate sharpened in Hellenistic philosophy through the Stoics. Chrysippus made a clear-cut division between animals who were credited with sensation, impulse and a consciousness of their own nature, but all in a merely instinctive and irrational form (e.g. Diogenes Laertius 7.85–6), and on the other hand humans whose mind was seen as wholly rational in structure and operation to the extent that even their emotions and passions are regarded as rational mental conditions resulting from some kind of false value judgement.[1] It followed that irrational beasts could not even be said to be angry, for example, but only fierce and aggressive.[2] The Stoic Posidonius, in the first century BC, jibbed at this, and claimed passions for animals, human babies and adults alike; but this was at the cost of abandoning Chrysippan psychology in favour of allowing for an irrational aspect of mind in humans. But animals still remained staunchly irrational, and at most a view developed[3] that animals in addition to perception and impulse may be credited with a kind of natural or instinctive sagacity that is common to all members of a species, but without individual distinctions; or to put it another way, this is universal reason operating through natural constitution but devoid of any separate individual reason in an animal. Such instinctive (irrational) behaviour was still sharply contrasted with the full rational, judgemental operation of the human mind.[4] In addition, the Stoics, like Plato, held that beasts, being irrational, cannot be credited with any moral or virtuous behaviour. They also held that in the divine rational teleological structure of the universe, lower elements were for the sake of higher; so while human rationality was subordinate to the divine reason of God, irrational animals were subordinated to and created for humans.[5] Thus animal irrationality was a serious tool of exposition in arguments relating to psychology, morality and theology.

The Stoics had plenty of opponents, of course, and the philosophical arguments rolled on and on, as we see from Sextus Empiricus, *Outlines of Pyrrhonism* 1.62–77, for example. Much of the ammunition came from instances of animal behaviour claimed to reveal not only intelligence, but also the other main moral virtues: courage, self-control and justice. These examples derived from two sources. One comprised the important zoological observations and investigations of the early Peripatetics, most of all Aristotle's works on natural history, like *Historia Animalium*. To this one could add later works which were much used, such as Sostratus of Alexandria (second half of the first century BC) on insects, snakes and the like, and Alexander of Myndos (in Caria, perhaps first half of the first century AD) on birds. Distinguishable from this were collections of marvellous or remarkable stories like the *Mirabilia* by Antigonus of Carystus (mid third century BC) and the Pseudo-Aristotelian *Mirabilia*. These two classes were by no means clearly distinct from the start, as we can see from Book 9 of Aristotle's *Historia Animalium*, and as time went on merged happily in collections like Pliny's *Naturalis Historia* Books 8–11, and Aelian, *De Natura Animalium*. Any writing on the subject helped itself indiscriminately.

Finally, since the topic was so popular and apparently inexhaustible, the schools of rhetoric used it as a stock theme for debates. We know that from Plutarch himself, in another essay on the same subject, *Are Land or Sea Animals More Intelligent?*, whose literary presentation sets up a formal debate between two of Plutarch's young men in his 'school' in Chaeronea for subsequent adjudication (959C ff.). This essay also demonstrates clearly that Plutarch was not only well aware of the background sketched above, but steeped in it through his reading much more than we can be with our truncated tradition, and also was prepared to use it in and for his arguments. The first seven sections (959B–965B) are occupied by an attack on the Stoa. He follows that with a vast wealth of instances of animal behaviour showing intelligent

moral and social action, much of which can be paralleled elsewhere as stock examples. Indeed he refers to the tomes of
Aristotle on the subject (959D), as well as to the storytellers (*hoi
mythologoi*, 968F).

Another roughly contemporary essay on the theme by Philo
of Alexandria, entitled *On Whether Irrational Animals Possess
Reason*, makes an illuminating comparison. Philo's piece survives
only in a sixth-century Armenian translation,[6] but the original was
written probably about the middle of the first century AD. It
starts as a dialogue between Philo and a young relative, Lysimachus. Then, rather in the form of Plato's *Phaedrus*, they read out
a supposed set speech from Alexander (Philo's nephew, Tiberius
Julius Alexander) advocating the case that 'irrational' animals
have reason, which in turn is discussed, criticized and refuted by
Philo. All the features outlined above are central to the presentation. There is a rhetorical atmosphere in the setting, the zoological
stock instances are plentifully supplied and the philosophical issues
seriously pursued. Alexander not only argues rationality, but also
dutifully proceeds through the four cardinal virtues allegedly
displayed by animal behaviour (§§30–65). Philo finally rejects rationality in animals mainly because it conflicts with his theological
views.

Now, when we return to our Plutarchan essay, it is not difficult
to point out superficial comparisons with the tradition. With
Philo's essay alone the following references can, and have been
made (Plutarchan reference first, followed by Philonic section):
986F–992E/§30; 987C–988E/§53; 988E/§100; 988F–991D/§§48 f;
991A/§66; 991B/§70; 991B–D/§§47, 62; 991E–F/§§38, 77 f.;
992A–B/§23; 992B/§27; 992C–E/§31; 992D/§78; 992E/§§85, 100.

It is no surprise either that the comparatively few stock instances of animal lore cited by the learned Grunter are among
the most widespread in the literature. So tortoises and marjoram
(991E) are instanced in Aristotle, *Historia Animalium* 612a24;
Antigonus, *Mirabilia* 40; Pseudo-Aristotle, *Mirabilia* 831a27;
Pliny, 8.41; Aelian, *De Natura Animalium* 6.12; Nicander, *Theriaca*
626; Plutarch himself again 974B. Cretan goats curing arrow
wounds by eating dittany (991F) are well known from Aristotle
*HA* 612a3; Theophrastus, *Historia Plantarum* 9.16; Antigonus 30;

Ps.-Aristotle 830b20; Philo, §38; Aelian, *Varia Historia* 1.10; Virgil, *Aeneid* 12.415. Or again, the partridge story of parents teaching their young camouflage (992B) surfaces in Antigonus 39; Pliny 10.103; Philo §35; Aelian, *NA* 3.16, 11.38.

And without doubt the essay is aware of the philosophical background. There is even, I believe, a covert allusion to Plato's *Laches* (987F, see p. 388, n. 1), while in general not only the topic of rationality, but also that of the virtues (courage, self-control) in animal behaviour are developed. But all that said, our essay is not in the least like that of Philo, nor indeed like Plutarch's other essay, *Are Land or Sea Animals More Intelligent?* The latter is a serious essay developing philosophical argument and zoological example within the tradition, and marked by personal feeling in Plutarch's own strongly held humane attitude with regard to our conduct towards animals. Our essay, on the contrary, tends to turn the tradition on its head. It is not at all serious. There is a good deal of leg-pulling going on and irreverent topsy-turvy, for the sheer intoxicating wicked fun of it.

Nothing indeed is sacred, certainly not our Homeric hero Odysseus, whose intelligence and moral motives are discredited from the start. Circe sees through him: his plea for his comrades does not spring from bravery or humanity but from self-seeking ambition and concern for his reputation (985E). His present behaviour also reveals his stupidity, since he is rejecting immortality with her for life with an ageing crone of a wife at home, should he ever reach it (985F). That is hardly a rational decision. Our intelligent pig, Grunter, has the same low opinion of him. Odysseus' rejection of Circe is due to cowardice, being frightened of change (986D). And it is quite illogical of him to throw away the natural abundance of Circe's magic island for the unremitting toil of scraping a living from barren Ithaca (986F–987A).

This leads cleverly into a main theme, the distinction between the bounty of natural advantages and the dangers of acquired skills. It can be applied also to the mind and to moral virtue. And here Plutarch *accepts* the philosophical distinction between animal behaviour as spontaneous, instinctive and natural, and the painfully acquired rationality of humans; but he uses the distinction against the normal philosophical arguments for animal irrationality, by praising the former as reasonable and virtuous and condemning the latter as stupid and corruptive. So he turns from the stereotyped defence of animal behaviour, with all its stock examples, to an attack on human rationality as by no means a good thing.

So Grunter turns on Odysseus *ad hominem*, one of the bravest and most sharp-witted of men. What is 'rational' human courage but discrimination between fearful alternatives, in other words, calculated cowardice (§4, 987C ff.)? But animals are simply brave by nature, with a natural and honest passion shown equally in males and females (not like Penelope sitting at home by the fire while Odysseus does the fighting). Human courage is passion diluted by rationality. As for the virtue of self-control (continuing *ad hominem* and *ad bestiam*), Odysseus need not pride himself on resisting Circe; a sacred goat from Mendes turned up its snout at a whole bevy of beautiful women and his precious Penelope turns out to be nine times less restrained than a crow (§5, 988F ff.) It need hardly be said that while the examples may be stock, the outrageous comparisons which form their contexts are not.

Grunter now reinforces his position with more perverse plunder from the philosophers to be used as rotten eggs to pelt them with. He trots out an Epicurean classification of desire into desires which are natural and necessary, and desires which are neither natural nor necessary but acquired. By again accepting that animals are restricted to necessary and instinctive desires, he argues that they are more self-restrained, that is, virtuous, precisely *because* they are so restricted, while humans are the slaves of alien desires which corrupt and deprave (§6, 989B ff.). So Grunter, thankfully now in his bestial mind, recognizes his vicious former human envy of Odysseus' unnecessarily extravagant finery (the examples are, of course, Homeric, not zoological). What folly, compared to his present natural contentment with his nice, soft, squelchy patch of mud!

Or take the sense of smell, for example (§7, 990A ff.): for animals it is a natural and necessary tool for food discrimination. But human intellectual ingenuity has created a whole industry of perfumery which panders to vicious lust and sex. Animals instinctively follow the natural rational laws of sex; human mentality contrives sexual perversity. (Plutarch produces local Boeotian examples of his own (990D–E), suitably diffracted.) Eating is the object of a natural and necessary desire which produces in animals a practical, sensible and defined diet. But human indulgence and skills have led them to the obscenity of omnivoracity, and to kill unnecessarily for it (§8, 991B ff.). So intelligence in animals is natural, direct and self-sufficient; human reason is acquired, specialized and so dependent on others, and immorally distracting (§9, 991D ff.).

Plutarch's pig-philosophy then is not at all like Plato's famous Pig City, or the first basic 'city' of the *Republic* (see 372d4), formed from the fundamental economic principle of simple division of labour. But it may be reminiscent of it, for it is a hilariously ingenious logical development, wickedly presented, of the initial basic hypothesis of much Hellenistic philosophy, that nature, the natural norm, natural affinity (*oikeiotes, oikeiosis*) is a key to morality. But in that case, argues Grunter, our pig-philosopher, animal mentality is more natural, direct and more purely in tune with the rational laws of our world than human rationality, which, far from leading to moral behaviour, seduces its possessors by its acquired ingenuities to moral excesses and depravities. It leads in fact to vice.

Now it need hardly be said that Plutarch himself did not believe a word of this looking-glass world which he had conjured up. And he still has one last trick to play. The essay ends abruptly, and some[7] are convinced that its final pages have been lost; for Plutarch has not completed the catalogue of the four virtues: justice remains absent from our version. But this essay is not fashioned by the traditional framework. It is not Philo, nor for that matter Plutarch's other essay, *Are Land or Sea Animals More Intelligent?* The formal framework of our essay is Odysseus, and it ends by terminating him with a final knockout. Odysseus, with difficulty getting a word in edgeways, opines that animals cannot be rational since they have no concept of God (992E). Where then, retorts the quick-witted Grunter, does that leave him, the son of Sisyphus, the notorious atheist? Collapse of rational party. The *Odyssey* story is reversed. Pigs refuse humanization. Pig, indeed, floors Odysseus, the great hero, the clever resourceful commander, the favourite of Athena; a Boeotian pig,[8] if it comes to that, from the backwoods of Chaeronea – this is Plutarch's final tongue-in-cheek dig at his Athenian friends.

Plutarch certainly enjoyed writing this essay. It has been thought to be a youthful *jeu d'esprit*, but I doubt it. Stylometry suggests a more mature period,[9] and so does the command and confidence of its composition.

1. E.g. Long and Sedley, *The Hellenistic Philosophers* 1.419 ff.
2. Seneca, *De Ira* 1.3.4.
3. Probably generally within the Stoa, although M. Pohlenz, 'Tierische und menschliche Intelligenz bei Poseidonios', *Hermes* 76 (1941), pp. 1 ff., based on Seneca, *Letter* 121, Nemesius, *De Natura Hominis*, p. 121 Matth., and Origen, *Contra Celsum* 4.86 f., attributed it to Posidonius.
4. Posidonius F159 EK, and see Kidd, *Commentary*, *ad loc.*
5. *SVF.* 2.1152–67; Plutarch, on *Stoic Self-contradictions* 1044C–D.
6. Conveniently translated and edited by Abraham Terian, *Philonis Alexandrini De Animalibus*, California, 1981.
7. E.g. Ziegler, *Plutarchos*, col. 104.
8. The Athenian taunt on the bucolic Boeotians: Pindar (another sufferer), *Olympian Odes* 6.90; Plutarch, *Advice on Public Life* 803D; *Life of Demosthenes* 11.5: 'A sow teach Athena!'
9. F. H. Sandbach, 'Rhythm and Authenticity in Plutarch's *Moralia*', *Classical Quarterly* 33 (1939), p. 196.

# ON THE USE OF REASON BY
## 'IRRATIONAL' ANIMALS

─────────

[1] ODYSSEUS: I think I've understood what you're saying,
Circe,[1] and I'll bear it in mind. But please could you tell me
whether there are any Greeks among the people you've turned
into wolves and lions?

CIRCE: Oh yes, a lot, my darling Odysseus. But why do you
want to know?

ODYSSEUS: To tell you the truth, because of the superb prestige I
think I would gain among the Greeks if – with your kind
permission – I got hold of fellow Greeks and restored them to
their former humanity, and didn't connive at their growing old
in an unnatural fashion, in the bodies of animals, with such a
wretched, degrading way of life.

CIRCE: Listen to the man! He thinks his own ambition, guided
by stupidity, should lead not just himself and his friends, but
even total strangers to disaster.

ODYSSEUS: This is yet another of your potions, Circe. This time
it's a verbal potion you're stirring and brewing up, and you're
definitely trying to turn me into an animal now, by getting me
to believe that it is disastrous for someone to change from an
animal to a human being.

CIRCE: Haven't you already done weirder things to yourself than
that? You rejected a life free of death and ageing, with me as
your partner, and you are impatient to set out, despite the countless torments you'll face, for a woman who is mortal and, as I
keep telling you, getting on in age by now.[2] And why? So that

1. See the Introduction, p. 375, for the dramatis personae and the setting.
2. His wife Penelope, fending off her suitors, the local nobles, in Ithaca for some
   twenty years while Odysseus took part in the Trojan War and then tried to
   find his way home again.

986A    you will become even more admired and famous than you already are, which is to chase superficial happiness and an illusion, not the real thing.

ODYSSEUS: Have it your own way, Circe. Why do we constantly have to argue about the same things? Please, as a favour to me, set the men free and hand them over.

CIRCE: It's not that simple, by Hecate:[1] they are special. Why don't you first ask them whether they want to be set free? And if they say no, my friend, you'll have to enter into a discussion with them and win them over. And if you fail to win them over, but instead they get the better of you in the discussion, then that should prove to you that your plans for yourself and your friends were ill-considered.

B    ODYSSEUS: Is this some kind of joke at my expense, Circe? How can they be at the giving or receiving end of a rational argument as long as they are donkeys, pigs and lions?

CIRCE: Don't despair, my ambitious friend. I'll make sure they can both understand and conduct a rational argument. Actually, one of them will be all you need to carry on a discussion with, and he can represent them all. Here you are – you can have your discussion with this one.

ODYSSEUS: What shall I call him, Circe? Who was he when he was human?[2]

CIRCE: What relevance does that have? Call him Gryllus, if you like.[3] I'll leave you both to it, in case he gives the impression of saying things he doesn't agree with just to please me.

C    [2] GRYLLUS: Hello, Odysseus.

ODYSSEUS: And hello to you, Gryllus, to be sure.

GRYLLUS: What do you want to ask?

ODYSSEUS: I realize that all of you were formerly human, and I'm sorry that you're in this state, but naturally I feel more for those of you who were Greeks and have got into this mess. So I've just been pleading with Circe to set you free, restore you

1. The appropriate goddess to swear by, as she was associated with sorcery and black magic.
2. A witty adaptation to the context of the formal Homeric greeting 'Who among men are you?'
3. Gryllus was not unknown as a human name – it was common in Xenophon's family, for instance – but it could also mean 'Grunter' or 'Pig'.

to your original form and let you accompany me on my journey, if any of you want to do all this.

GRYLLUS: Stop right there, Odysseus! Even you are not impressing any of us! You have a reputation for cleverness, and you're supposed to stand head and shoulders above everyone else intelligence-wise, but that turns out to be nonsense, because out of sheer prejudice, you're scared – and what you're scared of is people changing from a worse state to a better one. Just as children are afraid of doctors' medicines, which alter them by making them healthy instead of ill, and avoid their lessons, which alter them by making them knowledgeable instead of ignorant, so you too have retired in the face of becoming one thing instead of another. And here you are, living with Circe in dread and terror, in case she sneaks up on you and turns you into a pig or a wolf, and you're trying to persuade us, whose lives are filled with countless advantages, to leave them behind, and at the same time to desert the woman who keeps us supplied with them, and to sail away with you after having changed back to human beings, when there is no creature worse off than a human being.

ODYSSEUS: Gryllus, I think that the potion you took has made you lose your mind as well as your body; I think your head is full of bizarre and utterly perverted thoughts. Or alternatively, it wasn't a potion that bewitched you into this new body of yours, but your enjoyment of what was familiar to you!*[1]

GRYLLUS: Wrong on both counts, Cephallenian king.[2] And if you've no objection to talking rather than being rude, it won't take us long – because we've experienced both lives – to persuade you that we are right to prefer our present life to our former one.

ODYSSEUS: I'm all ears.

[3] GRYLLUS: And we're just as eager to explain. Let's start with the virtues, which you humans obviously pride yourselves on:

---

1. Odysseus is suggesting that swinishness was already familiar to Gryllus.
2. A formal title of Odysseus and his family (Homer, *Iliad* 2.631; *Odyssey* 24.378), since they ruled over the island of Cephallenia which lay next to Ithaca. There it is probably also a pun from the Greek for head (*kephalē*) where the brains (*enkephalos*) were, with which Odysseus was supposed to be so well endowed.

you consider yourselves vastly superior to animals in morality, intelligence, courage and all the other virtues. Now, you're really clever, Odysseus, so answer this question of mine. You see, I once overheard you telling Circe about the Cyclopes' land and how it is never ploughed and never sown at all,[1] but is such good and innately generous land that it spontaneously yields 987A produce of every kind. So my question is: which do you prefer, the Cyclopes' land or harsh Ithaca, which supports only goats[2] and which grudgingly gives its farmers a return on their considerable efforts and hard labour, a return that is small in quantity, poor in quality and of no value? And please make sure that you don't take offence and out of patriotic affection give us an answer which actually contradicts your opinion.

ODYSSEUS: There's no need for me to dissemble. Although my own native land occupies a higher place in my heart and my affection, my acclaim and admiration go to the Cyclopes' land.

GRYLLUS: So we'll say that this is how it is: the most intelligent man in the world expects to value and appreciate different things B from those he is drawn to and loves. And I assume that your answer is also relevant to the mind, given that the same goes for it as for the land: the better mind is that which produces its spontaneous crop, so to speak, of virtue without involving hard work.

ODYSSEUS: I grant you that assumption as well.

GRYLLUS: Well, you're now admitting that the animal mind is better equipped by nature for the production of virtue, and is more perfect. I mean, without being instructed or schooled – without being sown or ploughed, as it were – it naturally produces and grows whatever kind of virtue is appropriate to a given creature.

ODYSSEUS: Virtue in animals, Gryllus?[3]

[4] GRYLLUS: Yes, virtue of every kind, more than you'd find C in the greatest human sage. Let's start with courage, if you like, which is a particular source of pride to you: you scarcely shrink

1. Homer, *Odyssey* 9.105 ff.
2. Plutarch uses stock epithets of Ithaca from *Odyssey* 4.606, 13.242 ff.
3. See the Introduction, pp. 376–7, for the philosophical background to this question.

at being described as 'daring' and as 'a leveller of cities'[1] – and you are the rogue whose tricks and subterfuges corrupted people when the only fighting method they knew was straightforward and guileless and they had no experience of deceit and lies. And then you glorify this iniquity with the name of the virtue which of all the virtues admits iniquity least. You can see, however, that when animals fight with one another or with you humans, they do not employ tricks and stratagems: they rely in their battles on blatant, bare bravery backed up by genuine prowess. They don't need an edict to be passed to summon them to battle, and they don't fight because they're afraid of being court-martialled for desertion: they see the fight through to the bitter end and refuse to give in because they instinctively loathe defeat. I mean, they don't give in and mentally admit defeat even when they are being physically defeated, but instead they fight on until they die. And often, when an animal is being killed, its bravery and passion[2] recede to a particular location, gather at a single part of its body, and resist the killer by jerking and writhing, until the spark is altogether extinguished and the creature is no more.

You don't find animals begging or pleading for mercy or admitting defeat. Cowardice never led a lion to become enslaved to another lion, or a horse to another horse, as it does human beings, who readily welcome the condition which is named after cowardice.[3] Suppose humans trap or trick animals into captivity: if the animals are mature, they reject food, resist thirst and choose to bring about and embrace death rather than accept enslavement. On the other hand, if they are fledglings and cubs, whose age makes them amenable and submissive, then people feed them and drug them with all kinds of treacherous and tempting scraps and sops, give them a taste for unnatural pleasures and an unnatural way of life, and eventually sap their vitality,

1. Used as an epithet of Odysseus in *Iliad* 2.278.
2. Plutarch uses the word (*to thymoeides*) which in Plato's psychological analysis represented the 'good' passion of righteous anger which made you stand up for yourself, and was especially associated with courage.
3. Somewhat implausibly, Gryllus associates *deilia* (cowardice) with *douleia* (slavery).

F   until the animals accept and submit to what is called 'domestica-
tion', which is another way to say emasculation of passion.

So there can be absolutely no doubt that animals are naturally inclined towards boldness. On the other hand, lack of inhibition is actually unnatural for human beings – and the clearest
proof of this, my dear Odysseus, is as follows. Where animals are
concerned, nature keeps the scales of courage evenly balanced: a
female animal works for the necessities of life and fights for her
offspring no less than a male one. I'm sure you're aware of the
988A   Crommyonian sow,[1] which gave Theseus a great deal of trouble,
despite being a female animal. And that Sphinx[2] would have got
nowhere with her cleverness, sitting up there on Mount Phicium
weaving riddles and conundrums, if her strength and courage
hadn't enabled her clearly to dominate the Thebans. In more or
less the same part of the world there was also the Teumessian
vixen, 'a crafty creature',[3] and near by was the legendary snake
which fought Apollo in single combat for the oracular seat at
Delphi.[4] The king of you humans let the Sicyonian give him
Aethe as payment for being released from military service,[5]
which was an excellent piece of thinking, since he saw that a
good, spirited mare was preferable to a cowardly man. You
yourself have often seen how leopardesses and lionesses keep up
B   with their male counterparts where passion and courage are
concerned.

1. A legendary beast which terrorized part of Attica until it was killed by
   Theseus (cf. *Life of Theseus* 9). Plutarch probably has in mind here Plato's
   *Laches* 196e1–197c1, where Nicias will not call even the Crommyonian sow
   brave, because animals are irrational, but certainly bold (*thrasys*), the word
   chosen by Plutarch a few lines above.
2. A female monster with the body of a lion, wings and a woman's face. She
   killed any Theban who could not solve her riddle. When Oedipus did so, she
   killed herself in disgust.
3. Teumessus was near Thebes, to the east. Pausanias (9.19.1) records the local
   legend of the vixen and her terrorization of the people of Thebes. The source
   of the snatch of quotation is unknown, but a similar phrase occurs in Oppian,
   *Cynegetica* 1.490.
4. The Pythoness which guarded Delphi and was killed by Apollo (*Homeric
   Hymn to Pythian Apollo* 300 ff.; Plutarch, *Greek Questions* 293C, *On the Obsolescence of Oracles* 421C).
5. Echepolus of Sicyon presented King Agamemnon – the leader of the Greek
   forces at Troy – with his fine racing mare Aethe to escape accompanying him
   to the Trojan War (Homer, *Iliad* 23.293 ff.).

But your wife is quite different.★ While you are away fighting, she sits at home by the fireplace, doing even less than a swallow would to defend herself and her home against invaders.[1] And she is a Spartan.[2] So what conceivable point is there in me going on to talk about Carian or Maeonian women?[3]

All this demonstrates that manliness is not a natural human male attribute:[4] if it were, then women would be just as brave. Your courageous behaviour is due to pressure from your laws, and this pressure has no free will or freedom of choice, but is a slave to convention and criticism and is formed by others' beliefs and arguments.[5] You don't endure hard work and danger because   C you face them with courage, but because you're more afraid of their alternative. Any of your fellow voyagers who beats the others and boards first grabs a place at the light oar, not because he thinks it insignificant, but because he's afraid of the heavier one and tries to avoid it; in the same way, anyone who endures a beating to avoid being wounded, or fights an opponent in preference to being tortured or killed, is not being brave in respect of the former alternatives, but is being cowardly in respect of the latter alternatives.

So it turns out that your courage is actually calculating cowardice, and your bravery is fear plus knowing how to use some things to avoid other things.[6] In short, if you think that you humans are superior to animals where courage is concerned, then   D

1. For the comparison, see Plato, *Laws* 814b.
2. Gryllus is quite good at genealogy. Penelope was in mythology the daughter of Icarius of Lacedaemon, and niece of Tyndareus, king of Lacedaemon, and so a cousin of Helen. Spartan girls did physical training, and were believed to be more independent, courageous and self-assertive than women in other parts of Greece.
3. Men from countries in Asia Minor like Caria, Lydia and Maeonia were considered to be somewhat effeminate; by the same token, their women must be correspondingly more effete than other women. Gryllus is naturally talking within the context of the Homeric Trojan War: the Carians and Maeonians supplied contingents in support of Troy (*Iliad* 2.864 ff.), and one of the Carian leaders came to the war dressed in finery like a girl.
4. The pun (the word translated 'manliness' was a standard word for 'courage') is Plutarchan; the sentiment Epicurean (Diogenes Laertius 10.120).
5. The same line of argument is found in Aelian, *De Natura Animalium* 6.1 (second to third centuries AD).
6. A rationale of most human courage offered by Plato in *Phaedo* 68d.

why do your poets use as epithets for the best fighters 'wolf-spirited', 'lion-hearted' and 'of boar-like bravery'?[1] Why do none of them describe a lion as 'human-hearted' or a boar as 'of man-like bravery'? What they're doing, in my opinion, is using a simile for exaggeration: they are comparing skilful fighters with their superiors, by exactly the same device as when they call fast runners 'wind-footed' and good-looking people 'godlike'.[2] And the reason is that passion is what gives courage its strength and its edge,[3] so to speak, and animals draw on pure passion in their fights, whereas for you humans it is diluted with rationality, as wine is diluted by water, and consequently it metamorphoses in the face of danger and misses opportunities. Some of you even claim that you ought not to make use of passion at all when fighting, but should dispense with it and rely on sober reason; this is correct, if security and self-preservation are your concerns, but is an utterly despicable thing to say if courage and standing ground are your concerns. I mean, don't you think it's illogical of you humans to blame nature for failing to fit your bodies out with stings or tusks or talons, while you yourselves do away with and repress your mind's innate weapon?

[5] ODYSSEUS: Incredible, Gryllus. I think in the past you were a formidable debater, because even now, as a pig, you have set about addressing your hypothesis in such a vigorous fashion. But why haven't you gone on to discuss self-restraint?

GRYLLUS: Because I assumed that you'd attack what I've been saying first. But you're in a hurry to hear about self-restraint because you're the husband of a wife who is a model of self-restraint, and because you fancy that you yourself have been demonstrating self-restraint in spurning Circe's sexual advances. But this doesn't make you any better than animals where self-discipline is concerned: they too have no desire to mate with their betters, but they take their pleasure and have sex with

---

1. The first epithet occurs only as a proper name, Lycophron, in Homer; the others are Homeric epithets (e.g. *Iliad* 5.639 for the second and 4.253 for the third).

2. As in *Iliad* 2.786, 3.16.

3. So Cicero, *Tusculanae Disputationes* 4.43, of the Peripatetics. See the Introduction to *On the Avoidance of Anger*, pp. 171–3.

members of the same species. So your behaviour is not surprising. There's a story that in Egypt a goat from Mendes was once shut up with a lot of beautiful women and showed no inclination to mate with them,[1] but was more aroused when faced with she-goats; in the same way, you are happy with familiar sexual activity and, as a human being, are reluctant to sleep with a goddess. As for Penelope's self-restraint, countless cackling crows will heap laughter and scorn on it, because any crow which loses her mate lives alone not just for a short while, but for nine human generations.[2] So your beautiful Penelope's self-restraint is nine times less than that of any female crow in the world.

[6] Now, you've noticed that I'm a professional debater, so bear with me while I organize my argument by defining self-restraint and distinguishing several categories of desire.[3] Self-restraint, then, is a restriction and an ordering of desires by eliminating those which are extraneous and unnecessary, and by imposing order – in terms of timeliness and degree – on those which are necessary. I'm sure that the huge differences between various types of desire are obvious to you: ⟨on the one hand, there are the desires for food and⟩ drink which are not only instinctive but also necessary;* on the other hand, sexual desires may be basically instinctive, but even if one abstains, one is in a sense all right without them, and so they have been called instinctive, but not necessary.

As for the category of desires which are neither necessary nor instinctive, but which flood in from outside on a wave of illusion thanks to coarseness – well, you humans have so many of these

1. The usual story about the goats of Mendes (which were especially venerated there) was precisely the opposite: Pindar F201 Maehler; Herodotus 2.46.4; Strabo 17.1.19. This must have been an extraordinary case when the goat in the ritual showed no interest in the women offered.

2. This lengthy celibacy after the death of a mate was also noted by Aelian, *De Natura Animalium* 3.9. The 'nine human generations' comes from Hesiod (F304 Merkelbach and West), quoted by Plutarch in *On the Obsolescence of Oracles* 415C. Aristophanes, *Birds* 609, gives five generations, possibly to save the metre. The longevity of the crow was proverbial (D'Arcy Thompson, *Glossary of Greek Birds*, p. 169), and still is in Greece today.

3. Gryllus' classification of desire is basically Epicurean; cf. Cicero, *Tusculanae Disputationes* 5.93 (and other texts collected by Usener under Epicurus F456). Plutarch used it again in *On Socrates' Personal Deity* 584D ff.; see the Introduction to that essay, pp. 303–4.

desires that they have almost obliterated every single one of the natural desires, and the situation reminds one of a mass of visitors from foreign lands joining the populace and suppressing the native citizens of a country. Animals, on the other hand, have minds which are completely inaccessible to and unapproachable by alien feelings and lifestyles: like colonists who have settled far from the sea, they are out of illusion's reach.[1] They keep their distance from* elegance and extravagance in their way of life,

D   and assiduously protect their self-restraint and their better self-government by restricting the number of the desires which live with them and by forbidding entry to extraneous ones.

I too, I must admit, was once just as impressed by gold as you; I thought it was an asset which was infinitely superior to all other assets. Silver and ivory ensnared me as well. I thought that anyone who owned a great deal of these things was a happy man, high in the gods' favour, whether he was a Phrygian or a Carian of meaner birth than Dolon or worse off than Priam.[2] In this situation, because I was constantly dependent on my desires, I used to gain no pleasure or satisfaction from all the rest of my property, despite the fact that I had plenty of it and enough for

E   my needs. I found my life unsatisfactory because, as I thought, I lacked and was missing out on the most important things and was short on advantages. That was why when I saw you in Crete, as I recall, dressed in striking clothes, I didn't envy your intelligence or your virtue, but it was the delicacy of your amazingly worked tunic and the close texture and beauty of your purple cloak that I prized and admired. Even the clasp, which was golden, had some trumpery finely engraved on it, I think.[3] I was entranced, in a womanly fashion, and I became your follower. Now, however, I am free and clear of these illusions. I

F   have just as little interest in and time for gold and silver as I do for any other stone. And rather than your clothes and rugs, as

1. Fears concerning the material and moral dangers of maritime cities (e.g. Plato, *Laws* 704d ff.; Cicero, *De Re Publica* 2.5 ff.) were widespread enough to draw a defence from Aristotle in *Politics* 1327a11 ff.

2. The story of the cowardly Trojan spy Dolon is told in *Iliad* 10; for the tragedy of Priam, king of Troy, see *Iliad* 22.59 ff. and 24.486 ff.

3. Gryllus is remembering *Odyssey* 19.225–35.

Zeus is my witness there's nothing I would more gladly lie down on and relax on when my stomach's full than deep, soft mud. None of those extraneous desires inhabit our minds: instead, our life is chiefly governed by the necessary desires and pleasures, and we get involved with those which are only instinctive, but not necessary, in a way which is neither unruly nor excessive.

[7] We ought first to have before us a thorough description of these pleasures. Our pleasure in sweetly scented things, whose effluences are congruent with our sense of smell and stimulate it, is not only wholesome, free and uncontrived, but also makes a useful contribution by enabling us to judge the quality of food. The tongue is deservedly said to be the arbiter of sweetness, bitterness and sourness when flavours come into contact with the part that is sensitive to taste and somehow fuse with it; but as an arbiter of anything's attributes, our sense of smell works before flavour has been formed and is a far more discerning judge than kings' tasters.[1] It lets in anything congruent, but rejects anything alien and stops it making contact with or hurting our sense of taste: it lodges information about and denounces its badness before any harm is done.

990A

B

Moreover, it is no trouble to us, as it is to you. It forces you to gather together from all over the place and make a compound of incenses and cinnamon, spikenards and leaves and Arabian reeds,[2] and to enlist the formidable skill of a tincture-making alchemist or a potion-brewing witch, with their art called perfumery, so that you can spend a lot of money buying an unmanly, effeminate luxury which serves no practical purpose whatsoever. And despite the unmanly nature of this luxury, it has corrupted not just every single human woman, but most men as well by now, with the

---

1. Fearful kings and dictators appointed a taster to sample all food for poison before the king ate it. Athenaeus 171 B ff. discusses the practice.
2. See R. J. Forbes, *Studies in Ancient Technology* III, pp. 30 ff., on the vast and lucrative perfume trade from the East, known from Herodotus (3.107 ff.) onwards; the individual plants and ingredients are documented by authors such as Theophrastus (*Historia Plantarum* and *De Causis Plantarum*) and Pliny (*Naturalis Historia* 12–13). Cinnamon and spikenard mostly came from India; Arabian reeds were probably the aromatic sweet flag (Theophrastus, *HP* 9.7.1; Pliny 12.104 f.); the 'leaves' may have been malobathrum (Pliny 12.129), or the leaf of *Cinnamomum tamala*.

result that you even refuse to have sex with your own wives
C  unless they come to you smelling of perfume and scented powder.
On the other hand,[1] sows attract boars, she-goats attract he-goats,
and the females of all other species attract their mates by means
of their own particular scents; smelling of pure dew, of meadows
and new shoots, the couples are mutually drawn towards union
by shared affection. The females don't dissemble and disguise
their desire with lies and tricks and refusals, and the males aren't
led by lust and frenzy to buy the act of procreation with money
and work and service. At the appropriate time they pursue a
course of love which is untainted by deceit and finance, and
which in springtime awakens creatures' desire as it does the buds
D  of plants, and then extinguishes it without delay. The female
stops allowing penetration after she has been impregnated, and
the male stops attempting it. That is how little and how slightly
we animals value pleasure; for us, nature is all that counts.

This explains why, so far, animals' desires have not resulted in
sex between males or between females. This kind of thing, however, is rife among your upper classes and aristocrats, let alone
among worthless humans.[2] Agamemnon came to Boeotia with
Argynnus as his fugitive quarry and made false accusations against
the sea and the winds; then he gave his good self a good bath in
E  Lake Copais so as to quench the fire of his passion and free
himself there and then of his desire.[3] Similarly, Heracles went in
search of a young companion of his, and so got left behind by
the heroes and deserted the expedition.[4] On the vault of the

1. Plutarch used a description of animal behaviour similar to what follows in On
   Love of Offspring 493E–F.
2. Classical Greek society condoned homosexuality between an adult male and
   an adolescent boy; see K. J. Dover, Greek Homosexuality.
3. The beautiful Boeotian boy Argynnus drowned in the river Cephissus which
   debouches into Lake Copais in Boeotia. Agamemnon in grief buried him and
   erected a shrine to him. The story is told in Athenaeus 603D (in a long list of
   such liaisons), and in Propertius 3.7.21 ff. Gryllus claims that this love affair
   delayed the Trojan expedition until the storms blew up which were then
   blamed for the delay.
4. At Mysia, during the voyage of the Argonauts, Hylas, sent to draw water, was
   grabbed by enraptured nymphs; the distraught Heracles, in attempting to find
   him, missed the boat. This was a very famous story: Theocritus 13; Apollonius
   of Rhodes, Argonautica 1.1207 ff.; Propertius 1.20; Apollodorus 1.9.19.

temple of Apollo on Mount Ptoön one of your men secretly inscribed the words 'Achilles is handsome', although Achilles already had a son – and I am told that the graffito is still there.[1] However, if no hen is available and a cock mounts another cock, some soothsayer or augur asserts that this is an important and foreboding occurrence and the cock is burned alive. So even humans themselves admit that self-restraint is an attribute of animals more than it is of human beings and that animals sin less against nature in their pleasures.

Not even when she has convention on her side, however, can nature keep licentious behaviour among you humans within bounds. It is as though, thanks to your desires, your behaviour were in many respects carried away by a flood, so that, where your sexual activity is concerned, you do terrible violence to nature, and cause chaos and confusion in her. I mean, men have made sexual attempts on goats, pigs and horses, and women have been driven into a sexual frenzy by male animals. This is the kind of coupling that results in the birth of your Minotaurs and Aegipans and, I imagine, Sphinxes and Centaurs too.[2] It is true that starvation has now and again induced a dog to eat a human being, and necessity has led a bird to taste human flesh; but no animal has ever tried to use a human being for sexual purposes. But humans in pursuit of gratification treat animals violently and sinfully for this and for many other purposes.

[8] This is how rotten and undisciplined human beings are with respect to the desires I've been discussing; but they can be shown to be even worse where the necessary desires are concerned, and to fall far behind animals in self-restraint. These necessary desires are the desires for food and drink. Whereas we animals always combine our pleasure in food and drink with practicality, you humans pursue pleasure rather than naturalness in your sustenance. The consequence is that you are punished by a wide variety of serious illnesses which are all irrigated by a single wellspring – your excess – and fill you with all kinds of

1. It looks as if the graffito was still legible in Plutarch's time, to judge from Gryllus' amusingly anachronistic aside.
2. Mythical creatures of half-human, half-animal form – respectively bull, goat, lion, horse.

gases which cannot easily be purged.[1] The point is, primarily, that every species of creature has a single food which is specifically suitable for it – grass for some creatures, a certain root or fruit for others. Carnivores turn to no other type of nourishment and don't rob weaker creatures of their food: the lion lets the deer
C  feed in its natural way, as the wolf does the sheep.[2] Human beings, however, are so greedy that they are seduced by their hedonism into a wholesale approach: they sample everything, leave nothing untasted, as though they were still trying to discover what is proper to and congruent with them. The human creature is the only omnivorous creature there is.

The first point to notice is that it is not incapacity or incompetence that make him resort to flesh, since season by season there are such riches that it is always possible for him almost to exhaust himself by gathering and taking and picking various kinds of food from various plants and seeds. But prompted by pampered luxury and by over-indulgence in essential foods, he sets out in pursuit of nourishment which is inappropriate and which, since it involves killing creatures, is defiled, and he does so in a way which is far more savage than that of the wildest of animals. I
D  mean, blood and gore and flesh are the special victuals of kites, wolves and snakes, but for humans they are just a savoury.[3]

Secondly, in being omnivorous, man differs from the animals in that they refrain from most kinds of food and make war on only those few of their fellow creatures that are essential for their nourishment. But it is hardly an exaggeration to say that no creature, whether of the air or the waters or the land, has escaped your supposedly refined and hospitable tables.

[9] So anyway you treat these creatures as savouries with which to make your food more enjoyable. Why, therefore, ⟨if not because of your incon⟩tinence, ⟨have you gone to the trouble

---

1. Gases arising from undigested residues in the stomach was a theory of medical pathology ascribed to Hippocrates in the medical doxography originating from Menon in *Anonymus Londinensis* 5–7.

2. Until they eat them.

3. The same quip recurs in *On Eating Flesh* 994B, 995C; Plutarch may have advocated vegetarianism in his youth, and certainly advocated moderation in eating meat (*Advice on Health* 131E).

of inventing an art – that of the savoury-cook –⟩ which is dedicated to this purpose?* On the other hand, animals' intelligence refuses to accommodate any expertise which has no point or purpose; and it doesn't regard the necessary skills as matters to be imported from others, or as things to be taught for money, nor does it make practice a reason for cementing and joining fast   E a particular individual to a particular branch of study, but rather it generates the necessary skills on the spot, out of itself, as if they were native and natural products.[1] We are told that every Egyptian is a healer, and every animal is his own expert, not only in healing, but also in nutrition, in fighting, in hunting and guarding, and in music (depending on the extent to which each animal is naturally talented in music).

For example, who taught us pigs to go to rivers for crabs when we're ill?[2] Who told tortoises to eat marjoram if they've fed on snake?[3] Who told Cretan goats to look for dittany when they've been struck by arrows, after eating which the arrows fall   F out?[4] You see, if you reply with the truth – that nature is their teacher – then you're attributing animals' intelligence to the source of all authority and skill. And if you want to deny the name of reason or intelligence to what animals have, then it is time for you to try to find a more attractive and distinguished name for it, since there is no doubt that the faculty it constitutes is both practically better and more impressive than human intelligence. Ignorance and lack of information play no part in it:   992A rather, it is a self-taught and self-sufficient faculty. And this is not a sign of weakness, but it is because of the strength and perfection of its natural virtue that it does without any educational contribution that external agents might make to its intelligence.

At any rate, all those animals which are forced to undergo education and training by human beings (for reasons of affection or for sport) have more than enough understanding to apply

1. Compare Seneca, *Letter* 121.23, and see the Introduction, pp. 379 ff.
2. For the list of such examples, compare that in Pliny, *Naturalis Historia* 8.97 ff.
3. This occurred first in Aristotle, *Historia Animalium* 612a24, and then was often repeated (by Plutarch himself in *Are Land or Sea Animals More Intelligent?* 974B).
4. This common lore is also found in Aristotle, *Historia Animalium* 612a3, and used by Plutarch once more in *Are Land or Sea Animals More Intelligent?* 974D.

their minds to grasp their lessons even when they're being asked to do something physically unnatural for them. I won't go on about puppies being taught to follow tracks, foals to walk according to a rhythm, crows to talk and dogs to leap through spinning

B    hoops. Circus horses and cows learn, remember and perform without mistakes a series of prostrations, dances, dangerous poses and movements which are very difficult even for humans[1] – a display of pliancy which is absolutely useless for any other purpose.

In case you're not convinced that we can learn skills, then listen while I demonstrate that we can even teach them. For instance, hen partridges teach their chicks to avoid danger by concealing themselves – to lie on their backs and hold a lump of earth in front of themselves with their claws.[2] And consider storks: you can see them on the roofs, the mature ones in attendance instructing those which are tentatively starting to fly. Night-

C    ingales give singing lessons to their chicks, and those which are caught while they are still young and are brought up in captivity by humans don't sing very well, as they've been separated from their teacher too soon.[3] ⟨. . .⟩* Now that I'm inside this current body of mine, I'm unable to believe those arguments with which the professional debaters used to persuade me to regard every creature except man as irrational and unintelligent.[4]

[10] ODYSSEUS: So have you completely changed your mind, Gryllus? Do you claim that even sheep and donkeys are rational?

GRYLLUS: My dear Odysseus, these are exactly the ones to provide very strong evidence of the fact that animals' nature is not lacking in reason and understanding. A given tree is not more or

D    less mindless than any other tree: they are all equally unconscious, because none of them has a mind. Analogously, a given creature would not give the impression of being intellectually less alert and quick than any other creature, if they did not all have reason and understanding, but in varying degrees. You should realize that it is the cunning and sharpness of some animals which

1. Much the same, but for circus elephants, in 968B–C.
2. Also at 971C.
3. Again at 973B.
4. See the Introduction, pp. 376–7.

proves the stupidity and slowness of others, when you compare a fox or a wolf with a donkey or a sheep.\* It's no different from comparing Polyphemus with yourself, or that idiot Coroebus with your grandfather Autolycus. I mean, in fact I don't think there is as much difference between animals as there is between humans, in respect of intelligence, rationality and memory.

ODYSSEUS: But be careful, Gryllus. It might be an awful and outrageous thing to do, to allow reason to creatures which have no understanding of God.

GRYLLUS: In that case, Odysseus, are we to deny that you are the son of Sisyphus, given that you're so extraordinarily clever?[1]

1. This presents Odysseus with an awkward dilemma. It was claimed that Sisyphus, not Laertes, was Odysseus' real father (Plutarch himself in *Greek Questions* 301D). But Sisyphus was not only regarded in popular lore as the prince of tricksters, but as an atheist as well (Critias, *Sisyphus* F1 Nauck). So by Odysseus' own statement he could not have been a rational being – nor the father of one. Are we to regard this as a final knockout which leaves Odysseus speechless, or is the end of the essay lost? See the Introduction, p. 381.

# BIBLIOGRAPHY

There are three standard editions of Plutarch's *Moralia*; all three contribute to our understanding of the essays. The most convenient for English readers is the Loeb, now complete in fifteen volumes. The Greek text has a facing English translation. The later volumes, edited by such scholars as P. De Lacy, B. Einarson, H. Cherniss, W. Helmbold and F. H. Sandbach are particularly authoritative and informative in notes and introductions. The German Teubner edition, still in progress, is the basic edition for textual reporting and for cross-references both within Plutarch and to other authors. The French Budé edition, also incomplete, is of considerable value, especially in the more recently published volumes, for the introductions and supplementary notes. The first volume (Tome I¹, 1987) contains two long fundamental essays, on 'Plutarque dans ses "Oeuvres Morales"', by R. Flacelière, and on 'Histoire du Texte des "Oeuvres Morales" de Plutarque', by J. Irigoin. These three editions also publish standard volumes of the *Lives*.

The basic and essential work of detailed reference for Plutarch is the article by K. Ziegler, 'Plutarchos' in Pauly-Wissowa-Kroll, *Real-Encyclopädie der classischen Altertumswissenschaft (RE)*, 1951. This was published more conveniently as a separate monograph, *Plutarchos von Chaeroneia*, Stuttgart, 1949, and revised in 1964.

By far the best general introduction to Plutarch is: D. A. Russell, *Plutarch*, London, 1972.

The following small selection of works on and concerning Plutarch includes some older ones which have become classics, and range from general essays to detailed treatment:

Aulotte, R., *Amyot et Plutarque*, Geneva, 1965

Babut, D., *Plutarque et le Stoïcisme*, Paris, 1969

Barrow, R. H., *Plutarch and His Times*, London, 1967

Bowersock, G. W., *Greek Sophists in the Roman Empire*, Oxford, 1969

Bowie, E. L., 'Greeks and Their Past in the Second Sophistic', *Past and Present* 46 (1970), pp. 3 ff.

Brenk, F. E., *In Mist Apparelled: Religious Themes in Plutarch's Moralia and Lives*, Leiden, 1977

'An Imperial Heritage: The Religious Spirit of Plutarch of Chaeroneia', in *Aufstieg und Niedergang der römischen Welt [ANRW]*, II.36.1 (1987), pp. 248–349

Dihle, A., *Studien zur griechischen Biographie*, Göttingen, 1956

Dillon, J., *The Middle Platonists*, London, 1977

Dodds, E. R., 'The Portrait of a Greek Gentleman', *Greece and Rome*, 2 (1932/3), pp. 97 ff.

Fuhrmann, F., *Les Images de Plutarque*, Paris, 1964

Gill, C., 'Peace of Mind and Being Yourself: Panaetius to Plutarch', forthcoming, in *ANRW*

Gréard, O., *De la morale de Plutarque*, Paris, 1866

Helmbold, W. C., and O'Neil, E. N., *Plutarch's Quotations*, Baltimore, 1959

Hillyard, B. P., *Plutarch: De Audiendo*, New York, 1981

Hirzel, R., *Der Dialog*, Leipzig, 1895

    *Plutarchos*, Leipzig, 1912

Jones, C. P., 'Towards a Chronology of Plutarch's Works', *Journal of Roman Studies* 56 (1966), p. 61 ff.

    *Plutarch and Rome*, Oxford, 1971

Jones, R. M., *The Platonism of Plutarch*, Wisconsin, 1916

Kassel, R., *Untersuchungen zur griechischen und römischen Konsolationsliteratur*, Munich, 1958

Leo, F., *Die griechisch-römische Biographie nach ihrer literarischen Form*, Leipzig, 1901, p. 145 ff.

Long, A. A., *Hellenistic Philosophy*, London, 1974

Long, A. A., and Sedley, D. N., *The Hellenistic Philosophers*, vol. 1, Cambridge, 1987

Russell, D. A., 'On Reading Plutarch's *Moralia*', *Greece and Rome* 15 (1968), p. 130 ff.

Soury, G., *La Démonologie de Plutarque*, Paris, 1942

Stadter, P. A., *Plutarch's Historical Methods*, Cambridge, Mass., 1965

Theander, C., *Plutarch und die Geschichte*, Lund, 1951

Volkmann, R., *Leben, Schriften und Philosophie des Plutarch von Chaeronea*, Berlin, 1869

# TEXTUAL APPENDIX

We read the Greek text printed in the Loeb editions of Plutarch's *Moralia*, except at the following places, which have been marked in the translations by an asterisk.

40A: Reading ἐμμανεῖς, Wilamowitz.

41F: Reading ἐπιλέγουσαι, Wilamowitz.

44B: Reading τὸ φρονεῖν after καταφρονεῖν, Paton.

44B: Reading ἀπειρίας, Xylander.

44C: Reading ἐξανιστάμενος, Emperius.

51D: Reading ὑλήμασι with most MSS.

53E: Omitting καὶ δοκοῦντες with the MSS.

56E: Reading παίγματα, Hercher.

59A: Omitting μή with most of the MSS, and reading the sentence as a statement, not a question.

59A: Reading ἄνθρωπον (Paton) ἄτοπος ἄν εἴη ἐπαινῶν (MSS).

59A: Reading τοῖς ἐπαινοῦσιν with some MSS.

59B: Omitting καί before ἀκράτῳ, Waterfield.

65D: Reading Ἅγισι, Wyttenbach.

73F: Reading τὸ 'οὐκ ἐπέστησας' καί, Amyot.

73F: Retaining καί with the MSS.

74A: Reading προφυλακτική, Pohlenz.

74A: Reading παρισταμένους, Waterfield.

76A: Reading τοὺς δὲ ⟨μὴ⟩ πάντων (Wyttenbach) ... ἀφειμένους ἅπαντας (Paton).

77C: Reading ⟨εἰς⟩ λήθην φίλων, Edmonds.

77C: Reading πλοῦς, Turnebus.

77F: Including τῆς ἀγορᾶς with the MSS: its omission in the Loeb is probably a misprint.

79B: Reading αὐτοῦ with the MSS.

81D: Reading ⟨κατη⟩φιάσειεν (Kronenberg) ... ὥστ' εἰπεῖν μειδιάσας καὶ ὑποπλησθεὶς ἐρυθήματος (MSS).

81F: Omitting εἶτα ῥήτορας as the better MSS do.

82B: Reading ἐγκλήματα, Waterfield.

83E: Retaining λέγομεν with the MSS.

83F: Reading ἐξᾷττον with the better MSS.

84A: Reading καίρια with some MSS.

84D: Reading Σεμονίδην, Wilamowitz.

85A: Reading τοὺς ὄντως ἀγαθοὺς γεγενημένους, Paton.

345C: The lacuna that begins our text of this essay has been filled chiefly by reference to a passage from 270B–C of Plutarch's *Roman Questions*: see also *Life of Themistocles* 18.6 and *On the Fortune of the Romans* 320F.

345E: Reading Κλείδημοι, Wyttenbach.

346A: Reading, without much confidence, πεινητικῷ τι προσέοικε, Waterfield, after Kronenberg.

347A: Retaining ταῦτα with the MSS.

347A: Retaining γοῦν with the MSS.

347B: Reading πολὺν τὸν ἀγῶνα from Thucydides

347B: Reading διὰ [τὰς συντάξεις] ⟨τὸ ἀκρίτ⟩ως συνεχὲς Froidefond, Naber.

347C: Reading Ἐροιάδης, Kirchner.

349A: Retaining Ἀντιγόνην with the MSS.

349B: Reading ἐπίστημα, Froidefond.

350C: Reading Κόνωνος (Madvig), and therefore omitting Helmbold's addition ὁ δῆμος.

456E: Reading καὶ before μέλει, Madvig.

457D: Omitting οὐκ with the MSS.

458C: Retaining μυῶδες with the MSS.

461C: Retaining ἤ with the MSS.

461C: Reading φοβουμένους with most MSS.

463A: Reading φθόνου δὲ καὶ τὴν χειραψίαν, Waterfield.

465A: Reading κάλτιος πατρικιᾶτος, Waterfield.

465B: Reading ἀπὸ τῶν παρόντων with some MSS.

465D: Reading ἀναισθησίας σώματι φάρμακον ἀπονία with the MSS.

466D: Omitting προσφιλῶς with most MSS.

467C: Reading λαμβάνοντες with most MSS.

467D: Reading δὲ καί, Reiske.

469B: Retaining πολύν with the MSS.

470F: Including here too εὐτελὴς ἡ πόλις with some MSS.

472F: Retaining ἀτελῶς with the MSS.

475F: Reading ἕως with some MSS, as the *difficilior lectio*, and scanning it (as rarely) as a monosyllable.

477F: Reading πορίζειν ποθὲν ⟨οὐκ ἐθέλουσιν⟩, Wilamowitz.

549B: Reading μάρπτει, John of Stobi.

551C: Omitting καί, Waterfield.

552A: Reading πολυτελῶν, Cobet.

555C: Reading διανεμόντων, Reiske; but it is likely that more of this sentence is corrupt.

556A: Reading καὶ ἐλπίδος χρηστῆς with MS D.

560F: Reading περιούσῃ, Post.

562E: Reading ἐνίους τὴν ἕξιν αὐτῶν with the MSS.

563C: Retaining διαφθείρειν with the MSS.

565D: Reading ἀφειδοῦς, Waterfield; cf. Democritus F159 DK, which is preserved in a fragment of one of Plutarch's lost essays, for a faint parallel.

566B: Reading πρόσωθεν ἰδεῖν ἴδιον, Waterfield.

567A: Reading οὐκ ἐκεινῇ, Waterfield.

567F: Reading Ἰνδικῆς, Ziegler. But the earliest extant form of the story (Herodotus 3.109) talks about the Arabian viper.

568A: Reading ἐν πάντι κακοῦ γενέσθαι, Waterfield.

575C: Reading τοὺς δὲ ταῖς αἰτίαις ⟨καταδήλους γιγνομένους ἐπὶ⟩ μέρους ἀγῶνας ἀρετῆς πρὸς τὰ συντυγχάνοντα καὶ τόλμας ἔμφρονας παρὰ τὰ δεινὰ καθηκόντως καιρῷ καὶ πάθει μεμιγμένου λογισμοῦ, Waterfield.

575E: We read the text of the Loeb edition (p. 376, n. 1), but without much confidence: from 'since Simmias and Cebes' onwards, the Greek of the sentence is hopelessly corrupt.

575F: Reading οἰκεῖον ἔχειν, Madvig.

576F: Retaining σῶμα with the MSS.

577A: Reading διακόπτων, Waterfield.

577D: Omitting ἔχω λέγειν with the MSS.

577D: Reading ἐνεῖναι, Post.

578F: Reading ἀποστεῖλαι πρὸς ἑαυτὸν· ὁ δέ, Kronenberg.

579C: Reading ᾗ τὸ τριχῇ διαστατὸν διπλασιάζεται, Waterfield.

579C: Reading οὐ γὰρ τήν, Holwerda.

580A: Reading ᾗ, Waterfield.

580D: Reading ἐν οἷς, Wyttenbach.

581B: Reading γὰρ δή, Waterfield.

581B: We mark a lacuna between δοκοῦμεν and ὑπό, and tentatively fill it with τοιούτου γὰρ οὔκ ἐστιν.

582F: Reading εἰς ὅν, Post.

584E: Reading αἱ μὲν ἐκ, Post.

585A: Reading the received text and omitting ἀσκήσεως with Russell.

585C: Reading ἀναδέδυκε, Waterfield.

585D: Omitting ὅσον, Reiske.

589B: Reading δεχομένοις, Waterfield.

590E: Reading τὰς νήσους διαπεραινομένας, Waterfield.

593D: Omitting γάρ, Pohlenz.

595C: Reading αἰσχίστοις with the MSS.

595E: Reading ἀνθρώπους, Russell.

596A: Reading ἐκπλαγείς with the MSS.

609A: Reading τὸ ἀφελές, Reiske.

611C: Reading ταὐτά, Waterfield.

611D: Reading ἐπιθυμίαν, Reiske (and retaining ἐπίνοιαν a line earlier).

611F: Retaining πεπονθέναι with the MSS.

611F: Here, and again a few lines later, there is a gap in the Greek text; in both cases, however, the general sense is easily supplied.

612A: Reading αὐτῶν, Waterfield.

612A: Reading νόμοι περί, Wilamowitz.

986E: Retaining συνηθείας with the MSS.

988B: Reading ἀλλ᾽ οὐχ ὥσπερ, Post.

989B: Following Usener, we fill the lacuna with αἱ μὲν γὰρ περὶ τὴν βρῶσιν καὶ τήν, and then read ἔχουσιν with some MSS.

989C: Retaining τοῦ with the MSS.

991D: The gap in the MSS must have contained something like what we have supplied, though certainty is of course impossible.

992C: There is a lacuna of indeterminate length in the text, which may have contained futher examples of animals' intelligence.

992D: Omitting καὶ μελίττῃ, as suggested by Helmbold.

# DESCRIPTIVE INDEX OF PROPER NAMES

**Achilles:** the most renowned warrior in the Greek army at Troy, and hero of Homer's *Iliad* (66, 81, 96, 107, 110–11, 180, 213, 226, 395)

**Adonis:** in legend a beautiful youth loved by Aphrodite, but killed by a bear or a jealous god. The festival of his death and resurrection was celebrated annually, mainly by women (276)

**Aegipan:** Goat-Pan, supposedly the offspring of Zeus and a goat, or of Zeus and Aega, the wife of Pan (395)

**Aemilius Paullus:** Roman general and statesman, consul in 182 and 168 BC, respected for his culture and honour in public life. He defeated Perseus, King of Macedon, and settled Greece (232)

**Aeschines:** fourth century BC; Athenian philosopher of the Socratic circle (31, 97, 197)

**Aeschines:** fourth century BC; Athenian orator and statesman, and opponent of Demosthenes (164, 165)

**Aeschylus:** 525/4–456 BC, Athenian tragic dramatist (131, 132, 136, 161, 163, 180)

**Aesop:** according to Herodotus (2.134), a slave at Samos in the sixth century BC. His name became the peg for oral fables. The first collection of Aesop's fables of which we know was made by Demetrius of Phalerum (131, 269, 369)

**Aethe:** a racing mare given by Echepolus of Sicyon to King Agamemnon to excuse him from military service in the Trojan War (388)

**Agamemnon:** king of Mycenae and overlord of the Greek forces at Troy in Homer's *Iliad* (96, 108, 110, 166, 180, 193, 215, 394)

**Agathocles:** 361–289 BC; dictator of Syracuse, despite humble origins as a potter (189, 270)

**Agesilaus:** 444–360 BC; Spartan king from 399, and commander in Asia Minor from 396 (69, 74, 129, 135, 144, 314, 316)

**Agetoridas:** a Spartan who conveyed a message from King Agesilaus to the Egyptian seer Chonuphis (316)

**Agis II:** king of Sparta c. 427–c. 399 BC (218)

**Agis:** an Argive poet, contemporary of Alexander the Great (83, 93)

**Ajax:** Locrian chieftain, and Greek hero at Troy (270)

**Alcibiades:** c. 450–404 BC; brilliant but unpredictable Athenian statesman and general; ward of Pericles and friend of Socrates (69, 134, 142, 154, 163, 167, 218, 259, 322)

**Alcmene:** in legend the mortal mother of Heracles, wife of Amphitryon at Thebes, later consort of Rhadamanthus; she was buried at Haliartus (313–14, 316)

**Aleus:** a Boeotian name for Rhadamanthus (314)

**Alexander:** tyrant of Pherae in Thessaly, 369–358 BC (64)

**Alexander:** 'The Great' of Macedon, 356–323 BC (70, 77, 81, 83, 93, 94, 105, 130, 144–5, 179, 188, 191, 215, 226, 227, 228, 269)

**Amasis:** a pharaoh of Egypt in the sixth century BC (29)

**Ammonius:** philosopher and teacher of Plutarch, based in Athens. Plutarch refers to him with respect several times, dedicated an essay to him (*Lamprias Cat.* 84) and he plays a principal role in *On the E at Delphi* (103–4)

**Amphilochus:** in mythology the son of Eriphyle. He was celebrated as a seer, and his most famous oracle was at Mallos in Cilicia (283)

**Amphitheus:** Theban democratic leader imprisoned by the oligarchs in 379 BC (313, 333, 349, 356)

**Amphitryon:** husband of Alcmene, and so the human father of Heracles (316)

**Anacharsis:** Scythian sage of the early sixth century BC who travelled through Asia Minor and Greece. Anecdote later became attached to his name, and he was regarded as one of the Seven Sages of Greece (130)

**Anaxagoras:** fifth century BC; philosopher from Clazomenae, resident in Athens, where he was a friend and teacher of Pericles. He was indicted for impiety, but Pericles helped him to escape to Lampsacus where he continued teaching (143, 199, 231)

**Anaxarchus:** fourth century BC; philosopher from Abdera, follower of Democritus and admirer of Alexander the Great, whom he followed in his eastern campaigns (215)

**Andocides:** c. 440–c. 390 BC; Athenian orator, implicated in the scandal concerning Alcibiades and the parody of the Mysteries (320)

**Androclidas:** a Theban democrat of the early fourth century BC; he was assassinated while in exile in Athens on the orders of Leontiades (352)

**Androclus:** in Athenian legend son of King Codrus and founder colonist of Ephesus (163)

**Antigone:** daughter of Oedipus (161)

**Antigonus I:** 382(?)–301 BC; 'The Blind'; one of Alexander's generals, and king of Asia (186, 189)

**Antigonus II:** c. 300–239 BC; Gonatas, king of Macedonia (282)

**Antipater:** 397–319 BC; Macedonian general and statesman, very influential through the reign of Philip II and Alexander, and after Alexander's death (91, 130, 228)

**Antipater:** son of Cassander of Macedon (275)

**Antipater:** of Tarsus, second century BC; Stoic, Head of the School in Athens, and teacher of Panaetius (221)

**Antiphanes:** fourth century BC; writer of comedies who became an Athenian citizen (130)

**Antiphon:** c. 480–411 BC; Athenian orator and politician (165)

**Antiphon:** a tragic poet at the court of Dionysius I of Syracuse (98)

**Antiphon:** of Athens; father of Pyrilampes, Plato's stepfather (322)

**Antony, Mark:** c. 82–30 BC; one of the triumviri of Rome from 43 BC; notorious for a dissolute youth (76–7, 85)

**Anytus:** Athenian general and politician of the later years of the fifth century BC, and one of the accusers of Socrates (234)

**Apelles:** of Colophon and Ephesus; famous painter of the second half of the fourth century BC (80, 226)

**Apelles:** of Chios; a pupil of the philosopher Arcesilaus (89–90)

**Aphrodite:** goddess of love and sex (226, 265)

**Apollo:** Greek god whose chief shrine was at Delphi, and whose functions included music, prophecy and medicine (77, 269, 270, 289–90, 316–17, 388, 395)

**Apollocrates:** son of Dionysius of Syracuse (275)

**Apollodorus:** Athenian painter of the last third of the fifth century BC (155)

**Apollodorus:** a tyrant of Cassandreia (i.e. Potidaea in Chalcidice) of the early third century BC, noted for his cruelty (265, 268)

**Araspes:** a Mede, friend of the elder Cyrus, and a commander in his army (143)

**Arcadion:** an Achaean critic of Philip II of Macedon (186–7)

**Arcesilaus:** c. 315–241/40 BC; philosopher, who became Head of the Platonic so-called Middle Academy in Athens (74, 89–90, 195, 221–2)

**Arcesus:** a Spartan commander of the garrison in Thebes in 379 BC (333, 358)

**Archedamus:** fourth century BC; an Athenian well inclined to Boeotia (309–10, 350–53)

**Archias:** Theban oligarch who seized power with Spartan help in the coup of 382 BC (310–13, 333, 335, 349, 350, 352–4, 356)

**Archias:** an Athenian high priest at the time of the *coup d'état* at Thebes in 379 BC (353–4)

**Archilochus:** of Paros; iambic and elegiac poet of seventh century BC (43, 277)

**Archinus:** Athenian statesman associated with Thrasybulus in restoring independent democratic government to Athens in 404/3 BC, from the Thirty Tyrants and the Spartan garrison (154, 165, 309)

**Archytas:** of Tarentum; mathematician and Pythagorean philosopher of the first half of the fourth century BC (257)

**Ares:** the Greek god of war (162)

**Aresas:** a leader of the Pythagorean community in the south of Italy in the fourth century BC (325)

**Arethusius:** an Athenian against whom Demosthenes directed a speech (167)

**Argynnus:** a beautiful Boeotian boy pursued by King Agamemnon. He drowned in the river Cephissus, and Agamemnon erected a shrine to him (394)

**Aridaeus:** of Soli; relative of Protogenes who was an acquaintance of Plutarch. He became a reformed character after an other-worldly experience (285)

**Aristides:** Athenian statesman of the early fifth century BC, who became a legend for honesty and justice. He commanded the Athenian forces at Plataea, the final decisive victory over the Persians in 479 BC (124, 143, 164, 188, 200)

**Aristion:** Athenian who made himself dictator of Athens in 88–86 BC, before the city was taken by Sulla (272)

**Aristippus:** of Cyrene in North Africa, *c.* 435–356 BC; one of the Socratic circle; a sophist and traditional founder of the Cyrenaic school of philosophy, although the real founder was more likely his grandson of the same name (133, 197, 220–21)

**Aristocrates:** king of the Arcadians, mid seventh century BC (251)

**Aristogiton:** with Harmodius (q.v.), popularly known as the tyrannicides or liberators of Athens (98)

**Aristomenes:** teacher of Ptolemy V Epiphanes (105)

**Ariston:** a mercenary commander from Oeta who plundered Delphi in the Third Sacred War in the mid fourth century BC (262)

**Ariston:** of Chios; Stoic philosopher of the third century BC (37)

**Aristophanes:** *c.* 450–*c.* 385 BC; Athenian dramatic writer of comedies (105)

**Aristotle:** 384–322 BC; philosopher; pupil of Plato and founder of the Peripatetic School (70, 130, 179, 189, 192, 228)

**Artemis:** Greek goddess, sister of Apollo; virgin goddess associated with women in childbirth and with wild animals (164)

**Asclepiades:** of Samos, third century BC; poet (234)

**Asclepiades:** friend of Menedemus (74)

**Asclepiodorus:** fourth century BC; painter of the Athenian school (155)

**Asclepius:** god of healing (179, 262)

**Astydamas:** the common name of a father and son, both highly acclaimed Athenian tragic dramatists of the fourth century BC (163)

**Athamas:** in legend the husband of Ino, q.v. (267)

**Athena:** Greek goddess connected with war, arts and crafts; the patron goddess of Athens (156, 183, 237, 270, 319, 357)

**Atreus:** in mythology, the father of Agamemnon (215, 225)

**Atropos:** one of the Fates (342)

**Augeas:** in legend son of Helios and king of Elis. Heracles had to clean his stables as one of his Labours, but was refused payment (282)

**Autolycus:** the prince of thieves and lies in the *Odyssey*; grandfather of Odysseus (261, 399)


**Bacchyllidas:** a Theban conspirator in the *coup d'état* of 379 BC (324)

**Bagoas:** a eunuch and favourite of Alexander the Great (93)

**Baton:** a dramatist of comedies in the first half of the third century BC (74)

**Bessus:** of Paeonia, killed his father and betrayed himself (262–3)

**Bias:** of Priene, mid sixth century BC. One of the Seven Sages of Greece (29, 85, 251)

**Bias:** a character in a play by Menander (77)

**Bion:** of Borysthenes, *c.* 325–*c.* 255 BC; Cynic philosopher and writer (81, 138, 279)

**Biton:** and his brother Cleobis were part of an Argive legend made famous by Solon and Herodotus 1.31 (80)

**Brasidas:** fifth century BC; a Spartan general in the Peloponnesian War with Athens. He was remembered as a brave soldier (124, 132, 157, 163, 250)

**Briareus:** a legendary monster with a hundred arms (223)

**Briseis:** a captured girl, part of Achilles' booty, who was appropriated by Agamemnon, and so created the dramatic beginning of the *Iliad* (193)

**Cabirichus:** Theban magistrate at the time of the *coup d'état* of 379 BC (354–5)

**Cadmus:** mythical founder of Thebes (159)

**Caeneus:** in mythology a Lapith who originally had been a girl, Caenis, granted a sex change by Poseidon (123)

**Callimachus:** Athenian commander killed at the battle of Marathon in 490 BC (158)

**Callippides:** an Athenian actor of the second half of the fifth century BC (161)

**Callippus:** Athenian associate of Plato's Academy, who assassinated Plato's friend Dion in Syracuse, and gained short-lived power there (262)

**Callisthenes:** nephew of Alexander the Great, and a historian of his exploits. He was executed by Alexander (93, 179, 188)

**Callistratus:** Athenian financier and statesman prominent in public affairs in the 370s and 360s BC (355)

**Callondes:** of Naxos, nicknamed the Crow; killed the poet Archilochus in battle (277)

**Camillus, Marcus Furius:** Roman conqueror of the Veii, and second founder of Rome after the Gallic invasion in 387 BC (188)

**Caphisias:** brother of the Theban patriot Epaminondas; fourth century BC (308–58)

**Carcinus:** Athenian tragic dramatist of the fourth century BC, referred to several times by Aristotle (163)

**Carneades:** of Cyrene; philosopher and Head of the Academy in the mid second century BC (81, 232, 237)

**Cassander:** ruler of Macedon 317–297 BC; murderer of Alexander's surviving family. He caused the rebuilding of Thebes in 316 BC (260, 275)

**Cassius Severus:** Roman orator of the time of Augustus and Tiberius, who spent twenty-five years in exile because of his bitter speeches (84)

**Cato, Marcus Porcius (the Younger):** 95–46 BC; Roman politician, and Stoic with strict moral views. Plutarch wrote his *Life* (200)

**Cebes:** of Thebes; pupil of the Pythagorean Philolaus, and friend of Socrates (309, 320, 339)

**Cecrops:** mythical king of Athens; often represented as of serpent shape below the waist (258)

**Centaur:** legendary creature, half man, half horse (72, 395)

**Cephisocrates:** friend of Lacydes (90)

**Cephisodorus:** son of Diogiton; Theban conspirator in the coup of 379 BC (351–2, 353, 355–6)

**Cercopes:** ape-like human creatures of legend caught thieving by Heracles, who, amused by their jokes, let them go (83)

**Chabrias:** Athenian general who defeated the Spartan navy at Naxos in 376 BC. He was influential in the Second Athenian Confederacy, and was killed in 357 (163, 166)

**Charillus:** an early king of Sparta (75)

**Charillus:** fourth century BC; a Theban musician (320)

**Charon:** one of Plutarch's sons (368)

**Charon:** a Theban democrat in the conspiracy to overthrow the oligarchic dictatorship at Thebes in 379 BC (311, 332–5, 350–54)

**Chlidon:** a Theban at the time of the coup of 379 BC (334–5, 350)

**Chonuphis:** an Egyptian seer of Memphis who taught Eudoxus of Cnidus (316–17)

**Cimon:** c. 512–449 BC; Athenian statesman and general, influential in Athens' rise to power after the repulsion of the Persian invasion (160, 163, 259, 272)

**Cinesias:** Athenian dithyrambic poet of the second half of the fifth century BC, much derided by the comic dramatists (160)

**Circe:** the sorceress goddess in Homer's *Odyssey*, who turned human beings into animals (69, 383–4, 386, 391)

**Cleanthes:** of Assos, 331–232 BC; Stoic philosopher who succeeded Zeno as Head of the School in Athens in 263 BC (49, 74)

**Clearchus:** Spartan officer who commanded the Greek mercenaries in the army of Cyrus II at the battle of Cunaxa in 401 BC (100)

**Cleisthenes:** tyrant of Sicyon in the early sixth century BC (261)

**Cleobis:** with his brother Biton formed an Argive legend made famous by Solon and Herodotus 1.31 (80)

**Cleomenes III:** c. 260–219 BC; king of Sparta from 235 BC (71)

**Cleon:** Athenian politician and general prominent in the first part of the Peloponnesian War. He was satirized by Aristophanes in his plays, and died in 422 BC (105, 154, 163)

**Cleonice:** a young woman of Byzantium, killed by Pausanias, c. 478 BC (266)

**Clidemus:** historian of early Athenian history, writing in the mid fourth century BC (155)

**Clitus:** c. 380–328/7 BC; Macedonian noble and cavalry commander in Alexander's army. Alexander killed him (105, 188)

**Clotho:** one of the Fates (342)

**Clymene:** in legend wife of Helios the sun, and mother of Phaethon (366)

**Clytemnestra:** wife and murderess of Agamemnon of Mycenae in epic legend (265)

**Conon:** *c.* 444–392 BC; Athenian admiral operating in the latter part of the Peloponnesian War. After Athens' defeat, he revived her power with a naval victory over Sparta at Cnidus in 394 BC (154, 163, 165, 309)

**Conon:** an Athenian against whom Demosthenes directed a speech (167)

**Copreus:** father of Periphetes of Mycenae in the *Iliad* (261)

**Corinna:** lyric poetess from Tanagra in Boeotia; probably roughly contemporary with Pindar (159–60)

**Coroebus:** a proverbially stupid man (399)

**Crates:** *c.* 365–285 BC; Cynic philosopher and pupil of Diogenes of Sinope. He was based in Athens (101, 215)

**Cratinus:** Athenian comic dramatist in the fifth century BC (161, 166)

**Cratippus:** Athenian historian who wrote a continuation of Thucydides' *History* until the restoration of Athenian sea power in 394 BC at least (154)

**Crison:** of Himera; winner of the foot race at the Olympics of 448, 444 and 440 BC (81, 226)

**Croesus:** king of Lydia, *c.* 560–546 BC (80, 102, 269)

**Cronus:** in Greek legend, the god who was father of Zeus (225, 237, 238, 259)

**Ctesiphon:** an all-in boxer (185)

**Cyaxares:** prince or king of Media, and, according to Xenophon, friend of Cyrus I (102)

**Cyclopes:** gigantic one-eyed people of legend, whose land Odysseus visited in his wanderings (386)

**Cylon:** head of a faction in the south of Italy attempting to drive out Pythagorean communities in the fourth century BC (325)

**Cynegeirus:** brother of Aeschylus; lost a hand in the battle of Marathon in 490 BC (158)

**Cyrus (the Younger):** Persian prince in command of Asia Minor at the end of the fifth century BC. He led the expedition against the Persian King Artaxerxes in 401 BC, in which Xenophon took part, and Cyrus was killed (189)

**Cyrus I (the Elder):** founder of the Persian Empire, 559–529 BC (102)

**Dactyls:** mythical Cretan dwarfs (144)

**Daiphantus:** national hero of the Phocians (272)

**Damoclidas:** one of the Theban exiles who helped to overthrow the oligarchic dictatorship in 379 BC (349, 353)

**Darius I:** king of Persia, 521–486 BC (65)

**Demaratus:** Corinthian friend of Philip of Macedon (103)

**Demeter:** Greek goddess (333)

**Demetrius:** a favourite of Alexander the Great (93)

**Demetrius:** of Phalerum; Athenian statesman, writer and philosopher of the second half of the fourth century BC. He was pro-Macedonian and was installed as governor of Athens by Cassander. Exiled in 307 after the capture of Athens, he went first to Boeotia, and then to Alexandria, where he was librarian of the celebrated Library (101, 162)

**Demetrius I:** 336–283 BC; king of Macedonia, and nicknamed Poliorcetes (Taker of Cities). Plutarch wrote his *Life* (233, 282)

**Democritus:** fifth century BC; philosopher from Abdera in Thrace. He held an atomic theory in natural philosophy, and in ethics was regarded as a precursor of Epicurus (135, 227)

**Demosthenes:** fifth century BC; Athenian general at the time of the Peloponnesian War (154, 157, 163, 167)

**Demosthenes:** 382–322 BC; great Athenian orator and statesman (101, 134, 164, 165, 167)

**Diogenes:** an Athenian tragedian in the fifth century BC (35)

**Diogenes:** of Sinope, *c.* 400–325 BC. The original and most famous Cynic philosopher (111, 128, 129, 132, 137, 138, 193, 215, 217, 237)

**Diogiton:** father of Cephisodorus, q.v.

**Dion:** nobleman of the Syracusan court under Dionysius I and II; close friend of Plato (69, 70, 102, 262)

**Dionysius I and Dionysius II:** father and son, tyrants of Syracuse, the son succeeding in 367/6 BC; ambivalent hosts of Plato. Their court was highly cultured, but Plato's idealistic hopes for model rule broke down in the harsh realities of politics (36, 68, 69, 71, 76, 97, 98, 217, 225–6, 260, 275)

**Dionysus:** god of liberated emotions and ecstatic forms of worship, and of wine (77, 83, 160, 196, 288, 373)

**Dirce:** in legend the wife of Lycus. She was killed by Amphion and Zethus by being tied to a bull's horns, and had a secret tomb near Thebes (314)

**Diyllus:** Athenian historian. His *History* in twenty-seven books covered the second half of the fourth century BC (155)

**Dolon:** a Trojan in *Iliad* 10, whose teeth-chattering cowardice on meeting Odysseus and Diomedes made him a legend in literature for cowardice (124, 392)

**Electra:** daughter of King Agamemnon, and niece of Helen (161, 179)

**Ellopion:** of Peparethus; accompanied Plato and Simmias in philosophical discussions with Chonuphis of Memphis (316)

**Empedocles:** philosopher from Acragas in Sicily in the fifth century BC (89, 201, 227, 231, 319)

**Epaminondas:** fourth century BC; Theban patriot and general, who was also famed for the nobility of his character (30, 69, 144, 156–7, 162, 217, 227, 308–58)

**Epicharmus:** fifth century BC; Sicilian writer of comedy mainly at the court of Syracuse in the time of Gelon and Hieron. He also had philosophical interests (98, 274)

**Epicurus:** 342/1–271/70 BC; Athenian philosopher, and founder of the Epicurean school (45, 213–14, 231, 250)

**Epicydes:** father of the Spartan Glaucus, q.v.

**Erechtheus:** in mythology an early king of Athens (156)

**Erianthes:** a Theban, father of Hypatodorus, q.v.

**Eriphyle:** in mythology, bribed by a necklace, she sent her husband Amphiaraus to his death with the Seven against Thebes. She in turn was killed by her son (262)

**Eros:** a friend of Plutarch (177, 211)

**Eucles:** an Athenian, who supposedly reported the victory of Marathon (158)

**Euclides:** c. 450–380 BC; philosopher from Megara, associate of Socrates and founder of the Megarian school of philosophy (197)

**Euctus:** a companion of Perseus (102)

**Eudoxus:** of Cnidus; brilliant mathematician and astronomer of the first half of the fourth century BC, and pupil of Plato (317)

**Eulaeus:** a companion of Perseus (102)

**Eumolpidas:** fourth century BC; a Theban (312)

**Euphorion:** third century BC; poet from Chalcis in Euboea, who married a rich widow and became librarian at Antioch in Syria (227)

**Euphranor:** Corinthian painter and sculptor working in Athens about the middle of the fourth century BC (155–7)

**Eupolis:** Athenian comic dramatist of the second half of the fifth century BC (71)

**Euripides:** Athenian tragic dramatist, 485–406? BC (43, 45–6, 47, 63, 87, 100, 104, 109, 144, 161, 200, 230, 233, 250, 252, 253, 268, 322)

**Eurypylus:** leader of a contingent in the Greek army at Troy (189)

**Euthydemus:** disciple of Socrates (195)

**Euthyphro:** an Athenian seer and acquaintance of Socrates. He gave his name to a dialogue of Plato (320)

**Evenus:** an innovative sophist and elegiac poet of the fifth century BC, from Paros (63)

**Fabricius Luscinus, Gaius:** Roman hero in the war with Pyrrhus, king of Epirus in the early third century BC. He was a legend for his poverty, austerity and incorruptibility (217)

**Fundanus, C. Minucius:** Roman, suffect consul AD 107, proconsul of Asia 122/3; a friend of Plutarch and of the younger Pliny (176–201, 211)

**Galaxidorus:** one of the Theban conspirators who overthrew the oligarchic dictatorship in 379 BC (312, 318–24, 336, 348)

**Gelon:** c. 540–478 BC; dictator of Gela and then of Syracuse; brother of Hieron (258–9)

**Glaucus:** son of Epicydes, a Spartan, who tried to renege on a trust left in his care by a Milesian. According to Herodotus 6.86, the Delphic oracle condemned him and his family vanished from Sparta (268)

**Gobryas:** a Persian, associated with Darius in the overthrow of Smerdis the Magian (65)

**Gorgias:** of Leontini in Sicily; one of the most famous sophists and theoretical rhetoricians of the fifth century BC (91, 160, 325)

**Gorgidas:** Theban democratic patriot of the first half of the fourth century BC (310, 315, 349, 357)

**Gracchus, Gaius:** Roman politician and reformer; tribune 123 and 122 BC (182–3)

**Gryllus:** companion of Odysseus, transformed into a pig by Circe (383–99)

**Gyges:** king of Lydia in the seventh century BC (222)

**Hades:** in mythology a son of Cronus and king of the underworld (343, 374)

**Hagno:** a favourite of Alexander the Great (93)

**Harmodius:** with Aristogiton popularly known as the tyrannicides or liberators of Athens. But their plot to assassinate the ruling family miscarried and both were killed; the tyranny was overthrown three years later (98)

**Hecate:** a goddess of the underworld, especially associated with sorcery and black magic (384)

**Hector:** the leading Trojan hero of the *Iliad* (106, 110, 111)

**Helen:** wife of Menelaus, but abducted by Paris to Troy, which was the cause of the Trojan War (179)

**Helenus:** a son of Priam, king of Troy (347)

**Helicon:** of Cyzicus, fourth century BC; pupil of Eudoxus of Cnidus. He accompanied Plato to the court of Dionysius at Syracuse (199, 317)

**Hera:** queen of the gods, and consort of Zeus (270)

**Heracles:** most popular legendary hero in Greek mythology, often connected with Thebes. He represented a kind of invincible strong man (77, 83, 107, 160, 223, 270, 272, 277, 316, 357, 395)

**Heraclides:** fourth century BC; philosopher and savant from the Pontus, who spent much time at Athens with Plato in the Academy (158)

**Heraclitus:** philosopher from Ephesus, flourishing at the turn of the sixth and fifth centuries BC (34, 40, 186, 274–5)

**Herippidas:** Spartan commander of the garrison at Thebes in 379 BC (333, 358)

**Hermes:** the messenger and herald of the gods, also connected with eloquence (42)

**Hermodorus:** of Clazomenae, claimed to be a shaman. But Plutarch is probably thinking of Hermotimus of Clazomenae, and confused the name (345)

**Herodicus:** doctor from Selymbria in the fifth century BC; one of the first to study scientifically the therapeutics of exercise and diet (264)

**Herodotus:** of Halicarnassus; historian of the rise of the Persian Empire, and of the Persian invasions of Greece, culminating in their final defeat and retreat after the battles of Salamis and Plataea in 480/79 BC (27)

**Hesiod:** one of the earliest Greek poets, who wrote didactic and theogonic poems (128, 213, 228, 263, 280, 347)

**Hieron:** dictator of Gela, and then of Syracuse in the first half of the fifth century BC; brother of Gelon (98, 258–9)

**Hieronymus:** third century BC; philosopher from Rhodes who lived most of his life at Athens. He wrote a book *On Avoidance of Anger* which Plutarch had read (50, 180, 193)

**Himerius:** an Athenian notorious for flattery (84)

**Hipparchus:** son of Pisistratus, the sixth-century-BC dictator of Athens. He was murdered in 514 BC by Harmodius and Aristogiton for his offensive behaviour (265)

**Hippocrates:** father of Pisistratus, q.v.

**Hippocrates:** fifth-century-BC physician from Cos, who became the most famous medical figure in the ancient world. Under his name was collected the medical library now known as the Hippocratic corpus (138, 182)

**Hipposthenidas:** one of the Theban conspirators in the *coup d'état* of 379 BC (332–5, 350, 357)

**Hismenias:** a leader of the Theban democrats put to death by the Spartans in 379 BC (310)

**Hismenodorus:** one of the Theban conspirators in the *coup d'état* of 379 BC (324)

**Homer:** epic poet of *Iliad* and *Odyssey* (133, 134, 159, 177, 179, 180, 232, 261, 276, 319, 347, 372)

**Hypates:** Theban oligarchic leader in the dictatorship of 382–379 BC (353, 356)

**Hypatodorus:** a Theban at the time time of the coup of 379 BC (333)

**Hyperides:** 389–332 BC; Athenian orator, speech writer and statesman (45, 96, 164)

**I(a)dmon:** of Samos; a descendant of the family who bought Aesop as a slave (269)

**Ino:** in legend, the wife of Athamas. Jealous of her stepchildren, Phrixus and Helle, she attempted to have them sacrificed by her husband (267)

**Ion:** of Chios, fifth century BC; dramatist established at Athens (132, 215)

**Iphicrates:** *c.* 415–353 BC; Athenian general who established the military importance of peltasts, light-armed spearsmen, with whom he annihilated a Spartan garrison division in 390 BC (166)

**Iphitus:** a Phocian, identified by Plutarch as the Iphitus who had mares stolen by Autolycus in popular legend (262)

**Isaeus:** *c.* 420–350 BC; Athenian orator (165)

**Ismenias:** Theban statesman of great wealth in the second century BC (227)

**Ismenus:** personified river in Theban legend (159)

**Isocrates:** 436–338 BC; Athenian orator (165–6)

**Jason:** tyrant of Pherae in Thessaly in the early fourth century BC (327)

**Lachares:** Athenian general who made himself tyrant of Athens briefly between 297 and 295 BC, before being driven out and escaping to Boeotia (272)

**Laches:** fifth century BC; Athenian general (322)

**Lachesis:** one of the Fates (342)

**Lacydes:** succeeded Arcesilaus as Head of the Platonic Academy in Athens in 241/40 BC (90)

**Laertes:** father of Odysseus in legend (213)

**Lagus:** father, or reputed father of Ptolemy, the founder of the Egyptian dynasty (187)

**Lamprocles:** a son of Socrates (339)

**Leontiades:** Theban oligarch who seized power with Spartan help in the coup of 382 BC (310, 313, 315, 353, 355–6)

**Leptines:** Athenian politician attacked by Demosthenes (167)

**Lyciscus:** fourth century BC; citizen of Orchomenus (251–2)

**Lycurgus:** the traditional founder of the Spartan constitution (144)

**Lydiadas:** tyrant of Megalopolis in the mid third century BC (259)

**Lysander:** Spartan general in the Peloponnesian War against Athens in the last third of the fifth century BC (105)

**Lysanoridas:** a Spartan commander in charge of the garrison in Thebes in 380 BC (310, 312, 314, 349, 357)

**Lysias:** c. 459–380 BC; orator based in Athens (34, 43, 165)

**Lysimachus:** a successor of Alexander the Great, in command of Thrace (266)

**Lysis:** fourth century BC; a Pythagorean from Tarentum who migrated to Thebes and taught the Theban patriot Epaminondas (309, 315, 318, 325–7, 330–31)

**Lysitheus:** Theban conspirator in the overthrow of the oligarchic dictatorship in 379 BC (354)

**Lysithides:** Athenian public figure of the fourth century BC, nephew of the patriot Thrasybulus (309)

**Magas:** half-brother of Ptolemy II Philadelphus, a commander under him, and king of Cyrene, of which Paraetonium was a port (187)

**Marius:** 157–86 BC; Roman general and politician with seven consulships. In his final year he took Rome by force, and cruel purges followed (195, 261)

**Marsyas:** a satyr musician associated with new forms of music for the pipes (183)

**Medea:** daughter of Aetes, and wife of Jason (161)

**Medius:** of Larissa in Thessaly; boon companion of Alexander the Great (93, 227)

**Megabyzus:** Persian commander of the first half of the fifth century BC (80, 226)

**Melanthius:** fifth century BC; Athenian tragedian (35, 178, 256)

**Melanthius:** a parasite of Alexander of Pherae (64)

**Meletus:** of Athens; an accuser of Socrates in his trial of 399 BC (124, 234, 319)

**Melia:** a nymph in Theban legend, mother of the personified river Ismenus (159)

**Melissus:** a Theban conspirator in the *coup d'état* of 379 BC (324)

**Melon:** a leader of the exiled Theban democrats who overthrew the oligarchic dictatorship in 379 BC (310, 334, 353, 354)

**Menander:** 342/1–291/90 BC; Athenian comic dramatist (82, 159, 214, 230, 232, 235–6)

**Menedemus:** of Eretria, *c.* 339–*c.* 265 BC; founder of an Eretrian philosophical school, which was allied in dialectical methods to the Megarian School (74, 136, 227)

**Menelaus:** brother of Agamemnon, and husband of Helen (74)

**Merope:** usually in legend a Pleiad, and the wife of Sisyphus of Corinth (88)

**Merops:** legendary king of Ethiopia, and putative father of Phaethon (211)

**Metellus, Q. Caecilius Macedonius:** great Roman statesman and general of the second century BC (188)

**Metrocles:** Cynic philosopher from Maroneia in Thrace in the late fourth century BC (218)

**Miltiades:** *c.* 550–489 BC; Athenian general who defeated the Persians at Marathon in 490 BC (142, 160, 162, 163, 166, 259)

**Minos:** son of Zeus; legendary king of Cnossus, lawgiver and judge of the dead (254)

**Minotaur:** a creature half man, half bull, of Cretan legend (395)

**Mithridates VI:** king of Pontus 120–63 BC, and a major opponent of Rome in a series of campaigns beginning in the eighties (79)

**Mitys:** an Argive killed in civil unrest (262)

**Mucius, Gaius:** in Roman legend he attempted the assassination of Porsenna (187)

**Musonius Rufus:** Stoic philosopher from Volsinii in Etruria of the first century AD. He was banished more than once, but had considerable influence at Rome. His pupils included Epictetus, and a number of eminent Romans, such as Plutarch's friend Fundanus (177)

**Mynniscus:** an Athenian tragic actor (161)

**Myron:** tyrant of Sicyon in the later seventh century BC (261)

**Myronides:** Athenian general campaigning in Boeotia in 458–456 BC (154)

**Neileus:** in Athenian legend, son of King Codrus and founder colonist of Miletus (163)

**Neleus:** in mythology king of Pylos and father of Nestor. He was killed by Heracles for refusing him purification (282)

**Neoptolemus:** in mythology, son of Achilles (189, 351)

**Nero:** Roman emperor, AD 54–68 (77, 84, 196, 293)

**Nestor:** a venerable, respected, although somewhat long-winded counsellor in the Greek army at Troy in the *Iliad*. He was son of Neleus, king of Pylos (110, 282)

**Nicander:** teenaged acquaintance of Plutarch, possibly son of C. Memmius Euthydamus, Plutarch's fellow priest at Delphi. *On Listening* was addressed to him (27)

**Nicias:** *c.* 470–413 BC; Athenian statesman and general in the Peloponnesian War (154, 326)

**Nicias:** Athenian painter of the second half of the fourth century BC (155)

**Nicomachus:** a character in a play (88)

**Nicostratus:** an Athenian tragic actor (161)

**Nysaeus:** son of Dionysius of Syracuse (275)


**Odysseus:** Homeric hero, king of Ithaca, and represented in both *Iliad* and *Odyssey* as brave, sagacious and cunning (38, 68, 74, 96, 108, 110–11, 232, 234, 262, 270, 319, 383–99)

**Oedipus:** in legend an exposed child who became king of Thebes by solving the riddle of the Sphinx. But he fulfilled a prophecy by unwittingly killing his father and marrying his mother, at the discovery of which he blinded himself and went into exile (107, 161)

**Olympichus:** a friend of Plutarch (252–3, 276, 279, 283)

**Opheltas:** a king of Thessaly who settled in Boeotia (272)

**Orpheus:** mythical Thracian singer, killed and dismembered by Thracian women. He attempted to bring his wife Euridice back from the other world (271, 289)

**Orthagoras:** seventh century BC; tyrant of Sicyon (261)


**Paccius:** a Roman friend of Plutarch, with political influence and a forensic reputation (211, 219)

**Panaetius:** *c.* 185–109 BC; of Rhodes. Stoic philosopher and Head of the School in Athens 129–109 BC (199)

**Pandarus:** in Homer's *Iliad* he was the great bowman in the Trojan army (107, 181)

**Pantheia:** wife of Abradatas, king of Susa. She became the captive of Cyrus (143)

**Parmenides:** early fifth century BC; philosopher from Elea, who wrote in verse (43)

**Parmenion:** c. 400–330 BC; Macedonian noble and general of Philip II and of Alexander, who had him murdered because of the treason of his son Philotas (93)

**Parrhasius:** of Ephesus, c. 420–370 BC; painter of the Athenian school (155)

**Patrocleas:** relation of Plutarch by marriage – probably son-in-law (250–52, 260, 262, 277)

**Patroclus:** the friend of Achilles in Homer's *Iliad* (81, 96)

**Pausanias:** Spartan commander of the final victorious battle of Plataea (479 BC) in the Persian Wars, and then of the capture of Byzantium in 478 BC. Hostility to his behaviour abroad led to his recall, and suspicions of intrigue with the helots to his death by starvation in Sparta (266, 278)

**Peleus:** father of Achilles in Homer's *Iliad* (96, 187, 213)

**Pelopidas:** one of the leaders of the exiled Theban democrats who overthrew the oligarchic dictatorship in 379 BC (189, 310, 312, 349, 351, 353, 355–6)

**Penelope:** wife of Odysseus (391)

**Periander:** tyrant of Corinth in the seventh and sixth centuries BC (260)

**Pericles:** c. 495–429 BC; Athenian statesman who consolidated Athens' power after the Persian War and directed her strategy at the beginning of the Peloponnesian War (154, 160, 166–7, 261, 273)

**Persephone:** in myth, the daughter of Demeter carried off by Hades to be his consort in the underworld (342)

**Perseus:** king of Macedon, 179–168 BC, eventually in conflict with Rome, defeated at Pydna, and captured (102, 232)

**Petronius, Titus (or Gaius):** the touchstone of taste and fashion in the court of the Emperor Nero (84)

**Phaedra:** in mythology, wife of Theseus (68)

**Phaethon:** attempted to drive the chariot of his father, the sun, but disastrously lost control, and Zeus blasted him to his death (215, 271)

**Phalaris:** tyrant of Acragas in Sicily, c. 570–554 BC, who became a byword for cruel injustice (76, 124, 261)

**Phanias:** a character in a play by Menander (214)

**Pherenicus:** one of the Theban democratic exiles in Athens who helped to overthrow the oligarchic dictatorship in Thebes in 379 BC (311, 312)

**Phidias:** fifth century BC; Athenian sculptor (155)

**Phidolaus:** of Haliartus in Boeotia; privy to the democratic conspiracy which overthrew the oligarchic dictatorship at Thebes in 379 BC (313–16, 322–3, 336–9)

**Philemon:** c. 361–262 BC; from Syracuse, but he became an Athenian citizen and a prominent dramatist of the so-called New Comedy (187)

**Philip:** son of Cassander of Macedon (275)

**Philip II:** king of Macedon, 359–336 BC, who established the power of Macedon in Greece; the father of Alexander the Great (34, 98, 103, 186–7, 188)

**Philip V:** king of Macedon, 238–179 BC (71)

**Philippus:** Theban oligarch and magistrate in power before the overthrow by the democrats in 379 BC (349, 350, 352, 353, 354, 356)

**Philochorus:** Athenian historian of the fourth and third centuries BC. His *History of Attica* ran to seventeen books (155)

**Philolaus:** one of the heads of Pythagorean communities in the south of Italy in the fourth century BC (325)

**Philopappus, Antiochus:** Syrian prince, eminent friend of Plutarch (61, 95)

**Philotas:** c. 360–330 BC; Macedonian noble, son of Parmenion, a commander in the army of Alexander, who had him executed for conspiracy and treason (93)

**Philotimus:** eminent Greek physician of the fourth and third centuries BC (39, 109)

**Philoxenus:** of Cythera, 436/5–380/79 BC; poet at the court of Dionysius of Syracuse (226)

**Phlegyas:** legendary grandfather of Asclepius. He burned the temple at Delphi, and was condemned to torture in Hades (261)

**Phocion:** Athenian statesman and general of the fourth century BC. Plutarch wrote his *Life* (91, 144, 165, 191)

**Phocylides:** sixth century BC; gnomic poet from Miletus (43, 49)

**Phoebidas:** Spartan general who seized the Theban Cadmeia for the oligarchs (310)

**Phoenix:** tutor to the young Achilles whom he accompanied to the Trojan War (106)

**Phormio:** Athenian admiral in the opening years of the Peloponnesian War (154)

**Phrynichus:** the most famous of the earliest tragic dramatists at Athens, producing plays in the late sixth century BC, and in the first three decades at least of the fifth century. He was particularly remembered for plays relating to the Persian Wars (164)

**Phrynis:** mid-fifth century BC; musician from Mitylene. A virtuoso performer, he is said to have attempted to add strings to the instrument (141)

**Phylarchus:** historian of Athens in the third century BC; his *History* in twenty-eight books covered the period between 272 and 220 BC (155)

**Phyleus:** son of Augeas. He adjudicated against his father who had refused payment to Heracles for cleaning his stables (282)

**Phyllidas:** member of the Theban conspiracy which overthrew the oligarchic dictatorship in 379 BC (312–13, 332–5, 349, 353, 354, 356)

**Pindar:** lyric poet from Boeotia, 518–438 BC (99, 159–60, 164, 185, 217, 237, 254, 271–2, 280, 309)

**Pisistratus:** dictator of Athens 561–527 BC (187, 258–9, 265)

**Pittacus:** seventh and sixth centuries BC, statesman of Mitylene, who became regarded as one of the Seven Sages of Greece (224)

**Plato:** the Athenian philosopher, *c.* 427–348/7 BC (33, 34, 43, 45, 61, 65, 66, 68, 69, 70, 76, 97, 102, 104, 106, 124, 130, 132, 139, 143, 144, 160, 184, 199, 200, 216, 217, 226, 227, 231, 237, 254, 255, 257, 263, 264, 316–17)

**Plato:** Theban magistrate in the fourth century BC (315)

**Pleistaenetus:** early to mid fifth century BC; Athenian painter, brother of Phidias (155)

**Pleisthenes:** legendary ancestor of Agamemnon and Orestes (265)

**Polemon:** Head of the Platonic Academy, 314–276 BC. He was said to have been reformed from a wild youth by Xenocrates (106, 197)

**Polus:** an Athenian tragic actor (161)

**Polyclitus:** of Argos. He was regarded as the greatest sculptor of the Peloponnesian tradition in the second half of the fifth century BC (146)

**Polymnis:** of Thebes, father of Epaminondas and Caphisias (316, 317, 321–3, 326–7, 330)

**Polyphemus:** the savage Cyclops in the *Odyssey* who threatened to eat Odysseus and his men (399)

**Polyzelus:** an Athenian hero at the battle of Marathon (490 BC). The name elsewhere is Epizelus (158)

**Pompey, Gnaius (the Great):** 106–48 BC; Roman general and statesman (261)

**Porsenna:** in Roman legend an early Etruscan king opposed to Rome (187)

**Porus:** ruler of the eastern Punjab area of Pakistan, defeated by Alexander the Great (188)

**Poseidon:** Greek god, son of Cronus, younger brother of Zeus, and especially associated with the sea (140)

**Priam:** king of Troy and father of Hector in Homer's *Iliad* (197, 347, 392)

**Proteus:** in legend an Egyptian king at the time of the Trojan War (316)

**Protogenes:** a friend of Plutarch (283, 284)

**Ptolemy I Soter:** *c*. 367/6–283/2 BC; Macedonian king of Egypt (187–8)

**Ptolemy IV Philopator:** *c*. 244–205 BC; king of Egypt (71, 76, 83)

**Ptolemy V Epiphanes:** king of Egypt, 210–180 BC (105)

**Ptolemy XII Auletes:** king of Egypt, 80–51 BC (77)

**Ptolemy Ceraunus:** son of Ptolemy I Soter. He retreated to the court of King Lysimachus of Thrace, and in 281 BC murdered Seleucus, a Macedonian associate of Alexander, who had after his death acquired Babylonia (265–6)

**Pyrilampes:** Athenian, son of Antiphon, and stepfather of Plato (322)

**Pyrrho:** *c*. 360–*c*. 270 BC, of Elis; founder of a school of Sceptics known by his name (138–9)

**Pythagoras:** sixth century BC; philosopher from Samos who emigrated to Croton in southern Italy and founded a society there (41, 104, 319, 324)

**Pythia:** name of the priestess of Apollo at Delphi (277)

**Python:** of Thisbe in Boeotia, first century AD; said to be descended from the dragon's teeth men (282)

**Quietus, Avidius:** prominent Roman and friend of Plutarch (250)

**Samidas:** Theban participant in the overthrow of the oligarchic dictatorship of 379 BC (312, 355)

**Sam(i)us:** foster-brother and 'friend' of Philip V of Macedon; third and second centuries BC (70)

**Sappho:** lyric poetess from Lesbos in the early sixth century BC (136, 184)

**Satyrus:** fourth century BC; an orator from Samos (189–90)

**Seleucus:** one of the successors of Alexander the Great (266)

**Semele:** the mortal mother of Dionysus, who made her immortal (288)

**Semonides:** of Amorgus; iambic and elegiac poet of the seventh century BC (143)

**Seneca, Lucius Annaeus:** *c.* 5/4 BC–65AD; Roman writer and Stoic philosopher with an intermittent public career (196)

**Senecio, Q. Sosius:** one of Plutarch's most notable Roman friends, consul AD 99 and 107. Plutarch dedicated his nine books of *Table Talk* to him, and he appears frequently as a participant in their discussions. The *Lives* of Theseus and Romulus, Demosthenes and Cicero, Dion and Brutus are also addressed to him (122)

**Sextius, Quintus:** a Roman famous for abandoning a public career under Augustus for philosophy. A fund of anecdote centred on him grew in the first century AD. Seneca admired him and frequently referred to him (128)

**Sibyl:** a prophetess (290)

**Sileni:** older satyrs, bibulous attendants of the younger Dionysus (83)

**Simmias:** Theban friend of Socrates. He helped to overthrow the Spartan-supported oligarchic dictatorship in Thebes in 379 BC (309–49)

**Simonides:** lyric poet from Ceos, *c.* 556–468 BC (62, 93, 131, 157, 267)

**Sisyphus:** the craftiest of men, according to the *Iliad*, and condemned to torture in Hades. One legend has him as the true father of Odysseus. He was also supposed to have believed that the gods were a mere invention (261, 399)

**Socrates:** 469–399 BC; Athenian philosopher and teacher of Plato (45, 97, 104, 106, 143, 181, 188, 195, 215, 223–4, 233–4, 256, 319–24, 336–9, 346)

**Solon:** *c.* 640/35–560 BC; Athenian statesman, reformer and poet (80, 102, 129, 227, 255)

**Sophocles:** *c.* 496–406 BC; Athenian tragic dramatist (43, 49, 70, 110, 131, 142, 161, 163, 189, 193, 199, 218)

**Speusippus:** nephew of Plato; philosopher who succeeded Plato as Head of the Academy, 347–339 BC (102, 106)

**Sphinx:** a female monster with the body of a lion, wings and a woman's face. She killed any Theban who could not solve her riddle. When Oedipus did so, she killed herself in disgust (388, 395)

**Spintharus:** of Tarentum; an acquaintance of Epaminondas (30, 346)

**Stesichorus:** early sixth century BC; lyric poet (265)

**Stilpo:** *c.* 380–300 BC; philosopher and Head of the Megarian School. Zeno the Stoic is said to have acquired dialectical skills from him (140, 218, 233)

**Strabo:** father of Pompey the Great (262)

**Strato:** of Lampsacus; Peripatetic philosopher and Head of the School, 286–268 BC (227)

**Strouthias:** a character in Menander's play *The Flatterer* (77)

**Sulla, Sextius:** a Carthaginian living in Rome, and a friend of Plutarch (176–7)

**Telamon:** in legend, king of Salamis and father of Ajax (74)

**Telephus:** in the epic tradition, king of Mysia; he was wounded by Achilles when fighting for the Trojans (47)

**Teletias:** a Sicyonian victor in the Pythian games, dismembered by his countrymen in a dispute with the Cleonaeans (261)

**Tellus:** an obscure Athenian, pronounced blessed by fate by Solon (80)

**Terpander:** seventh century BC; lyric poet from Lesbos who settled in Sparta (272)

**Terpsion:** of Megara; associate of Socrates, and was with him in the last hours. He appears in Plato's *Theaetetus* (321)

**Tettix:** a Cretan, buried at Taenarum (277)

**Teucer:** son of Telamon, and brother of Ajax (74)

**Thales:** of Miletus, philosopher and sage of the early sixth century BC (315)

**Thamyris:** a legendary bard blinded by the Muses for attempting to rival them (181)

**Theanor:** a Pythagorean from Croton, visiting Thebes at the time of the *coup d'état* of 379 BC (324–48)

**Themis:** a goddess associated with the goddess Earth, famed as a prophetess; in legend occupied the oracular shrine at Delphi before Apollo (290)

**Themistocles:** *c.* 528–462 BC; Athenian statesman and general at the time of the Persian Wars who won the decisive battle of Salamis in 480 BC (142, 154, 160, 162, 163, 259)

**Themistogenes:** a putative historian from Syracuse, but more likely a pseudonym used by Xenophon for the authorship of his own *Anabasis* (155)

**Theocritus:** a Theban seer, part of the conspiracy to overthrow the oligarchic dictatorship at Thebes in 379 BC (311–15, 319–20, 324, 332–5, 339, 346, 348, 350, 352, 355)

**Theodorus:** of Cyrene; fifth century BC, mathematician and teacher of Plato (216)

**Theodorus:** a celebrated Athenian actor in the fourth century BC (161)

**Theon:** a friend of Plutarch (370)

**Theophrastus:** 372/69–288/5 BC, of Lesbos; pupil of Aristotle and important Peripatetic philosopher (28, 130)

**Theopompus:** one of the Theban exiles who helped to overthrow the oligarchic dictatorship in 379 BC (349, 355)

**Theramenes:** Athenian politician prominent in the political upheavals during the last part of the Peloponnesian War in the last decade of the fifth century BC (154)

**Thersippus:** said in some accounts to have brought back the news of the battle of Marathon (158)

**Theseus:** legendary national hero of Athens (155, 388)

**Thespesius:** the name given to Aridaeus in his other-worldly experience (285–93)

**Thespis:** sixth century BC; Athenian poet, reputedly the creator of the tragic dramatic form (164)

**Thetis:** mother of Achilles (96)

**Thrasybulus:** sixth century BC; Athenian who married the daughter of the dictator Pisistratus (187)

**Thrasybulus:** Athenian general and statesman who organized the repossession of Athens in 404/3 BC by the exiled democrats from the oligarchic government of the Thirty Tyrants and the Spartan garrison (154, 163, 165, 309)

**Thrasyllus:** Athenian commander in the final years of the Peloponnesian War (154)

**Thucydides:** Athenian historian who recorded the contemporary rise of Athens in the fifth century BC and the Peloponnesian War (76, 105, 108, 132, 154, 157–8, 159, 251, 256, 273)

**Tiberius Caesar:** 42BC–AD 37; emperor of Rome, AD 14–37 (83–4)

**Timaea:** wife of King Agis of Sparta (218)

**Timagenes:** of Alexandria; historian and rhetorician, patronized by Augustus at Rome (98)

**Timarchus:** of Chaeronea, fourth century BC; probably fictitious author of a myth (339–46)

**Timarchus:** An Athenian against whom Aeschines directed a speech (165)

**Timoleon:** Corinthian general of mercenaries in Sicily. He defeated the Carthaginians in 341 BC, and restored autonomy to Sicilian states after tyrannical rule. Plutarch wrote his _Life_ (260)

**Timon:** Plutarch's younger brother (250, 253, 268–71, 272)

**Timotheus:** Athenian statesman and general, son of Conon, and influential after the foundation of the Second Athenian Confederacy in 377 BC. He died in 354 (166, 309)

**Timoxena:** Plutarch's wife, and also a daughter who died in infancy (365–74)

**Tissaphernes:** Persian viceroy of the Aegean coastal provinces 413–395 BC (69)

**Tolmides:** Athenian admiral in the 450s BC (154)

**Trophonius:** a Boeotian oracular god with a shrine near Lebadeia (339, 346)

**Tydeus:** father of Diomedes, a Greek hero in the *Iliad* (78, 106, 108)

**Xanthippe:** Socrates' wife (195)

**Xenocrates:** philosopher and Head of the Academy, 339–314 BC (28, 49, 106)

**Xenophon:** *c.* 430–c. 354 BC; Athenian writer, admirer of Socrates adventurer and general in Cyrus' expedition against Artaxerxes, after which he lived the life of a country gentleman (33, 74, 100, 132, 154, 212)

**Xerxes:** Persian king who invaded Greece in 480 BC (181–2, 223)

**Zeno:** of Citium, 335–263 BC; founder of the Stoic school of philosophy (130, 139, 198, 217)

**Zeus:** the king of the Olympian gods (72, 74, 83, 156, 213, 215, 225, 226, 229, 237, 254, 278, 286, 339, 369, 393)

# Visit Penguin on the Internet
### and browse at your leisure

---

- ◆ preview sample extracts of our forthcoming books
- ◆ read about your favourite authors
- ◆ investigate over 10,000 titles
- ◆ enter one of our literary quizzes
- ◆ win some fantastic prizes in our competitions
- ◆ e-mail us with your comments and book reviews
- ◆ instantly order any Penguin book

### and masses more!

---

*'To be recommended without reservation ... a rich and rewarding on-line experience'* – Internet Magazine

## www.penguin.co.uk

# READ MORE IN PENGUIN

In every corner of the world, on every subject under the sun, Penguin represents quality and variety – the very best in publishing today.

For complete information about books available from Penguin – including Puffins, Penguin Classics and Arkana – and how to order them, write to us at the appropriate address below. Please note that for copyright reasons the selection of books varies from country to country.

**In the United Kingdom**: Please write to *Dept. EP, Penguin Books Ltd, Bath Road, Harmondsworth, West Drayton, Middlesex UB7 ODA*

**In the United States**: Please write to *Consumer Sales, Penguin Putnam Inc., P.O. Box 12289 Dept. B, Newark, New Jersey 07101-5289.* VISA and MasterCard holders call 1-800-788-6262 to order Penguin titles

**In Canada**: Please write to *Penguin Books Canada Ltd, 10 Alcorn Avenue, Suite 300, Toronto, Ontario M4V 3B2*

**In Australia**: Please write to *Penguin Books Australia Ltd, P.O. Box 257, Ringwood, Victoria 3134*

**In New Zealand**: Please write to *Penguin Books (NZ) Ltd, Private Bag 102902, North Shore Mail Centre, Auckland 10*

**In India**: Please write to *Penguin Books India Pvt Ltd, 11 Community Centre, Panchsheel Park, New Delhi 110017*

**In the Netherlands**: Please write to *Penguin Books Netherlands bv, Postbus 3507, NL-1001 AH Amsterdam*

**In Germany**: Please write to *Penguin Books Deutschland GmbH, Metzlerstrasse 26, 60594 Frankfurt am Main*

**In Spain**: Please write to *Penguin Books S. A., Bravo Murillo 19, 1° B, 28015 Madrid*

**In Italy**: Please write to *Penguin Italia s.r.l., Via Benedetto Croce 2, 20094 Corsico, Milano*

**In France**: Please write to *Penguin France, Le Carré Wilson, 62 rue Benjamin Baillaud, 31500 Toulouse*

**In Japan**: Please write to *Penguin Books Japan Ltd, Kaneko Building, 2-3-25 Koraku, Bunkyo-Ku, Tokyo 112*

**In South Africa**: Please write to *Penguin Books South Africa (Pty) Ltd, Private Bag X14, Parkview, 2122 Johannesburg*

# PENGUIN AUDIOBOOKS

**A Quality of Writing That Speaks for Itself**

Penguin Books has always led the field in quality publishing. Now you can listen at leisure to your favourite books, read to you by familiar voices from radio, stage and screen. Penguin Audiobooks are produced to an excellent standard, and abridgements are always faithful to the original texts. From thrillers to classic literature, biography to humour, with a wealth of titles in between, Penguin Audiobooks offer you quality, entertainment and the chance to rediscover the pleasure of listening.

You can order Penguin Audiobooks through Penguin Direct by telephoning (0181) 899 4036. The lines are open 24 hours every day. Ask for Penguin Direct, quoting your credit card details.

*A selection of Penguin Audiobooks, published or forthcoming:*

**Emma** by Jane Austen, read by Fiona Shaw

**Pride and Prejudice** by Jane Austen, read by Joanna David

**Beowulf** translated by Michael Alexander, read by David Rintoul

**Agnes Grey** by Anne Brontë, read by Juliet Stevenson

**Jane Eyre** by Charlotte Brontë, read by Juliet Stevenson

**Wuthering Heights** by Emily Brontë, read by Juliet Stevenson

**The Pilgrim's Progress** by John Bunyan, read by David Suchet

**The Moonstone** by Wilkie Collins, read by Michael Pennington, Terrence Hardiman and Carole Boyd

**Nostromo** by Joseph Conrad, read by Michael Pennington

**Tales from the Thousand and One Nights**, read by Souad Faress and Raad Rawi

**Robinson Crusoe** by Daniel Defoe, read by Tom Baker

**David Copperfield** by Charles Dickens, read by Nathaniel Parker

**Little Dorrit** by Charles Dickens, read by Anton Lesser

**Barnaby Rudge** by Charles Dickens, read by Richard Pasco

**The Adventures of Sherlock Holmes** volumes 1–3 by Sir Arthur Conan Doyle, read by Douglas Wilmer

# PENGUIN AUDIOBOOKS

**The Man in the Iron Mask** by Alexandre Dumas, read by Simon Ward

**Adam Bede** by George Eliot, read by Paul Copley

**Joseph Andrews** by Henry Fielding, read by Sean Barrett

**The Great Gatsby** by F. Scott Fitzgerald, read by Marcus D'Amico

**North and South** by Elizabeth Gaskell, read by Diana Quick

**The Diary of a Nobody** by George Grossmith, read by Terrence Hardiman

**Jude the Obscure** by Thomas Hardy, read by Samuel West

**The Go-Between** by L. P. Hartley, read by Tony Britton

**Les Misérables** by Victor Hugo, read by Nigel Anthony

**A Passage to India** by E. M. Forster, read by Tim Pigott-Smith

**The Odyssey** by Homer, read by Alex Jennings

**The Portrait of a Lady** by Henry James, read by Claire Bloom

**On the Road** by Jack Kerouac, read by David Carradine

**Women in Love** by D. H. Lawrence, read by Michael Maloney

**Nineteen Eighty-Four** by George Orwell, read by Timothy West

**Ivanhoe** by Sir Walter Scott, read by Ciaran Hinds

**Frankenstein** by Mary Shelley, read by Richard Pasco

**Of Mice and Men** by John Steinbeck, read by Gary Sinise

**Dracula** by Bram Stoker, read by Richard E. Grant

**Gulliver's Travels** by Jonathan Swift, read by Hugh Laurie

**Vanity Fair** by William Makepeace Thackeray, read by Robert Hardy

**War and Peace** by Leo Tolstoy, read by Bill Nighy

**Barchester Towers** by Anthony Trollope, read by David Timson

**Tao Te Ching** by Lao Tzu, read by Carole Boyd and John Rowe

**Ethan Frome** by Edith Wharton, read by Nathan Osgood

**The Picture of Dorian Gray** by Oscar Wilde, read by John Moffatt

**Orlando** by Virginia Woolf, read by Tilda Swinton

# READ MORE IN PENGUIN

## A CHOICE OF CLASSICS

| | |
|---|---|
| Aeschylus | **The Oresteian Trilogy** |
| | **Prometheus Bound/The Suppliants/Seven against Thebes/The Persians** |
| Aesop | **The Complete Fables** |
| Ammianus Marcellinus | **The Later Roman Empire (AD 354–378)** |
| Apollonius of Rhodes | **The Voyage of Argo** |
| Apuleius | **The Golden Ass** |
| Aristophanes | **The Knights/Peace/The Birds/The Assemblywomen/Wealth** |
| | **Lysistrata/The Acharnians/The Clouds** |
| | **The Wasps/The Poet and the Women/ The Frogs** |
| Aristotle | **The Art of Rhetoric** |
| | **The Athenian Constitution** |
| | **Classic Literary Criticism** |
| | **De Anima** |
| | **The Metaphysics** |
| | **Ethics** |
| | **Poetics** |
| | **The Politics** |
| Arrian | **The Campaigns of Alexander** |
| Marcus Aurelius | **Meditations** |
| Boethius | **The Consolation of Philosophy** |
| Caesar | **The Civil War** |
| | **The Conquest of Gaul** |
| Cicero | **Murder Trials** |
| | **The Nature of the Gods** |
| | **On the Good Life** |
| | **On Government** |
| | **Selected Letters** |
| | **Selected Political Speeches** |
| | **Selected Works** |
| Euripides | **Alcestis/Iphigenia in Tauris/Hippolytus** |
| | **The Bacchae/Ion/The Women of Troy/ Helen** |
| | **Medea/Hecabe/Electra/Heracles** |
| | **Orestes and Other Plays** |

# READ MORE IN PENGUIN

## A CHOICE OF CLASSICS

| | |
|---|---|
| Hesiod/Theognis | **Theogony/Works and Days/Elegies** |
| Hippocrates | **Hippocratic Writings** |
| Homer | **The Iliad** |
| | **The Odyssey** |
| Horace | **Complete Odes and Epodes** |
| Horace/Persius | **Satires and Epistles** |
| Juvenal | **The Sixteen Satires** |
| Livy | **The Early History of Rome** |
| | **Rome and Italy** |
| | **Rome and the Mediterranean** |
| | **The War with Hannibal** |
| Lucretius | **On the Nature of the Universe** |
| Martial | **Epigrams** |
| | **Martial in English** |
| Ovid | **The Erotic Poems** |
| | **Heroides** |
| | **Metamorphoses** |
| | **The Poems of Exile** |
| Pausanias | **Guide to Greece (in two volumes)** |
| Petronius/Seneca | **The Satyricon/The Apocolocyntosis** |
| Pindar | **The Odes** |
| Plato | **Early Socratic Dialogues** |
| | **Gorgias** |
| | **The Last Days of Socrates (Euthyphro/ The Apology/Crito/Phaedo)** |
| | **The Laws** |
| | **Phaedrus and Letters VII and VIII** |
| | **Philebus** |
| | **Protagoras/Meno** |
| | **The Republic** |
| | **The Symposium** |
| | **Theaetetus** |
| | **Timaeus/Critias** |
| Plautus | **The Pot of Gold and Other Plays** |
| | **The Rope and Other Plays** |

# READ MORE IN PENGUIN

## A CHOICE OF CLASSICS

| | |
|---|---|
| Pliny | **The Letters of the Younger Pliny** |
| Pliny the Elder | **Natural History** |
| Plotinus | **The Enneads** |
| Plutarch | **The Age of Alexander (Nine Greek Lives)** |
| | **Essays** |
| | **The Fall of the Roman Republic (Six Lives)** |
| | **The Makers of Rome (Nine Lives)** |
| | **Plutarch on Sparta** |
| | **The Rise and Fall of Athens (Nine Greek Lives)** |
| Polybius | **The Rise of the Roman Empire** |
| Procopius | **The Secret History** |
| Propertius | **The Poems** |
| Quintus Curtius Rufus | **The History of Alexander** |
| Sallust | **The Jugurthine War/The Conspiracy of Cataline** |
| Seneca | **Dialogues and Letters** |
| | **Four Tragedies/Octavia** |
| | **Letters from a Stoic** |
| | **Seneca in English** |
| Sophocles | **Electra/Women of Trachis/Philoctetes/Ajax** |
| | **The Theban Plays** |
| Suetonius | **The Twelve Caesars** |
| Tacitus | **The Agricola/The Germania** |
| | **The Annals of Imperial Rome** |
| | **The Histories** |
| Terence | **The Comedies (The Girl from Andros/The Self-Tormentor/The Eunuch/Phormio/The Mother-in-Law/The Brothers)** |
| Thucydides | **History of the Peloponnesian War** |
| Virgil | **The Aeneid** |
| | **The Eclogues** |
| | **The Georgics** |
| Xenophon | **Conversations of Socrates** |
| | **Hiero the Tyrant** |
| | **A History of My Times** |
| | **The Persian Expedition** |